$50.00
60·B

HUMANIST PLAY AND BELIEF
The Seriocomic Art of Desiderius Erasmus

Erasmus' comic works have often been used to deny any serious claim of greatness in his writings. In this book Walter M. Gordon argues that Erasmus' levity is in fact the key to appreciating the stretch and depth of his spirit.

Gordon's approach is, for the most part, literary: it fixes upon Erasmus' comic scenes, with their images and metaphors, in an attempt to elucidate his vision. Frequently, and especially in the later chapters, Gordon refers to what Hugh of St Victor calls the demonstration of the symbol – the visible used to portray the invisible or spiritual.

An introductory chapter examines the Judaeo-Christian tradition within which theological reflection readily makes use of ludic imagery in expressing itself. Gordon then explores the gradual maturing of Erasmian seriocomedy, especially with regard to the influences of Greek classical writers upon the author. The next section concentrates on the link between the comic works and the reform of Christendom.

Gordon concludes with a study of those writings which extend to the sublime extremes of comedy. These illustrate most powerfully how the playful images of theatre, music, and dance prove conducive to the expression of theological and mystical thought. Far from diminishing the weight of Erasmus' greatness, the comic writings offer a means of arriving at his most profound insights.

WALTER M. GORDON is Associate Professor of English, University of Georgia.

Erasmus Studies

A series of studies concerned with Erasmus and related subjects

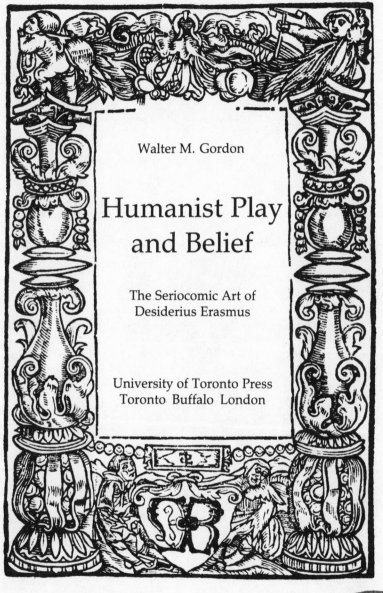

Walter M. Gordon

Humanist Play and Belief

The Seriocomic Art of
Desiderius Erasmus

University of Toronto Press
Toronto Buffalo London

© University of Toronto Press 1990
Toronto Buffalo London
Printed in Canada

ISBN 0-8020-5846-9

Printed on acid-free paper

Canadian Cataloguing in Publication Data

Gordon, Walter M., 1928–
Humanist play and belief

(Erasmus studies ; 9)
Includes bibliographical references.
ISBN 0-8020-5846-9
1. Erasmus, Desiderius, d. 1536–Criticism and interpretation.
2. Comic, The, in literature.
I. Title. II. Series
PA8518.G67 1990   877'.04   C90-093781-5

This book has been published with the help of a
grant from the Canadian Federation for the
Humanities using funds provided by the Social
Sciences and Humanities Research Council of Canada.

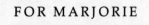
FOR MARJORIE

Contents

✿

PART FOUR
TOWARDS A LUDIC THEOLOGY

Acknowledgments

I wish to express my gratitude to those who prepared me for these studies: Professor Frank Sullivan, Professor Arthur Brown, and especially the Reverend Leopold Malevez, sj. I am also indebted to Professor Coburn Freer, my departmental head, who allotted me time for this work, to Professor Hugh Ruppersburg, who managed the exchange of the entire text from one computer disc to another, to Ms Lisa Barnett, the typist, and to Ms Judy Williams of University of Toronto Press, who oversaw the final editorial revision of the manuscript. My greatest debt is to my wife, Marjorie, who edited both the text and the notes and assembled the bibliography and the index.

PART ONE

PROLEGOMENON

ONE

Theology, Literature, and the Ludic

PLAY AND THE SACRED

The idea for this book came to me several years before I found it concisely expressed in Johan Huizinga's *Erasmus and the Age of the Reformation*: 'For only when humor illuminated that mind did it become truly profound.'[1] The great Dutch scholar found that Erasmian thought attains its most arresting and penetrating force in his comic writings. More recently, M.A. Screech's *Ecstasy and the Praise of Folly* tends to confirm Huizinga's insight. Screech has taken Erasmus' playful masterpiece and traced the sources of its culminating vision to earlier accounts of the mystical experience within the Christian tradition. The comedy of Erasmus terminates in the beatific vision; this marks the goal or end of its play. We may expect, therefore, that this finality will have an effect on the comic works as a whole. Much of Erasmus' playfulness can be related to his Christian belief, and the relationship can be grasped as reciprocal: the humour casts light on his faith, and the faith lends substance to the deft, gentle touch of his wit.

Erasmus' bent for comic expression led to misunderstandings which drew him into controversy with both Catholic and Protestant theologians at the time of the Reformation. While his opponents were pummelling each other over the questions of works and salvation, Erasmus was playing with these disputants and their cherished ideas. Many of the points of that debate can no longer be considered living issues, and the fever which sustained the argument has now cooled in the awareness that this interdenominational strife has only added to the modern weakening of belief in Christianity itself. Surprisingly enough, the humorous tone which alienated Erasmus from his contemporaries is a quality no longer repudiated in modern theological discussion. In fact, Hans Urs von Balthasar, the Swiss theologian, criticizes his own Catholic confrères as well as the Protestants for the gloominess and rigidity of their manners. 'How,' he asks, 'could Christianity have become such a universal power if it had always been as sullen as today's humourless and anguished Protestantism, or as grumpy as the super-organised and super-scholasticised Catholicism about us?'[2] The Protestant author Jürgen Moltmann takes us beyond the temper of approach into the very matter of theology itself and sees his co-religionists betraying a most vital aspect of the original vision of the first Reformers.

> The *Reformation* fought justification by works in the medieval ecclesiastical society with its systems of penances, indulgences, and almsgiving on the grounds of a new faith which justified without the works of the law. The Reformation also abolished the holidays, games, and safety valves of that society. This led to the establishment of the Puritan society of penny pinchers and to the industrial workaday world among the very people who had at first insisted on believing that men are justified by faith alone. Nowhere did the morality of achievement find greater support than in the Protestant countries, Scotland and Swabia, for example.[3]

Moltmann suggests a new reformation and liberation of man within a ludic understanding of existence. Both Balthasar and Moltmann, Catholic and Protestant, sense the appositeness of a comic awareness and a playful spirit in the expression of contemporary religious thought. There is little doubt that Erasmus offers a lead to the thinkers of today, a lead pointing towards a more modest, gentle, and humorous style of discussing the divine reality, which, in the end, will always escape us; and, because of the adroitness of his comic approach, at which the modern theologian is so unskilled, he belies Huizinga's rather disappointing assessment that Erasmus' 'influence has ceased' and that 'he will speak to the world no more.'[4] Ironically, the very qualities of wit and humour which caused him to be rejected by the cantankerous scholars of his own times make him most relevant to a modern Christianity grown heavy and short-winded in its ponderous triumphalism.

This introduction to a study which links religion with play must consider the grounds for bringing together two subjects frequently thought of as disparate. Some would consider the holy to demand nothing but awe and reverence. In such an outlook, playing only degrades the object of devotion. But might playing not make man, in some sense, connatural with the deity itself, since a ludic freedom can be discerned within the divine nature? The God who, according to 1 John (4:8), is love loves without constraint. His work is said to be 'always play in the sense that it is always joyous, spontaneous, and completely free.'[5] The traditional understanding of the scriptural play of Wisdom before God assigns the ludic rejoicing to the Person of the Son before the Father: 'I was with him forming all things: and was delighted every day, playing before him at all times; playing in the world: and my delights were to be with the children of men' (Prov 8:30–1). After examining the patristic commentaries of this text, Hugo Rahner concludes that in this passage 'the mystical play of the Logos finds a place in the innermost being of the Triune God.'[6] His conclusion is based on the interpretation of such commentators as Salonius, Bede, and Rabanus Maurus, who identify God's creative with his recreative act.

If play is involved with the creative act of the creator, we should expect to find the same characteristic in the activity of his creatures. Romano Guardini, in discussing the liturgy as being both playful and without purpose, touches upon something very similar to this liturgical freedom of spirit in the scriptural account of angelic movement. Guardini asks us to 'consider the flaming Cherubim,' as described by Ezekiel (1:4ff). Think of how

> every one of them went straight forward, whither the
> impulse of the Spirit was to go ... and they turned not when
> they went ... ran and returned like flashes of lightning ...
> went ... and stood ... and were lifted up from earth ... the
> noise of their wings was like the noise of many waters ...
> and when they stood their wings were let down.

Guardini reflects on the passage: 'How "aimless" they are! How discouraging for the zealous partisans of reasonable suitability for a purpose! They are only pure motion, powerful and splendid, acting according to the direction of the Spirit, desiring nothing save to express Its inner drift and Its interior glow and force.'[7] The joyous, playful freedom of movement in the angels suggests the intense happiness characteristic of those close to God. Hence, we find at the end of the *Moria* a paean to the Christian folly that terminates in rapture and ecstasy. Erasmus' faith teaches him that this is the good man's destiny. His faith could be nothing other than seriocomic.

A divine madness lies at the heart of Erasmian comedy. The thought that lays hold of Erasmus' most profound religious insights has less to do with positive or dogmatic theology than with what is traditionally called negative theology. The human mind, enlightened by faith, can know God in so far as he reveals himself, but this very revelation veils a mystery. So Erasmus says that God babbles ('balbutit') that mystery to us.[8] Knowledge of the revelation leads to a knowledge of one's ignorance, a kind of inner 'nada,' an emptiness. Man is in no way equal to the enigma of the divine fullness. His situation, then, in confronting God, includes a comic aspect. He is a kind of vacuous buffoon facing an august reality which escapes his full comprehension. Christ, in becoming man, assumes this emptiness and charges it with his divine love until it becomes the kenosis of his passion and death by which human darkness and mortality are sanctified.

ERASMIAN SERIOCOMEDY AND THEOLOGY

Granting the possible compatibility between the sacred and the comic in general, let us proceed to the ways in which Erasmus joins these two elements in particular. Here we will attempt an initial description of Erasmian seriocomedy and leave the question of its decorum for chapter 4. The comedy we will be studying can be considered under a tripartite division, all parts of which involve some aspect of religion. First, there is the witty satire of man in his bemused or wrongheaded ways of reaching out to God. Here, comedy holds sway so long as Erasmus' wit maintains its underlying balance, but this satire can become astringent and cutting, especially when the author turns against those Christians who make their belief in the crucified Christ a reason for their violence against their fellows. The anger arises out of Erasmus' own conviction that Christendom, through its fostering of savage, internecine wars, has lost touch with its own calling. A second kind of Erasmian comedy assumes a more convivial mood and, within a setting of human, earthly happiness, celebrates the life of goodness which the atmosphere of easy friendship tends to confirm. Such comedy will sometimes be portrayed within the context of a dinner party, a feast of love reminiscent of Plato's *Symposium* but not without some tie also with Christ's last meal with his apostles on the night before he died.[9] This celebration of friendship can also take place within a pastoral scene as it does in the *Antibarbari*. There is a third kind of comedy more difficult to define or to appreciate as having anything to do with the serious. At some moments in the *Colloquia* or even in one or two whole dialogues, a festive temper can arise, the ascendancy of which does not seem reducible to any sound purpose. The laughter which this writing incites suggests the spirit of the 'comique absolu' of Baudelaire, the mind's revolt, as it were, from reason.[10] We are simply invited to laugh at man the fool, and, in doing so, we let go of any serious pretence about the human species, even about ourselves. This type discloses another side when, in addition to the erasing of human, rational pretence, a joyous celebration of sublime folly or excess takes place. We see this jubilation when Erasmus rhapsodizes over the madness of the saints in the *Moria*, or when his prose joyously shouts of the excesses of divine love in the incarnation. In such passages he tends to abandon all restraint in a wildly comic gesture provoked by the one thing that made his life important, or, if you will, serious.

When we study the quality of the prose in the third or most festive kind of Erasmian comedy, we note that it frequently reveals a style of writing found in the literature of the mystics. Images borrowed from human intoxication and love-making tend to arise, and the reader is made to sense that, for all of his sharp and subtle wit, Erasmus can also write, and write power-fully, the language of the heart. His greatest masterpiece, the *Moria*, contains all three kinds of comedy as distinguished above. It both laughs and scowls at man's aberrations. It affably sings of the madness that makes human love and friendship permanent. In the course of the declamation, human reason is gradually undone by Folly's own incongruity until the mind is silenced by the very end of all reasoning: the celebration of the divine ecstasy of the saints.

The plan of study here will not follow a strictly chronological order, although Erasmus' first attempts at seriocomedy will occupy us immediately after the opening discussion. Part 1, comprising the present chapter, will serve to introduce us to the nature of and the religious background to Erasmian seriocomedy. Part 2 will focus upon early works and passages as well as upon the Greek writers who might have offered our author leads with regard to the festive texture of composition. Part 3 concerns those dialogues and declamations in which either a satirical or a utopian mood prevails. Most of these reveal a serious interest by reason of their religious and moral content. In part 4, we reach the summit of Erasmian seriocomedy, and will concentrate on those works or passages that best approximate a literature of a highly spiritual nature. Throughout all the sections of this investigation, an interest in Erasmus' word pictures will obtain: the figures, the tropes, the metaphors, the allegories. At the start, the monastery will be set in contention with the stormy world outside it, and the images of Plato's Silenus and Aesop's beetle and eagle will crop up. In the middle chapters, Erasmus will be seen capturing the splendour of Canterbury Cathedral's exterior and the gloom of its interior, the beauty of a country villa where friends meet, the antics of a madcap exorcism, and the wild devotion to relics manifested by passengers on a sinking ship. The final chapters will consider the most sublime images of Erasmus' comic vision: Christ the harpist playing his song of love, the mad saint whose praises Folly sounds, the theatre of the world whose drama centres on the Son of God, the cosmic dance of the saviour with his spouse. To put it briefly, the emphasis will fall upon Erasmus the poet, the purveyor of symbols that point to heavenly mysteries.

The design of the book follows a line of ascent that starts with Erasmus' first attempts at the seriocomic and ends with passages and works that are jubilantly religious and even at times mystical. For this reason, the last section of the book, consisting of four chapters, has been entitled 'Towards a Ludic Theology.' The heading has been chosen with deliberation. Some readers may wonder what comic dialogues and declamations of a literary nature have to do with theology or what kind of theology would be receptive to a study of ludic works. True, we have already seen where two modern theologians, one Protestant, the other Catholic, have called for a theology less sombre and more festive in its approaches, but a desire does not constitute a reality, or even a possibility, for that matter. Whether or not a ludic theology is attainable will depend largely on how we define the discipline of theology. Since we are concerned with Erasmus, it seems best to see first how he understands this study. In the course of the discussion of education on which his *Antibarbari* focuses, James Batt, the main character in the dialogue, lets fall, by way of a few asides, some ideas that can serve as an initial sketch of a theology close to the heart of Erasmus.

During the course of the conversation that takes place in the *Antibarbari*, Erasmus brings together notions of play, literature, and theology. Early in the dialogue, William Conrad, the burgomaster of Bergen, expresses his envy of Erasmus for being able to give himself entirely to a life of leisure and study. Conrad imagines the details of such a pleasant existence:

> you are strolling about all the time with your Muses, entirely at leisure and unoccupied, now chatting on whatever topic you like with a friend, now holding a conversation with one of the ancient writers, at times beating out the rhythm of some ditty, or at others committing to paper, as to faithful companions, whatever you are turning over in your mind.[11]

Notice how easily the account glides from reading to conversation because the two activities are envisioned as a way of communing with another, just as composition, even when done in solitude, is conceived as a way of talking to 'faithful companions.' Indeed, the entire dialogue seeks to capture on its pages the easy recreation that Conrad describes as Erasmus' life of leisure; and the place towards which the personae move is Conrad's own pleasant country estate, which the *Antibarbari* calls a retreat where one can 'relax a little more freely and play.'[12] James Batt, the protagonist of the discussion, undertakes stout battle against the barbarians standing in opposition to 'bonae literae.' Twice during the discussion, he allies the literary studies of which he speaks with theology. He refers to a young scholar as 'no less a rhetorician than a theologian'; he surmises that, were he a theologian, he would in no way be 'straying from the domain of the poet.'[13] In still another place, Batt plays the theologian and interprets Paul's saying, 'Knowledge puffs up' (1 Cor 8:1). He understands the apostle to mean that knowledge avails little or nothing without love: 'Paul does not mean that knowledge should be nonexistent, but that it should not exist alone, that is, without charity.'[14] If this is true of knowledge in general, it would surely apply to that branch of knowing concerned with God and the things of God.

The pastoral setting of the *Antibarbari*, together with the amicable feeling that prevails among the personae, suggests that the author is indulging in a humanist dream that calls up his version of social happiness. At the same time, the work portrays at different levels the divisiveness that shatters every dream of peace. In contrast to the quiet rural backdrop to the conversation, we are told of the wars that have ravaged the Dutch territories. The antagonist of the piece is the barbarian, the despiser of genuine learning whom Erasmus tends to see as the instigator of the catastrophic wars. The barbarian, too, is the man of myopic vision, clinging like a leech to one specialized topic and acting thereby as an impediment to the integration of learning, the very linchpin of Erasmian humanism. Recall Batt's efforts to see the poet, the theologian, and the rhetorician as one and to see the knowledge of them all to be of little use without love. We have here a tendency to unite disciplines and to relate them to the surrounding world.

The theology that Batt suggests to his friends is one that readily admits of poetical wisdom and insight and is given to rhetorical expression. It takes little effort of the imagination to see that in the *Antibarbari* Batt speaks for the mind of Erasmus. Late in his life, Erasmus adverts to the motive that sustained him in the pursuit of the knowledge of literature: 'I gave myself to humanist letters for one reason alone: that these studies would serve the more important disciplines of learning and especially those of theology.'[15] His desire was to achieve a renaissance of theological studies by returning them to a more direct and immediate dependence upon a sound knowledge of the languages in which the scriptures were written. His edition of the Greek New Testament gives clear evidence of this effort. Of course, his reform would apply to critical as well as linguistic skills. In this sense, the man of letters and the theologian would be joined in a single person, a person quite different from the scholastic theologian of the day with his proclivity towards abstract speculation. Erasmus, in defending his *Moria* against the charges of the Louvain theologians, divided the history of theology into the New and the Old.[16] The New refers to the thought and methods of the scholastics of Erasmus' day, much given to philosophical distinction and definition; the Old finds its sources in the fathers and seems much more at home with the figurative expression of literature. At any rate, this is how Erasmus would distinguish the two.

The Erasmian joining of the literary to the theological should cause no problem if we confine such a union to the editing of the scriptures; however, such a combination might arouse some resistance were we to include Erasmus' own literary works among the significant theological contributions to his own and to later times. An eminent Erasmian scholar in France, Jacques Chomarat, demurs from calling Erasmus a theologian and gives as one of his reasons the Dutch humanist's great love for literature. Chomarat understands theology as a well-structured science not to be confused with literary art, especially that of an entertaining kind.[17] Chomarat's judgment suggests the attitude of many readers of Erasmus who question the depth of his thought by reason of the brilliance adhering to the literary surface of his prose. This latter attitude prevailed during our author's lifetime and was used to great advantage by Martin Luther. See how Luther rates his friend Melancthon, his enemy Erasmus, and himself: 'Substance with words – Philip. Words without substance – Erasmus. Substance without words – Luther.'[18] Luther seems to be indicating that Erasmus has nothing to say because he says it so well.

In his controversy with Erasmus over the freedom of the will, Luther quite systematically denigrates his opponent because of his literary skills. He acknowledges the 'highly decorative arguments' of Erasmus, arguments which he dismisses in the same breath as 'trivial and worthless.'[19] He will strip away 'the seductive charm' of this language to get at 'the dregs beneath.'[20] Luther's strategy – rhetorical? – is to establish himself as the voice of theological authority in contrast to an Erasmus who, because of his adroit usage of language, must be derided as a master of deception. Throughout whole sections of the De servo arbitrio, Luther personifies Erasmus' work on the freedom of the will by taking its words as coming from the lips of a woman he calls 'Diatribe.' She is given to dreaming, to follies, to thoughtlessness. She commits blunder after blunder, contradicts herself, rambles on insanely, confuses issues, and, worst of all, pretends and pretends again.[21] Luther is attempting to turn Erasmus' treatise into a second version of the Moria by dramatizing Erasmus' argument in the persona of a woman given to masking the truth with her painting and her lies. By implication, Erasmus, the master of style, is one with his persona, a mere player, and on no account to be taken seriously.

The opposition which Luther establishes between himself, the voice of theological authority, and Erasmus, the trafficker in words, resembles the contrast Richard A. Lanham draws in *The Motives of Eloquence* between 'homo seriosus' and 'homo rhetoricus.' The first of these two, like Luther, is 'pledged to a single set of values,' favours the univocal in his reading of scripture, and harbours not the least doubt about either the nature or the rectitude of his position.[22] 'Homo rhetoricus,' on the other hand, must appeal, Erasmus-like, to his audience in an open and liberal manner because his listeners are free to choose for or against his argument. 'Homo seriosus' is assertive, even aggressive, but responsible; 'homo rhetoricus' is, by comparison, relaxed, cajoling, tactful. Luther 'seriosus' stands for nothing less than the truth and will not tolerate the least reluctance or hesitation to side with him. Erasmus 'rhetoricus' entertains a play of mind out of fear of alienating his audience, which he wants to win freely, without constraint. Luther will go to any length and let the world perish in the process if only the word of God, as he utters it, can prevail. On the other side of the fence, Erasmus, confronted by mysteries his mind fails to penetrate adequately, cannot act with the independence of mind his opponent manifests. He speaks more gently and even playfully because he senses that more is to be had from consent than from the certitude of a single, bad-tempered individual.

Although the playful aspect of Erasmus' literary theology will be extensively looked at in part 4 of this study, a preliminary account of it seems desirable here in order to show how this ludic material relates to and encourages serious reflection. Erasmus believed that the learning process functioned more smoothly the more it took on a ludic quality. It is only natural then that he often conceives of God's education of man through revelation in a playful way. The creator, in accommodating himself to his creatures, assumes a childlike, picture-book language man can understand. Erasmus describes scriptural allegory as a literary figure that simultaneously reveals and obscures the secret to which it is linked, after the manner of a game of hide-and-seek. The reader, when puzzled by an implied comparison, must hunt for an answer which, when found, gives him the pleasure of having discovered something by himself and makes him feel that the truth is his own and not merely something he has learned by rote. This discovery, Erasmus tells us in the *Ratio verae theologiae*, constitutes the delight in the play of allegory.[23] Marjorie O'Rourke Boyle writes about this ludic aspect of the scriptural trope: 'Allegory provokes a recognition which is pleasurable; this is true learning. "Thus more enjoyably is truth seized upon which first tested us under the wrap of enigma." With its play in the discrepancy of signifier and signified, allegory is a pleasant way to do theology.'[24]

In addition to the play involved in the reading of allegory, the literary theology of Erasmus includes certain treatises, declamations, dialogues, and scriptural commentaries each of which denotes something of a ludic nature. As we shall see in chapter 4, Erasmus conceived of his 'schola declamatoria' as a school or playground where the young could exercise their minds by pleading on either side of a proposition. The declamation, in so far as it avoids the absolute, the necessary, the dogmatic, partakes of the nature of play by reason of the free range it encourages in the mind. Erasmus' supreme accomplishment in this genre, the *Moria*, establishes in a ludic manner its own fictional boundaries, the scene within which Folly will deliver her address. On this field, as it were, takes place an agon or contest between two kinds of folly, a drama that will be analysed in chapter 8. Conflicts usually of a gentler kind abound in the *Colloquies*, where one side is frequently meant to win as the dialogue takes on a hortatory or persuasive tone. When Erasmus rises to the defence of the *Colloquies*, he attempts to show their effectiveness by reason of their power to teach the young playfully.[25] The ludic spirit of these works anticipates the attitude and insight of Friedrich Schiller, who understood art as a means of reform and thought that to change people for the better one should catch them in the hours of leisure during which their tastes could be transformed by means of the awakening of a play impulse made sensitive to beauty.[26] Play in Schiller's thought eludes coercion and allows man to be free, to be human.[27] Such a way of thinking at the social level corresponds, at the level of belief, with the Erasmus who saw Christ in his saving act as playing a song of love, the power of which could raise the spiritually dead to life.[28]

THE LEAP FROM THE VISIBLE TO THE INVISIBLE

Erasmus' literary theology plays in its representation of God babbling his revelation to man, in its view of scriptural allegory, in its ludic portrayal of Christian ideals through the declamations and dialogues, and in its musical representation of the powers of divine grace. We are already beginning to indicate the highest extremes to which Erasmian seriocomedy reaches, but more has to be said of its nature, the radical foundation of its vision, and the precedent in tradition for such a way of beholding things. In Erasmus' teaching of allegory, for instance, a lower reality often stands for a higher one, or a surface appearance leads to a corresponding interior discovery. The fifth rule laid down in his *Enchiridion* calls for a movement of the soul's attention from the visible to the invisible,[29] and this general habit of mind is given a specified expression in the Erasmian explication of allegorical figures. According to Georges Chantraine, the manifestation of the invisible by the visible constitutes the objectivity of allegorical language, its end and its norm.[30] The movement from visible to the invisible, of course, is discernible in Christian thought from its beginnings; the tendency follows inexorably from an awareness of God's incarnation and is expressed as a rule of mind in the ancient preface for the Mass of Christmas: 'ut dum visibiliter Deum cognoscimus, per hunc in invisibilium amorem rapiamur.'[31]

When Erasmus plays with words within a religious context, he is often leading the reader on a journey from the earthly to a heavenly reality, and such playing has characterized Christian revelation and speculation throughout its history. The symbol derives its mental force from the acceptance in faith of a correspondence between visible and invisible reality. The mind must play in going from one thing to another in a kind of jump which the symbol incites. Jean-Paul Sartre, when discussing play, observes that it 'is not by chance that materialism is serious; it is not by chance that it is found at all times and places as the favorite doctrine of the revolutionary. This is because revolutionaries are serious.'[32] In so far as he is pure materialist and locked into a single stratum of reality, Sartre's revolutionary appears to impair the resiliency of mind needed for play. This person is totally immersed in physical, worldly phenomena with no hope of attaining the human, as Sartre would say, or the spiritual, as the Christian would add. 'Thus,' says Sartre, 'all serious thought is thickened by the world; it coagulates; it is a dismissal of human reality in favor of the world. The serious man is "of the world" and has no resource in himself. He does not even imagine any longer the possibility of *getting out of* the world, for he has given to himself the type of existence of the rock, the consistency, the inertia, the opacity of being-in-the-midst-of-the-world.'[33] Called to make the leap from visible to invisible reality, the Christian must foster an interior spirit diametrically opposed to that of Sartre's materialist. Plato isolates the earliest manifestation of the play impulse in the child's spontaneous urge to jump,[34] and man's mental leap from the lower to the higher can be regarded from a ludic point of view. We will catch Erasmus doing this very thing time and again throughout this study. It is a sign both of his Christian faith and of his sense of play. This characteristic of his thinking hardly singles him out in the history of Christian thought. The play of mind I am describing is found in revelation, the fathers, and in the early scholastics.

In the gospel of John, the people whom Jesus encounters are often asked to make this mental leap, but, in failing to do so, they fail to comprehend what the master is saying. When, in the fourth chapter, Christ meets a Samaritan woman at the Well of Jacob, the conversation straightway turns on the subject of water. 'Everyone,' says Jesus, 'who drinks of this water will thirst again. He, however, who drinks of the water that I will give him shall never thirst; but the water that I will give him shall become in him a fountain of water, springing up unto life everlasting' (13–14). Obviously this is no ordinary water. The woman vaguely senses as much, but she does not grasp the full implication of what this stranger has told her. 'Sir,' she pleads, 'give me this water that I may not thirst, or come here to draw' (15). Christ speaks of a spiritual water; the woman remains at the level of the senses. Later in the same chapter, Jesus tells the disciples that he has a food of which they do not know. The disciples immediately wonder who it was who brought him lunch (32–3). As so often happens in John, the words of Jesus are misunderstood because they are taken in a narrowly literal sense. His listeners do not have the dexterity of mind to take the meaning to a higher plane. The materialist mentality cannot engage in the symbol's demonstration. Christ has spoken of the refreshment and nourishment of the spirit, and his words have been received, not uncomically, by incorrigible literalists who are incapable of the literary play that leads to meaning.

The fourth chapter of John elevates the idea of food from the material to the spiritual level by suggesting that there is a sustenance for the soul as well as for the body. Augustine takes the suggestion and, in his 'Sermo 28' (*De vetere testamento*), applies this image to God himself as the one who not only sustains but ultimately fulfils human life. The preacher chooses as his text the third verse of Psalm 104 – 'Let the heart of those seeking the Lord be glad' – and uses it as a point of departure for a discourse on spiritual sustenance. As the eye rejoices in the luminous, the ear in pleasant sounds, so the heart, Augustine argues, is made to find its joy in God.[35] 'To our heart,' he says, 'the Lord is light, sound, fragrance and food.'[36] He is all of these things and, as their creator, none of them. God is the nutriment of the inner man, a food which replenishes without consuming itself.[37] To digest such nourishment means to become what it is, to take on godliness.[38] Augustine talks of light as the sustenance of the eyes, which perish if confined to darkness. Such a food is this light that all partake of it without diminishing or exhausting it.[39] As light to the eyes, so is sound a food to the ears, and a miraculous kind at that. Thought wrapped in sound is dispersed to Augustine's congregation without ever leaving the preacher. Unlike normal food, which gradually disappears when shared, the concept uttered remains whole in the speaker, one in itself and divided among the many, and made whole again in the heart of each listener.[40] And if man can do this with human words, cannot God achieve a far greater thing by means of his divine Word? 'Behold,' Augustine proclaims, 'the Word of God ... remaining ever with the Father, in order to come forth to us, sought out flesh, as it were, his sound, and set himself in it and came forth to us without ever leaving the Father.'[41] 'Sermo 28' reflects the play of a divine Wisdom that paradoxically unites leaving with staying, sharing with possessing, consumption with replenishment. If we note in this sermon an adroit play of a mind that leaps from matter to spirit and back, it might be that no other mentality is capable of grasping the object of what Augustine believes. At the close of the sermon, Augustine describes the Word of God as leaning towards creation and remaining at the same time in the bosom of the Father. Erasmus, in the introduction to his commentary on Psalm 38, describes this sublime movement as the Son's cosmic leap, a leap that later will be revealed as a dance to the music of love.[42] Paradox, wonder, mystery all contribute to the heavenly play and show why, for Erasmus, the spirit most foreign to the man of faith inclined towards a moroseness which likewise rendered playfulness disagreeable.[43]

The use of symbol serving as the stimulus for the mind's ascent from the visible to the invisible becomes in the twelfth century the matrix for a theological program the bent of which is literary and which depends more upon the support of nature as created by God and of history as entered into by God than upon any complex metaphysical schema. This symbolic theology has been described for us by Marie-Dominique Chenu, especially in those essays of his where he discusses the Victorine commentaries on the writings of Dionysius, sometimes called the Areopagite, the fifth-century author whose works so profoundly influenced medieval thought.[44] Because the approach to theology in Chenu's account anticipates Erasmus' own method, an understanding of this important variant in the medieval tradition is relevant to the work at hand. If, as de Lubac suggests, Erasmus was not what he calls 'un théologien d'école,' we need not for this reason cancel any claim he might have to being a theologian.[45] Chenu's achievement was to expose another option quite distinct from a rigidly dialectical system, one which was available to the medieval scholar and chosen by such authors as Bernard of Clairvaux, Hugh and Richard of St Victor in the twelfth century, and Bonaventure, in his more imaginative writings, in the thirteenth. Later, Erasmus would be drawn along a similar path.

In saying that Bernard, the Victorines, and Bonaventure frequently, if not exclusively, engaged in a disciplinary mode distinct from the one which was ultimately to dominate scholastic thought by the close of the Middle Ages, I do not mean that their symbolic theology must be considered as something foreign or opposed to the teaching of the greatest of the scholastics, Thomas Aquinas. Aquinas' own delineation of the boundaries of theology is most generous and admits of a great variety of styles, including, to name a few, the symbolic, the historical, and the preceptive, as well as the argumentative, the mode most often associated with him.[46] Chenu, even when concentrating on the Victorines, is careful to point out those writings of Aquinas which conform to the approach taken by his twelfth-century predecessors.[47] In the prologue to his commentary on the *Sentences* of Peter Lombard, Thomas tells us that, because the principles of theology lie beyond the reach of human intelligence 'which in this present life is accustomed to observe and deal with things of sense, we have to treat these phenomena as symbols of the high truths on which we are bent. Consequently, theology also employs a metaphorical and parabolical style of discourse.'[48] This statement echoes the doctrine of Dionysius and the Victorines. In another place, Thomas says that the spiritual sense of scripture arises out of the readiness of things literally expressed in the text to stand *per figuram* for other things 'because visible reality is accustomed to be taken as a figure of the invisible.'[49] In other words, the spiritual meaning is reached through a figurative reading of the text, a reading bound to an imaginative process not unrelated to the creating of poetry. Even when the mind focuses upon a spiritual being, Thomas maintains that the divorce from the imagination is not complete: 'for we cannot,' he writes, 'in our present state know other incorporeal substances except negatively and by analogy with corporeal reality.'[50] It would appear that all reflection upon the invisible realm demands 'the analogy with corporeal reality,' though the theologian is called to rise beyond the image and not to rest on it. In the above passages, Aquinas shows his receptivity to a line of thought more literary in its concerns and more taken with concrete history and its relationships than with the ontological abstraction in which he so acutely excels elsewhere. It is to this more pronouncedly literary discipline that we now turn.

Chenu, in commenting upon Hugh of St Victor's use of the term 'translatio,' says that it means an 'elevation from the visible sphere to the invisible, through the mediating agency of an image borrowed from sense perceptible reality.'[51] The transference from the lower plane to the higher is achieved by means of the image's guidance, or as Hugh's Latin expresses it, 'manuductione.' Literally, man is hand-led like a child, pointed by what lies below to what lies on high. Such a vision is formulated in Hugh's definition of this distinctive sign: 'a symbol is a juxtaposition, that is, a coaptation of visible forms to demonstrate some invisible matter.'[52] The word 'demonstration' is used by Hugh not to mean – as it often does – logical proof; rather it indicates a showing or an opening of the invisible realm by means of the tangible image. According to Chenu, Hugh's dictum refers to a symbolic expression that reaches beyond mere imagination and 'touches upon the sources of poetry.'[53] Chenu distinguishes this mental activity from the workings of strict logic. 'Such "demonstration,"' he writes, 'did not operate like the premises of the dialectician, for there was no logical continuity between the two realities involved; rather, it fixed upon a likeness underlying the contrasting realities and made a leap between them.'[54] The same play of mind noted in John and Augustine becomes in Hugh of St Victor part of a theological method. The insight upon which this approach rests can be traced to Hugh's immediate source, the writings of Dionysius, whose ontology dictates a kinship, a likeness, a 'continuatio' between visible and invisible reality.[55] All things are charged with a divine spark, and so all creation by its very nature is congenial to the mind's quest for its creator. Of course, Dionysius' claim for the congruity between the seen and the unseen goes back to Paul's words to the Romans, where he teaches that the invisible attributes of God have been revealed 'through the things that are made' (1:20). This Pauline doctrine appears to be a carry-over of a belief common to all archaic societies. According to Mircea Eliade, 'all symbolism is, or at least was, a religious symbolism ... From the beginnings of archaic cultures, the hierophany is simultaneously an ontophany, the manifestation of the Sacred is equivalent to an unveiling of Being, and vice versa.'[56]

Although all creatures reflect the glory of the Lord by reason of their goodness, Dionysius paradoxically prefers what he calls the dissimilar similitude as the symbol best suited to declaring the truth of the unseen realm. See how Hugh's disciple, Richard of St Victor, explains the function of this image: 'Every figure demonstrates the truth more clearly in proportion as by dissimilar similitude it figures [figurat] that it is the truth and does not prove [non ... probat] the truth; in so doing, dissimilar similitudes lead the mind closer to the truth by not allowing the mind to rest on the similitude alone.'[57] Dionysius and the Victorines and Aquinas after them hold that 'the figures of base bodies rather than those of fine bodies more happily serve the purpose of conveying divine things to us.'[58] And so the 'rock,' the 'worm,' the 'fool' will be preferred to the 'light,' the 'heavens,' the 'monarch' because the former figures will not be mistaken for the deity itself while the latter group could lead into such an error. The likeness in the image is not mistaken for a sameness. Rather, it is taken as a shadow which so feebly portrays the divine mystery that the soul will not come to rest on it but will continue to mount to the object of its loving pursuit. Furthermore, this kind of speculation does not seek absolute proof: 'non veritatem probat'; it images a truth held in the mind by belief. Thus figurative or poetic knowledge enhances the understanding without violating the freedom involved in the act of faith. The concept is not forced upon the mind as necessarily true, but the mind is rather invited to imagine playfully and opaquely an idea whose full actuality escapes it. The thinker entertains the thought, the image, as one might a guest known to be foreign, a visitor from a higher realm. The play here is opposed to a seriousness involved with that self-satisfaction that we associate with personal accomplishment. The mind in toying with the symbol is most sensitive to its own inadequacy. We will return to the dissimilar similitude in chapter 9 when we discuss Erasmus' use of metaphor within this same patristic tradition.

As well as acknowledging the symbolic value of all things, both Dionysius and Hugh give most of their attention to the figurative element found in the history of man's redemption taken as a whole. The first type of symbolism derives from the divine source of the creation of nature, the second from the same source as achieving a re-creation through grace. Man's salvation takes place in a history that involves the selection of a chosen people from whose numbers a saviour will arise. The events of that history are both important in themselves and as referents to other major happenings which will ensue from them. Already we are involved in a kind of double vision. This way of seeing is expounded by Hugh of St Victor when he describes for us his meaning of the 'doctrina sacra': 'The foundation and principle of sacred learning, however, is history, from which, like honey from the honeycomb, the truth of allegory is extracted. As you are to build, therefore, "lay first the foundation of history; next, by pursuing the typical meaning, build up a structure in your mind to be a fortress of faith."'[59] As Hugh conceives it, a knowledge of the historical or literal sense of the biblical text provides the foundation upon which all sacred learning must build. The symbolic meaning ('significatio typica') is to be erected upon the firm base of the letter or the historical event as walls rise up in a cathedral.

Chenu points out that Hugh's original contribution to the history of theology consists in his using the traditional multiple readings of the scriptural texts as an element intrinsic to the structure of his theology.[60] The building imagery employed in his discussion of allegory in the sixth book of the *Didascalicon* reflects this mental attitude. Allegory, always founded upon history, is as necessary to the development of his theology as walls are to an edifice. The teaching on which this entire approach rests goes back to the Pauline doctrine of 1 Corinthians 10, which recounts the adventures of the Jews led by Moses through the desert as prefiguring in a mysterious way the Christ who would issue from them: 'for they drank from the spiritual rock which followed them, but the rock was Christ' (v 4). The allegorical reading of the Bible, then, is based first on the Old Testament's pointing towards its Messiah and then upon the New Testament's pointing towards the church's final consummation in beatitude. All such readings imply an awareness of the integration of seemingly scattered events by means of the divine providence.

Christ, the Son of God, occupies the centre of history, prefigured in the characters antecedent to him and the model and source of the heroism following upon him. In terms of the theology being described, he is as the Word made flesh, the archetype of all symbols in the sense that he supremely confirms the affinity between the visible and the invisible, between the temporal and the eternal, between nature and grace. And he is more. Chenu, in explaining Victorine symbolism, points out the two basic, controlling norms for their allegorical interpretation: the primacy of the literal sense of scripture and the guiding rule of faith.[61] It is belief in Christ and the incarnation that directs this reflection and distinguishes it from Platonic thought, to which it bears some resemblance. Hugh of St Victor, in the preface to his commentary on the *Heavenly Hierarchy*, distinguishes between a worldly and a divine theology, the one originating in nature and reason, the other originating in grace and divine revelation. Basing his discussion on the Pauline contention between two wisdoms in 1 Corinthians 1, Hugh paraphrases the apostle: 'Therefore God made foolish the wisdom of this world because in it the wisdom of God was not able to be discovered, and he revealed another wisdom which, while it seemed foolish, was not, so that true wisdom might be found through it. Christ crucified was preached in order that the truth might be sought in lowliness of mind.'[62] Hugh writes of a texture of thought completely resistant to a man-centred logic of the self. The divine wisdom, through the light of revelation and grace, finds its most sublime, earthly expression in the folly of the cross. Unaided, human reasoning could never arrive at such a conclusion. The mental inversion of things wrought by the cross opens the way for a theological language given to oxymoron, paradox, and other modes of expression aimed at stunning the mind, at striking it into an awareness not only of the mystery it has entered but also of a divine rationale totally at loggerheads with the wisdom of this world. Out of such a vision will issue the playful sallies so characteristic of Erasmus' *Moria*.

The symbolic theology inherited by the Middle Ages from the fathers through the various monastic schools takes on a play of mind that develops out of an optimism begotten by faith and summed up in two lines of *Piers Plowman*: 'Was neuere werre in this world ne wikkedere enuy / That Loue, and hym luste, to louhynge it ne brouhte' ('No evil under the sun can resist Love's power to turn it to laughter').[63] The couplet echoes a notion dear to St Bernard of Clairvaux, who sees the great reversal wrought by Christ's cross, which encourages his followers to rejoice at what the world abhors and thereby makes the cloister a paradise on earth. We find the same paradox in Erasmus' description of religious life in his *De contemptu mundi*, a work which, as we shall see, shows a clear affinity with the spiritual writers of the twelfth century. Walter Ong has written of the literary qualities in the writings of the Victorine school when it reached the moment of its greatest theological acumen in this same century. He touches on the writings of Hugh, the mystical works of Richard, the poetry of Adam, all of St Victor, to show how the teaching of the two prose authors affected the verses of the poet. Ong stresses the element of wit as characteristic of Adam's poetry and notices that 'at the point to which the trail of wit leads, the very texture of the poetry itself – the element which makes literature – is seen to come into functional contact with the heart of Christian doctrine, the mysteries distinctive of Christianity as those lie in their own distinctive way within the human mind.'[64] The very life of Adam's verse feeds and flourishes on sacred doctrine. Here the poet plays upon themes issuing from the incarnation.

> Infinitus et immensus
> Quem non capit ullus sensus
>   Nec locorum spatia,
> Ex aeterno temporalis,
> Ex immenso fit localis,
>   Ut restauret omnia.[65]

The dance of wit juxtaposes time and eternity, the finite and the infinite, and resolves the opposition by means of the mystery of the incarnation, or rather rejoices in the opposition without really knowing the answer. A play of mind is called for simply because no amount of mental work will enable us to get any closer to a solution. The poet rather celebrates the paradoxical union of God with man. And Hugh says the same thing in his theological prose: 'He whom the whole world could not contain placed himself in the womb of a virgin.'[66] Just as in Richard of St Victor's commentary on the dissimilar similitude of Dionysius, an apparent contradiction is accepted in a sense of wonder. Another doctrinal mystery, the life-bearing aspect of Christ's death, is given paradoxical treatment by Adam.

> O mors Christi vivifica
> Tu Christo nos unifica;
> Mors morti non obnoxia
> Da nobis vitae praemia.[67]

The energy of these verses stems from a joy over a death which succeeds at vivifying and uniting mankind, a death paradoxically ordered to bestowing life. In the above sampling, Adam plays upon the mind-arresting aspects of Christ's birth and death. The poet has placed his wit at the service of the divine by playing on the immense difference between God and man and by rejoicing in the unsoundable love that undergoes death to restore life. The wit of Adam's verse reflects the same interests of the Victorine prose writers who express belief through paradox and oxymoron and who explicate the dissimilar similitude as an expression involving the joyous leap of the mind from the visible plane which we grasp to an invisible plane too immense and overwhelming to be comprehended satisfactorily.

The symbolic theology of the twelfth century marks the crest of a literary form of the discipline reaching back to the church fathers. As indicated earlier, Hugh of St Victor made explicit its methodology. In the same century, however, a more argumentative and rigidly systematized discourse began to gain favour, and by the close of the Middle Ages the latter dominated scholastic thought. Against this abstract and dissecting manner of presentation Erasmus directed a criticism which at the same time called for a return to the Old Theology of the fathers. Because a patristic influence lies at the source of both Hugh of St Victor and

Erasmus, a similarity of approach can be discerned in both writers. As with the Victorine school, Erasmian theology is literary and places an importance upon allegory as God's way of accommodating the divine mystery to a human intelligence which depends upon sense perception for its knowledge. As in Hugh's symbolic theology, Erasmus' expression takes on a poetic quality in the broad sense that it is oriented towards the double meaning of things which both declare themselves and signify a higher reality. Again like Hugh, Erasmus is sensitive to the radical difference between a mind locked into the immediate data presented to it by its surroundings and a mind which has, as it were, been broken into by the mystery of the cross. So much of the play of Erasmus' intellect depends upon the paradoxes of Christianity, the wisdom of a way that looks foolish, the mysteries which man cannot penetrate. We must not, then, allow Erasmus' abhorrence of the scholasticism of his day to lead us to the mistaken conclusion that he owed nothing to the thought of the Middle Ages, especially when it comes to his play of mind in the area of Christian mystery. Samuel Dresden's notes to the *De contemptu mundi* strongly suggest Erasmus' dependence on Bernard of Clairvaux in the composition of that work. At any rate, the medieval authors, such as Bernard and the Victorines, offer a clear antecedent to the style that Erasmus will assume when he undertakes a ludic approach to a religious topic.

A RHETORICAL THEOLOGY: THE *QUERELA PACIS*

This initial attempt to define the nature and range of Erasmus' seriocomedy has ventured into the area of literary theology because it is here in the comic pieces of this particular discipline that the topic of our study finds its fullest expression. The relationship between Erasmian comedy and his rhetoric was initially discussed here in contrast to Luther's disdain for the literary aplomb of his opponent. Luther wanted to reduce Erasmus' *De libero arbitrio* to what he considered another *Moria*, to a mere piece of comic literature not worthy of a theologian's attention. A case has been opened in this introduction in support of the intellectual value of Erasmus' seriocomedy. I also mentioned earlier that Erasmus' rhetoric is not an arbitrary form into which he casts his theological reflection, but rather that it intrinsically adheres to that thought as an essential part of it. The rhetoric, that element mocked by Luther, holds to the theology as a quasi-comic constituent of his serious thought.

Thomas Aquinas suggests the relevance of a rhetorical approach to theology in his comments on the relationship between faith and persuasive reasoning. He divides rational argumentation into two kinds: the demonstrative and the persuasive. The first of these aims at convincing the mind beyond doubt of the truth of its conclusion, and, therefore, it cannot arrive at articles of faith because reason cannot lay hold of statements requiring belief. On the other hand, since persuasion does not set out to convince finally and irrevocably as does strict demonstration, it can argue on behalf of matters of belief without disturbing the freedom of faith's assent. This same congruity with freedom was mentioned earlier in the discussion of Hugh of St Victor's symbolic theology where the sign figures forth the truth without proving it. Aquinas appears to have something similar in mind when treating persuasion, for he sees this line of argument as deriving from likenesses ('sumpta ex aliquibus similitudinibus') and, therefore, as dependent upon an eye for resemblances, the power, which Aristotle characterizes as the genius of the poet.[68]

It would be a mistake, however, to restrict Erasmus' rhetorical theology to persuasion alone, as if it were void of the certitude characteristic of the demonstration defined by Aquinas. Although the mind cannot conclude to an article of belief by means of demonstrative logic, it is certainly capable of reasoning upon premises that have been accepted in faith. Aquinas lays down his own teaching in this matter: 'Though arguments of human reason reach no position to prove the things of faith, nevertheless ... holy teaching does work from the articles of faith to infer other things.'[69] Erasmus, likewise, will sometimes construct an argument soundly resting upon a principle of Christian belief and proceed to the obvious consequences of his premise. In the *Querela pacis*, a declamation which we will presently study as an illustration of his rhetorical theology, Erasmus calls up the image of the eucharistic cup. The presence of Christ on the altar is accepted by his audience as an article of faith. Erasmus argues from this belief to the madness of those who in the morning partake of communion and by noon stand on the battleground slaying their fellow Christians.[70] Erasmian rhetoric, although it will sometimes playfully engage in the paradox intrinsically connected to Christian mystery or sometimes follow a line of probability in matters left open to debate, can come down hard upon those who refuse to follow the logic which faith forces upon them. This rhetoric, then, is in no way alien to the 'homo seriosus' of which Lanham speaks, but has everything to do with its author's deepest convictions.

Just what were Erasmus' deepest convictions and out of what corollary to his faith do these arise? Let us return for a moment to the idyllic setting of the *Antibarbari*: its quiet countryside, the group of affable friends, their common love of letters, and the easy interchange or communication between disciplines by which the student of the humanities can with ease take to the study of theology. All of this was represented above as the ideal of Erasmian scholarship. It will prove instructive to take a closer look at the enemy of this ideal as the *Antibarbari* presents him. He is first of all the brutal schoolmaster whose dealings with his pupils are characterized by whippings and verbal abuse;[71] he is the monster who will exterminate good letters and genuine learning. Now the violence which sets apart the enemy in this description proves to be a constant in the thinking of Erasmus. Jacques Chomarat, in what might be the most enlightening pages of his monumental study, sees violence in Erasmus' mind not only as an enemy but also as the very antithesis of truth.[72] Be that as it may, there can be no gainsaying of Erasmus' abhorrence of violence in all sectors of life and especially where it intrudes upon the legitimate freedoms associated with learning and thinking. It might even be said that his insight and teaching on this subject occupy the gravitational centre of his theology.

The importance which Erasmus attaches to peace and unity affects his conception of the theological forum. He encourages ways of writing less aggressively dogmatic and more persuasive in tone. In this sense, the play of his thought goes hand in glove with his religious belief. His view on the way to deliberate upon delicate issues of doctrine differs widely from what we find in the theological mêlées that obtained in his day. Rather than brandish the pen as if it were a knife, the theologian was asked to join in a discussion until a consensus became evident, and, in this agreement, the presence of the Spirit and the mind of the church was to be discerned. James Kelsey McConica calls this formula for the resolution of differences the 'grammar of consent.'[73] If peace is to be maintained among the participants in the pursuit of the truth, then the bond of love must dictate the manner and the tone of the discussion. Marjorie O'Rourke Boyle understands Erasmian theology as essentially rhetorical in its form because she perceives it as being composed within a context that looks primarily to the preservation of the unity of the truth and the catholicity of the church.[74] The theologian, therefore, will plead rather than intimidate, listen rather than dogmatize, and discuss rather than denounce. Now if the setting of Erasmian theology in general be one of a peacefulness that sets itself inexorably against violence, it is easy to see how acceptable a ludic manner will prove. In most of its manifestations, play would seem inimical to wrath and to force. Nothing destroys the ludic spirit quicker than violence. The game straightway dissolves when the contestants turn to brawling. Enemies find it impossible to enjoy a joke together, and, if they do happen to catch themselves laughing, they are no longer enemies. Play intimidates, as nothing else can, the presumptions of wrath.

The *Querela pacis*, Erasmus' great cry for peace in the Europe of his day, may serve to recapitulate and to illustrate some of the above points in this preliminary delineation of Erasmian serio-comedy within a rhetorical and theological framework. The *Querela pacis* first appeared in the Froben edition of 1517. By that time the *Moria* had become very well known and would have no doubt come to the mind of a reader who noticed the stage direction at the head of Erasmus' new work: 'Pax loquitur,' an echo of the opening to the *Moria*: 'Stultitia loquitur.' There are other surface resemblances between the two works. Both are declamations, rhetorical exercises which Erasmus associates with the playground of youthful learning. Both share the ludic feature of a female persona created for the occasion to be the spokesperson for the author. The persona in either piece lends a certain dramatic perspective which these addresses would lack if presented in the straightforward fashion of an essay. The dramatic element is intensified in the *Querela pacis* and in the *Moria* because both speeches contend fiercely against unseen enemies and so stir up an agon or conflict that is maintained throughout. Although Dame Folly projects a much more pronouncedly comic temper, Lady Peace's early remarks on the harmony in nature endow the *Querela pacis* with a vision of an ordered cosmos that serves as a pattern for happiness no matter how far below the ideal mankind falls. If men fume in madness throughout most of this speech, Lady Peace never desists from urging them to a happier life.

After hanging her backdrop, the tapestry of nature's cosmic unity, Peace takes us on a tour of the human community and reveals the stark contrast between creation's unanimity and mankind's strife. In the city, at court and at college, in church, home, and monastery, the scene is ever the same: men fly out in anger at each other and rage within themselves. Peace is nowhere to be found. This picture of universal discord is sandwiched between the view of the placid designs of nature preceding it and the declaration of the peaceful character of the Christian vocation following it. The peace of Christians originates in the bond that holds them together. It is not a natural tie that joins them; the affinity is stronger and more intimate than that of blood, although this supernatural bond, too, is closely involved with the beginnings of life. Christ, Peace tells us, prayed not just that his disciples be of the same mind but that they be one as he and his Father are one.[75] Christian peace and unity derive from the hold of love existing within the Trinity itself.

In the style of the Victorine theology discussed earlier, Peace will make a telling use of the argument of the symbol. We saw that the thrust of the 'demonstratio symboli' in Hugh of St Victor carried the discussion from the visible to the invisible. The same thing obtains in Peace's speech when she refers to the church on earth as the prototype of the celestial Jerusalem.[76] The *Querela pacis*, however, manifests an urgent concern for life as it is lived on earth, with the result that even the anagogical meaning of the church as symbol entails a social reference. If the heavenly Jerusalem, the argument goes, means 'the vision of peace,' should not its prototype on earth foreshadow something of that concord and tranquillity?[77] If Christians partake of so exalted a life with so high a destiny, should not some glimmer of that life become evident here and now? The harmony of nature, first developed as an initial backdrop for Peace's accusations, seems to be replaced in the course of the talk by the presence of grace implied in the wealth of religious imagery, and the heights which such imagery represents measure the distance of man's fall from his acknowledged calling.

The symbol argues on behalf of Peace's charge that men, in allowing war to become commonplace, have fallen away from grace in the most perverse ways. Religious ceremony and custom have lost their meaning: the white vestment, a token of peace, the formal greeting of love, the cross itself, go unregarded.[78] Worse still, religious symbols have somehow become involved with acts indicating the very opposite of the symbols' original significance. Christ calls his followers his sheep by reason of the gentleness of this animal. Now the sheep have fallen to devouring each other, much to the consternation of the wolf.[79] The image of the saint is fixed to a new cannon as a kind of benediction for the gun, and the gory business of murder and dismemberment is dedicated to heaven.[80] Perhaps the greatest perversion of the symbol consists in making the cross a military standard so that soldiers follow it into the field of carnage. Peace turns on the brutal warrior. 'You, polluted soldier! What have you to do,' she asks, 'with the cross? ... This sign conquers by means of dying not by means of fighting.'[81] The mad reversal of symbolic meaning has been brought about by the clergy. The priest has made of the trumpet of the gospel a trumpet of Mars.[82] The bishop has traded his mitre for a helmet, his crosier for a sword, his Bible for a shield.[83] Adding to the general confusion, the benighted ministers drape their churches with regimental battle flags and place them next to the relics of the saints. It would appear, Peace reflects ironically, that this new piety consists not in becoming martyrs but rather in making them.[84]

There can be no doubt about the position Peace occupies in her speech. She presents herself as the one who brings life's happiness while war plunges mankind into sorrow. What is the cause of this tragedy? Peace indicates that the leaders of society carry much of the blame, but she also explores a chilling psychological factor in this human madness. At the opening of her talk, she asks her listeners to reflect on the insanity of men who consider themselves unworthy of the good things she offers, and, instead of her blessings, they choose the horrors of war.[85] Towards the end of the speech, she returns to the same disquieting notion. 'Why,' she asks, 'do you think yourselves unfit for the joy of the present life?'[86] In both of the above passages, Peace uses the word 'invidere' which I have translated as 'to hold oneself unworthy,' but the word denotes more than this. 'Invidere' can mean 'to cast an evil eye' or, better yet, 'to see evilly.' The word suggests a distorted vision. In another place, Erasmus says that a spiritual blindness can rise in an eye that sees physically; this is the blindness of envy ('excaecati invidia'),[87] that grudge of the mind at goodness. Peace is implying that man looks maliciously upon himself and, in his despair, gives in to a death wish. It is as if, after the fall, he looks with darkened eyes upon his nakedness and is not only ashamed but sees himself to be unworthy of salvation and happiness. The logic, then, of man's restoration would have to include his coming to see himself as saveable, as capable of receiving happiness. But for this, he needs other eyes, not those darkened by sin, but those enlightened by faith. He must come to see himself as Christ sees him – to see with the eyes of Christ. At the close of her speech, Peace refers to the saviour as the author of happiness, as the source of the new vision man so badly needs.

Because the *Querela pacis* appears to be nothing more than a slight rhetorical exercise, it has something of the external bearing of what Erasmus will call a trifle. It partakes of a play of mind by reason of its declamatory nature, but the depth of its concerns indicate that it must be classified among those trifles which, as the *Moria* claims, lead 'to serious ideas.'[88] Still, it shares little of the comic spirit that will be evident in most of the other works to be taken up in this study. Only because of its ludic resemblance to the *Moria* does it qualify as an illustration of the serious playfulness that will occupy us here.

THE LUDIC IMAGE IN THEOLOGICAL LITERATURE

The foregoing examination has established a link between the irenic aspect of Erasmus' belief and the rhetorical and ludic forms of his expression. His conviction, which sees peace at the summit of the Christian religion as its genuine fruition and goal, causes him to favour playful rather than aggressive means in the pursuit of truth. Of course, such a conviction is a moral one, but it is moored also to his theological stand against Luther. Erasmus' playful demeanour follows clearly upon his understanding of human activity within God's saving act. Think of the way the *De libero arbitrio* expresses the soul's being drawn by God, and immediately the ludic element in the act of conversion suggests itself. Erasmus refers to the words of Christ dealing with the nature of man's attraction to him: 'No one can come to me unless the Father draw him' (John 6:44). Erasmus wonders if the word 'draw' suggests a necessity that would rule out freedom.[89] 'Drawing' appears as 'trahendi' in his Latin text, a word meaning 'to drag' or 'to haul' or 'to plunder' as well as 'to allure' or 'to attract.' One set of meanings bespeaks violence; the other set indicates a delightful inducement. The same might be said for the word Erasmus uses to express God's influence or movement upon the soul: 'ita deus pulsat animum nostrum sua gratia,' which Rupp translates: 'so God knocks at our soul with his grace.'[90] Like 'trahere,' 'pulsare' can summon realities of contradicting significance. On the one hand, it can mean 'to push,' 'to beat,' 'to set in violent motion,' 'to agitate,' and 'to disturb'; on the other hand, it can mean 'to strike' or 'to play upon a musical instrument.' One group of meanings points to violence, the other to play. It is not difficult to guess which of these sets Erasmus will opt for.

The predictability of Erasmus' choice here can be traced to his notion of the divine nature. In the *De libero arbitrio*, he asks why God grants anything to free choice and straightway confesses that the Almighty does so 'in order that the calumny of cruelty and injustice may be excluded from God.'[91] In this matter of grace and free will, sides are taken according to one's understanding of the deity. One way of looking at God sees him stripped of some of his power by granting human freedom in the reception of grace; the other way sees that power enhanced and identified mysteriously with love when it is shared. Erasmus prefers the latter way. In explaining the Father's attraction on the soul, he states:

> this drawing is not an act of violence, but it makes you will what yet you may refuse, just as if we show a boy an apple and he runs for it, and as we show a sheep a green willow twig and he follows it, so God knocks at our soul with his grace, and we willingly embrace it ... But we are so drawn that we then run willingly. Thus you read in The Song of Songs: 'Draw me after you, let us make haste.'[92]

The very act of conversion is depicted as a kind of joyous increase of freedom. Note also how the picture of man being graced borders upon genuine ludic expression. The divine touch upon the soul, the spiritual 'pulsans,' perhaps best answers, not to a knock as it were on a door, but to the striking of a musical note: the sounding of divine love that resounds in the soul. Aquinas writes of the gifts of the Holy Spirit as infused instincts, new 'dispositions whereby every power of the soul can be played on by God.'[93] Aquinas' commentary on the Father's drawing of men towards Christ (John 6:44) uses a language not unlike Erasmus'. The meaning of 'traho' for Thomas does not include violence but rather denotes the attraction of love, an attraction that leaves human freedom and the power to resist intact. The divine action upon the spirit is expressed as an incitement that strikes and sets in motion: 'interior instinctus impellens et movens, ad credendum.'[94] Aquinas' 'impellans' and Erasmus' 'pulsans' both indicate a striking movement, and, if we are to avoid the suggestion of violence which both wish to eschew, then something like a musical sounding would appear to be appropriate in this case. In defending the freedom involved in the act of conversion, Erasmus gathers together texts from the Old Testament that see man being saved and restored as part of a turning motion originating in divine action and in human compliance. The Lord says in Jeremiah (15:19), 'If you will be turned, I will turn you.' 'Turn to me says the Lord of Hosts,' in Zachariah (1:3), 'and I will turn to you.'[95] In commenting on the divine attraction in John (6:44), Aquinas invokes a similar verse: 'Turn us to you, O Lord, and we shall be turned' (Lam 5:21); he also sees the term of this awakening as the Song of Songs expresses it: 'Draw me and we will run after thee in the odour of your ointments' (1:3).[96]

The above parallels between Aquinas and Erasmus in their respective analyses of the moment of grace suggest that the latter's description answers to the traditional Catholic account, that Erasmus is attempting neither to be unique nor to stand apart from that tradition. Yet notice how his explication edges its way towards the realm of the playful. The turning to God by means of an impulse awakened by the divine attraction, this pulsating moment of grace, suggests the divine initiative in the traditional terms of God's call to man, yet this very conservative tone does not rule out, but rather encourages, the illustrative image of musical soundings leading towards the divine musician's dance. Erasmus conceives of the movement of grace as a twofold act performed in unison, with God as principal and man as secondary agent. Such a doctrine invites the examples of music and dance which this study will explore in its final stages. As part of this introduction, we have been looking at the theology which would support such a choice of imagery. The one sustains the other: doctrinal explanation is supported by the expository force of the musical figures; the symbols call for theological explanation to ground their playful energies squarely within the area of the serious or, rather, within the region of the divine. But what is theologically apt about such imagery which a more restrained account would fail to capture? The answer to this question has been given by the modern theologian Hans Urs von Balthasar.

According to von Balthasar, man as creature has a natural desire for the God who is the source of his being. Now, when man is raised to the life of grace, his whole being becomes attuned to the divine by the gift of the Spirit. The Spirit bestows on man a new sensorium, an instinct sensitive to the divine will. This gift is cultivated by the Spirit's presence and the various experiences of consolation and desolation. It nurtures the development of an interiority that is Christ's, an inner obedience and resiliency responsive to the promptings of God's love. The creature becomes ontologically resonant to the divine touch. 'An existence is envisaged,' writes von Balthasar, 'which is like an instrument tuned by the Spirit: at the breath of the Spirit, the instrument like the Aeolian harp rings out in tune. This is an attunement ... which is a concordance ... with the rhythm of God himself.'[97] The new sensorium is set or pitched at Christ's own instinct for obedience to the Father. This divinely endowed sensitivity would seem to affect radically the reader of the sacred page of scripture and to lead to what von Balthasar calls the 'fruitio' or the fulfilling disclosure of the spiritual meaning of the text which the same author regards as the very goal towards which the study of divinity leads. To arrive at the Spirit's sense of the text constitutes 'the central act of theology as a science.'[98] From such a conviction, von Balthasar concludes that 'the rich substance – the inner sanctum of theology, so to speak – lies rather on the side of rhapsody than on the form of discourse which externalizes itself in distinctions and definitions.'[99] The passage ends with a series of rhetorical questions reminiscent of Erasmus when he champions the teachers of the Old Theology against the practitioners of the New. 'Is Ignatius of Antioch a theologian?' asks von Balthasar. 'Is Origen a theologian in his homilies and commentaries? ... And Augustine in his non-polemical writings? ... Bonaventure in his shorter writings? And what are we to make of Denys the Areopagite's hierarchies?'[100] What indeed?

Most of the authors mentioned by von Balthasar in the passage just cited belong to the patristic age, and, where they do not, they partake of its spirit. It is worth noting that, when Hugo Rahner wrote his pioneer essay, *Man at Play*, his illustrations of a ludic theology were almost exclusively taken from the fathers. They offer the precedent for exploring the divine mysteries in terms of a play that assumes cosmic dimensions. The harmony of the universe suggests the very music of being to which all things dance. If there is song in the macrocosm, then it must exist also in the microcosm. So goes the turn of this thought which appears in pre-Christian philosophy and is soon adopted by the fathers of the church. The presence of the ludic image to theological reflection has a long history.

According to Plato, certain gods were given to men to be the companions of their festivals. Among them we find Apollo, Dionysus, and the Muses.[101] These deities were meant to be the leaders of the holiday dances. Dancing becomes a way of communing with the gods, of sharing with them those invigorating rhythms intimately connected to their inner life. Man, thus, is divinized through dancing. In the *Timaeus*, the human being is invited to participate in the cosmic rhythms that lead to a tranquillity of spirit, to a well-measured balance of mind.[102] The movement of the stars is related to the movement of human desire and passion. What Eliot calls the 'dance along the artery' is in this way of thought 'figured in the drift of stars.'[103] This correspondence between cosmic and psychic motion is adapted by the Jewish philosopher Philo of Alexandria. In Philo's religious cosmology, the ritual candles of Hebrew worship shine as mirrors of the seven planets. Moses, the leader of the sacred dance of the Jews, is likened to the sun in the star dance of the heavenly bodies.[104] The seven-stringed lyre produces harmonies governed by the same principles that govern the great concord in the skies. It is number in Philo's thought that connects the sweep of the heavens to the inner world of man.[105] According to James Miller, Philo's tendency to see the seven-branched candlestick as a figure of the choral dance of the planets constitutes a synthesis by which 'the laws of cosmic harmony became one and the same as the moral laws brought down from Sinai by the prophet. To participate in the one was to obey the other.'[106] In both Plato and Philo, we notice a common desire to link the forces of the universe to the inner workings of human conduct.

As we enter the Christian era, we can detect a similar bent of mind towards the integration of man with the universe through the imagery of music and dance. Ignatius of Antioch, in his *Letter to the Ephesians*, refers to the star of Bethlehem as the new centre of the cosmic dance: 'A star blazed forth in the sky, outshining all the other stars, and its light was indescribable, and its novelty provoked wonderment, and all the starry orbs, with the sun and the moon, formed a choir round that star.[107] The unity of the heavens wrought by the star of Christ beckons mankind towards a corresponding harmony within the church. Ignatius tells the Ephesians that their presbytery 'harmonizes with the bishop as completely as the strings with a harp.'[108] Out of this union among the priests arises a song of peace and love that is sung to Christ, and the laity is called to follow the lead of its ministers and join in the heavenly song. 'But you,' writes Ignatius, 'the rank and file, should also form a choir, so that, joining the symphony by your concord, and by your unity taking your key note from God, you may with one voice through Jesus Christ sing a song to the Father.'[109]

In Ignatius we read of a celestial dance with Christ's star at the centre and of an ecclesiastical harmony represented under a musical metaphor. In Clement of Alexandria, Christ's action upon the souls of men, the sway of grace itself, is portrayed by means of musical imagery. Clement champions Christ as the new Orpheus whose music revives men deadened by sin and makes them sensitive to the divine attraction. Christ stirs sinners to a new life and delivers them from their slavery to passion. For this reason, he is the true Orpheus who 'made men out of stones ... men out of wild beasts' through the power of his song.[110] Christ, the divine musician, is descended from David, the singer of Israel's songs, but he is a far greater minstrel than his forbear. Christ disdains 'those lifeless instruments of lyre and harp' and performs his song to his Father on the 'many-voiced instrument of the universe.'[111] He plays this same music to mankind so that the human heart may join in the chant of praise. The new song of the Word of God, the music of redemption, is played to 'open the eyes of the blind, to unstop the ears of the deaf, and to lead the halt and erring into the way of righteousness; to reveal God to foolish men, to make an end of corruption, to vanquish death, to reconcile disobedient sons to the Father.'[112] With this song we move past the sounds and rhythms of creation; this is the music of grace.

Plato writes of a cosmic music related to the inner harmony of the soul. Philo's Platonic vision is incorporated into the Hebraic belief in the one God, the source of all unison and music. For

Ignatius of Antioch, Christ, the Son of God, becomes the centre of both the physical and the moral cosmos. In Clement of Alexandria, Christ plays his song to the Father; the spiritual music sounds in registers exceeding the limits of matter and awakens souls to a divine life. Basil, one of the Cappadocian fathers, conceives of the higher ranges of the spiritual life as 'the comprehension of mysteries, the perception of hidden things, the understanding of divine favours, the participation in heavenly order, the choral dance with the angels ... the joy without end, the permanent abode in God.'[113] In this enumeration of gifts to the soul, we notice an ascending scale. At first the spirit, still on earth, sees into the secret things of God; then it rises to the heavenly order, which is described as a participation in the angelic dance. Of the above schemata, Clement of Alexandria and Basil resemble Plato in the connection they make between heavenly movement and the inner life of the soul. The celestial dance for Ignatius, however, refers to the stars, while an angelic dance in the invisible spheres obtains in Basil. Ignatius of Antioch, on the other hand, is fond of linking the cosmic dance not just to an individual soul but rather to the church as a community. Gregory Nazianzus takes up a similar theme when he writes about spring, the queen of seasons, leading to Easter, the queen of days. The movement of the skies that results in the coming of spring is related to the movement of the church towards the celebration of the feast of the resurrection.[114] A stronger tie between the heavens and the church is found in Dionysius the Areopagite, only now the link is not between the motion of the skies and the harmony of the faithful, as in Ignatius, but rather between the celestial dance of the angels themselves and the congregation of the faithful at worship.

Dionysius sees the Christian liturgy, especially its synaxis or assembly service, as a focal point at which heavenly reality and the church on earth meet. The hymns chanted during the early part of the liturgy dispose the congregation to become one with the rhythms of the celestial realm.[115] Clergy and laity are set, as it were, in tune with the music that sustains the circular motion of the angels dancing in heaven around the deity. Thus the angelic rhythm is induced within the hearts of the faithful and inspires them to focus upon a mystery around which the angels dance. Now the ludic image referring to the heavenly creatures reflects a ludic quality in the deity itself and that quality is mimed in the procession of the bishop performed during the liturgical service of the synaxis. The prelate leaves the high altar and goes into the main body of the church and then returns to the sanctuary. Dionysius sees in this movement an imitation of that play of the divine goodness which reaches to the farthest end of creation without ever leaving itself or abandoning its own inner unity. Goodness, as it were, diffuses itself with a union in mind: the many are drawn to a oneness. So, in the incarnation the Son descends to earth to draw scattered mankind to him, to a unity which he ever enjoys in the bosom of the Father.[116] In the play of this paradox, Christ goes out without ever leaving. His body appears to be scattered in the bread and wine of the eucharist, only to achieve what Dionysius calls 'a fellowship in food.'[117] Diffusion dances with cohesion in the play of this thought. Erasmus will pick up on these themes when treating Christ, the divine harpist, whose dance consists of a cosmic leap from heaven to earth while his centre holds fast to the Father.

If a father of the church is given to writing about a cosmic music, he will almost inevitably tend to consider the world or the universe as a vast theatre. Clement of Alexandria announces that the locus for sublime drama is no longer found on the mountains of Greece. Rather, the action originates on Mount Sion and now extends to 'the stage of the whole world,' where Christ has become the great hero.[118] As the 'theatrum mundi' trope develops within a Christian context, it takes on an implied philosophical view of the world. In his *Heavenly Hierarchy*, Dionysius the Areopagite refers to the scripture's 'use of poetic representations of sacred things' as a kind of 'rude scenic' designation of heavenly reality.[119] Because the sacred writer has employed an imagery borrowed from physical creation, it is called 'rude' and 'scenic.' In fact, we can only use these same adjectives in describing the world about us if creation is being compared to heavenly existence. The world, in this way of thinking, becomes a theatre because, when beheld from a celestial perspective, its apparent permanence becomes fictive. Something of this idea gets into the thought of Erasmus' friend John Colet, when he expands and expounds upon the passage just noted in the Areopagite.

Colet calls theology 'the revelation of divine truth' and observes that this revelation takes into account human weakness by accommodating heavenly truth to minds that are dependent upon the senses for their perception. So, in the gradual apprehending of divine truth, 'there may first exist a sort of stage, and rude show.'[120] Revelation would seem to begin with a faint glimmer of the truth and move forward through various stages to a more complete vision. Colet sees the truth of the Old Testament as a foreshadowing of the New. Passing from one dispensation to the other is like moving from night to day because the earlier period gives us only shaded things, mere wisps in the dark that flesh out with the coming of Christ, who is God's own image and the Sun of revelation. The definitive fullness of truth, however, is not attained on earth. See how Colet sums up the entire process:

> Thus by God's wonderful dispensation of things, and care, as it were, of the human race, that it may be fashioned again for happiness, has there first gone before a faint shadow of the divine countenance, drawing men to a closer image of the same countenance, that at length they may be transformed into the reality of the selfsame countenance; to the end that no longer either in a shadow, or in an image, or in the Church here on earth, 'as through a glass darkly,' but 'face to face' they may behold the true countenance of God itself; then, namely, when 'it shall have appeared what men shall be,' as saith St. John, and 'they shall see him as he is.'[121]

For Colet, the Bible teaches us about a world which foreshadows a higher reality as a kind of 'stage or rude show' that leads on to a brighter image of the final, glorious apprehension of the source of all being. In so far as the fullness of truth still lies hidden, the earth remains a stage peopled with characters in masks, not completely aware of their ultimate destiny. In so far as the image of Christ, the image of the Father, has been revealed to mankind, the drama has already achieved its moment of anagnorisis or discovery where a genuine mirroring of the truth's fullness has broken through the mask of human mortality.

Because the beatific vision does not occur in this life, a masquerade continues even under the Christian dispensation. The Christ of history both reveals and hides a mystery. Even the most intense moment of that revelation, his passion and death, includes, from a human point of view, a deception. This deception paradoxically gives religious substance to Erasmus' own view of the 'theatrum mundi.' In commenting on Psalm 33,

Erasmus touches the nerve of Christian folly and the kind of disguise it involves:

> There was in Christ no dissembling of nature; for a time he hid his divinity; he did not lay it aside. He took on a real human nature; he did not merely pretend to be a man. Under one aspect only could any dissembling be detected; he who would be the one to make all mankind just and whole took on the persona of a guilty man.[122]

Erasmus' reading of the passage in 1 Corinthians that dwells on the nature of Christian folly stresses a power that passes as weakness and an honour that is mistaken for dishonour. The basis for this disarming way of seeing things is the divine intrusion into human history, the kenosis of God in Christ, that process initiated by the deity running counter to human expectation:

> In a mysterious manner, God cast himself down from his sublime heights to our lowliness; he descended from his wisdom to our folly and, nevertheless, what in him was seen as foolish surpasses all the wisdom of this world, and what in him was taken as feeble proved stronger than all the combined forces of human kind. What is more contemptible than to be lifted up on a cross as a criminal between criminals? And, by this conjunction, he alone conquered death which had never before been vanquished by anyone.[123]

This descent of Christ into misery in order to pass into glory becomes a law for his true disciples, a spiritual codex for all believers. 'From the refuse of this world,' writes Erasmus, 'springs the glory of the gospel so that, by reversing the order of things, littleness overcomes greatness and simplicity proves human cleverness false.' Later his paraphrase adds: 'Whatever according to popular opinion seems impotent, [God] chose to be most powerful so that he might all the more ridicule those who think themselves strong by reason of their own forces or riches or political sway.'[124] In such a vision, the theatre of this world becomes at once a sublime deception and a mystical play in which Goodness itself can walk abroad under the name and persona of Sin.

Erasmus' own use of the world-as-theatre topos in its most religious application is based upon a vision that sees human history as a unified action with God the Father as the play's director and God the Son as the principal actor. What is implied in Erasmus is made explicit in the thought of Hans Urs von Balthasar, who discusses Christian doctrine under the image of theatre through no less than five volumes in his magnum opus, *Theodramatik*. The unified action which Erasmus understood as the divine drama within the history of mankind is stressed by von Balthasar in ways that shed light upon Erasmus' defence of and insistence upon the topos. The Swiss theologian does not understand divine revelation as a static form to be beheld but as a dramatic event, 'an action of God on and with the human being.'[125] Revelation calls for engagement much in the same way that a dramatic script must be lifted off the page by the actors who would present it in its intended form. Von Balthasar contends that the 'revelation of God is not a thing to be looked at, but it is his acting in and on the world which can be responded to only by acting.'[126] In order to experience the divine goodness as the truth, man must actualize that truth through love. As in Erasmus, there is no genuine knowledge without charity, no theology without love. A casual or distant knowledge will not do; truth is to be absorbed from within. Von Balthasar writes of an inner connection, an 'innerer Zusammenhang,' between the theatre of man's world and that of God's.[127] God 'has already included the drama of existence on the world stage in his completely different play that he wanted and wants to enact on the same stage on which we play. Like the play within a play: our play plays in his play [unser Spiel spielt in seinem Spiel].'[128] Both stages include masks or disguises. As in Erasmus, the supreme deception or revelation focuses on the appearance of God as man, which gives rise to consternation and questions. Does God 'hide in pure "incognito,"' von Balthasar asks, 'behind the mask of man? Should he remove the mask only when about to be killed, and when the drama reveals who had played in reality – "this was the Son of God" (Mt. 23.54)?'[129] Behind these questions lies a whole tradition of theological reflection based upon the God who, in revealing himself, hides himself in an august mystery made known in his own person to mankind. Out of this paradox arises the thought we are about to explore: Erasmus' various attempts at capturing the play of life through the play of his mind.

PART TWO

THE SHAPING OF ERASMIAN SERIOCOMEDY

TWO

The Early Writings of Erasmus

※

PLAYING WITH WORDS AND IDEAS

Erasmus' penchant for seriocomic expression is related to an even more pervasive aspect of his style: his habit of juxtaposing notions in a state of contention and of reducing one idea to its opposite. This predilection is evident from the start of his career. In an early poem, written around 1487, he reflects upon love's power to unsettle the psyche and to overturn its emotional and spiritual condition. It can make the wise stupid and the eloquent dumb.[1] In another poem from the same period (c 1489), he entertains the opposing notions of joy and sadness. Happiness can turn into bitterness; pleasure never comes unmixed. Man's peace is ever riddled with strife, and death has the power to upset everything.[2] The same frame of mind, given to reversal or to the joining of opposites, invites the bringing together of serious and comical elements within a single composition. This particular alloy appears first in letters written by the young Erasmus to his fellow Augustinian monks. His success in this kind of writing was not instantaneous. The problem, in Erasmus' case, originates in his so mingling the joke with more urgent material that the reader becomes confused as to where one leaves off and the other begins. Although this criticism would dog Erasmus for the rest of his life, it is easier, in reading these first efforts, to sympathize with the confusion and difficulties of his reader than in his later, more accomplished works.

As a young man, Erasmus seems convinced that comical and serious material can be admitted into a single work, but he is not yet certain about the manner of achieving this blend. In a letter to William Hermans, he corrects his fellow monk for allowing the possibility of a jest to obscure what might be a serious admonition. Erasmus wants him to be very explicit in his intent: 'If you are joking, please tell me so.'[3] Erasmus still has to learn that most forms of the seriocomic, especially the ironic form, cannot admit of such an explicit avowal. The writer must hide the signal of intent in the text for the reader to discover on his own. This skill is not present in Erasmus' earliest attempts to join the playful with the serious. Although he seems wise enough to avoid following the bad advice he gives to Hermans with regard to being explicit, the fusion of jest and earnest in an early letter to Cornelius Gerard reveals an immaturity and reckless confusion that threaten the meaning of his statement. Erasmus starts to play with the idea of pastime.[4] He first tells Gerard that leisure and solitude, according to Cicero, enervate the mind. Then he comes to the defence of his own leisure because it is dedicated to letters. Then, because teaching will not bring him success, Erasmus sees no reason to spend his life 'idly in the study of literature.' Then, he claims that, if the enemies of humanist learning only took the time to read his little oration in defence of good letters, they would soon find out 'that it requires no small skill to speak or write in a good Latin style.'[5] In other words, Erasmus' leisure is taken up with good hard work. While his underlying, serious defence of literature is not lost in the passage, the attempt at joking hardly complements his thought. The self-conscious, not to say self-indulgent, switches in attitude and meaning from one clause to another indicate why Erasmus' correspondents had difficulty in distinguishing comical from serious matter in some of the letters. At the start of his literary career, our author's effort to blend the two tones in one letter is something less than successful.

Erasmus' play on the idea of leisure is not restricted to the letter to Gerard. The opposition between business and pastime attracts him again and again. It first appears in a letter to Servatius Rogerus, a monk of Steyn. Erasmus scolds Rogerus for not writing him and then speculates on the cause for this neglect:

What must I guess to be the reason? Surely, that you have been too busy, or too idle. Indeed I suspect both of these are true at once: namely, that you are engaged in a kind of leisure than which, it is agreed, there is nothing less leisurely, nothing in fact busier. For every person who is at leisure is caught up in love's longings, love being 'the sickness of an unoccupied soul.'[6]

The leisure of Rogerus, by taking on the feverish emotions of love, begins to look like business. On the other hand, the leisure of the worldly, like that of Rogerus, induces a state of worry and concern normally associated with work. His tranquillity really suggests anxiety. Here again we see the cast of thought that wants one idea to become its opposite. This mental game turns leisure into business, happiness into sorrow, wisdom into folly, eloquence into dumbness.

In the group of early letters and poems that we have been studying, Erasmus usually plays with words and ideas rather fitfully without any sense of design extending beyond a given sentence or short passage. The same is not true of the *De contemptu mundi*, written in all likelihood while Erasmus was living at Steyn.[7] This work is structured on the intransigent opposition between the cloister and the world.[8] Out of this friction arises a whole series of verbal antagonisms in which contending notions are clamped together. Word-play abounds in this paean to the monastic life and diatribe against secular involvement. Perhaps because of a style that betrays a comic rather than a zealous spirit, the work has been thought irresponsible in its depiction of the religious life. The *De contemptu mundi* is the first composition of Erasmus that clearly poses the problem of writing comically about serious affairs.

Like the two works of Erasmus most important to this study, the *Moria* and the *Encomium matrimonii*, the *De contemptu mundi* is a declamation, a piece of rhetoric, which might be assigned any student within the humanist plan of education. Erasmus dismisses it, as he did the *Moria*, as a trifle.[9] It amounts only to a school exercise and merits the attention usually afforded such writing. There is a sense in which we are to take him at his word when he reduces the importance of the *De contemptu mundi* to a school exercise. It partakes of a sportive and competitive spirit; it exults in conflict, in the carom of words, and thrives on a play of thought. Because its genre belongs in the classroom setting, it may assume a ludic form, but this does not necessarily compromise its serious intent. We know that Erasmus loved to make much of his trifles, to say things of weight and moment under the guise of a game. In this case, the word-play develops out of the strain of the contest and intensifies rather than dissipates the basic antagonism between the cloister and the world.

In an early elegy on joy and sorrow, Erasmus naïvely separates the two conditions according to a temporal division, with youth enjoying a monopoly on happiness and sadness left to decrepit old age. Similarly, his *De contemptu mundi* draws another simplistic distinction, now in the spatial order, when it designates the cloister as the locus of true happiness and the world beyond the monastic gatehouse as the region of snare and delusion. Erasmus would revise this immature demarcation, as the *De contemptu mundi*'s final chapter, a later appendage to the work, indicates.[10] In the work's initial conception, however, the separation of truth and illusion according to place comprises the master plan and controls the thought through the first eleven chapters. Out of this spatial opposition, the contest develops. Each place has its own representative voice as Erasmus invents an invisible, imaginary opponent who frequently interjects words of protest and objection to the argument of the main persona. The latter, of course, dominates in his condemnation of the world and his praise of the religious life. He establishes the two ways of living as mutually exclusive. The monk is a man of the spirit; his counterpart in the world is a man of the flesh.

On one page of the *De contemptu mundi*, its author attempts to convince his reader of the insidious train of temptations laid by the devil in which a kind of social pressure forces the individual to move inevitably from one danger to another.[11] The desire to be companionable leads to the tavern; the tavern encourages drinking large quantities of wine; drinking invites dancing; dancing lies one short move away from embracing, and so on up the stairs to the bedroom. The paragraph in which this admonition is found constitutes one of the liveliest descriptions of worldly joy in the entire work, but it stands as an exception to Erasmus' usual treatment of fleshly satisfaction in the *De contemptu mundi*. Normally, when Erasmus writes about the pleasures of lust or greed in this work, he is quick to move on to the painful consequences of these passions. Unchecked appetite follows madly after the call of the Sirens only to fall upon their painfully sharp rocks.[12] Because of this disenchantment, the satisfaction achieved through a sinful passion is almost always presented as tainted by pain. This combination of joy and sorrow is a major source for the verbal play most common to the *De contemptu mundi*, its unstinting use of the oxymoron.

When Erasmus writes of the pleasures men seek through sexual indulgence with women, he calls them tainted delights, bitter sweets, poisoned honeys.[13] He later shows the pain involved in these pursuits when he explores the servitude into which lust drives a man. Subjected to his passion, he cannot let his eyelids rest in sleep but must rise and seek out his whore in her place across the city. Slave to his shameless desire and menially obeying every wish of his mistress, he is fettered in a double bondage. At her whim, he must arrive, depart, and return again.[14] The author draws what should be play as work in his description of sinful joy. This paradox is even more evident in the account of the struggle involved in amassing riches. To ensure the growth of his holdings, the wealthy man must abandon home, risk his life on the high seas, and travel unknown countries, only to end with more money and greater worries.[15] Such are the hard, foolish tasks, ridden with anxiety, to which the rich shackle themselves. Their peace, at best, is, like that of other men of the world, a perilous one – 'periculosa tranquillitas.'[16]

We have already noted that Erasmus sets the cloister and the world at odds with each other from the start of the work. The world is characterized by restlessness, clamour, and danger. It is frequently pictured as a wild sea fraught with peril, while the monastery offers a harbour safe from shipwreck and drowning. In order to make the religious house more attractive than the secular city, Erasmus opposes its joy to worldly joy, its pastime to worldly pastime, its pleasures to worldly pleasures, and, in the comparison, the cloister comes off the winner. But on this very point, the De contemptu mundi has met with criticism from a writer who dismisses it as empty of any truly religious spirit, a mere exposition of pagan interests and attitudes. Emile V. Telle gives the book another title, the De voluptate vitae eruditae, because he believes that it is concerned only about the delights of scholarly pursuits.[17] One reason for this kind of negative reception probably originates in Erasmus' initial description of monastic happiness. There he borrows heavily from Vergil's Eclogues, with the result that he could be understood to be speaking of a kind of pastoral bliss completely divorced from Christian asceticism.[18] This same impression might be reinforced when Erasmus later extols the monks for their Epicurean way of life. More truly than the man of the world, the man of the monastery lives a life of pleasure.[19] To use such passages, however, to prove that the De contemptu mundi pleads for a degenerate Christianity, one would have to treat these sections in isolation from the full development of the work's discussion of happiness; furthermore, the reader would have to ignore or take exception to the obvious fact that Erasmus is playing with the idea of pleasure.

Let us look at the development of Epicurean thought in the work. No doubt Erasmus starts out in agreement with this school of ancient philosophy when he says that all men live for pleasure and that lower pleasures are to be sacrificed for the higher kind.[20] But, when Erasmus describes this sacrifice as an exchange of earthly comforts for heavenly ones, then he has reached a position where the true disciple of Epicurus will refuse to follow. Erasmus is talking about a total conversion of life in the Christian sense, as I hope to show presently, and, if this is the case, then he has transformed, in a playful manner, the thought of Epicurus to suit the ideals and demands of Christianity.

The man of the world, especially if he is wealthy, is frequently called a fool in the De contemptu mundi. The pleasure he gets from life is likened to the happiness of a criminal, condemned to execution, who proceeds to the scaffold laughing and joking while the crowd looks on in silent horror.[21] Worldlings refuse to consider death as the terminus to all their activity. If they did so, how differently they would conduct themselves. The thought of death would so shock the mind that it would view everything under a different light. What before seemed insipid would now be hungered for; what before seemed vile would now be precious. The meditation on death can bring about a complete reversal of value, of disposition, of taste. Within this purview, a life of penance is sought instead of one of ease; a life of fleshly satisfaction is traded for one of spiritual delight. It is just this kind of conversion that Erasmus requires of the monk long before the hour of his death. In order to obtain spiritual riches, the wealth of this world is to be forsaken. To win eternal honour, the desire for temporal acclaim must be snuffed out. To reach a paradise even here on earth, all commerce in sinful pleasures must cease. Such is the Epicurean teaching of Erasmus. It demands effort, but even this labour proves more delightful than the worldling's pleasures – 'nostri labores vestris praestent delitiis.'[22] As with his representation of the mixed nature of sinful pleasure, so Erasmus also defines the sanctity of the monk in terms of ease and effort. Here too the thought expresses itself by joining contraries together.

Monastic joy is really an amalgam that includes discipline and pain. At its core lies the paradox of Christianity – a dying to reach life. This paradox encourages the continuation of the verbal dialectic that earlier characterized the discussion of worldly happiness with its frequent use of the oxymoron. This rhetorical figure of contradiction appears many times over in a single sentence that penetrates into the ambivalent nature of the satisfaction attached to the religious life: 'There is nothing more wealthy than our poverty, more liberating than our bondage, more restful than our labour with its fastings so satisfying, its confinement so spacious, its sorrow so joyous, its bitterness so sweet, and its vigils more gratifying than sleep.'[23] At first sight, the oxymora here would appear to be easily unravelled by recourse to a simple distinction, so often made in this work, between animal and spiritual pleasure. For instance, a night of wakeful prayer, while taxing on the body, may prove restful to the psyche, so that such experiences can justifiably be called 'vigils more gratifying than sleep.' But this division tends to break a single reality in two and fails to capture the fullness of the paradox. To appreciate the richness of this word-play, we must place it within the monastic tradition of the literature to which it belongs. Incongruous as it may seem, young Erasmus comes closest to an accurate account of contemplative delight and reflects best the teachings of the cenobitic masters in this sentence that reads as if it were a mere word game.

Let us return for a moment to a key expression in the above passage from which a whole series of oxymora flow. Erasmus joins the contrary notions of work and rest, ideas close to being synonymous with the earnest and the playful, when he tells us that nothing is more restful than the labour of the cloister: 'labore nihil quietius.' Now other authors have represented the central activity of the monastic life, that of contemplation, in a manner similar to Erasmus' paradoxical wording. Peter of Celle, the twelfth-century Cluniac, says that contemplation is 'a labour more excellent than rest, but more delightful than sleep, even more enjoyable than any pleasure.'[24] Here too work and rest are equated, and here too the contemplative life resembles the Epicurean's joy. The monastic theology that ultimately justifies the yoking of these opposite notions takes us back to the origin of all things in the divine creative act. When commenting on God's rest after the six days of creation, Aelred of Rievaulx, the twelfth-century Cistercian, warns his reader against misconstruing the words of Genesis:

Earlier you pictured God to be working in time and, as it were, taking his rest in time to ease his fatigue. This is not to understand God but to erect an idol. Beware lest in banishing the idol from the temple at Jerusalem, you cultivate one in your heart. God made nothing by exerting himself; he spoke and creation came to be. God did not rest on one day due to the fatigue brought on by another because the day of his rest is eternal.[25]

In Aelred's mind, the activity of creation and the divine repose can be reduced to God's love seen as outgoing, in the first instance, and, in the second, as self-contained – the triune gaze of reciprocal attraction and fulfilment. This fusion of rest with activity the monastic writers restrict to the deity, but they do allow that man can imitate, howsoever feebly, the divine perfection in this regard. Peter of Celle exhorts the monk to place his soul's effort and work in the hands of his Maker who rests within him and to rest in those same hands of him who works within.[26] The justification, therefore, for the joining of those contradictory notions reducible to Erasmus' work-rest oxymoron is found within the divine nature, which is at once supremely active and placidly at rest, or, to speak more anthropologically, busily engaged and playfully relaxed. Later in the *De contemptu mundi*, Erasmus evokes a similar idea when describing the allure of contemplative delight in terms of a most subtle perfume which reanimates ('recreat') the soul.[27] Samuel Dresden, the editor of the work, points out the double meaning of 'recreat' in this context.[28] Contemplation operates like a second creation by effecting a complete regeneration, while at the same time it refreshes the spirit; that is, it both re-creates and recreates. Dresden, in like manner, comments on the significance of 'meditari' in the same passage: it means both to meditate and to exercise.[29] Both of these words, 'recreare' and 'meditari,' as used by Erasmus in depicting the joy of prayer, amount to a religious equivalent of the yoking together of work and play.

The oxymoron in which Erasmus joins sadness and joy, 'maeror jucundissimus,'[30] might nicely sum up the story which climaxes the discussion of the monk's Epicurean happiness in the eleventh chapter of the *De contemptu mundi*.[31] There the author asserts that young men and women are drawn away from the pleasures of the world into the cloister because they have conceived of their calling as a most happy thing. They are convinced, in spite of the disbelief of their family and their friends, that what they leave is nothing in comparison to what they are seeking. Such is the conviction of a certain Margaret, of whom Erasmus writes as an eyewitness to her story. In order to win her father's approval of her religious vocation – until now he has been adamantly opposed – the young woman has invited to supper in her home many of her friends who she hopes will entreat her father on her behalf. The man of the house, surrounded by a host of intercessors, yields to this pressure and grants Margaret her request. He then embraces her, and under a surge of emotion, unabashedly surrenders himself to tears. As if this were a cue for the others, the girl's mother, brother, and friends all follow suit until Margaret's is the only dry face in the room. Her brother urges her not to abandon the family, and those friends who have just spoken in defence of her vocation now oppose it at the realization of her imminent departure. Margaret, on the other hand, reminds her father that he has little cause to grieve and much more to rejoice, because he is not losing a daughter but winning a beadswoman who will pray very diligently for him. She turns to her mother in an effort to ease her sad heart – all in vain. Try as she may, she cannot lift the gloom that has fallen over the gathering: 'the feast extended long into the night with the unrelieved sounds of sobbing, crying, and complaining, with only one cheerful table companion in the lot, Margaret herself.'[32]

The sudden outburst of weeping in this scene, rendered comical by the exaggerated language of the account, epitomizes in a humorous way the two contending attitudes of the book, so seriously developed in the earlier chapters. Margaret possesses within her person a serenity that reflects the peace of the cloister; her family and friends betray the giddy, emotional spirit of the worldling who cannot comprehend the joy of one dedicated to the heavenly life. This failure of understanding measures the distance between two frames of mind: one believing in the eternal, the other holding fast to the temporal. Where one rejoices, the other grieves.

Following the story of Margaret, Erasmus concludes chapter 11 and, no doubt, his original draft by rhapsodizing upon the joys of monastic life. Twice in this chapter, Erasmus cites St Bernard of Clairvaux on the pleasures of monastic life. One key notion borrowed from the great twelfth-century Cistercian supports much of the paradox that permeates the *De contemptu mundi*. According to Bernard, those living outside the monastery only behold the suffering of the monks and none of their inner consolations: 'Vident ... cruces nostres, unctiones non vident'.[33] Earlier in the work, Erasmus refers to the monastery, in another Bernardine allusion, as 'our Jerusalem,' with the heavenly Jerusalem in mind, the place towards which the monk's spirit leans.[34] To live in the monastery is to inhabit a paradise of delights. In a setting of rural peace, the monk is to apply his mind to the study of the scripture, the old fathers, the more recent schoolmen, and the authors of pagan antiquity. Where the sinful pleasures of the world entice us only to strangle the life of the soul, the happiness derived from religious observance leads to peace, to freedom, to everlasting life. Although, in the later appended chapter 12, Erasmus seems to recant and to qualify this idyllic picture of the cloister, his quest for the realization of happiness, as expressed by Christians living in amicable community with each other, will never cease. We will encounter it again later in the discussion of the 'Epicureus,' the *Antibarbari*, and the *Convivium religiosum*, dialogues which either depict or examine the means of attaining happiness on earth. Again, in chapter 10 of this study, the same concern arises in Erasmus' writings on matrimony. The *De contemptu mundi*, although its title seems to indicate otherwise, opens this discussion, so dear to the humanist's heart, of the possibility of the Christian community's achieving happiness in the here and now.

HORACE

The stages of Erasmus' education antecedent to the study of theology are characterized by a preoccupation with the Latin authors of classical antiquity. It is said that in his youth he memorized the entire corpus of both Horace and Terence.[35] In the monastery at Steyn, he would steal from the hours of sleep so that he could read a Roman comedy.[36] Of all the Latin authors to whom he gave himself at this period, Horace seems to have been the most influential in the formation of Erasmus' seriocomic art. Eckart Schäfer, in his masterful study of the literary affinity between the two men, sees very early in Erasmus' career the hand of Horace leading the young writer away from a sentimental display of emotion towards a more objective, humorous, and ironic mode of expression.[37] Erasmus was learning through the imitation of Horace to give a lightsome turn to his more serious concerns. He was to develop further in this direction, and, as his style matures, we find less imitation and more adaptation of Horace to Erasmus' own bent and genius. In many cases, Erasmus' use of Horace amounts to his own personal accommodation of a text in which he manipulates the original sense of the adage to serve his own intent. Some of these instances, as we shall now see, point up difficulties involved in the bringing together of jest and earnest.

In his letter to Martin Dorp written in defence of the *Moria*, Erasmus cites verses from a Horatian satire when justifying the dissemination of truth through laughter.[38] He paraphrases the same passage in pleading for one of his humorous colloquies, the 'Apotheosis Capnionis.'[39] The lines in Horace – 'ridentem dicere verum / quid vetat?'[40] – refer particularly to the pedagogical strategy of making a lesson more pleasant by spicing it with the comical. It would be difficult to argue against such pedagogy, but, when Erasmus transfers his Horatian principle into the realm of his own polemics, its application becomes more questionable. For instance, when he refers to these verses from Horace to validate his exoneration of John Reuchlin in the 'Apotheosis Capnionis,' it is obvious that the humour and delight of that colloquy will be enjoyed by the partisans of Reuchlin. What Erasmus calls the truth of the dialogue, that is, Reuchlin's ascent into heaven, doubtless would not have been accepted by that controversial scholar's enemies, nor would they have found his glorification particularly entertaining. The Horatian 'ridentem dicere verum' would have been entirely lost on them.

Horace strikes a slightly different aspect of the seriocomic in the 'Ars poetica' when he praises the author who achieves a happy blending of the profitable with the delightful: 'omne tulit punctum qui miscuit utile dulci'.[41] The 'utile' or useful element within this context indicates some kind of instruction usually of a moral or sapiential nature. The mixing of ethical wisdom with a pleasant presentation of it became a humanist ideal especially dear to Erasmus and his friend Thomas More. The latter's *Utopia*, as its subtitle tells us, is intended to be 'nec minus salutaris quam festiuus,' and Erasmus defends his *Moria* against the censures of Martin Dorp by appealing to those princes who of old 'brought fools into their courts' in order 'that their freedom of speech might point out some lighter faults and put them right without offending anyone.'[42] It would appear that Erasmus' belief in the fool's ability to correct others by making fun of them was too sanguine. For one thing, it glosses over the volatile nature of satiric literature, especially as it is so sharply described by Robert C. Elliott in *The Power of Satire*. At any rate, Erasmus was forced for years to go to the defence of his own lady-fool for what was considered her indiscretions; furthermore, the balance between instruction and delight is difficult to strike, especially when the enjoyment assumes the form of laughter. Although rational man is distinguished from the other animals because he does laugh, the act seems to have an essential link to the irrational as well, and this element provides a constant threat to the intended illumination. We shall see examples later in the works of Erasmus where delight overwhelms lesson and saves our author from being what many critics would like him to be – a didactic moralist pure and simple.

A clear indication of the originality in Erasmus' borrowings from Horace's maxims on the seriocomic shows up in the Dutchman's adaptation of a dictum from the 'Ars poetica': 'hae nugae seria ducent.'[43] Horace points out in this passage that the neglect of small aspects of style can lead later to trouble when the author's work is ill received by the reading public. Literally, trifles (when not attended to) lead to serious problems. In the preface to the *Moria*, Erasmus paraphrases this verse of Horace when he considers the possibility of the insignificant inducing serious reflection: 'maxime si nugae seria ducant.'[44] Although Erasmus' wording approximates the diction of Horace, his meaning differs widely from the Roman poet's. Horace speaks of carelessness with regard to small details intrinsic to the work of art and the extrinsic effect this will have on its audience. Erasmus focuses on the *Moria* as an apparent trifle that leads intrinsically to a thoughtful state of mind. He refers in an ironic tone to the seriocomic nature of his declamation. If the quotation be from Horace, the meaning now belongs very much to Erasmus.

In what is considered his finest piece of poetry, the 'Carmen Alpestre,' Erasmus dwells on the theme, recurrent in Horace, of the slow, inevitable encroachment of death upon life.[45] In both writers the changes of seasons bring to mind the great mutation wrought by the aging process. The theme appears early in the verses of Erasmus written at Steyn. In his 'Elegia de mutabilitate temporum,'[46] the seasonal changes in the countryside lead to a meditation upon the waning of strength in man as youth evolves into old age. At the close of the poem, the poet urges the friend to whom it is addressed to seize the present hour and to make the most of life while he is still young and vigorous. The blend of the sombre and the pleasant in this early poem follows a Horatian scheme of the seriocomic. The one defence against death's final victory is to take hold of the present and to enjoy it to the full. C. Reedijk, the editor of Erasmus' poems, has assigned 1487 as a probable date for the 'Elegia de mutabilitate temporum' and notices that, in a later poem of 1489, many of the lines of the former reappear as Erasmus returns to the theme of the passing of things.[47] The 1489 poem, however, entitled 'Elegia secunda, in iuuenem luxuria defluentem atque mortis admonitio,'[48] the 'carpe diem' conclusion is abandoned, and the thought of the approach of death arouses the poet to think only of his immortal soul. A similar conclusion is reached towards the end of the more mature 'Carmen Alpestre' of 1506. After a mournful contemplation of the passing of youth, the mind of the poet can find solace only in the thought of his redeemer: 'Pectore iam soli toto penitusque dicato / Certum est vacare Christo.'[49]

The theme of 'vacare Christo,' to be empty and free of all things for Christ, has supplanted the earlier 'carpe diem' conclusion borrowed from Horace, and the new distinction suggests the difference between Erasmian and Horatian seriocomedy. For the vacuity which Horace projects into his future, Erasmus supplies a present fullness and joy. For him that vacuity is replaced by another emptiness in which the soul has abandoned all in order to be joyously free and open to love. One 'nada' has replaced the other – a notion that will receive its fullest expression in the *Moria*. The distinction also emphasizes the difference between the early Erasmus, totally given to the Latin authors of classical antiquity, and an older Erasmus whose initial enthusiasm for letters has not ceased but changed its direction. By 1500, he has turned to the study of Greek and will master the language in order to devote himself 'entirely to sacred literature.'[50]

THE MATURING INFLUENCE OF THEOLOGICAL STUDIES

Sometime in 1493 Erasmus left Steyn to serve as Latin secretary to the bishop of Cambrai. By 1495, we find him in Paris, where he spent most of his time until his first trip to England in the summer of 1499. During these years Erasmus undertook the study of theology and helped to support himself by tutoring young students in Latin when the time allowed. This appears to be a period of transition from a not always discerning passion for letters to a more balanced and profound approach that finds its fulfilment in the study of the Bible. The young Erasmus devoured the works of Rome's classical age while at Steyn and betrays something of a neophyte's immaturity when he shows nothing but scorn for works of art that do not conform to the classical temper and writes letters of passionate love in imitation of his ancient masters. His efforts at comedy during these earlier years of composition reveal, for the most part, a lack of import, with the result that they cannot easily escape the charge of frivolity. In one letter, written from Paris to Christian Northoff in the person of his pupil Heinrich Northoff, the addressee's brother, Erasmus knows no limit to the praise he heaps on literary masterpieces. These alone form 'man's proper wealth ... They alone ... give peace to the spirit and abide as a refuge ... without them we could not even be human.'[51] Granted that this letter is intended as a model of epistolary style and that Erasmus is playfully dramatizing both a dinner scene and an ensuing dream, a reading of the letter will disclose the extent of his development from this kind of writing when we compare it with the final revision of the *Antibarbari*, a dialogue also devoted to the praise of good literature.[52] The younger author, at least in his weaker moments, lacks the balance and depth that will distinguish his finest pieces of comedy. The study of theology seems to have played a decisive role in this maturing process by offering him a body of literature that both encouraged his passion for letters and also pointed to higher realities beyond the written word where, in fact, words fail utterly. Without this, Erasmian seriocomedy would have been restricted to wickedly amusing satirical dialogues and literary encomia of a rather light weight. With the religious dimension fostered by theological studies, the *Moria* becomes possible, the relevance of the Silenus to Christianity becomes clearer, and the heavenly realm towards which the ancients had pointed becomes the end of all reflection and composition.

It was a common interest in theology that drew Erasmus and John Colet together. Their friendship quickly produced an exchange of letters which shows us an Erasmus now reflecting more deeply than ever before on the beliefs of Christianity in areas most pertinent to this study. The Dutch scholar had been invited by his pupil, Lord Montjoy, to visit England; so, in the summer of 1499, Erasmus crossed the Channel. Most of his stay in England seems to have been spent at Oxford, where he met John Colet, who had already made a reputation for himself by reason of his public lectures on the epistles of Paul. On one occasion when Colet was visiting the College of St Mary's, Erasmus' place of residence in Oxford, an argument arose over the cause of the fear which came over Christ as he prayed in Gethsemane before being arrested. Erasmus thought simply that the prospect of suffering gave rise to feelings of apprehension. Colet, on the other hand, considered such a view unworthy of the saviour and followed the opinion of St Jerome, who gives Christ's awareness of the complicity of his own people in his death as the reason for his sadness and fear. The debate is recorded in a series of letters between Erasmus and Colet in October 1499.[53] There is no need to repeat the entire line of the argument, but Erasmus was forced by the discussion into exploring the theological concepts that would constitute the foundation for his later seriocomic expression of religious topics.

Throughout this epistolary debate with Colet, Erasmus is keenly aware of the need to conduct himself in a manner worthy of the issue in dispute. He lays down norms to be followed when scholars are locked in disagreement. In opposition to the spirit of contention and strife then so prevalent, Erasmus takes care not to be controlled by what he calls 'the eagerness to maintain one's own position.' He must free himself 'from every shred of prejudice' when putting together the arguments of either side. He must remember that in a literary battle 'the wise soldier would rather be defeated than win; that is, he prefers learning to teaching.'[54] In that way, he will come away better instructed, should he be overthrown. No doubt Erasmus sensed that the bitterly divisive rancour of the theologians was doing Christendom little good, and the ensuing years were to prove him right when the battle over doctrine began to draw blood as well as ink. He esteemed the advice in these letters to Colet enough to publish them later in a treatise which he called the *Disputatiuncula de tedio, pavore, tristicia Iesu.*[55]

Very closely related to this interior meekness advocated by

Erasmus is the gracious style he adopts with Colet. From the start of his career, Erasmus shows a connatural feeling for a style of composition that is gentle and cheerful in preference to a more agitated and intense way of expression.[56] His early admiration for Terence rests on the Latin playwright's polished and witty charm. Now, in this most earnest of discussions, Erasmus' gentle style does not abandon him, and Colet is quick to notice it. Replying to one of the letters, the Englishman observes in Erasmus 'a style worthy of a philosopher,' which possesses a happy turn of expression illuminating 'the bare facts, and, as far as the dryness of the subject permits, rendering them pleasant.'[57] Erasmus feels obliged to make the discussion as entertaining as possible. In contrast to the 'stammering, foul, and squalid style'[58] of the trifling theologues, he would lighten the reader's burden in holding to the argument. The relaxed ambiance within which Erasmus wants to debate opens the door to a spirit of play. Colet's freedom in refuting him gives Erasmus the greatest pleasure, and he compares his own part in the debate to 'a young soldier in training under you [Colet] in the tilting-yard.'[59] The military imagery then takes hold of him until he turns it against his friend by laughingly accusing Colet of fighting against himself and causing a general massacre just to salvage one mere opinion out of Jerome.[60] In another place, Erasmus mocks himself for introducing poetic myths into a theological argument.[61]

The portrait of Christ drawn in these letters suggests that Erasmus' personal inclination towards an uncontentious manner of expression had now become reinforced by religious conviction. The subject of the debate, focusing as it often does on the human nature of Jesus, forces Erasmus to call up his own image of the saviour, and a picture takes shape that corresponds with the affable tone of the argument. Erasmus sees Christ in his passion as a 'gentle lamb ... bruised by blows, disfigured, abandoned, and an outcast.' He never appears proud or high-spirited; rather, he is the meek one who 'desired that his own death should be of a most humiliating kind.'[62] Erasmus presents Jesus as the model for man to follow: 'Our Lord's purpose was to be a pattern of gentleness, mildness, patience, obedience, not fearlessness. If you trace his entire life from the cradle upwards, you will find many gentle and obedient actions, a great many instances of mildness, none of quick temper.'[63] So the subject matter of this debate, the human conduct of Christ, discloses the main reason for the debater's consciousness of the need for restraint. An ideal of gentleness in disputation supports the possibility for playful laughter as a natural channel of expression in this kind of discussion, no matter how serious the topic may be. Lightness of touch relieves the tension resulting from too much involvement and thereby helps to reassert balance and moderation. The humility of approach which the letters to Colet exemplify would as readily admit a congenial sort of playful banter as it would avoid rhetorical flourish and pomposity. Here we first encounter within a theological context the reasoning that leads to the formation of a style receptive to comedy even as the author's mind ponders a most serious aspect of the saviour's nature.

So far our review of this debate indicates the origins of our author's more mature approach to writing as these are found in aspects of the theological scene contemporary to Erasmus, in his own temperament, and in his belief about the conduct and character of Jesus. The vision of the Lord in these letters, however, is restricted not to just his humanity, or to his function as a model of gentle conduct for man to follow. In one striking passage, Erasmus goes beyond all ethical considerations as he explores the twofold essence of Christ as God and man. Here we enter the realm of Erasmus' belief and discover in this mystery the transcendental and ultimate moorings for his expression of the seriocomic. The passage takes us up to a summit of Erasmus' thought where it binds together in the single person of the redeemer certain antagonistic notions that we have already begun to study: joy and sorrow, pleasure and pain, the exhilaration of life and the anxiety of death. The author is attempting to describe to Colet his way of seeing Christ's sadness as the saviour contemplates the death that awaits him in the immediate future. Paradoxically, he finds coexistent with this intense sorrow an equally intense joy.

I contend that among the whole army of martyrs there never was such holy joy as Christ had in that hour when he sweated drops of blood. At that very moment he rejoiced with inexpressible gladness that the time, ordained by his father before time was, had now come to pass, when he should reconcile fallen mankind to his father by his death. Never was there any man whose longing for life made him wish as ardently to live as he wished to die. Never did anyone seek the kingdom of Heaven as passionately as he thirsted for death.[64]

Even while he admits the ardour of Christ's happiness, Erasmus argues that this great joy did not 'diminish or alleviate the experience of terror.'[65] The author readily accepts, in an act of faith, the simultaneous presence in Christ's soul of extreme happiness and sadness in the act of saving mankind from its sins. This is an enigma, and Erasmus thinks it impossible to speak about it in words that do justice to the reality. A matter of belief cannot be explained adequately; nevertheless, what is believed comes across in unmistakable terms: the agony of Christ, without losing any of its torment, was permeated with happiness. Another way of expressing this complex mystery would be to say that Christ in his passion is the supremely effective 'athleta Dei,' God's chosen hero, whose life reaches its greatest intensity in this magnificent, soul-stretching agon of love – deep pain and deep happiness felt in a single stroke. The act of redemption realizes the ultimate integration of the opposition between joy and sorrow. Tragedy, without being divested of its horror, must in some supernatural way cohabit with sublime delight. The most serious and sober event in Christian history, because of the heart of its central agent, must be understood as totally receptive to a delicate and heavenly rapture.[66]

Erasmus says that man cannot follow Christ to these psychological extremes, so caught up as they are with the mystery of the incarnation and the sustenance which the saviour's humanity received from the godhead. Yet the spiritual experience of Christ on the cross, being the pivotal act of human history for the Christian, of necessity is reflected and shared in the life of the church. We have already touched on the dialectic between pleasure and pain and joy and sorrow in the oxymora of the *De contemptu mundi*. There Erasmus is talking about the monk in his monastery, but later he will refer to the life of all true Christians in the same fashion. When commenting on the beatitude, blessed (or happy) are those who mourn, he extends the paradox of Christ's joyous suffering on the cross to the pain and sorrow of the Christian. 'But blessed are those,' he writes, 'who suffer out of love for the gospel, those who have now been delivered from selfish affections ... who, despising the pleasures of the world, spend their lives in tears, in vigils, in fasting, for the heavenly Spirit, the secret comforter will be with these.'[67] The Holy Spirit offers real consolation; especially in the time of trial, he breathes within the soul so that, even in the midst of the most atrocious bodily torment, the heart of the faithful Christian can rejoice. This receptivity to both sorrow and joy is essential to Erasmus' concept of the follower of Christ, the person of faith. The Christian kerygma, then, for all of its gravity and pathos, exhorts its listeners to joyousness as well. In the *Moria* and the 'Sileni Alcibiadis,' Erasmus will give expression to this twofold mystery in a most penetrating way.

One other letter, written from Oxford in the autumn of 1499, deserves mention here not by reason of the depth of its content but because it recounts a theological debate in a festive setting with Erasmus assuming a role he would often play in his later career. The scene is laid at Oxford, probably in a dining hall of one of the colleges where Colet, Erasmus, and Prior Charnock gathered with other scholars for a banquet. Erasmus believed that he never had 'experienced anything more pleasant, civilized, delicious ... It was seasoned by such refinements of comfort as might have delighted Epicurus and by conversation such as might have charmed Pythagoras.'[68] Such dinners as this seemed to embody for Erasmus a humanist ideal dear to his heart, a dream of happiness on earth in which the higher pleasures are enjoyed by men in an affable and relaxed milieu that conforms entirely with their vocation as Christians. The subject of the convivial repast will return time and again in the *Colloquies* until it receives its most polished and complete expression in the 'Convivium religiosum.' Erasmus' letter to Joannes Sixtinus from Oxford anticipates the festive mood that runs through the banquet dialogues of the *Colloquies*.

Early in the letter, Erasmus refers to the most honored guests seated at the high table where 'the defender and champion of the ancient theology,' John Colet, presides.[69] To Colet's right sits the prior and to his left another theologian who on that day had delivered a lecture in Latin. Next to him sits Erasmus, who is styled not as a theologian but as a poet. Even after he receives his doctorate in theology, Erasmus will often continue to take on the role of poet among the theologians in a manner which his part in this feast anticipates. As the happy group of men chat over their cups, the discussion leads into an argument concerning the nature of the sin by which Cain had angered God. Colet claims that his use of the plough implied a lack of faith and trust in God his Creator. Both Erasmus and the anonymous theologian argue against Colet's position, but to little avail. Colet appears intoxicated not with wine but 'with a sort of holy frenzy.'[70] As the debate continues, Erasmus senses that it is becoming 'too serious and too rigorous to suit a dinner party.'[71] The moment calls for a change of tone and spirit. 'I decided to play my part,' he writes, 'that is, the part of a poet, with the object of getting rid of this contentious argument and introducing some gaiety into the meal.'[72] So he begins to narrate a legendary tale about Cain. In the story, Cain, who is described as a 'thoroughly bad man, but a consummate orator,' talks the angel standing guard at the gates of Paradise into giving him a handful of seeds from the now forbidden garden.[73] Cain's purpose is to make a paradise of the earth to which his parents were banished. Man's industry, he claims, will cultivate this land, overcome disease, and make life immortal. This Cain, not unlike Colet's, places all his trust in man. The noticeable difference in Erasmus' contribution to the debate lies not so much in what he says as in the manner of saying it. He brings a colourful tale to a discussion, which until then had held rigidly to abstract considerations. The situation of man tempting angel, in a reversal of roles, introduces a note of comedy into the proceedings. Already Erasmus has begun to play the gamester among the grave theologians.

THREE

Greek Analogues

꽃

Erasmus' study of the Greek language and its literature had as its chief goal a mastery of sacred letters that would culminate in his edition of the New Testament, but, in the process of learning the language, he gave himself to the reading of its major literary authors. What concerns us in this chapter is not Erasmus' grasp of the koine but rather his contact with the classical authors from whom he would have gained a familiarity with the Grecian notion which is the subject of this book: the merry seriousness derived from what the Greeks called the 'aner spoudogeloios,' the festively grave man. Three authors seem especially relevant: Lucian, Aristophanes, and Plato. We will be studying them in order to see how the seriocomic manner and vision of each of these authors prepares us for comprehending the same quality in Erasmus. All of them partake, in varying degrees, of a merrily grave spirit, and our discussion will move from what I judge to be the least to the most serious. We will begin with Lucian, whose serious content appears to be less evident than that of a writer like Plato. With Aristophanes perhaps the word 'serious' applies less than even with Lucian, but his vision has an expansiveness and charge that induces a silent awe which Lucian, for the most part, is incapable of evoking. Plato, on the other hand, reaches beyond the Aristophanic range and, at the same time, focuses upon the comical appearance and speech of the great hero of his dialogue stage – the ironic Socrates.

LUCIAN

Lucian's presence in the development of Erasmus' literary art lies beyond controversy, as the studies of Christopher Robinson and Douglas Duncan have shown.[1] As a master of dialogue composition, Erasmus seems to owe more to Lucian than to any other author in this genre. The setting, characterization, and conflict of a colloquy by Erasmus most often reflect the Lucianic model.[2] In the matter of merry seriousness again a similarity is evident, although not as pronounced and striking as that found in Aristophanes and Plato. But before attempting to show the resemblance, I would first like to determine the extent of seriousness one can discover in the thought of Lucian. If we understand the serious in terms of the weighty, the intense, and the gravely assertive, I am afraid that Lucian will resist classification under this heading. In the *Menippus*, for instance, a dialogue that includes a most moving passage on the capricious nature of all human fortune and power, the leading character of the piece, after contemplating the vanity of things, concludes with a word of advice to his companion: 'make it always your sole object to put the present to good use and to hasten on your way, laughing a great deal and taking nothing seriously.'[3] From lines such as these, however, we cannot infer that there is not discernible in the substratum of the author's thought the faintest gleam of an ideal. Most often Lucianic laughter is based upon a clearly defined outlook that implies an ethical stance, a stance that is not easily distinguished from the author's assessment of his art as entertainment.

In his delightful panegyric, *The Dance*, Lucian tells us much about his own way of regarding entertainment and the kind of truth it should propose to the audience. He writes of an ancient mode of ballet in which a dancer dramatizes through his movements a tale that is narrated to the viewers by an actor with the help of a chorus and musical accompaniment. The ideal which Lucian places before the performer of this art consists of an inner equipoise that is inimical to excessive effort in acting. The goal here is similar to that of the literary artist. 'As in literature,' Lucian writes, 'so too in dancing what is generally called "bad taste" comes in when they [the dancers] exceed the due limit of mimicry and put forth greater effort than they should.'[4] The golden mean that Lucian places before the performer, when it is presented to the audience, helps to induce an equanimity within the beholders so that any departure from it will be taken as ridiculous.[5] So on Lucian's comic stage, much of the derisive laughter is pointed at some species of 'alazoneia,' the manifestation of an overreaching impostor who exceeds his nature. As we have just seen, the ideal behind the miming of the dance does not differ from the ideal behind the miming in literature and the literary dialogue. Both disciplines look to the imitation of the human. The viewer of the ballet, if he is to enjoy it properly, will find 'in the dancer as in a mirror his very self, with his customary feelings and actions ... Really, that Delphic monition "Know thyself" realizes itself in them [the audience] from the spectacle, and when they go away from the theatre they have learned what they should choose and what avoid, and have been taught what they did not know before.'[6] Because it too is mimetic, literature must remain true to man's understanding of himself and hold the mirror up to nature. This, then, is the truth and seriousness of Lucian. He unfailingly holds up for scorn and derision the 'alazones,' the impostors, who, by reason of their greed, their tyranny, their pomposity, their self-conceit, violate the truth of their manhood as social, earthbound, mortal creatures. This will to restore and uphold the human balance controls Lucian not only in what he says but in the way he says it. His laughter issues from this equipoise, and in this sense, his art and his morality are one and the same.

Lucianic seriocomedy does advance its own modest morality, which, while not equivalent to the ethical position of Erasmus, does cohere with the latter's view of the overreacher in his various forms as war-monger or hoarder of wealth. The exaggerated mental aberrations of the hair-splitting Scotists and other decadent scholastic theologians, so often the butt of Erasmian satire, carry a clear resemblance to the wild-eyed philosophers who people Lucian's stage. The characters of Erasmus' *Colloquies* will often assume postures imitative of Lucian when an impostor unconsciously exposes himself to a sharp-eyed and satirically inclined interlocutor. Christopher Robinson has discerned variations on this arrangement in Erasmus' 'Pilgrimage for Religion's Sake,' 'The Seraphic Funeral,' 'Cyclops,' and other of his dialogues, and attributes this kind of dramatic engagement to the influence of Lucian upon these works.[7] Both authors will mock the character who has no sense of his own place and limitations, although Erasmus does not seem as consistent on this point as does Lucian, for reasons that will be mentioned when we turn to the likeness between Erasmian and Aristophanic seriocomedy.

Involved with Lucian's awareness of man's place is his sense of perspective. Douglas Duncan considers the key metaphor of Lucianic detachment to be that of the 'over-viewer' who looks down from the heights of heaven and beholds the minuscule race of mankind caught up in a spectacle that looks like a bustling flea circus.[8] The metaphor is amply developed in the *Icaromenippus*, which was translated by Erasmus for his 1514 edition of Lucian. In this dialogue, Menippus equips himself with a pair of wings and flies to the moon where he beholds the human comedy and compares its stage, the earth, to an anthill. Erasmus borrows this image out of Lucian for the *Moria* and uses it to facilitate a transition as Folly moves from her account of human madness in general to her sketches of lunacy among the various professions. But, in Erasmus' treatment, the comparison becomes more than a means to establish an internal detachment from secular affairs. The *Moria* also suggests two contradictory ways of seeing: one heavenly, the other earthly, one far-sighted, the other near-sighted, one Christian, the other materialistic. No such suggestion, of course, is to be found in Lucian. His view of things concludes with man's circumscription as a mortal creature limited to a brief appearance on the stage of life, while Erasmus, agreeing with this as far as it goes, is not confined by it. There is another dimension, man's eternal destiny, that effects a radical difference in the substance of Erasmian seriousness.

Because Erasmus has a great deal more to affirm than does Lucian, he sometimes proves a too enthusiastic reader of the Lucianic text by attributing to it a gravity which the author never intended. The best example of this tendency occurs when Erasmus praises Lucian's *Toxaris* because 'it preaches friendship, an institution so holy that it was formerly held in reverence by the most savage tribes.'[9] Whether the *Toxaris* preaches or only amuses is, I think, a matter of question. This dialogue consists of a series of tales told by a Greek and a Scythian in a contest to discover which of the two countries holds friendship in the higher esteem. Each narrator gives himself to such broad exaggeration in the effort to prove his nation's superiority that the notion of friendship he champions becomes laughable. In his final story, Toxaris, the Scythian, plays the trump card in this game of tall stories with the tale of Abauchas and Gyndanes. When Abauchas' lodgings catch fire with his friend sleeping there, the master of the house shakes off his wife, tells her to fend for herself and the children, and rushes off to save Gyndanes. He

carries this fully grown man out of the place while we hear the
thud of a baby being dropped by the wife in her wild attempt to
save herself and the children. After the event, Abauchas claims
that he can always have more children. Anyway, children may do
him no good at all, but Gyndanes has already given him
'abundant proof of his devotion.'[10] The tale suggests the whimsical bent of the *Toxaris*. When Erasmus calls it a sermon on
friendship and then ruminates on the nature of love as it flowers
within the mystical body of Christ,[11] we may well wonder what
all of this has to do with the *Toxaris*.

The seriousness that can be attributed to Lucianic comedy must
be restricted to his art and its affirmation of balance, the golden
mean, and human limitation. In no way should we take in earnest
the social or philosophical issues arising in his works. His
philosophers do not scrutinize each other's thought to any depth;
they are rather caricatures of the various Greek schools of
thought. As such, they belong to a literary tradition going back to
Old Comedy and are meant to entertain, not to stimulate
reflection. In his *Saturnalia*, a collection of conversations, decrees,
and letters concerning the ancient festival, Lucian makes much of
the egalitarian aspects of a holiday in which the rich are invited to
share their goods with the needy. It would be a mistake to see in
these writings a social concern similar to what we clearly find in
Erasmus' *Moria* or in some of the *Colloquies*. Lucian will not
support so serious an interpretation. He is first and last a public
entertainer, and the conflicts he stirs within his works exist for
the sake of his art and are not meant as a reflection of an actual
social condition he intends to remedy. In this sense, his works are
divorced from the world about him. Such is not the case with
Aristophanes.

ARISTOPHANES

Unlike Lucian, Aristophanes is very much involved with the
world that surrounds his stage. The themes of his plays are
related to the Athens contemporary to him: the city's govern-
ment, its education, its literary art. Famous Athenian citizens are
the subjects of Aristophanic caricature. As a result, the satirical
point in his drama becomes more topical and abrasive than that
which we usually find in Lucian. Erasmus distinguishes the two
writers on this very aspect when he notices that Lucian recalls

'the outspokenness of Old Comedy' while avoiding 'its acer-
bity.'[12] One explanation for both the greater interest in community and the stronger tone in Aristophanes is suggested by the
development of his theatre within the context of a religious
festival that simultaneously celebrates the communion of its
devotees with the god Dionysus and includes elements of
violence associated with purgation and sacrifice. The wines of the
god stir up both camaraderie and wrath. Because this drama
reaches maturity as part of the Dionysia, its action lies closer as
well to the heavenly realm. Divinity in Lucian exists as a figment
in a man-centred universe. In Old Comedy, however, man can
reach beyond the merely human towards union with the deity;
furthermore, this theatre's proximity to a feast originating
in some kind of fertility ritual allows it a much freer expression in
matters of sex. Paradoxically, the plays of Aristophanes are at once
more heavenly and more earthy than the dialogues of Lucian.
His universe is fuller and more vibrant.

The range of Aristophanes' world will be seen to better
advantage if we extend the comparison with Lucian to the cosmic
journeys in each author. When Lucian sends one of his characters
into the sky, he does not propel him there for the glorification of
man but rather for the reduction of his pride. From outer space,
the sky-rover beholds human activity reduced in scale to the
dimensions of an ant. The opposite seems to be Aristophanes'
intention when he launches a comic hero into space. In *Peace*, the
farmer Trygaeus is drawn to heaven by a dung-eating beetle.
There he resurrects the goddess Peace from the pit where she had
been buried and wins Opora, the handmaid of the goddess, in
marriage. As he gains heaven and a lady-in-waiting to heaven's
court, Trygaeus shows little concern for moderation. The same
can be said for Aristophanes' other great sky-climber Peithet-
aerus, who, in the *Birds*, fashions a great city above the clouds,
challenges Zeus himself, and claims the goddess Basileia for his
bride. In both of these plays, the hero invades the celestial realm
and wins for himself a kind of union with divinity that is
symbolized by his marriage to a heavenly woman. Rhapsodic
excess and the breaking of limits prevail in these plays, not the
preservation of balance or a golden mean.

A further indication of the energetic expansiveness of the
Aristophanic cosmos when compared with Lucian's is found in
the former's description of the underworld as we read it in the

Frogs. His Hades is not the morose plain inhabited by gloomy shadows and strewn with skeletal remains that we find in Lucian's *Menippus.* Even in the land of the dead, Aristophanes brings his characters to life with great exuberance. A kind of immortality is symbolized in this play by the presence of the Eleusinian Chorus on its stage. This troop of religious companions is possessed of divine secrets and initiated into mystical rites and exercises. The Chorus' part in the *Frogs* has been interpreted as 'a collective representation of Athens redeemed beyond the grave,'[13] just as the resurrection of Aeschylus can be understood as a metaphor for the immortality of the Athenian spirit preserved in its greatest literature.[14] Here is a world large enough to include both the celebration of the phallus and a Dionysian rapture of a more spiritual nature, an affirmation of all life on all of its levels.

The difference between Lucian and Aristophanes becomes clearer still when we compare their understanding of Saturnalian holiday. In his *Saturnalia,* Lucian sees the festival as an attempt to retrieve the equality that existed among men in the Golden Age; in Aristophanes the festive temper aims at reversal and overthrow as man and beast storm heaven, as woman overcomes man, and as individual aspiration transcends the state. This latter spirit takes hold of Erasmus in some of his satires, the most striking of which is the 'Scarabeus aquilam quaerit,' one of the longer essays in his *Adagia.*[15] Because this piece, depicting the struggle between the lowly beetle and the mighty eagle, involves the Saturnalian reversal, the space journey, and the grotesque energy of Aristophanic fantasy, it calls for study in some detail. The essay also illustrates how Erasmus transforms the perspective of Aristophanes so that it appears to be at home within a genuinely Christian scheme of things.[16]

The tale of the eagle and the beetle is preceded by a history which treats the origins of the eagle's royal ascendancy over the other winged creatures and the natural enmity which it nourishes against the vulture, the wren, and other species. Throughout this part of the introduction, Erasmus concentrates on the parallel between the ravenous appetite of the eagle and that of the monarch whom Homer addresses as the 'People-devouring King.'[17] As the eagle wreaks havoc in the animal world, so the prince causes no end of tragedy by reason of his unbridled violence. The king's voice that can silence and kill is likened to the harsh, unmusical screech of the eagle. The savage bird, a symbol of the tyrant, finds in the swan, the symbol of poetry, its natural enemy. One recalls the sword, the other the pen. The smaller, more refined instrument, however, is known to cut more accurately than the steel weapon, and, in the 'Scarabeus aquilam quaerit,' Erasmus pierces through the swollen belly of regal pomp and majesty.

When Erasmus turns to the other contender in the contest he is about to recount, he begins, as he did with the eagle, by sketching its nature for the reader. The family portrait of these particular insects is littered with excrement: 'from dung they come, on dung they feed, in dung is their life and their delight.'[18] Erasmus makes a multifold use of the beetle and its scatological environs. In one sense, the beetle and its dung are what we expect them to be – thoroughly despicable. The insect's life, spent in the rolling of manure balls, is likened to the warriors 'who have often during a sharp siege borne hard winters and harder hunger, who have dragged out a life of ill-health from eating not only roots but rotten food, who have spent months at sea. Compared with the filthiness of this life, the beetle is clean; compared with its wretchedness he is enviable.'[19] Erasmus first suggests a likeness between the soldier on his pallet in the open field and the beetle on its dung heap, but then withdraws it. The bug is by far the cleaner of the two. The same holds true when the insect is set next to the eagle: 'when we see the beetle keeping clean in the midst of its dung, with its shell always shining, and the eagle smelling bad even in the air, well, I ask you, which of them is the cleaner?'[20] Both the soldier and the eagle, two agents of force and aggression, reek next to the manure-loving beetle. Such a judgment is verified by the recourse to the moral order of things where both king and warrior have proven themselves foul by reason of their murderous actions.

The scatological beetle, then, is clean when compared with the filth of kings, generals, soldiers. But he is more than that. For all his lowliness, the insect is even said to be worthy of admiration. Erasmus sings the praises of dung because of its fertilizing and medicinal powers. And the beetle in the fable narrated by the author is one with a heavenly destiny. He is of the same pedigree as the beetle in Aristophanes' *Peace* who feeds on dung and powers the cart in a startling transformation by which a lowly insect becomes, as Whitman observes, a mighty Pegasus.[21]

So in Erasmus' tale, the beetle rises high. First, he seeks out the eagle's mountain nest where he destroys her eggs. Later, he ascends to 'the very stronghold of mighty Jove,' the king of the gods, who had promised the distressed mother eagle to protect her eggs himself since she had no defence against the wiles of the beetle. In the heavens the insect hero defeats even Jove when he deposits in his bosom 'a ball expressly made for the purpose out of dung.'[22] When the god tries to rid himself of the offensive pellet, he inadvertently throws out the eagle's eggs with it.

This essay's spirit of Saturnalian overthrow, the grotesque yoking of earth and heaven, together with the energetic fantasy affirming all of life and the burning concern for the commonwealth, indicate an Aristophanic strain that has been converted by a Christian understanding. With regard to this transformation, Erasmus will take, in another of his *Adagia*, the image of the beetle as used in Old Comedy and incorporate it within a scriptural context to make of the contemptible insect an image of the saviour as the psalmist beholds the opprobrium and ignominy that the Servant of Yahweh will suffer: 'But I am a worm and no man' (Ps 21:7). Erasmus recalls here that some commentaries on this verse identify the worm with the beetle.[23] The mentality, so characteristic of Erasmus, that wants to find importance within the apparently insignificant and despicable will be further confirmed by the Silenus image that he discovers in Plato.

What has been said of the Aristophanic elements in the 'Scarabeus aquilam quaerit' applies in a less apparent but more festive manner to the *Moria*. When Erasmus, in his preface to the work, suggests that his critics will accuse him of reviving Old Comedy, he is also indirectly acknowledging his debt to Aristophanes. The *Moria*, considered from the aspect of its spatial movement, consists, like the 'Scarabeus aquilam quaerit,' of a voyage to heaven in which silly, fallen humanity is finally apotheosized. At the start of the speech, Folly seems to stroll among her fellow fools in a state of benign rapport. At the beginning of part 2, she invites her audience to look down from the moon upon the stage of fools below. By the end of her talk, she has led us to behold transcendent folly in the ecstasy of the blissful souls in heaven. Such happiness arrives not by reason of the merits of the sanctified. Like the rascality by which Aristophanes' hero triumphs, the Christian saint wins redemption by reason of his ignorance in sinning and by force of the divine Fool who submits to the heavenly madness of the crucifixion. The heroes of the *Moria*, like the protagonists of Old Comedy, do not mount heavenwards primarily because heaven would reward their moral uprightness but rather because they are caught up in the folly of their Champion; furthermore, earthiness becomes grotesquely involved in this grammar of ascent. Stupid, lowly animals such as the ass and the lamb become the companions of Christ, who lifts the fallen to great heights. The god Silenus, first seen as a white-haired wooer dancing a jig, reappears later in the form of an ugly doll which, when opened, reveals objects of great spiritual beauty. In a later chapter devoted exclusively to the *Moria*, a parallel will be shown in some detail between the out-going lovers of part 1 and the transported saints of part 3. Finally, the joy experienced by the saints absorbed in the contemplation of divine beauty amounts to a Christian version of that expansive wholeness that constitutes the goal of the greatest heroes in the plays of Aristophanes.

PLATO

In passing from Aristophanes to Plato, we encounter forms of thought and style more conducive to expressing serious ideas about the life of the spirit. Yet the philosopher, for all the flight of his inquiring mind, is not unreceptive to the genius of Aristophanes. A link between the two writers appears in Plato's sympathetic creation of the comic poet in the *Symposium*. The attack of hiccups that seizes Aristophanes causes him to lose his turn at delineating love and makes for a comical introduction to his not uncomical speech on love. Both before and after his encomium, he betrays a fear that what he says will be taken as absurd, and there are grounds for his uneasiness. His depiction of early men and women rolled into odd-looking pairs of various combinations has more than a little of that grotesque character already noted in the playwright himself. These strange creatures resemble grasshoppers when they copulate and evoke the antics of the clown turning cartwheels when they try to run. Yet the speech as a whole, like the plays of Aristophanes, does aspire beyond the merely ludicrous. Man, according to the persona in the dialogue, is now incomplete and goes about looking for his other half. 'For there was a time ... when we were one, but now, for our sins, God has scattered us abroad, as the Spartans scattered the Arcadians.'[24] He sums up all of life in terms of love when he says that 'the happiness of the whole human race, women no less than men, is to be found in the consummation of our love, and in the healing of our dissevered nature by finding each his proper mate.'[25] As the *Symposium* continues, this oneness, which is definitively asserted in the speech of Socrates, goes beyond the union of two people to the cleaving of the soul to the good.

The *Symposium* indicates how much of Aristophanic comedy Plato absorbed as well as how far beyond the dramatist the philosopher can rise in his *Dialogues*. In range, he is not so earthy as Aristophanes but much better exercised in probing the heavenly realms. He is sympathetic to comedy because he conceives his quest for the truth as a kind of game and writing about it as a pastime; however, this entertainment of ideas, because it is far removed from the trivial, is most noble and godlike. In Plato, the spirit of merry seriousness finds its fullest expression. The speech he gives to Aristophanes in the *Symposium*, apart from its comedy, is laden with ideas that elicit adaptation and development within a Christian frame of reference. John Colet, in his treatise on the mystical body, describes mankind in a state of dispersion, and it can only be reunited by the love of the Holy Spirit.[26] The parallel between this notion and those noted above in the *Symposium* is obvious.

Erasmus' use, as well as his revision, of Plato is seen in one of its happiest instances when the humanist borrows the image of the Silenus of Alcibiades and makes it serve his own religious insight. Towards the end of the *Symposium*, Alcibiades likens Socrates to the Sileni that were commonly sold in the statuary shops at Athens. On the outside appeared the ridiculous form of Silenus, the drinking companion of Bacchus, but within were hidden miniature figures of the gods. Socrates, according to Alcibiades, is also like Marsyas, the ugly flute player, who composed heavenly tunes that enjoyed a magical power over those listening to his music. The idea of the ugly possessing an unexpected beauty intrigued Erasmus, and he takes up the theme in one passage of the *Moria* and in the famous essay 'Sileni Alcibiadis.' In both of these works, Erasmus outdoes Plato in the stress he lays on the bawdy appearance of the god Silenus. The *Moria* catches him dancing the coarse, bacchanalian cordax,[27] a dance which, according to Lane Cooper, would have no place in Plato's ideal community.[28] In the 'Sileni Alcibiadis,' Silenus is designated the schoolmaster of Bacchus, 'whom the poets call the jester of the gods (they have their own buffoons like the princes of our time).'[29] Socrates is compared to the Silenus statue because of his 'yokel's face, with a bovine look about it, and a snub nose always running.' From such an appearance, 'you would have thought him some stupid, thick-headed clown.' The Silenus statue, in spite of its absurd outer casing, discloses a divine beauty when opened. So too with Socrates. Although his penchant for jesting suggests the clown, this impression fades once he begins talking about philosophy. At that moment, the Silenus opens, and within 'you find a god rather than a man.'[30]

Erasmus' development of this image in the 'Sileni Alcibiadis' remains almost exclusively Platonic until he applies it to Christ, whom he claims to be 'the most extraordinary Silenus of all.'[31] He cites the saviour's poverty and humble beginnings, his unlearned companions, his weary life and miserable death on the cross. At this point he begins to mingle a Greek line of thought with the Hebraic: 'The mystic prophet was contemplating him from this angle when he wrote, "He hath no form nor comeliness; and when we shall see him, there is no beauty that we should desire him. He is despised and rejected of men."'[32] This quotation from Isaias (53:2–3) shows how easily the notion of Christ, the Silenus, fits into the Judaeo-Christian tradition. Although certain parts of Erasmus' discussion of it carry an element of surprise, the underlying idea is known to other ages of Christian belief. Richard of St Victor, writing in the twelfth century, refers to the earthly eye of man being arrested and held by the wounds and broken body of Christ, and to how, through this deformity, the inner eye awakens to the saviour's majesty and eternal beauty.[33] Something similar happens in Erasmus' treatment of Christ, the Silenus. On the outside, he is ridiculously weak and ugly, but,

> if he deigns to show himself to the purified eyes of the soul, what unspeakable riches you will find there: in such service to mankind, there is a pearl of great price, in such humility, what grandeur! in such poverty, what riches! in such weakness, what immeasurable strength! in such shame, what glory! in such labours, what utter peace! And lastly in that bitter death, there is the source of everlasting life.[34]

Christ, the Silenus, begets a great variety of paradoxes. The *Moria* likewise exploits the paradoxical nature of the statue. There the figure is said to have 'two aspects quite different from each other. Hence, what appears "at first blush" (as they say) to be death, will, if you examine it more closely, turn out to be life; conversely, life will turn out to be death; beauty will become ugliness.'[35] Here, too, the deformed can become beautiful. In other words, that which ordinarily causes pain and discomfort can produce pleasure. Obviously, we are not far here from one essential form of the seriocomic amalgam. Aristotle thought that the effect of the comic originates in the species of the ugly which he calls the ridiculous, and this last term he defines as 'a deformity not productive of pain.'[36] This and much more can be said of Christ, the Silenus: a deformed figure capable of causing the greatest joy.

Erasmus' treatment of the Silenus lays the groundwork for the development of a Christian grotesquerie. There is a beauty in fallen, decrepit, sick, dying man. This paradoxical insight lies at the heart of Erasmian comedy, which so often blends the earthly and the heavenly in outlandish ways. The Silenus, too, high-lights the ever-changing nature of human vision with its built-in potential for reversal. Opposites can trade places: 'riches will turn to poverty; notoriety will become fame; learning will be ignorance; strength, weakness; noble birth will be ignoble; joy will become sadness; success, failure; friendship, enmity; what is helpful will seem harmful.'[37] In such an outlook, the serious can stand where the playful stood only an instant before. These last two opposites are also a pair or, as Plato would say, 'sisters.'[38] The Christian application of this inversion in Erasmus sees Christ as foolish and ridiculous in the eyes of his enemies and wise in the light of heaven. So, in a later chapter of this study, we will behold Folly herself lifted up and subsumed within eternal mystery.

The reversal of meaning, so intrinsic to Erasmian word-play, originates in a view of things that is expounded by Plato in the allegory of the cave.[39] There the stage of human activity is compared both to a kind of shadow play and to puppet theatre; but the divine puppet in this picture tale is surely the character who wins freedom from his shackles and turns around to look up to the light. This turning is later referred to as a conversion, and upon this basic change of position depends the total 're-vision' of things. Now substance is known for what it is, and shadow is taken for shadow. The opposite is true for those still manacled to an illusory world. Because of the fundamental difference of outlook in these two types of men, each must regard the other as mad. This Platonic conversion along with its eristic consequences permeates Erasmus' play on words and sense of paradox. When the point of view is reversed, the meaning of words somersaults. 'The reversing of values,' says Erasmus in the 'Sileni Alcibiadis,' 'brings about a reversed use of words,'[40] and in the *Enchiridion* he says that 'in Christ all things are changed and their names are reversed.'[41] Although the end or goal of this conversion is Christian, its intellectual and literary composition harks back to Plato. The Silenus image itself is based on this kind of 're-vision' that probes deeply to find a reality which opposes appearance.

Although the Silenus, when viewed spatially, awards the place of preference to the inside, this order is normally reversed in Plato's poetic arrangement of the cosmos. He situates the earth at the centre of things and establishes the gods in the outer regions of the heavens.[42] The allegory of the cave places humankind in a lower darkness that calls for an ascent to light. In the *Phaedrus* that ascent is inspired by beauty; in the *Symposium*, it is described in terms of love. The *Republic* conceives of an upward climb towards the truest existence as an educational process, part of which is analysed in the *Sophist* as a game of dialectical cross-examining. This passage from the lower to the higher, from the visible to the invisible, must needs be accompanied by play in a variety of forms: the contest of dialectic, the play of words, the drama of dialogue. The noble reaching up to the highest realms of love and beauty that we follow in the *Symposium* takes place within the setting of a drinking bout. Such an ambience symbolizes the conviction that somehow an air of carelessness must accompany this most careful and caring of investigations. Solemn man is not equal to the search because nothing in life is completely serious save God; and the divine will, according to the *Laws*, desires that man make of his existence a noble game in which he plays the part of heaven's toy.[43]

Erasmus, in his *Enchiridion*, conceives of things for the most part in this Platonic manner when he urges his reader to move away from earthly reality towards the truer reality of the spirit. Likewise, he imagines this movement in terms of an ascent. The faithful Christian is told that he must

not wish to crawl on the ground with filthy beasts but, ever relying upon those wings which Plato thinks are engen-

dered in souls by the fervor of love, steadily aspire to mount
– as if by certain steps of Jacob's ladder – from body to spirit,
from the visible world to the invisible, from the letter to the
essence, from the sensible to the intelligible, from multiplicity to oneness.[44]

What the author labours at in the *Enchiridion* he plays with in the
Moria. We have already seen the Aristophanic aspect of this
rising motion whereby man leaves earth to invade the heavenly
realms and how such a journey served as a model for both the
'Scarabeus aquilam quaerit' and the *Moria*. When this ascent
involves the forsaking of the body on behalf of the spirit, then the
thinking of Plato replaces the gusto of Aristophanes, whose
comic vision resists the abandonment of the flesh in the name of
the spirit. The flying heroes of Aristophanes want bodily
enjoyment as well as a likeness to the gods.

Plato's use of the 'theatrum mundi' theme in which he
compares human existence to a shadow play or a puppet show
tends to reduce the importance of that existence much in the way
that Lucian does in the *Menippus*. As we have already seen, the
latter will shrink the dimensions of man's social life to the size of
an anthill when his hero views the planet earth from the moon.
Likewise, Plato describes the vastness of the cosmos in order to
show us that men 'live round the sea like ants or frogs round a
pond.'[45] Erasmus does not remain unaffected by such a conception of the universe, but we would fall short of the truth were we
to conclude that he remains satisfied with the implications
involved in this world view. There is something about this
tendency to trivialize human activity that runs counter to the
Christian belief in the incarnation, where the heavens themselves
with all their vastness submit and are contained in the finite space
of the Virgin's womb. This belief will force Erasmus, in his
treatment of the 'theatrum mundi' theme, to move beyond his
classical models towards a vision that heightens rather than
lowers the significance of man's action on earth.

Plato's symbolical use of the sun and the heavens in his
mythical 'picture-thinking' is based on the conviction that a
harmony exists between the spiritualized man and his cosmos
because, according to the saying of Thales, all things are 'full of
gods' and the universe itself is ordered according to intelligence.[46] 'It is mind,' says the Athenian in *Laws*, 'to which the

heavens owe all their ordered array.'[47] Here is a cosmos quite different from the one imagined by Lucian, yet, in one of its aspects, this Platonic universe does bear a resemblance to the Lucianic one. It is vast. And this vastness so reduces man in size that we seem to 'live round the sea like ants or frogs round a pond'; furthermore, the higher reaches of this cosmos are pervaded with mystery that confounds the mind and defies adequate expression. Our words will never satisfactorily capture it. For this reason, man had better speak quietly and admit only to that which he does know. Hence the need for ironic speech which knowingly falls short of total verity. This Socratic mode is neither a pose nor an accident but a necessity that requires men to play with words in the hope of getting nearer to the truth. The heavenly mystery that is the source for the ironic tone of Socrates in the *Dialogues* encourages a similar tone and a willingness to play in Erasmus.

Just as Plato cannot conceive of a cosmos apart from intelligence, so he cannot discuss civic affairs apart from the soul. His *Republic* is as much concerned with a state of mind as a state of society. The two are interlocked. Just as the inner man undergoes a dialectical ascent to the truth, so the ideal city is pursued through a process of elevation until it is realized that the happiest of societies, by reason of its relationship to the inner republic, exists in its most valid form in the heavens. The inner state, whose wholesome condition is so necessary to the well-being of the outer one, must achieve and maintain a balance of mind which eschews the extremes of rage and mere frivolity, of the purely tragic or the purely comic. It is rather a poised positioning between these two extremes that makes seriocomic expression possible. The *Republic* opens with a struggle of minds that sets the quiet, ironic Socrates against the tempestuous Thrasymachus, who personifies in his seething mind both the thought and the temperament diametrically opposed to Socrates' inner calm. The latter will catch himself even when he grows too earnest and excited about the building of the city of justice.[48] One senses at such moments an awareness that a single mind cannot achieve its own goal in this lofty endeavour. The ideal state exists in its purity in a world above man, in the regions of the gods. To work at its construction, man must remember that he is their puppet acting on their comic stage.[49]

PART THREE

COMEDY AND RELIGIOUS REFORM

FOUR

Laughter and the Sacred:
The Erasmian Sense of Decorum

In the first chapter of this study, some attention was given in general to the compatibility between the ludic and the sacred and to the possibility of harmony between literary art and the discipline of theology. In this chapter we take up a related but more pointed and distinct problem: On what grounds does Erasmus justify the introduction of the comic and of laughter into the realm of the sacred and, more particularly, into the study of theology? We are focusing now on the mind of the author and his own attitude with regard to the conditions necessary for a proper joining of the holy to the risible. Although we will look briefly at the issue as it has been discussed within a Judaeo-Christian tradition, the main concern here will centre on Erasmus' own approach to the problem and his resolution of it. From what we have seen already, we have reason to expect that his attitude will differ sharply from those of his contemporaries. For most of these men, the seriousness of the theological argument called for an absolutely serious tone, and, if any laughter at all were to be permitted, it had to be grim. Erasmus, on the other hand, made fun of religious eccentricities in a very light manner, and this ridicule caused many to dismiss him as an idle scoffer not really concerned whether sound belief flourished or died. In Luther's eyes, Erasmus seemed 'to treat weighty and sacred matters too casually.' After their long years of disagreement, the great reformer was shocked that Erasmus, by then old but still professing to be a theologian, could continue to cling to his 'childish trifles, histrionics, and jests.' Such antics forced Luther to agree with the conclusion of other learned men that 'Erasmus was truly mad.'[1] The learned men in question were not necessarily all Protestant. Catholic authors such as Dorp, Stunica, and Pio all took exception to Erasmus' willingness to intermingle the holy and the comic.[2]

The problem under consideration concerning the employment of wit and humour within a sacred context obviously extends beyond Erasmus and his age; it is perennial to the human species in its approach to the deity. On the one hand, we have the awe and reverence due to the supreme being; on the other, we have the comic disproportion between finite man and infinite God. Within the Catholic tradition anterior to Erasmus, important figures seek to suppress the second of the above considerations out of a regard for the first, at least as far as theological discussion is concerned. St Ambrose bans all levity from the study of theology, and Aquinas reiterates the order.[3] The same attitude is perpetuated within the Protestant stream of thought by Francis Bacon when he says that turning religion into comedy or satire 'is a thing far from the devout reverence of a Christian, and scant beseeming the honest regard of a sober man ... There is no greater confusion than the confounding of jest and earnest.'[4] In spite of recent efforts to formulate a theology of play, this opposition between a comic spirit and serious reflection on religious topics is restated today by Christopher Robinson, who holds that 'common sense tells one that an ardent believer in any religious or philosophical values would be unlikely, even with the best of literary precedents, to use religious or philosophical motifs, of whatever kind, for purely comic effect.'[5] In the case of Erasmus, the old hostility to his witty genius survives in our own times as well and continues to influence our assessment of his dialogues and declamations when read within the larger context of Reformation polemics. As important a scholar as David Knowles considers that Erasmus' use of the weapons of satire, irony, and fiction seems 'to place the great debate upon the dialectical, if not even upon the rhetorical and the recreational level, rather than upon the purely spiritual or even the purely moral one, where the high seriousness can be maintained that alone carries conviction and troubles consciences and so justifies its severity.'[6] In the mind of this eminent author, only a gravity that occupies a lofty perch can assure us of commitment; Erasmus forfeits his claim to it when he resorts to satire and playful narrative.

The above complaint against associating divinity with the risible in general and against Erasmus' practice of it in particular does not go unanswered. A tradition as old as scripture itself pictures a deity given to an ironic, mocking evaluation of human undertakings. In his eleventh provincial letter, Pascal points out that the very first words which God addresses to Adam after the fall are fraught with a sharp, biting irony: 'Behold Adam has become as one of us' (Gen 3:22). Pascal sees in the passage a 'discours de moquerie' and an 'ironie piquante.' Holy scripture, it would appear, lays down a precedent here for the use of comic irony within a decidedly religious context. Pascal then goes on to cite a list of church fathers who read these lines ironically. Chrysostom calls the irony in the sentence 'cutting and irritating.' According to Rupert of Deutz, Adam's foolishness deserves God's ridiculing observation, and Hugh of St Victor is of the same mind.[7] Pascal then observes the mocking tone that colours the language of several of the prophetical books. He caps his argument by citing two fathers, Chrysostom and Cyril, who discern the saviour's ridicule of Nicodemus in John (3:10). Writing in the same vein as Pascal, John Milton rebuts Lord Bacon's plea for the banishment of laughter from theological debate by pointing to another scriptural precedent, Elijah's derision of the prophets of Baal (1 Kings 18:27).[8] Leaving the Hebraic for the Grecian religious outlook, we learn that the first flowering of comedy is situated within a feast celebrating the god Dionysius. The link between comedy and worship is frequently declared within the celebration of the holy day. Out of the medieval instinct for ritual and play arises the drama of the feast of Corpus Christi. C.L. Barber explores a similar connection between English religious and seasonal holiday and the development of Shakespearean comedy.[9] Erasmus is conversant with the festal customs of ancient Athens and Jerusalem, a knowledge that enables him to sketch a theory of festive literature against the background of the holy day as it flourished in both the Hellenic and Hebraic worlds. In this ethical investigation concerning decorum, then, we will follow Erasmus' discussion of the ancient festival and his notion of transforming it as a kind of prelude to his actual treatment of religious topics within a comic framework.

FESTIVE LITERATURE AND THE ANCIENT FESTIVAL

A good deal of information about the nature of Greek religious celebration comes to Erasmus from Lucian's *Saturnalia*, to which we adverted in the preceding chapter. Implicit in the conversations, laws, and letters of this work is the principle of inversion by which the poor are allowed to occupy the places of the rich during the holy season. Erasmus adopts this same principle in his vision of topsy-turvydom that logically follows from a belief in the incarnation of Christ and the folly of God. But Lucian does not describe the reversal of position during the Saturnalia as accomplished in good spirit and in good order. Beneath the surface of these writings lurks the enmity between the poor and the rich, which the holiday attempts, not always with success, to alleviate. Complaints about the unequal distribution of wealth are put before Cronus, the god of the festival, to no avail. He can only rectify this inequality during the Saturnalia. He has no authority beyond the seven days of the feast. The golden days of his reign, during which there existed no bondage because the people themselves were of a golden disposition, are gone forever.[10] Now all that Cronus can do is warn the rich of the hatred they stir up in the poor because they refuse to share their wealth with the less fortunate.[11]

Violence looms on the periphery in Lucian's description of the Saturnalia. Not only is it present in the contention between slave and free, rich and poor, but it is also reflected in the myths of Cronus himself, the castrator of his father Uranus. Although he denies that he devoured Rhea's children and that his pity for slaves harks back to his own period of bondage when he lay fettered in Tartarus, the mere repetition of these legends adds to the imagery of contention and destruction.[12] Such tales tend to confirm René Girard's theory that the ancient festival is born out of the subconscious desire to curb and to channel unrestrained human aggression.[13] According to Robert C. Elliott, the earliest recorded manifestation of satire in Greece took place during a feast of Demeter, whose priest Archilochus recited verses that cursed his intended in marriage and her father for breaking their bridal agreement.[14] Archilochus' savage verbal attack against his enemies took effect and resulted in their deaths during the festival. Erasmus shows some familiarity with the wild striving in the early festival in a passage from his De concordia where he refers to drunken revellers, who, 'with filth-smeared faces scattered ribald verses from carts among those they met on the street. As a prize the winner received a goat, a lid worthy of the pot, as the saying goes.'[15] The wine-drinking of the Dionysia resulted in a release that found expression in hostile as well as gregarious feelings. The joyous bacchanal hid another face and mood – the wrath that we behold in the *Bacchae*.

There seems a dark side to the joy and merriment connected with the feasts of Greek antiquity – something which resists conversion into a Christian scheme of things. The shadow on the face of primitive laughter seems to darken even more when we recall Baudelaire's mythical derivation of this peculiar feature of the human animal. Writing in a theological vein, he traces laughter back to the very beginning of history, and advances the theory that both tears and mirth are consequent to Adam's fall from grace. Laughter springs from a loss of innocence and a belief in one's superiority that permits the fun-maker to look down at the object of his ridicule. Baudelaire relates the risible quality in man to a Satanic origin, but he does not abandon it there. It can be ransomed by reason of a Christian paradox: 'the effects resulting from the Fall will become the means of redemption.'[16] Something of this same confidence lies behind the judgment of certain early fathers of the church and of Erasmus, too, when they consider incorporating the games and merriment of the pagan holiday into a Christian framework.

The ambivalence that we notice in Baudelaire's treatment of laughter can be found also in an early Christian assessment of the Roman festival. A violent rejection of the games obtains in the earlier parts of Tertullian's *De spectaculis*, where he condemns every kind of amusement associated with the feasts of the gods whether they were celebrated in the circus, the amphitheatre, the stadium, or the theatre.[17] Most of this entertainment was either obscene or violent; all of it begot in the hearts of its audience a lamentable frenzy.[18] The controlling argument, however, in Tertullian's invective against the games arises out of his conviction that they were performed in honour of gods who were in fact nothing but demons.[19] This mentality becomes very clear when he treats the art of horsemanship connected with the events of the circus. Tertullian attaches no guilt to the skill of handling a horse; he even calls it a gift of God, but as soon as the skill is used in the races of the circus, it straightway is conscripted into the service of the demons.[20] All of these games, even those which seem innocent, are played under the aegis of Satan. Though the talent exhibited in any contest be good in itself, its presence in games played in honour of false gods corrupts it. Somewhat inconsistently, Tertullian modifies his extremist position in the latter part of *De spectaculis* when he admits that certain aspects of the festival competitions are gentle, becoming to a man, even honourable.[21] And, finally, at the end of the treatise, the author encourages his reader to engage in the pleasures of spectacles dedicated to Christ. These pleasures include the enjoyment of verses, songs, and melodies.[22] We discern here ideas that anticipate Christianity's own appropriation of the festival.

In Tertullian we observe, on the one hand, a detestation of the Roman festival because of its excesses and its association with the Roman gods, and, on the other, a readiness to convert the festival, to direct it away from the gods and to win it to Christ. At times this conversion only means a thorough internalization of joyous song and other festive activities; at other times it can mean the express involvement in religious celebration. Gregory Nazianzus is more explicit than Tertullian in affirming this second kind of transformation to his mirth-loving audience:

> But if you must dance because you are a lover of feasts and festivities, then you may; but do not dance the dance of the shameless Herodias who brought death to the Baptist. No; dance the dance of David before the ark of God, for I believe that such a dance is the mystery of the sweet motion and nimble gesture of one who walks before God.[23]

In Christianizing the festal dance, Gregory purges it not only of its lewdness but also of its association with extreme violence – in this case, the murder of a prophet. A similar attitude prevails when Erasmus directs his attention to what he sees as the Hebrew adaptation of the Hellenic festival.

In the preface to his *De concordia*, a commentary on Psalm 83, Erasmus discusses the old Jewish harvest feast of the Tabernacles as the original setting for the singing of this sacred hymn. This discussion leads him to the consideration of the Christian celebration of the holy day in the world contemporary to him. He urges his readers to avoid the licence and self-indulgence which turns the festival into a godless orgy. Like Gregory Nazianzus, he calls for a conversion of the feast, and, again like Gregory, he bases his argument on the example of a biblical figure in order to bring out the difference between the Israelite in his festivities and the revels of his Greek counterpart:

Moreover, since the Gentiles were in the habit of celebrating harvest time with profane and shameless rites in honor of a sportive Bacchus, wantoning with frenzied games, lewd dances, and smutty language – several vestiges of which secularity we grieve to see holding over to the present day – Moses converted this public merry-making to the reverent offering of thanks, changing bawdy posturing to the ceremonial dancing of prophets (for we read that David danced before the ark in honor of God), and suggestive songs and indecent lyrics to mystic psalms. Thus he converted the impious worship other nations were giving to devils into the worship of the true God.[24]

Erasmus goes on to contrast the drunken ribaldry of the Greek poetry competition to the contests of singing and dancing among the Jews and the early Christians.

If the Erasmian transfiguration of the holy day does not explicitly advance a form of Christian comedy, its affirmation of festive joy opens the way for it. As Erasmus says in the *De concordia*, because 'the feast day is a time for rejoicing,' that is 'a spiritual rejoicing,' the participants are to be 'glad in the sight of God.'[25] The psalm on which he is commenting refers to the delight of those dwelling in the tabernacle of the Lord, which, for Erasmus, means the church founded by Christ. Only within this church, he writes, does man experience the joy of harmonious love. The people who live in God's tabernacle are transformed by grace from a selfish to a selfless life in Christ, who was 'anointed with the oil of gladness.'[26] They experience a happiness like that of Sarah in Genesis (17:15), who laughed to hear that she, in her old age, would bear a son whom she would call Isaac, literally 'laughter.' We find in this biblical episode a source for the comical that differs appreciably from the pride which Baudelaire locates at the root of mirth. Instead of ridiculing another from her own position of advantage, Sarah laughs at her aging, withered self – joyously. Laughter has been ransomed from depravity, because its source, the heart of the woman herself, has been enlivened by God along with her aging womb. Erasmus mentions the case of Sarah while discussing the nature of divine transformation by which the 'old man' of whom Paul writes in Romans and Ephesians dies to himself that he may live in Christ, 'by whose undeserved grace he has been thus transformed. Sarah,' continues Erasmus, 'did not give birth to Isaac – "joy of the spirit," that is – until after her womanhood had failed her.'[27] The reality, then, of which he writes here, has a double nature consisting of both loss and increase, dying and living, pain and gladness. Likewise, the festal singing of the *De concordia* is set within a competition, a struggle, and the song of David which Erasmus is explaining reveals at its centre a spiritual agon. Even the violence of the Hellenic feast has not been totally abandoned; it too has been transfigured. Corresponding to the Song of Degrees commemorating the pilgrims' going up to Sion and to the steps of its temple, there is an inner music and an inner striving by which the soul is led 'upward in a steep ascent' to the House of God.[28] 'Let us psalmodize in mind,' urges Erasmus.[29] The song as it takes root in the heart of the singer is spiritualized and leads to a scaling of 'the fifteen mystical steps to the everlasting Tabernacle.'[30] The Christianized celebration has its own inner combat conducted under the auspices of a new deity: 'Our Director of Games summons us to a contest and has offered tremendous prizes to those who compete according to the law. He presides not only as overseer and judge but also as helper. He gives us strength and keeps up our spirits.'[31]

The spirit in which Erasmus theorizes about the metamorphosis of pagan celebration into a Christian festival carries over into his most creative literary writings and there finds concrete expression. As in the composition of sacred songs for the holy season, so in those works of his inspired by a holiday mood we notice the same components of joy and strife. What happens to the wild, happy temper of the old feast in Erasmus' literary conversion of it is suggested by the meanings which he and his contemporaries give to the Latin word 'festivitas.' Although the term indicates a restrained and witty urbanity not usually associated with the release of a Dionysian kind, its etymology recalls the cultural phenomenon out of which the word develops. 'Festivitas' sheds and leaves behind it the connotation of primitive carnal excess but clings still to the elements of earnest strife and laughing enjoyment that are highlighted in the discussion of the ancient holy day. The clash may consist of something as slight as an ironical conflict of meanings, but it is there nonetheless. In fact, the seriocomic nature of 'festivitas' consistently delves into a world of ambivalences that gives birth to its ironic utterance. René Girard has impressed on us the concern for the well-being and continuance of the community that is present in the festival customs of sacrifice and revelry.[32] A similar gravity of intention lies disguised behind the laughing countenance of 'festivitas.' In a most civilized tone that avoids a direct assault on the listener, the 'vir festivus' will deliver matters of urgency as if they were trifles. Once inserted into the mind, these little seeds of thought are meant to take root and grow in order to become of major interest.

In Samuel Dresden's enlightening delineation of Erasmian 'festivitas,' we are told that its playful mood, while averse to an earnestness of manner, is not inimical to a seriousness of content.[33] It maintains a cheerful spirit entirely open to weighty concerns like the virtuous contending in Erasmus' *De concordia* where God himself is the gamesmaster. Dresden's 'vir festivus' looks on life as a spectator from his seat in the theatre and, because of this vantage, is aware of the discrepancy between words and things that opens the way to a host of meanings which in turn sets afoot the game of playing with terms and ideas.[34] The merry detachment is not a sham but, at least within the Erasmian ideal of 'festivitas,' rests directly upon the settled temper of a soul that rejoices in the presence of its God. As Hedonius says tauntingly to Spudaeus in Erasmus' 'Epicureus,' you should 'not think it wonderful that where God, the fount of all joy, is present, there insuperable happiness exists … Wherever is a pure heart, there God is. Wherever God is, there is paradise, heaven, happiness.'[35] Ultimately, the true 'festivitas' consists in a rejoicing in God, in an internal sabbatical or freeing of the spirit, as the term or end of its development out of the older, external vacation of the festival.[36]

If, as Dresden holds, divinity resides at the core of Erasmian 'festivitas,' then we must adjust the above description of it in order to allow for the presence of God. If we focus on the human aspect of the term, the chief characteristic of 'festivitas' consists of its Lucianic equilibrium that derides all forms of excess and in this way champions what is moral. When, however, we turn to the divine aspect of this concept, limits tend, in one sense, to disappear, because the object of the celebration is infinite. Now a new mood prevails that comes closer to the release of Aristophanic comedy; excess threatens the primacy of moral consideration, and ecstasy disregards and transcends normal respectability. The higher realm of Erasmian thought extends into the heavens. It is there that the *Moria* attains its climax and there that the 'philosophia Christi' achieves final consummation. These extremes of Erasmus' festive spirit define the reaches of his comedy and answer to Edith Kern's sketch of Baudelaire's view of comedy's range: 'It swings from what the poet called the "grotesque," "carnivalesque," or "absolute comic" to the "significative."'[37] Significative comedy is usually clear in its meaning and can thereby yield to instructional ends. On the one hand, Erasmus will frequently defend his *Colloquies* and other humorous pieces by reason of their didactic value in teaching sound doctrine and good morals. The *Moria*, he claims, was written 'to show men how to become better.'[38] On the other hand, he will occasionally defend his comedy on the grounds that he was merely joking.[39] In doing so, he suggests the other extreme of the comic, the laughter which in its relation to the irrational defies clarity and approaches the regions of the carnivalesque and the absolute. Whole sections of the *Moria* belong under this second heading; passages from other works of Erasmus approach this same area where moral instruction is all but lost. Consider just one of his Saturnalian images, that of the Silenus, the doll whose revelling gesture bespeaks an exuberance that is mindful of no restraint. The Silenus, taken literally, belongs to the old pagan festival, but, taken by Erasmus, it is transformed, and its riotous appearance is reconciled to the divinity within it by reason of a heavenly overflowing, an infinitude of love. There are, then, two kinds of Erasmian 'festivitas' based on the wide stretch of his comic genius, and each kind must be approached differently in trying to decide its relevance and suitability to the sacred. Moral instruction and human limit obtain in the one, divine largess and boundlessness in the other.

SCHOLA DECLAMATORIA

A cursory look at the titles listed in Erasmus' *Opera omnia* will indicate the very low percentage of his writings that can be classified as comical or even festive. Just as the feast day comes as the exception to the norm of a workaday life, so these writings of a relaxed and humorous nature come from the pen of Erasmus far less frequently than his other more serious efforts. They appear at something like a sabbath ratio of one to six. Obviously, Erasmus is more taken up with strictly theological studies, especially those pertaining to scripture, and, in this area, he rules out all playing and joking. So he tells us in the *Ratio verae theologiae*, and he repeats this order in his commentary on Psalm 22 when he says that it is impious to introduce laughter into a discussion of scriptural allegory.[40] Yet Erasmus is not entirely consistent in holding to this opinion. The humorous interpretation of scripture given us by Folly in the latter sections of the *Moria* and the absurdities of the Bible which Erasmus discusses in the 'Sileni Alcibiadis' both tend in varying degrees to associate the words of scripture with the comical.[41] Here we must either make some kind of distinction or charge Erasmus with the failure to abide by his own rules.

Erasmus himself distinguishes between two kinds of trifling, the different meanings of which are germane to the present discussion. He makes frequent use of the Latin word 'nugae' (nonsense, trifles) and its cognates and synonyms, but in two distinctly different ways. He will attack the irresponsible and delirious imaginings of decadent theologians for reducing their august subject to the importance of a trifle, to a mere joke. He accuses both those who cling too rigidly to the literal meaning of the sacred text even if it leads them into a ridiculous position and those who recklessly turn every passage in scripture into allegory and thus make a mockery of it. In other words, the latter introduce laughter where it was never intended to be. There are, nonetheless, stories and verses in the Bible which, at first sight, seem to be ludicrous. If, on the literal level, they appear so, then this is a sign that the passage calls for an allegorical interpretation. And so, what at first seems to be a foolish trifle proves in the end to teach, as the 'Sileni Alcibiadis' says, 'that profound wisdom, truly divine, a touch of something which is clearly like Christ himself.'[42] From a passage or verse which initially strikes the reader as nonsense, a new depth of meaning can be discovered. The trifle turns out to be a gem. Now Erasmus applies this hermeneutical principle to his own approach to writing. He will, in some of his festive pieces, take what on the surface is a mere game, a kind of frolic, and so develop it that the work ultimately discloses a store of spiritual wealth. The *Moria* realizes most successfully this ideal, and the *Encomium matrimonii*, in its own more modest way, sportively celebrates ideas which, as we know from his other works, Erasmus took seriously. These two compositions can be rhetorically classified as declamations. This particular genre leads us to another important distinction when trying to determine the relationship between Erasmian comedy and his theological reflection.

Early in the *Ratio verae theologiae*, Erasmus refers to the sacred edifice of theological studies and to the humility of spirit required of those wishing to enter its interior chambers.[43] The awesomeness and majesty of the place demand reverence. If we judge by the topics which this work takes up, we will conclude that Erasmus restricts theology to the study of the sacred books of the Bible. Here he admits of no playful tactics, no attempts at humour, no toying with ideas until one notion is transformed into its opposite. What the scripture leaves clouded in mystery must be worshipped at a distance and not curiously pried into. What the text states clearly and simply must be received without question. In his paraphrase of the New Testament, Erasmus exemplifies the respect for holy writ which he teaches in the *Ratio verae theologiae*. In this latter work, he draws an interesting distinction that makes room for the creation of such works as the *Moria* and other of his trifles. Beyond the precincts of sacred theology, in the restricted sense, stands the 'schola declamatoria,' a kind of academic playground and school which invites contests in rhetorical skills and the clash of wit. In this area, more freedom is allowed the imagination when marshalling arguments.

Erasmus distinguishes between the discipline of theology and the 'schola declamatoria' when commenting on a very strained and erroneous reading of Peter's denial of Christ where the commentator, in an attempt to whitewash the apostle's guilt, claimed that Peter, in saying he did not know the man Jesus, only meant to acknowledge his divinity: 'Nescio hominem, quia scio deum.' Erasmus calls such an interpretation frivolous, because, in saving Peter, it makes Christ, who predicted the denial, guilty of lying. Foolishly subtle and far-fetched distinctions like this, continues Erasmus, may be admitted in the 'schola declamatoria,' but 'in sacred matters, there is no room for playing or quibbling or for twisting ideas lest we undermine belief in the truth by defending falsehood. The utterance of truth ... is simple, and nothing is truer or simpler than Christ.'[44] Word-play, outlandish arguments, and ludicrous readings are not to be applied to scripture in the schools of theology. Such diversions are meant for boys when sharpening their wits in the schools of rhetoric.

Erasmus thought it his calling in life to restore the union between theology and good literature as it existed in the early church.[45] His most serious efforts in this area were his edition and the paraphrase of the New Testament, the *Ratio verae theologiae*, and the book of instruction for preachers, the *Ecclesiastes*; this attempt to rejoin theology and sound eloquence, however, called for reforms on all levels of society starting with the instruction of children. Because he wanted to attract young people to both good morals and fine letters, he wrote his *Colloquies*. In addition to these sportive dialogues, Erasmus composed other humorous 'encomia' that indulge in the word-play which he forbade the student of theology. Yet, for all of his principles, Erasmus' genius took most readily to this kind of writing, and these 'colloquia' and 'encomia' constitute a body of work which, if the judgment of posterity be consulted, overshadows most of the other more ambitious tomes in the canon of his *Opera omnia*.

Almost all of the works of Erasmus that remain to be discussed in this study may be considered as products of the 'schola declamatoria.' Some are declamations outright like the *Moria* or the *Encomium matrimonii*; others, such as the selections from the *Colloquies*, are dialogues created as games 'to allure the young.'[46] Both the declamations and the dialogues were published as school exercises, little trifles that lay outside of the weighty interests of the learned philosopher or theologian. Erasmus, when driven to defend one of these 'opuscula,' frequently pointed to their fictional and educational nature, which, according to him, should have protected them from being read to any serious purpose. Most often, this argument itself is transparently a joke. The subject matter of the *Colloquies* alone – celibacy, clerical greed, religious superstition – reflects too many of the social and ecclesiastical concerns of the day to be dismissed as meant only for a child. Erasmus writes, as it were, inside of the schoolhouse but with an eye looking out through its window to the tumultuous streets of the world about him.

The 'schola declamatoria,' then, is a place of exercise for the young, the atmosphere of which must encourage the freedom to discuss all aspects of an argument. As a 'schola,' it is etymologically also a place of leisure, insulated from the pressures and demands of daily occupation. Because of this immunity, it partakes of the holiday spirit described above. Erasmus attempted, through his literary trifles, to please young students rather than to intimidate them with 'strict or harsh treatment.'[47] Ideally, studies were to approach as nearly as possible to recreation, although the drudgery involved in them could never be completely removed. 'I'm not sure,' writes Erasmus, 'anything is learned better than what is learned as a game.'[48] It is not by mere chance, therefore, that Erasmus' most creative works should have been produced in the 'schola declamatoria' in a spirit close to the childhood's play and dream which Freud makes the common denominator between the poet and the rest of humanity. Language itself leads Freud to his insight. In German the word for play, 'Spiel,' is associated with the kind of writing that depends on the power of the imagination to represent insight by means of concrete objects. The German for comedy is 'Lustspiel,' for tragedy 'Trauerspiel,' and the actor is called 'Schauspieler.'[49] It seems that only one of Erasmus' educational declamations was written with a specific performance in mind, the *Concio de puero Jesu*, which was probably delivered by one of the scholars at John Colet's St Paul's in London. It is the most pious of the works composed for the 'schola declamatoria,' too pious to be called comedy in the usual sense of that word. Yet it is decidedly festive and ties together for us the two main topics of the present discussion: Erasmian 'festivitas' and his school works.

Richard DeMolen, in an article on the feast of the Boy Bishop in Tudor England, discusses Erasmus' *Concio de puero Jesu* within the setting of the Christmas holiday which appears to have provided the occasion for the sermon.[50] This festival in honour of Christian childhood flourished through the latter part of the Middle Ages on into the first half of the sixteenth century. It was celebrated wherever a school or choir permitted a sufficient assembly of child scholars to mime their grown-up ecclesiastical superiors. In the Sarum liturgy of the *Episcopus puerorum*, the Boy Bishop was elected upon St Nicholas' Day, 6 December, by his classmates.[51] His rule reached its climax at the vigil and on the ensuing feast of Childermas, now called Holy Innocents' Day, the fourth day in the old Octave of Christmas. Dean John Colet left among the statutes for his school orders that the pupils 'shall every Chyldremasse day come to paulis church, and here the Chylde Bisshoppis sermon, and after be at the hye masse, and eche of them offre a 1d. to the Childe Bisshopp.'[52] It is probably with this festival in mind that Erasmus composed the *Concio de puero Jesu* and offered it to the pupils of Colet's school of St Paul's.

DeMolen argues that the Feast of the Boy Bishop, held in honour of the Holy Innocents, has been misunderstood because it has been confused with the Feast of Fools and because of the failure 'to distinguish between the festival as masquerade and the festival as religious devotion.'[53] While DeMolen's point about separating the Boy Bishop and his celebration from the Feast of Fools clarifies the nature of each, his desire to separate masquerade from devotion is less illuminating, because the costume of the child prelate and those of his entourage are a necessary part of this play or act of devotion. Not only is the child singled out as a model or ideal whom Christ himself selected in the gospel of Matthew (18:3–4), but we have here a joining of the ancient Saturnalian reversal to a fundamentally Christian form of happiness, expressed in the 'Magnificat,' where Mary rejoices in the putting down of the mighty and the exaltation of the little ones (Luke 1:52).

It has been suggested that Erasmus started work on the *Concio de puero Jesu* at the moment when he had grown tired of the flattering, dull phrases of a panegyric he was composing in honour of Phillip of Burgundy.[54] He decided he would be able to give himself more spontaneously to a panegyric in praise of the child Jesus. The sermon celebrates the divine person who becomes an infant and thereby sanctifies childhood and establishes it as the model for the sanctity that he will later preach. The events in the life of the young Jesus contain lessons for both the young and the old, but the message involves more than external imitation. The speech anticipates some of the deepest insights of the *Moria* and bears comparison with Erasmus' masterwork in other aspects. As in the *Moria*, we have an unlikely preacher, this time a child instead of a fool, appearing before a congregation in a festive setting. The speaker declaims a heavenly wisdom throughout, the same wisdom that Dame Folly extols at the end of her sermon. Although the *Concio* wears a more serious face, befitting its church setting, the structure of its thought relates, like the *Moria*, to a carnivalesque frame of mind. In both works, a Saturnalian inversion results from the religious insights. In the *Concio*, moreover, the boy who has dressed up like an ecclesiastic in a pious sort of Christmas game calls for a transformation symbolized in his own costume change.

The Christmas Saturnalia in which a boy occupies the exalted throne of the bishop reinforces the controlling idea of the *Concio*:

this Jesus, the divine child, has overturned the entire order of things ('omnem rerum ordinem hic puer invertit').[55] The coming of Christ realizes the Saturnalia to the fullest. In the opening sentences of the declamation, we are told of a new Christian eloquence that differs as much from worldly eloquence as Christ's wisdom differs from the secular kind.[56] The new mode of address follows upon the paradoxical nature of the incarnation. A person whose being is without limit is now confined in space; the All-Powerful whose eternal greatness defies explanation has become an infant within the order of time. He has come down from above in order to lift up mankind; he has assumed a human nature in order that man may share of his divinity.[57] The All-High has become low that he might raise up the fallen race of Adam, with the result that the original sin can now be called, 'not absurdly,' a happy fault.[58] This is, as it were, the new order of Christ's divine wisdom, based on a sublime inversion of things. In the light of his revealing descent, all the wisdom of the world straightway turns foolish and all things suddenly are seen under a new light.[59] 'What was sweet is now bitter, what was bitter sweet. What terrified now attracts, what attracted now terrifies.'[60] Likewise, the despised now turns splendid, the weak mighty, the deformed beautiful. Death and suffering no longer chill the spirit of the believer; care and worry subsequently recede.

The Saturnalian reversal which the sermon teaches leads necessarily to a transformation already represented by the boy and his costume. The image of a child in the setting of authority and power declares that Christian greatness lies in becoming little. Implicit here is a call to what the *Concio* tells us is a new form of childhood. 'An non palam videtis,' asks the preacher in the Latin, 'novum pueritiae genus?'[61] The new kind of childlikeness is patterned after the boy Jesus, and, by becoming a child again through a second birth, the Christian is transformed into Christ. A principle of exchange is at work: Christ through the incarnation dresses himself in human clay ('in limum,' literally 'mud') that man may put on his divinity.[62] This second metamorphosis is wrought by the saviour by means of his living presence in the scriptures, where he lifts up, arms, teaches, admonishes, attracts, ravishes, and transforms the reader into himself.[63] Recalling, then, the original scene of the *Concio*, we see the ceremony begin as a child's pious game in which a boy mimes a prelate and then evolve into a vision of the play of grace within man's heart where the spirit of Christ is born anew and grows. Man becomes like God, who is the object of his love, as the creature transfers his affections from a diversity of objects to the one being of the creator in whom all others are cherished. The episode of the child teaching in the temple instructs the listeners about the nature of this heavenly change. Separated from his parents, Jesus seeks first his Father's business. All of his affective thrust arises from this dedication. Seated in the temple and surrounded by the learned doctors, the divine child symbolizes for Erasmus an interior attitude for all Christians to assume. 'What does it mean,' asks the Boy Bishop, 'to sit in the temple? Nothing,' he replies, 'but to rest and to settle on holy things and to render the soul tranquil, free from care. Nothing agitates more than vice, and wisdom loves peace and stillness.'[64] The teaching child is the God 'who energizes all things while he himself is still.'[65] The divinely calmed heart that we saw earlier in the 'homo festivus' appears again within the child Christ, the central figure of this festive sermon.

The Saturnalian inversion of the *Concio* and the paradoxes which derive from it invite a good deal of word-play which this account has only partially indicated. The playfulness becomes the role of a boy who must turn preacher. It also befits the holiday mood that surrounds this kind of paraliturgy. And, finally, it conforms to a notion found in the last sentence of the little work. The listeners are there exhorted to make of the child Jesus the end both of their literary studies and of their play. In either occupation, they are to taste joyfully of his wisdom: 'Hunc [Jesum] et litterae nostrae, et lusus etiam sapiant.'[66] In him, play and work, piety and celebration are united. In him also, the antagonism between comedy and the sacred is to be resolved.

The Feast of the Boy Bishop within which we have read the *Concio* is of medieval and not Renaissance origin. In so far as this line of medieval thought found no opposition between laughter and the holy, we can say that Erasmian religious comedy belongs to it. The same tradition gave birth to the mystery plays in a festive ambience very much like the setting for Erasmus' sermon. The drama of the Middle Ages had no trouble accommodating games with earnest subjects and comic episodes with the serious narrative of man's salvation. A fifteenth-century treatise, *Dives et Pauper*, includes a justification of mirth on the holy day in its discussion of the proper keeping of the sabbath. It teaches that 'the rest the mirth the ese and the welfare / that god hath ordeyned in the halidayes. is token of endlesse reste joye and myrthe and welfare in heuenes blisse that we hope to haue withouten ende.'[67] In anticipation of eternal happiness, man is to celebrate joyfully on the sabbath and not to confine himself to greater restrictions than those which obtain on working days. The sabbath is a day of liberation and freedom. This same attitude prevails in Erasmus' approach to laughter and holiness.

But why is it that Erasmus allows laughter and religion to go hand in hand in the 'schola declamatoria' and yet insists that they be kept apart in the schools of theology? Or is the distinction that clear and neat? Is it every kind of laughter that he banishes from the religious setting of theology or just that kind which demeans the august subject? Remember that, in the *Ratio verae theologiae*, Erasmus both denounces the theologian who trivializes sacred letters and, at the same time, tells us that God babbles his message to us.[68] In both cases, a diminution takes place. In the first, what should be appreciated as a sacred mystery shrinks to an obsession with angels dancing on a pinhead; in the second, the infinite mystery is turned into a broken lisp because no speech can adequately express it. Both cases admit of a comic rendition, but it appears that essentially Erasmus means to banish the nugatory from the study of theology. To help chase the small-minded zealots from its halls, he institutes the 'schola declamatoria' where among other things he may pillage the triflers. In addition to satirical attack, Erasmus will explore in the works written for the 'schola' the mystery of Christian paradox. The *Concio de Jesu puero,* written for a child to deliver, illustrates Erasmus' more profound usage of the word 'nuga,' the trifle which leads to serious reflection and, therefore, justifies its presence even within the sacred precincts of theology.

FIVE

Satire and Reform

❧

From the more general concern for decorous comedy within a religious context, we move to a more particular and concrete question: What contribution did Erasmus' satirical and comical dialogues make to his own program of reform in sixteenth-century Europe? What evidence do these works present to incline us to consider them fit instruments for awakening the consciences of the Christian society in that era? Luther thought that Erasmus was mistaken in the means he had chosen to stir his readers. A reformer, in setting out to attack abusive practices, he believed, should do so with great authority and seriousness. He 'must seize the sword in both hands, and not do as Erasmus does who ridicules ceremonies only because they are foolish.'[1] Erasmus, on the other hand, had great confidence in the curative powers of congenial laughter in leading men to a point where they are convinced of their erroneous ways. Comedy provides the honey to the medicine of reprimand. It is the care-dispelling drink of which Plato speaks when he 'approves the habit of taking wine with a man at drinking-parties on a generous scale, because he thinks some faults can be dissolved under the cheerful influence of wine which severity could not correct.'[2] This defence of his own comedy may be too optimistic about the corrective force of a convivial style. His recourse to wine-drinking as an example does not securely forward the argument. Wine, after all, induces not a keener awareness but a relaxation from tension and even oblivion, if taken in the generous quantities to which Plato is said to have subscribed. Mirth is known to have similar effects. The comical, as it begins to win an ascendancy, can assume forms that defy the didactic. In the opinion of Morton Gurewitch, 'True

Comedy should banish *all* thought – of mortality and morality.'[3] He writes here of the comical in a most absolute sense and not of satire, but the anarchical strain of mirth cannot be ignored when trying to determine the part of laughter in satirical works. My own position with regard to Erasmus upholds the effectiveness of his satire as long as he exercises control over his comical impetuosity. Still, there are places in these dialogues where a spirit hostile to satire takes over, where the comedy frees itself from moral concern. Such moments do not occur frequently, but they are there and call for our reflection. What place, if any, does humour for its own sake have in Erasmus' program of reform? The paradox at which the present discussion will conclude holds that this non-conforming, unbridled comedy may, in one essential aspect, be more relevant to Erasmus' doctrinal stand than the satire.

The topic of this chapter is an important and necessary part of the main subject of this study because satire is essentially a seriocomic art. On the one hand, it originates, according to Pope, in 'The strong Antipathy of Good to Bad'; on the other hand, it wittily rises above mere invective in its attack on evil.[4] Our investigation into Erasmus the satirist will look for the blend of moral vision with a spirit of merriment that transforms the ethical abrasiveness and aggression into comical enlightenment. This union between amusement and serious concern admits a great variety, especially in the case of Erasmus. The range of his satire extends from the splendid 'A Pilgrimage for Religion's Sake,' filled with grim indignation, and the vitriolic pieces against war, through several richly comical dialogues until we reach what might be called the merriest work in the *Colloquies*, the 'Exorcism.' An attempt will be made, especially in the earlier phases of this discussion, to link the content of these satirical writings to some of Erasmus' strongest religious convictions as expressed in his most sober compositions in order to make explicit the earnestness of feeling which the *Colloquies* manifest indirectly through voices other than that of the author.

The scope of the present chapter will be restricted to the *Colloquies* and the *Julius exclusus*, a work which most scholars today attribute to Erasmus.[5] Of the *Colloquies*, only those will be treated which have a claim to satire or comedy. The discussion of some of these will be deferred until the next chapter, which considers the positive side of Erasmian reform, the society for whose realization he strives. Other colloquies devoted to the subject of wedlock will not be taken up until the final chapter, when the entire spectrum of Erasmus' comedy will be reviewed under the rubric of Christian matrimony.

DARK COMEDY, BRIGHT COMEDY

As might be expected, Erasmus inveighs in his satirical colloquies against those superstitious practices that undermine the supernatural virtue of faith. Repeatedly he holds up to ridicule any excessive preoccupation with external rites and devotion that so fixes the soul on the outward deed that it fails to reach the significance and the goal of the activity. Erasmus so frequently deplores the misuse of religious ceremonies that many of his Catholic contemporaries judged that he was against them altogether. Such a misunderstanding led not infrequently to charges of heresy. On the other hand, the depth of feeling that is sometimes discernible in his attack indicates that his indignation is sincere, and, as I hope to show in the course of this discussion, the insight supporting his accusation reveals a belief most fundamental to Christianity.

Erasmus' critique of Catholic piety centres on the fixation upon mere externals and is aimed directly against the confusion which this kind of obsession can easily engender. The merely human can be mistaken for the divine; heavenly splendour may be reduced to fit man's misunderstanding. Sister Geraldine Thompson has observed that in those colloquies which attack superstitious practices 'we see God and the things of God shrunk to human dimensions.'[6] In one of these, 'A Pilgrimage for Religion's Sake,' this bathetic movement from greatness to smallness is so prevalent that we might call it, in the terminology of Alvin B. Kernan, the 'master trope' of this particular dialogue.[7] Repeatedly, we are led to feel the loss of grace and majesty by the reduction of religion to human, material terms. Such a view is comically announced in the opening scene where Menedemus ('stay-at-home') encounters the outlandishly attired Ogygius, just returned from a round of pilgrimages in Spain and England. Menedemus cannot refrain from commenting on his friend's dress: 'You're ringed with scallop shells, choked with tin and leaden images on every side, decked out with straw necklaces, and you've snake eggs on your arms.'[8] Ogygius' ridiculous appearance recalls the similar opening to Lucian's *Menippus*, in which the hero arrives back from Hades in a strange costume. But Erasmus' description is more pointed. It highlights the shells and little images, the trinkets, the knick-knacks, and the gewgaws to which religion is being reduced, or, as the text hints, by which it is choked. The pilgrim with his necklace is clutching at straws. Here is greatness become a trifle, and, as we saw earlier, Erasmus composes his own 'trifle' in protest against the truly offensive ones.

The theme of diminution is skilfully orchestrated by means of spatial imagery in Ogygius' account of his visit to Canterbury. A note of awe is struck in the introductory description of the cathedral:

> The church sacred to St. Thomas rises to the sky so majestically that it inspires devotion even in those who see it from afar. Thus by its splendor it now dims the glory of the neighboring one [church] and, so to speak, overshadows the spot that was anciently the most sacred. It has two huge towers, as though greeting visitors a long way off and making the region ring far and wide with the wonderful sound of its bronze bells.[9]

Seen first from a distance, the immense edifice dominates its setting. The impression of vastness is maintained as the pilgrim advances into the body of the cathedral. 'When you enter,' he says, 'the spacious grandeur of the building is disclosed.'[10] Until now, the depiction of Canterbury has stressed the towering heights and great sweep of the church in a way that suggests the true object of the pilgrim's devotion – the divine majesty. Once the pilgrim is within the place, however, his point of view changes and focuses no longer on greatness but on little relics: the skulls, jawbones, teeth, and skeletal fingers of departed saints. Nothing can be insignificant, provided it has some link with one of the holy ones, especially St Thomas. Even his soiled handkerchief is thought fit to be revered. The Canterbury episode concludes with one reasonable pilgrim refusing to kiss the old shoe of some saint. 'What,' he exclaims, 'do these brutes want us to kiss all good men's shoes? Why not, in the same fashion, hold out spittle and other excrements to be kissed?'[11] In this part of the colloquy, we move from an impressive vision of grandeur suggestive of deity to a grotesque collection of bones, rags, and shoes which measures the extent that piety has dwindled away for want of holding to its true purpose.

The reductive tendency in the sketches of Canterbury moves from a grand external setting into an interior where religion falls away to a fixation with collector's items and the store of loot accruing from the exhibition of these relics. A similar movement occurs in Ogygius' account of the shrine to the Virgin at Walsingham, only here the passing from the outside to the inside implies going to the heart of the devotion. We are led gradually to 'the inner sanctum of the Holy Virgin,' and there we find a canon waiting 'to receive and keep the offering.'[12] Later, the visitors are brought by special favour to see the secrets or inner mysteries of the Virgin and there we find a beautiful jewel at Mary's feet.[13] One brief scene in the Canterbury episode reinforces this scheme that takes us to a centre, a core as it were, occupied by wealth. Ogygius follows his guide into the crypt to the Virgin's special residence and there in the shadows he comes upon the 'dark riches' of the Madonna enclosed by a double row of iron rails.[14] At the heart of this great shrine we discover something looking like a bank. Both at Walsingham and at Canterbury, the altars bespeak not a real presence but a rather curiously profane transubstantiation by which the numinous has turned numismatic. The shrines have become what Erasmus would call reverse Sileni: temples all holy without but reduced to a narrowing concern for gold within.[15]

The foregoing dialogue's harsh treatment of materialistic devotion, be it of a pecuniary or purely physical nature, is repeated time and again not only in the Colloquies but in many other works of Erasmus. Indeed, it occurs with such frequency that one could easily think that Erasmus nourished a decided antipathy to all things liturgical. But to do this is to miss his point. The real abuse in Catholic worship lay not in the rite or the external form of the sacrament but rather in a torpor of mind which prevented the faithful from going from the liturgical sign to the fullness of its meaning. The rind was blocking the way to the fruit. The full significance of the sacraments constituting the basic structure of Catholic worship cannot be attained without reference to the ecclesial unity which these rites were instituted to effect. For Erasmus, then, it is incomprehensible that Christian peoples so joined together could so readily be led into warring against each other. This, however, was the case, and the phenomenon convinced Erasmus that the true meaning of the sacraments was lost on most Christians. His sensitivity to this blindness is very evident in his 'Dulce bellum inexpertis,' where he writes against the scandal of warfare among Christian nations:

> What an absurd thing it is that there should be almost continuous warfare between those who are of the household of one Church, who are members of the same body and glory in the same Head, that is Christ; who have one father in heaven, who are quickened by the same Spirit, initiated into the same mysteries, redeemed by the same blood, regenerated by the same baptism, nourished by the same sacraments ... eating the bread, sharing the same cup.[16]

Again, in the *Querela pacis*, Erasmus refers to the work of Christ being carried on 'in so many ceremonies' whose meaning has been lost on the congregation.[17] Erasmus' frequent harping upon the failure to understand church services has to be read in the light of the unity towards which the sacraments work. A divided, warring Europe meant that sacramental ritual had been emptied of meaning. This religious conviction helps to explain also the vehemence of his satirical onslaught against soldiering and warmongering.

Erasmus directs his most aggressive satire against warfare and the horror of Christian people murdering each other. Thrasymachus, the soldier in 'Military Affairs,' argues ironically in defence of the campaign he has just completed. 'Butchers,' he reasons, 'are paid to slaughter beef. Why is our trade denounced when we're hired to slaughter men?'[18] And to this reason he adds the blessing of authority: a preacher had decreed from the pulpit that the war was a just one. As for the personal sins committed during the war – the drinking, the whoring, the plundering – these offences will be wiped away in the confessional. And so the sacrament that should strengthen the unity of the church by the power of forgiveness only quiets the sense of guilt in this soldier for having ravaged and murdered his fellow Christians. But the effects of these sins are not so casually dismissed in 'The Soldier and the Carthusian.' The military man in this colloquy returns from his expedition with the marks of the Spanish pox on his face. The disease has stooped the warrior and contracted his bones.

Erasmus dwells on such repulsive details in an effort to strip from warfare its drapes of glory and to expose it for the hideous thing it is. In 'Charon' we move to a more sweeping vision made possible by the vantage of Charon, the underworld ferryman, and Alastor, an avenging spirit. The Furies have been let loose on contemporary Europe, and the plague of war rages everywhere: in Spain, Britain, Italy, France. The preaching friars spread the contagion by proclaiming at court 'in their evangelical sermons that war is just, holy, and right.'[19] This lesson is delivered to both sides, and the carnage continues, much to the profit of the friars who grow fat on the wills and mass offerings of the deceased and the bereaved.

The spirit of violence driving the soldier to engagement with the enemy is absorbed by the churchmen who urge him to it and carries over into the practice of religion. Doctrinal positions are not defended by reason illumined with faith but by recourse to physical beatings. Polyphemus, the zealot in 'Cyclops or the Gospel Bearer,' pummels a Franciscan who has babbled opinions from the pulpit which Polyphemus decided were wrong. His remedy is to punch the friar until his face swells and then to absolve him by 'banging him on the head three times' with a gospel book, 'raising three lumps, in the name of the Father, Son and Holy Ghost.'[20] Although this colloquy reads like a scene from domestic comedy, it is not without a serious, ironic turn. The same deliberate joining of religious conviction to headstrong violence was occurring at that time in less comical ways. Awful torture was being inflicted on people suspected of heresy, and Erasmus knew some of these; an entire city was submitted to a reign of terror when Jan Bockelson, the new Elijah, gained control of Münster.[21] And this same misbegotten alliance of faith and the fist appears to one reading the colloquy today as a harbinger of the religious wars that would break out after the death of Erasmus.

Of the dialogues seen to this point, the 'Cyclops or the Gospel Bearer' might be called the brightest of these dark comedies. What laughter we find in this group is not far removed from the grotesque and the macabre. The war colloquies especially, while not tragic in themselves, are written in such a way as to lead the reader's mind towards tragic reflection. The meditation of Williams, Shakespeare's foot-soldier in *Henry v* (4.1), on how few die well 'when blood is their argument' could have been inspired by the reading of 'Military Affairs' or 'The Soldier and the Carthusian.' We do not have long to read before sensing the indignation present in these colloquies. This is Erasmus at his most caustic, and the temper of this satire is not unrelated to the author's outrage and lamentation over the division of Christ's mystical body.

We now turn to a series of dialogues less abrasive than the first group because now the emphasis begins to lie on sin as folly rather than on its viciousness. This will make the introduction of comic representation more feasible. 'The Shipwreck' provides a good example of the difference between its kind and the grimmer sort of colloquy particularly because its subject matter, the popular abuse in Catholic devotion, resembles 'A Pilgrimage for Religion's Sake.' This permits us to discriminate more clearly between the mood and development of the two pieces. Where 'A Pilgrimage for Religion's Sake' pays a good deal of attention to the clerical greed that vitiates the practice of visiting shrines, 'The Shipwreck' focuses on man's hysteria in his heavenly invocations. Where the first colloquy follows an imaginative argument whereby greatness shrinks to insignificance, the second runs in an opposite direction: it balloons things of lesser importance until they reach such a size that divinity itself is lost sight of. This is that satirical master trope which Kernan calls 'magnification.'[22]

In this colloquy, Adolph narrates to his companion Antony the tale of tragedy at sea which he himself had experienced. During the night, the winds rose with such a violence that within minutes the captain lost control of his vessel and was forced to tell his passengers to commend themselves to God. The colloquy then studies the reaction of several individuals confronting the prospect of death and the personage to whom they direct their prayers. Hardly anyone follows the captain's advice to invoke the deity. The frightening storm causes the imaginations of the passengers to billow with the waves. The sailors cry out to the Virgin Mary with invocations suggesting that she is the terminus of all prayer. 'Mistress of the World,' she is called, and 'Port of Salvation.'[23] Adolph, the narrator, associates this kind of prayer with the superstitious devotion sailors had to Venus in antiquity, 'because she was believed to have been born of the sea.' Superstition evolves into downright idolatry when some frantic souls fall to their knees and call to the waters: 'O most merciful sea, O most kind sea, O most splendid sea, O most lovely sea, have pity on us! Save us!' Others begin to bargain with the saints that they might be saved from the horrors of the deep. Adolph is amused by 'one chap, who in a loud voice (for fear he wouldn't be heard) promised a wax taper as big as himself to the Christopher in the tallest church in Paris – a mountain rather than a statue.'[25] The gigantic size of the images here symbolizes the wild exaggeration of created objects of devotion that prevails in this scene. Only three of these characters turn to God: Adolph, the captain, and a mother with an infant at her breast. All the rest pray to the Virgin and the saints, not in a spirit of piety, but in ways that either resemble idolatry or reduce religion to a kind of bartering. A wooden statue of the Virgin and, 'certain queer beads' are clutched at as the means of salvation.[26] In this chaotic scene, the supreme confusion consists of men and material things swelling in importance until they occupy the position reserved for God alone.

Much of the comedy in 'The Shipwreck' is provided by the two priests, a Dominican and an old fellow named Adam. Just before the ship breaks apart, Adam stands up and preaches 'a sermon from Gerson on the five truths concerning the benefit of confession.'[27] Then the passengers begin to confess to Adam and the Dominican. Finally, each priest confesses his sins to the other while a lifeboat waits to receive them. Then one of the fathers feels obliged to confess his sins again, because 'some condition ... had been forgotten.'[28] This causes both of them to miss the boat, which is lowered into the sea without them. The Dominican cries out to a saint of his order, Catherine of Siena, to protect him as he strips and leaps into the waves, but, alas, with his Dominican cowl gone 'how could Catherine of Siena recognize him?' The poor man is lost at sea. In conformity with the dominance of a misplaced emphasis in 'The Shipwreck,' the treatment of the two priests stresses a crazed interest in non-essentials. The subject of sacramental confession must be dissected and treated in little parts. The infinitesimal grows and becomes the main interest. Confession must be repeated because some conditional part has been omitted, but the priests seem distracted by minutiae from simply being sorry before God for their sins. In the end, the Dominican loses his life for dallying with the unimportant, which he has blown beyond proportion until it has displaced the essential.

'The Shipwreck' is more comical and less aggressive in its

treatment of Catholic devotion than is 'A Pilgrimage for Religion's Sake.' The comedy, though, has not yet completely escaped the gloom. It is a laughable reconstruction of a tragedy at sea that takes place during a night of dreadful storms which reveal the darkness in the minds of the ship's passengers. These frantic, erring devotees are more victims of their own foolishness than downright vicious, so we are more prone to laugh at their mistaken beliefs. Other colloquies in this same group explore the madness of men by reason of their conscious or unconscious espousal of falsehood. The conscious ones play the role of a confidence man who, by his lying scheme, cheats his fellow; the unconscious ones are those whom the trickster fleeces.

The colloquies of this group are among the most dramatic of the entire collection because they almost all involve a situation calling for some kind of acting. A number of these dialogues overtly refer to role-playing as if the story being related were nothing but a scene from a drama. Phaedrus, in 'The Cheating Horse-Dealer,' speaks of enlisting 'a man to play a supporting role in this comedy'[29] which he narrates, and Levinus mentions a player coming on the stage in the tale Hilary tells in 'The Sermon.'[30] Similar references are found in 'The Old Men's Chat,' 'The Ignoble Knight,' and 'The Seraphic Funeral.'[31] 'The Ignoble Knight' consists of lessons in passing off the lie of noble birth for the truth. The impression will stick, provided the charlatan robs the innocent, lives splendidly, and incurs huge debts. In 'The Cheating Horse-Dealer,' we are treated to a story in which a dishonest salesman falls victim to his own kind of chicanery. Another confidence man appears in 'Alchemy' in the person of a conniving priest who dupes the learned Balbinus into financing the cleric's pretended experiments in search of the philosopher's stone. The game is drawn out as far as the creditor's purse can extend it. Balbinus is only rid of the fellow after he has drained great sums of his wealth and bedded the wife of a local courtier.[32]

In 'Alchemy,' a dishonest cleric gulls a learned but inexperienced scholar by means of role playing. Other colloquies develop another kind of deceit involving costumes which really serve as disguises. Here, too, the theme of life as theatre is suggested. Erasmus expounds his own philosophy of dress in 'The Well-to-do Beggars.' Clothing is meant to serve the need of the body for protection against the elements and to distinguish the different professions and classes of society. A decorum is to be observed according to the climate and the condition in which each person finds himself. Still, a particular kind of dress or uniform is not a sure indicator of the quality of the person wearing it. Many a fool has paraded about in an academic robe. Some of the dialogues show us clothes and makeup used for the sake of disguise on life's stage. Misoponus in 'Beggar Talk,' for instance, admits that, when he was poor and begging, he would touch up his face 'with paints, turpentine, sulphur, resin, birdlime, linen cloth, and blood' to make himself more pitiful looking.[33] In 'The Seraphic Funeral,' the learned and double-dealing Eusebius, upon hearing that he has only a few days left to live, straightway 'clothes his poor, weak body in complete Franciscan dress; he receives the tonsure, puts on an ashen cowl, a robe of the same color, a knotted cord, and sandals.'[34] Thus costumed, he dies and is carried on a bier in his funeral procession amidst the dirges and groans of those apparently saddened by his demise. The narrator of these ceremonies, however, finds them more laughable than distressing and sums up the entire performance as a show in which Eusebius, the corpse in friar's dress, is venerated for a life he had never lived.

Another colloquy concerned with Christian obsequies will serve as a résumé of our study to this point, because it possesses the cutting edge of the harsher colloquy as well as the wittiness of the merrier kind; its central irony is at once hilarious and mordant. I refer to the episode dealing with the last services afforded to George, the military hero of 'The Funeral.' Before turning to the circumstances of his demise, it will add to our enjoyment of this scene if we first recall an insight of Erasmus which is basic to his evaluation of the soldier's life. Early in his 'Dulce bellum inexpertis,' Erasmus compares man and beast in an effort to prove that among the animals of this earth the human species is the most poorly equipped for fighting. Without horn, claw, or beak, the argument runs, man is suited by nature not to fight but to love and to live in peace. Yet, the fact is that man has turned against his own nature, in a sense, blinded himself to it and become a murderer.[35] By definition the soldier's calling requires the quelling of respect for human life. For this reason, a most suitable poetic justice obtains in 'The Funeral' when George, the old warrior, is visited by an assemblage of physicians and friars none of whom manifest the least interest in his dying condition.

As George is told by his doctors to prepare to meet his God, he stares at them in 'wild surmise.'[36] The medical men cannot agree on the cause of his worsening condition. One says dropsy; another tympanites; another an intestinal abscess. So as George enters into his last agony, the physicians, each lost in his own analysis of the case, seek out George's wife and beg her permission to perform an autopsy after her husband passes away. Each doctor anxiously desires to validate his own diagnosis on the corpse he had failed to save. So their interest now is directed towards a dead body, not towards the pain and distress of the living one. The same humorous juxtaposition of a distressed and dying man surrounded by professional authorities distracted from their charge by egotistical fixations continues when the physicians of the soul are called. From the time they enter the sick room until their departure, the four friars and one parish priest battle one another for the honour of administering the last sacraments and the funeral services. Even when George opts for the parish priest, the friars retire to the hall outside of the room and continue their dispute. No notice at all is taken of George, and the wrangling ceases only after he pays off all five clergymen. Erasmus brings together here several of the strands which occupy him in the *Colloquies* – a passionate concern for money, an overwrought attention to ritual, and a total disregard for the dying – only in this scene the irony is exquisite, because this inhumane oblivion is turned on one whose military profession was made possible by the same attitude.

TOWARDS THE ABSOLUTE

Until now, Erasmus' comic mood has been displayed in artful conformity to his more serious intention. It unobtrusively coheres with the ethical sensitivity in the colloquies we have seen as it intensifies the madness of humanity in its aberrant conduct. Comedy, however, is too incalculable and unpredictable to make an ideal subordinate; and Erasmus' frequent appeal to the Horatian dictum of joining the useful to the pleasant is a principle of composition that is not quite so simple and uncomplicated as he would have us believe, especially in his own case where the pleasureful calls for the exercise of wit and humour. The more it is charged with laughter, the more comedy is capable of intimidating serious reflection. In this final section of the chapter, we will concentrate on some comical elements that threaten the moral intentions within a given work. We will restrict ourselves to only a few instances, enough to illustrate the tendency, without any attempt to make a complete and exhaustive review of this thrust in the comical prose writings of Erasmus. We will begin with a study of the *Julius exclusus,* not because the rebellion of mirth dominates the work, but because, while possessing an admirable balance between jest and earnest, the dialogue contains a strain of ethical anarchy which, although finally defeated, lies at the source of the work's merriment.

Looked at from one angle, the *Julius exclusus* amounts to a tirade against a warrior pope whose life stands as a contradiction to the life of him whose headship he claims as Christ's vicar on earth. Christ became poor, and Julius surrounded himself with riches; Christ chose a humble trade, and Julius craved the zenith of political and spiritual power.[37] The sins of the man were enormous: he bribed his way to the papacy and slew many of his own flock after he got there. Julius seems more fit for Erasmus' most excoriating invective than for his satire. Yet somehow the author rose to the occasion by surmounting his own bitter scorn of the worldly pope to create a truly comical figure. The *Julius exclusus* succeeds as comedy because of the protagonist of the work, and, surprisingly enough, the laughter which he excites does not issue from a simple disdain for the persona.

In this matter of character conception, it behooves us to compare Erasmus' Julius with that other humanist study in Renaissance tyranny, Thomas More's Richard the Third. It is much easier to detect More's animus against his subject than Erasmus'. The difference between the two personae shows most clearly in the respective ways the two villains present themselves to others. Where Richard darkly hides his motives and true intentions to deceive all about him, Julius openly admits his sins to everyone.[38] This follows from Erasmus' decision to make Julius, and not his Genius or St Peter, assume the major part of the burden of making known his own wickedness. In addition, Julius is unhesitatingly generous in his assessment of his enemies. They are, for the most part, good people who did not merit the maltreatment which they received from him. His attempts to destroy them were made only out of a selfish concern for his own power and prestige. In his almost total disregard of moral reflection, Julius II, as Erasmus portrays him, bears a certain resemblance to the hero of Aristophanic comedy described in chapter 3. Like this ancient figure, Julius enjoys his deceitfully won position of eminence and conducts himself there above and beyond any consideration for law and justice. This aspect of the character constitutes part of our enjoyment of him and allows the persona to rise above a purely didactic function. The ability of Erasmus to expose so much evil, both founded and unfounded, in one man, without divorcing him entirely from our sympathies, enables him to sustain a comic spirit throughout a very serious and prolonged attack on those papal abuses that proved so damaging to the entire church.

So the comedy of the *Julius exclusus* is founded on a character who, in one regard, is ill suited to the purposes of satire. Northrop Frye observes an opposition between the comic and the self-righteous spirit.[39] Satire, of course, partakes of this latter zeal for goodness, and, when its laughter begins to lull the mind's wakeful scrutiny, it is in danger of losing its intransigent animosity towards folly and vice. On the one hand, *Julius exclusus* exhibits a lofty scorn for the despicable ways in which a particular pope abused the powers of his office. But Julius himself has been created very much in a comic spirit that frees him from the unattractive postures of self-righteousness. He owns up to all of his vicious practices and sees no contradiction whatsoever between his appetite for earthly enjoyment and his desire to win admittance into heaven. His will knows no limit, and, in the terms of Baudelaire's theory, he seems better suited to the comedy of the absolute than that which the French poet calls 'significative.'[40] Satire belongs to this second class; Julius mounts towards the first, even though he never arrives there. In the *Julius exclusus*, Erasmus' presentation of the pope threatens to undermine the effectiveness of the satire but ends by only softening it and, in fact, saving it from becoming an unrelieved tirade.

We move now to a clear instance of comedy's insubordination. It has to do with a simple, humorous illustration apparently meant to support a serious position, but the example ends by overwhelming the point being made. The colloquy 'A Fish Diet,' from which the story is taken, cannot be classified as a satire. Although it begins lightly enough and presents to us a butcher and a fishmonger as its only characters, the discussion gets so bogged down in matters of ecclesiastical doctrine and regulation that the verisimilitude of its personae vanishes together with the

comical tone of its opening lines. It does have its moments of
humour, one of which occurs when the conversation turns on a
subject dear to Erasmus, that of the overturning of values so that
what is of major importance is lost sight of because of a
preoccupation with the less important. Externals take the place of
the internal and minor regulations distract from major injunc-
tions. This loss of proper perspective reminds the butcher of a
story he had once heard told in the pulpit by a Dominican:

> A young man had taken advantage of a nun; her swollen
> belly was proof of the deed. An assembly of nuns was
> convoked, the abbess presiding. The nun was accused. No
> question of denial; the evidence was inescapable. She took
> refuge in the *status qualitatis* – or the *status translationis*, if
> you prefer. 'I was overcome by someone stronger.' 'But at
> least you could have screamed.' 'I would have done so,'
> says she, 'but there's a strict rule against making noise in the
> dormitory.'[41]

This tale succeeds very well on its own – too well to support a
reasonable argument. The nun's reply displays a delightful
quickness of wit together with a vacuous incongruity by which
she reverses an obvious hierarchy of values. She strains at the
gnat while swallowing the camel. If we laugh at this, we will have
to suspend, while laughing, our moral judgment. In such a
mood, school is out and the teacher's voice is no longer heard.
Although this is only a slight tale told in a much weightier
colloquy, it does serve to exemplify the potential for antireformat-
ory laughter that is discernible in some of Erasmus' comedy. It
can occur at any moment in his more playful colloquies. As long
as it remains incidental to the composition as a whole, it probably
will not detract in a harmful way from the serious temper of the
work. But there is at least one colloquy in which the spirit of fun
for its own sake overtakes Erasmus and leads him down a merry
path to the undoing of the satire. I refer to the 'Exorcism.'

We have already noted Erasmus' tendency to treat the episodes
related in the *Colloquies* like little pieces of theatre. None of his
dialogues comes so complete with its own dramaturgy as does
'The Exorcism.' The story told by Anselm to Thomas is called a
play by the narrator, and he refers to Polus, one of the tale's
characters, as 'the author of this play as well as an actor in it.'[42]

Later he tells us that Polus is also the director.[43] He divides the story into five acts and gives it a prologue that serves to highlight the kind of human failing that will be satirized in the main plot. In the prologue, Polus, while riding in the country with a group of companions, feigns that he sees a vision in the sky. 'Good God,' he shouts, 'what do I see?' He calls to the others and asks them if they can make out 'the huge dragon there, armed with fiery horns, its tail twisted into a circle?' Of course, no one sees it, but Polus so insists that soon he has the rest agreeing with him. 'Within three days, report of the appearance of such a portent had spread throughout England.'[44] The introductory vignette tells an anecdote of the human credulity which will be merrily exploited in the main action.

Polus invites to supper a priest from his neighbourhood by the name of Faunus, an ecclesiastic who takes himself to be 'uncommonly wise, especially in divinity.'[45] During the repast, the host regales his guest with the local rumour that a spectre haunts the open fields in the vicinity of a nearby bridge. This whets the priest's curiosity. He goes there, to hear an eerie wail coming out of the darkness not far from the bridge – the voice of Polus howling in the night. A great fuss is made in preparation for the exorcism: a circle is drawn near the bridge where the spectre appears, crucifixes are set in its centre, and Faunus readies himself for the ceremony that will take place in the evening. The rite is interrupted, however, by Polus and a friend (another priest), who play demons astride their hellish chargers. When they ride off, Faunus claims to have scattered the fiends 'by his potent spells.'[46] Indeed, the comedy is heightened by the juxtaposition of the ludicrous happenings in the night and Father Faunus' ensuing account of them, told with much wonder and seriousness. For the next encounters, Polus has his son-in-law play the tormented ghost in a white sheet with a lamp in hand. The director continues in the role of the devil. This intensifies the vicar's obsession with the spectre and his wild efforts at freeing it from the devil. Such preoccupations begin to unhinge him, so the gamesters deliver the distraught Faunus by means of another ruse: a letter written, as it were, by the once agonized wraith, who now, at last, rests in the peace of heaven – thanks to the labours of Faunus. Credulous to the end, the priest carries 'the letter around and displays it as if it were something sacred; and he believes nothing more firmly than that it was brought from heaven by an angel.'[47] Thomas, to whom Anselm has told this tale, observes at its conclusion that one form of madness has been exchanged for another. 'Very true,' agrees Anselm, 'except that now he's mad in a more pleasant way.'[48]

From start to finish, the butt of Anselm's story has been Faunus, the deluded priest. For this reason, it will come as a surprise when Erasmus tells us in 'The Usefulness of the Colloquies' that in 'The Exorcism' he intended to expose the tricks that impostors delight in playing 'upon the credulous minds of simple folk by feigning apparitions of demons, souls, and heavenly voices.'[49] Yet surely the spotlight of the tale is not focused on the deceit of Polus, at least not in any inimical way. The satirical exposure of the trickster simply does not occur in 'The Exorcism,' and the reason for this is hinted at by Erasmus in the same paragraph of his essay when he tells us that he decided 'to describe the method of the trickery by an amusing example.' In this case, Erasmus the entertainer wins out over Erasmus the teacher.

There is present in 'The Exorcism' a spirit insubordinate to the didactical purposes of satire. That spirit is announced by Anselm before he starts the narration when he exclaims to Thomas, his audience of one, that he has been hoping 'for a long time to run across someone to share the fun with.'[50] His professed motive in telling the story, while not excluding the possibility of some instructional value, seems headed in an opposite direction: Anselm is eager to tell a joke. Once the play begins, we come upon a number of grown men all eager to get into the act, to have a part in the pranks directed against the priest. These too want to join in the fun without much bother about gravity and decorum; and, even though these people are enjoying themselves at Faunus' expense, the tale is not devoid of a sense of fellow-feeling. We find it at both the start and the finish. Polus' little farce would not have got past its opening scene had not Faunus been so anxious to relieve the poor spectre of his torments. The players, too, when they see the priest become so involved with ghosts and demons, devise a way to free him from his obsession. Although the butt of a joke, Faunus is not entirely isolated by his companions, as Malvolio is in the mock exorcism of Shakespeare's Twelfth Night. All the members of Polus' play have willingly jumped up on a stage of fools of differing sorts and have partaken in the lunacy present throughout the action. They are eager to be there. Polus' son-in-law would 'jump bail set at any sum if a play like this ['The Exorcism'] were to be seen or acted.'[51] We meet in this colloquy a spirit of communion in folly not unlike that which can so easily prevail at drinking parties, the joy of which Erasmus likens, as we have seen earlier, to the corrective laughter that satire raises. Yet it is within such a setting of carefree conviviality that all lessons are most likely to get lost.

The dampening of moral concern in 'The Exorcism' is reflected in the attitude which the little work assumes towards the human proclivity to err. Some of the same propensities satirized in other colloquies are held up for ridicule in 'The Exorcism,' but to an extremely different effect. Faunus, the priest, manifests an unhealthy credulity that involves him in rituals hardly to be distinguished from the magical incantations of a witch doctor. Yet his companions see this as an occasion not for serious rebuke but for energetic farce. Faunus' errors are not savagely excoriated but made the butt of a joke which several others can enjoy. His madness provides the material for an entertainment whereby the good-tempered folly of the revellers does actually work an exorcism in reverse. They chase a furious devil out of the would-be exorcist, and, in this way, one folly expels another.

By now we have experienced something of the entire range of Erasmian satire. It can move irately against superstition, as it does in 'A Pilgrimage for Religion's Sake'; it can expose the same failing as a madness that must be derided and laughed at, as it does in 'The Shipwreck'; or it can show this same credulous attitude as a particular manifestation of the folly which more generally afflicts all of mankind. At one end, the temper borders on invective; at the other, we approach the regions of a more liberating laughter associated with absolute comedy which discards the significant and the meaningful. For this reason, the comedy of 'The Exorcism,' although illustrative of Erasmus' literary genius, will probably not strike us as a convincing instrument for stirring the consciences of its readers. 'A Pilgrimage for Religion's Sake,' because of its unmistakable sense of outrage, and 'The Shipwreck,' because of its comical exposure of mistaken piety as a thing to be ridiculed, both sustain their animosity against foolishness and, therefore, better qualify as contributions to the reawakening of religious sensibility in the sixteenth century. But even with regard to these effective satires, my guess is that they possess far less power to move an audience than do the thunderous pronouncements of Luther against the evils and abuses of his times. Had it been only the *Colloquies* which the Renaissance popes had to endure, Rome would still be enjoying them, unrepentant and unreformed. Ironically, the savage denunciations of the papacy on Luther's part did more to inaugurate the reform of Catholicism than the whole repertoire of Erasmus' comical performances.

If, however, we move in history beyond the time of the Reformation, then colloquies of the less abrasive sort like 'The Exorcism' take on a relevance which they did not enjoy when they were first published. Although Luther's words did more than the *Colloquies* to stir the minds of sixteenth-century Europe, the effect of his verbal onslaught cannot be judged a simple, unmixed blessing. The wrath in his message left the church divided into churches that harboured little love towards one another. Indeed, the anger and bias led soon enough to the wars of religion, and it has taken centuries for the bitterness to slacken. In this process of mellowing the souls of Christians towards each other, the less aggressive colloquies of Erasmus had a role to play, and this role was recognized early in the history of the separated churches. When, in 1680, the Anglican Roger L'Estrange wrote the introduction to his translation of selected colloquies out of Erasmus' Latin, he touched on this new appositeness of the humorous, light-spirited colloquies to the evolution of Christendom towards a more tolerant and peace-loving unity. He tells his reader that he will 'find matter of Diversion enough' in these dialogues, which are able 'to mollifie the Evil Spirit, and to turn some Part of the rage and Bitterness that is now in course into Pitty, and Laughter.'[52] Erasmian amusement takes on new significance in this view even when the entertainment in a given colloquy may not reveal any clear moral intent. The laughter itself seems to contribute to the mollifying process that turns rage into pity. There is a kind of vacuity, it would appear, that can lead to fullness.

In this chapter, we have encountered some passages where mirth intimidates ethical consideration. In such instances, the delightful does not serve the useful, at least not in any obvious way. Yet the silencing of moral judgment need not be looked on as undesirable in every case even within a religious frame of things. The Sermon on the Mount, for example, exhorts against moral calculation whenever a man looks at his neighbour's deeds: 'Do not judge, that you may not be judged' (Matt 7:1). So when Catholic and Protestant both behold the folly of man in his attempt to worship God and simply laugh at his lack of understanding, they let go of the indignant moral rage that has set them at odds with each other. This is not all. The jocular forgetfulness, void of rhyme and reason, will, in the *Moria*, serve as a buttress to the analogue between human and divine foolishness, the metaphor on which the entire work rests. Aquinas compares contemplation – the end of all human activity – to play precisely because the two acts are performed to no ulterior purpose.[53] Pointless merriment, too, mimes the activity which crowns the religious life of man.

SIX

Entertaining an Ideal

✺

From Erasmus the satirical reformer lashing out against the errors and abuses of his age, we turn to Erasmus the visionary who brings forth for his contemporaries an image of a better life, one more worthy of their Christian vocation. Erasmus addresses his society with the aims of a prophet in mind: he desires the eradication of gross moral delinquency and the realization of a world more recognizably Christian. Although his manner of writing in the works we are studying in this chapter is too comical to be called prophetic, his intention is fixed at the same goals which Jehovah had set for Jeremias: to level and to build (Jer 1:10). Luther sees Erasmus as one who has perhaps succeeded in exposing the bad in the world about him but has failed to lead men to the good. In Luther's mind, Erasmus resembles Moses in that he is destined, like the great prophet, to die on the plains of Moab short of the promised land.[1] With regard to one point, the coupling of the two figures is most apt. Like Moses, Erasmus desires to lead his people to a new country of their own which would be dominated by a Jerusalem, a 'visio pacis.' This is for Erasmus the utopia for which he strives, a Europe at peace with itself.

We have already established the important place which Christian pacifism occupies in the thought of Erasmus. In the *Querela pacis*, he upbraids the church for failing to resemble her prototype, the Heavenly Jerusalem, whose name denotes the vision of peace.[2] In the 'Dulce bellum inexpertis,' he writes in a similar vein: 'In the City of God there is supreme concord. And Christ wished his Church to be simply this: a people of heaven, living on earth as nearly as may be on the model of the celestial city, hastening towards it, drawing strength from it.'[3] This chapter will focus on a group of seriocomic works that forward the cause of peace and the restoration of society and that offer the means whereby the goal can be attained. In the 'Epicureus,' Erasmus endorses a life of joy for the Christian living on earth. The dialogue embellishes and develops an idea we have already noted in the *Querela pacis* when Peace chides her listeners for failing to deem themselves capable of the happy life experienced by good people and for yielding in a kind of despair to the slaughter of their fellow men.[4] For Erasmus the reformer, the attainment of happiness on earth, in so far as the means to it lie within the hands of men, depends upon the kind of rearing and education the people receive. Reform of society, both ecclesiastical and civic, primarily means for him the revitalization and reshaping of the school on all levels. Three of his works approach this subject in a seriocomic spirit: the *Antibarbari*, the 'Puerpera,' and the *De pueris instituendis*. The first of these is a long dialogue written in the Platonic manner, the second a colloquy, and the last a declamation, the earnestness of which is mingled with a comical use of animal imagery and a sustained plea for the important place which play occupies in the early instruction of the child. Finally, the 'Convivium religiosum' offers us an imaginative projection of the good life as it is achieved by good men, a utopia, as it were, in miniature.

As the title of this chapter states, we consider in these pages the entertainment of an ideal, not a grave and sober presentation of the same. In the 'Epicureus,' for instance, a Christian vision of happiness and pleasure is set in contention with an opposite view, one which understands the same life as stoical and lacking in joy. This dialectic is so constructed as to induce a play of mind within the reader as he reflects on the agon of the colloquy. The tone of these works is usually light, and two of them, the *Antibarbari* and the 'Convivium religiosum,' are given a holiday setting. The thought that shapes the speech in all of them looks to the same end: a happy society of men on earth. At the close of each one of these works, we feel that its personae have moved a step closer to the desired goal. By reason of the play of mind, the lightness of tone, and the thrust of these pieces towards the happy end, they all partake of the comic spirit and form. In them, Erasmus toys with ideas about which he feels seriously.

ERASMUS THE EPICUREAN

The central argument of the 'Epicureus' can be reduced to one sentence: If nothing 'is more wretched than a bad conscience' and nothing 'happier than a good one,' then the Christian who lives up to his beliefs is the happiest of men.[5] We will get closer to the meaning of these words by consulting the original Latin. 'Nihil est miserius,' says Hedonius, *quam animus sibi male conscius.* Literally, he claims that nothing is more miserable than a mind that is fully conscious of the evil it has perpetrated. It seems to follow, then, that nothing is more pleasant to the mind than its awareness of the good it has achieved ('nihil esse felicius animo sibi bene conscio'). The reasoning in this passage lends itself to more than one interpretation, and certain readings of it will run the risk of clashing with the rest of the dialogue's argument. For instance, its application to a Christian frame of things appears to dissolve when we superimpose upon this way of thinking the prayers of the pharisee and the publican in the eighteenth chapter of Luke. The deluded pharisee gives thanks to God for not making him like the rest of men, robbers and adulterers. He fasts and pays his tithes. Surely here is a man whose conscience, in its freedom from guilt, rejoices in the good it has accomplished. By way of contrast, the publican is aware only of the evil of which he is guilty and his need of God's mercy and forgiveness. My guess is that there are other arguments in this dialogue similar to the one just examined which might likewise be shown to disadvantage, were we to approach them from an angle that would not do justice to their real intent. There is a sound explication to Erasmus' plea for the quiet conscience, but we must come at it not on our own terms but on the terms of the work itself.

A work is to be taken in the spirit in which it is written, and we are given straightway a hint about the spirit of the 'Epicureus' in the names of the colloquy's personae. Hedonius, translated 'the devotee of pleasure' by Craig R. Thompson, happens upon Spudaeus, 'earnest' or 'sober,' who is 'bent double over his book, mumbling something or other to himself.'[6] Throughout their conversation, Spudaeus remains a serious objector to the sometimes surprising, sometimes upsetting opinions of the more light-hearted Hedonius. The latter's part occupies the lion's share of the talk because he must explain and defend a position that strikes Spudaeus as an unheard-of novelty. We meet, then, at the start of the dialogue, two characters, one playful, the other serious. The conversation is so plotted that the playful one's ideas are absorbed by the serious one – the play is taken seriously. It is as though Erasmus were applying the adage he had read from Anacharsis: 'ludere ut agas seria' – play in order to stir up serious reflection.[7] This mentality is confirmed within the colloquy itself when Hedonius undertakes his final appeal on behalf of the happiness of the Christian vocation.

Hedonius begins the final stage of the dialogue by introducing a riddle in the form of a 'joke with a serious meaning,' and Spudaeus, of course, is anxious to hear it because he knows the tale will not be an idle one. Hedonius then tells the fable of Tantalus, who, after dining sumptuously with the gods, is invited by Jupiter to request a going-away gift. Tantalus quickly replies by voicing a desire 'to recline at such a table all his life.'[8] The wish is granted, but with one additional feature that takes from Tantalus all his pleasure. He is destined to sit at a festive board in the company of dancers and jesters while over his head dangles a huge stone ready at any moment to fall on his head. In Hedonius' allegorical reading of the tale, the Tantalean rock becomes the grudge of a dark and evil conscience that will not allow the mind that craves to steep itself in pleasures the rest and peace which only the saints know. What dominates in the last phase of the colloquy holds true of the entire work. Something which at first seems ridiculous is proven to be true by the time the talk is concluded This key joke is called by Spudaeus 'a paradox topping all the paradoxes of the Stoics.'[9] On the surface, it appears outlandish; there are no people more Epicurean than the godly, mournful Christians. This is the joke that wants serious validation.

The carom in Hedonius' line of thought moves between two different understandings of the work 'Epicurean' – one popular and the other much deeper and more reflective. In ordinary parlance, the term usually signifies a person fond of luxury and sensual pleasures; its more scholarly and scientific usage harks back to Epicurus himself. By means of the more popular notion, Erasmus achieves the paradoxical surprise of the dialogue's opening statements; by means of certain austere aspects in the original Epicurean doctrine, Erasmus goes on to justify these startling opinions. A tension, therefore, exists between the usual meaning of the term and the term as Erasmus redefines it. The first is shown to be a misunderstanding because it betrays a false concept of what pleasure really is.

This conflict between two different appreciations of the notion of Epicureanism may derive in part from Erasmus' reading of Cicero's *De finibus*, the work over which Spudaeus pores at the beginning of the dialogue. Hedonius is quick to inform his companion that he should not expect to discover the truth in that book, no matter how much learning and eloquence Cicero displays in it. In point of fact, the *De finibus* does not treat Epicurus and his teachings with much sympathy. Cicero stresses the idea that the Epicurean lives for pleasure; such an orientation must surely undermine the moral fibre of the individual. He sets pleasure in opposition to virtue and dismisses the Epicurean's high respect for human friendship as an idle claim, inconsistent with a life that is lived for one's own satisfaction. Cicero believes friendship must be measured 'by the test of its own charm' and not by the standard of profit.[10] Such an avowal, which reduces Epicurean pleasure to mere self-advantage while admitting that friendship yields 'its own charm' (or pleasure), makes the Ciceronian critique of Epicurus rather suspect. Cicero's description hardly squares with the last words Epicurus ever wrote:

This is the happiest day of my life ... it is the last. The pains in my bladder and stomach, always extreme, continue their course, and lose none of their violence. But against all that I place the joy in my soul when I recall the conversations we [Epicurus and his dearest friends] have had together. You, who have been faithful to me and to philosophy from boyhood, take good care of the children of Metrodorus.[11]

It is clear from this that Cicero fails to give to Epicurean friendship its due.

For good reason, Hedonius tells Spudaeus that he will not find the truth in the *De finibus*, especially with regard to what will become the main topic of their conversation. Shortly after dismissing Cicero, Hedonius answers Spudaeus' charge that Epicureans are universally detested. 'Let's disregard,' he advises, 'bad reputations – Epicurus was whatever you please – and consider the matter in itself.'[12] These words tell us much about the kind of argument we should expect from Hedonius. When he says casually that 'Epicurus was whatever you please,' we know that he will not present us with a tight analysis of the philosopher's body of thought. His ensuing plea seems to indicate a desire to probe the principal Epicurean tenet concerning the pursuit of pleasure. But for Erasmus, unlike Cicero, the Epicurean is not defined as one who establishes pleasure as his final goal in life. Nowhere in the work does Hedonius say that the Epicurean lives for pleasure as his last end. The dialogue rather subordinates the notion of pleasure to that of happiness, and, in portraying the Christian as the most Epicurean of men, Hedonius identifies human joy with the union between the creature and his creator. 'Whatever destroys the amity between God and man' inevitably leads to sorrow.[13] By introducing the supreme being in so radical a way, Erasmus seems to take away the grounds for his analogy between the teachings of Epicurus and those of Christ, but, with regard to two essential characteristics, the similarity holds.

The words quoted earlier of the dying Epicurus show the philosopher setting an inner happiness, the recollection of his friends, against the torments of his body. This inner joy is referred to as a kind of repose called 'ataraxia' in the Greek.[14] Such a state of mind would appear to be the constant form of happiness for which the Epicurean strives. Cicero reveals an awareness of it in the De finibus when Lucius Torquatus, the persona of the dialogue who pleads the cause of Epicurus, extols the virtues because of the pleasure which they give. In almost every case, that pleasure is conceived of in terms of an interior calm. Temperance is praised 'because it bestows peace of mind,' courage because it allows us 'to live without anxiety and fear,' and justice because of its 'essentially tranquillizing influence upon the mind.'[15] Now this same concern for inner peace runs through 'Epicureus' in the form of the argument which sees the bad conscience, tormented by guilt, as the cause of man's greatest unhappiness, and the good conscience, at rest in its God, as the cause of man's greatest happiness. This inner repose that Erasmus advocates has been accused of representing a watered-down version of Christianity, one in which passivity and ease replace the violence that takes the kingdom of heaven.[16] The Erasmian conversion of Epicurus' 'ataraxia' to a Christian scheme of things needs to be examined more closely to see whether or not it does lead to moral laxity.

We have already come across the ethical significance of Erasmus' conception of rest in the *Concio de puero Jesu*, where he interprets in a spiritual sense the meaning of Christ's being seated in the temple: the child Jesus reposes only on the sacred things of God.[17] In the *De praeparatione ad mortem*, Erasmus reiterates this idea in glossing the text from Matthew where Christ states that 'the Son of Man has nowhere to lay his head' (8:20). Here again he interprets rest as the settling of desire upon a selected object. Christ has no place on which to recline on earth because his spirit refuses to repose upon the things of this world.[18] To rest, then, in these passages, means to settle upon something as a source of enjoyment by a deliberate choice or movement of the will. At the close of the *De concordia*, Erasmus again links the restraint of desire to tranquillity, only now on a much wider scale; the quiet interior state of the individual brings about the very peace of the entire church. 'If, therefore,' he writes, 'with moderate counsels and passions controlled we concentrate upon restoring peace in the Church, what Isaiah prophesied will come to pass: "My people will sit in the beauty of peace, in the tabernacles of faith and the fullness of rest" (32:18).'[19] To such an end Erasmus orients his adaptation of the spiritual equilibrium in Epicurus. The church and society will be at peace when the hearts of its members are.

By suggesting a kind of weight or gravity that impels the soul to hold to its God as the satisfier of all its desires, the Erasmian notion of rest indicates that it partakes of a dialectical nature. The rest that is won presupposes labour. Recall the oxymoron of the *De contemptu mundi*: the monk's efforts and works are described as most tranquil ('labore nihil quietius').[20] We have seen a similar yoking of opposites in the letter of the dying Epicurus, which brings together physical pain and spiritual bliss. This manner of combination is a constant in the writings of Erasmus. In 'Epicureus,' he mingles joy with hurt or sacrifice. Hedonius speaks of 'that heavenly love proceeding from the spirit of Christ,' that can make of sorrow a cause for rejoicing.[21] The Franciscan, 'poorly and cheaply dressed, worn by fasting, vigils, and labors, without a penny in the world, lives more delightfully – provided only that he has a good conscience – than six hundred Sardanapaluses rolled into one.'[22] The friar's inner quiet makes all his penances light and endurable. The colloquy will even go so far as to claim that the love which Christ raises in the hearts of his followers can make death pleasing.[23] Erasmus can say this because he views Christ's death as the cause of all the happiness of which he writes in the 'Epicureus.' In his commentary on Psalm 22, he poses a question concerning the placing of this joyous song immediately after Psalm 21, a prophecy of Christ's crucifixion. This ordering of the Psalms strikes him as congruent, even beautiful, 'because the death of Christ is the source of all our joy ... The way to life is through death; the way to never-ending joy is through affliction.'[24]

The joy of Christian life is intermingled with suffering, but this does not weaken Erasmus' conviction about the happiness of this calling. In the 'Epicureus,' Hedonius insists first of all on the happiness of Christ's life on earth: 'Completely mistaken ... are those who talk in their foolish fashion about Christ's having been sad and gloomy in character and calling upon us to follow a dismal mode of life. On the contrary, he alone shows the most enjoyable life of all and the one most full of pleasure.'[25] We saw in chapter 2 that Erasmus believed that, even in the torment of the cross, Christ mysteriously continued to partake of the glorious vision originating in his divine nature. He exhorted Christians not to meditate gloomily on that death, but to rejoice in its victory over sin. If the master lived joyously, so should the servant follow him. With God in his heart, the Christian lays hold of 'paradise, heaven, happiness.' So argues Hedonius: 'Where happiness is, there is true gladness and unfeigned cheerfulness.'[26] And even on earth the disciple of Christ celebrates in 'songs, dances, exultings, revels' – joys that are known only to him.[27]

The discussion has gone beyond the question of the ethical vigour in the Erasmian notion of repose, but a knowledge of the happiness to which it is joined allows us a fuller perspective of it. Erasmian rest calls for recollection of mind and concentration of desire; it is an alloy, not a simple notion of ease but a vital union of repose and labour as an instance of the more sweeping and general fusion between joy and sorrow. This then is the Erasmian version of Epicurus' 'ataraxia' and one of two essential similarities upon which he bases his analogy between the Christian and the Epicurean. In order to approach the second similarity, we had best return to the unresolved problem already mentioned. Even if Erasmus' Epicurean Christian can be absolved from the charge of moral laxity, this blissful conscience of his seems to bespeak a pharisaical complacency and self-satisfaction. To answer this problem, we must look into the second fundamental likeness between the Epicurean and the Christian as Erasmus conceives each.

At the summit of Epicurus' thought is discovered a tenet which may strike some as an anomaly. He believes that the greatest of all pleasures ensues from friendship, and friendship, at least in its maturity, is enjoyed for its own sake.[28] Contrary to what Cicero writes about the Epicurean relationship, friendship, in the mind of Epicurus, does not mean that the two people are looking after their own interest and advantage.[29] So the search for pleasure, ending as it does in the joy of friendship, is transformed from a selfish preoccupation into a happiness, the fullness of which must be conceived as shared with another. Similarly, the bliss of Erasmus' Christian results not from a self-satisfaction but from a joyous relationship with God. To achieve this, everything which 'destroys amity between God and man' is to be avoided.[30] As in the works of Epicurus, the happiness of which Erasmus writes cannot be thought of as isolated: friendship constitutes its very definition; therefore, because it is a joy that rises out of a union, it too must be understood as shared. It means partaking of the interior beatitude which is God's.

Towards the conclusion of his first version of the *De contemptu mundi*, Erasmus cites a passage from a letter of St Jerome in which the church father feels himself transported to the ranks of the heavenly angels and to be singing joyously with them a line from the Song of Songs: 'We will run after thee to the odour of thy ointments' (1:4).[31] The passage from Jerome sums up for Erasmus the happiness experienced by the faithful upon earth, a pleasure that is shared by and common to all who live piously: 'Atque haec quidem voluptas omnibus piis communis est.'[32] This joy of its very nature must be communal because it issues from God and his own state of beatitude. The divine rapture, as a result of the triune character of the deity, is a state shared by the three persons. Erasmus' understanding of this aspect of the Trinity is clearly stated in his paraphrase of Christ's words in John (16:15): 'Nothing exists among us which is not held in common. All things flow from the Father but nothing is his which is not mine also, and nothing belongs to the Father nor to me which is not held in common with the Spirit. Through him I will speak to you just as the Father has spoken through me.'[33] The divine nature, given as it is to sharing, communicates itself most spontaneously to man. God elevates the redeemed from a state of slavery to one of freedom and friendship by his act of self-communication. The slave obeys orders he does not understand, but Christ calls his disciples friends and proves this when he communicates to them whatever the Father has told him in a manner in which a friend addresses a friend.[34] Out of this sharing in a spirit of amity the community of the church is begotten.

We have just seen that in the mind of Erasmus God's way of being corresponds to his way of acting and communicating. The divine generosity of God revealing itself in creation and in redemption follows from the unselfish character of the triune nature. Under the inspiration of grace, men take on the same trait. Erasmus comments on the sharing of wealth in the early church as a miracle performed by the Spirit, who drew the faithful together in unity and peace. In this passage, he does not restrict the community of goods to material commodities but includes spiritual endowments as well.[35] Words of enlightenment and consolation are freely dispensed to all. At this point, we touch on the theological grounds for a Christian humanist theory of literary composition. Communication follows upon and looks towards communion. By the spoken and written word, the speaker or the author attempts to confirm and to validate what Erasmus' friend John Colet calls the 'common feeling' and the 'common sympathy' which the Spirit stirs up in the Mystical Body of Christ.[36]

The playful works of Erasmus provide a small but very apt instance of the communication whose origin is founded on this Christian impetus to share. In the *Colloquies*, we noticed the tendency among characters friendly to each other to share a joke. This form of playing has a spiritual side illustrative of Erasmus' adage on the equality achieved by friendship – 'amicitia aequalitas.'[37] Erasmus attributes to Pythagoras the idea linking friendship to equality, but the best account of how this connection is fittingly expressed through play is given by Aquinas:

Friendship is more permanent when the give and take is equal and identical, for instance, pleasure for pleasure. Since there are different kinds and quantities of pleasure according to the difference of objects, a settled friendship requires, not merely that pleasure should be repaid with pleasure, but that the pleasure should be in the same thing;

thus, happiness in play when one delights in the sport of another, and not when, as sometimes happens in erotic love, a couple are not enjoying the same thing.[38]

All pleasures do not merit, in the thought of Aquinas, equal moral approbation. Some are suited to sharing while others are susceptible to the encroachment of self-interest like the satisfaction obtained by the aging lover in J.V. Cunningham's poem:

> It is a pact men make, and seal in flesh,
> To be so busy with their own desires
> Their loves may be as busy with their own,
> And not in union. Though two enmesh
> Like gears in motion, each with each conspires
> To be at once together and alone.[39]

In play, be it of the spoken or written variety, both the one sporting and the one finding amusement in the sport take pleasure in the same thing. This is a genuine, if less fervent, example of the Erasmian dictum about the joy which good people share with one another, the 'voluptas omnibus piis communis.' Erasmus describes his friend Thomas More as a person who, like the fictitious characters in the *Colloquies*, took the greatest pleasure in conversing with friends close to him and in sharing pleasantries and anecdotes with them.[40] This ambience of amicable discussion seems to have provided the inspiration and encouragement for *Utopia* and the *Moria*. In many instances, if not most, the playful literature of both Erasmus and More develops as an extension of friendly and witty engagement of minds. It is most natural, then, that the two men would favour literary forms, like the declamation and the dialogue, which present to the imagination the written word as being spoken to another or to an audience.

Both the form and the content of 'Epicureus' reflect this humanist approach to the communication of thought. The pleasure of a Christian is conceived of as dependent upon a relationship between God and man. Man's nature requires that God-given pleasure be shared generously among other men. The fun of the dialogue originates with an author who invites his readers to assimilate it in a festive spirit. The play of thought may shock some into thinking that Erasmus has corrupted the

Christian ethic by reducing it to self-interest. But the end of this little work is to lure us, along with the sombre Spudaeus, into seeing that its playfulness corresponds with the optimistic outlook of Hedonius, who believes even the most arduous elements of Christian life to be linked intrinsically to an unselfish state of joy.

The 'Epicureus' really advocates a new attitude towards the ascetical life by envisioning the spiritual combat as a joyous struggle free from the stern and morose temper that can so easily prevail in Christian spirituality. The aggressive instinct in man, according to Erasmus, is to be directed outwards only in good-hearted competition, and inwards only in a joyous hope of victory over passion and appetite.[41] To achieve this high ideal, men are to be put to training from their earliest years. Proper education is indispensable for the seeker of the happiness which Erasmus describes. Three works of a seriocomic nature are involved with the essential elements of a good formation, namely, the learned and affable teacher, a curriculum of Latin and Greek studies, and parents who are fully conscious of their great responsibility to raise the child and to see to its education. The *Antibarbari* addresses the first two needs; the 'Puerpera' looks at the role played by the mother in the early stages of the infant's life; the *De pueris instituendis* is meant for both parents and teachers and discusses all three aspects of the subject.

FORMING THE GOOD MAN

The first version of the *Antibarbari* took the form of a speech, and only later was it changed into a dialogue. Erasmus probably made one of his several revisions of the piece while he was staying at a country residence at Halsteren near Bergen-op-Zoom in the spring of 1494 or 1495, because the dialogue is set in the same environs.[42] At the opening of the work, the author tells us that he had taken refuge from the plague by retiring to 'a rural corner of Brabant, so salubrious and charming a place that it seemed highly suitable not only for preserving health but for a studious retreat.'[43] The idyllic setting for study, reflection, and the good life, first pictured in the *De contemptu mundi*, has shifted from the cloister to this haunt of the Muses, 'who are said to delight in clear springs, green grassy banks, and the thick shade of the woods.'[44] The beginning of the *Antibarbari* finds Erasmus walking in this rural paradise with two of his friends: James Batt, the town clerk of nearby Bergen, and William Hermans, an Augustinian canon of Steyn. As they cross a canal bridge, they spy two more of their friends: William Conrad, the burgomaster of Bergen, and a certain Dr Jodocus, physician to the same city. This amicable group continues its stroll through the countryside exchanging views on the plight of good literature in an educational world that is largely hostile to it. When they reach the grounds of the estate where Erasmus resides, he suggests that they make their academy in these groves after the 'model of Plato's.'[45] They sit and continue to challenge the arguments directed against the pagan literature of Greece and Rome, with Batt doing most of the talking, until the burgomaster's wife, from her neighbouring house, sends a servant to summon them to dinner.

Even this brief sketch will suffice to suggest the potential for literary richness in the *Antibarbari*. Erasmus gives careful attention to the delineation of his characters, especially Batt's. The serious consideration of the state of liberal studies and learning itself is laced with jokes and pleasantries which prevent the discussion from becoming too ponderous. This variety in tone, achieved by the mingling of the serious with the comical, makes for enjoyable reading. We sense the influence of the Platonic dialogue on this work in a way that is not felt in the *Colloquies* of Erasmus. Here we have a setting that recalls the *Phaedrus*, thrice referred to in the text, and a debate that centres on a subject not unlike the approaches to rhetoric which Socrates examines in the same dialogue. Something akin to the burning Platonic quest for the truth can be detected in the *Antibarbari* as well. Batt, in particular, reveals so strong an attachment to the wisdom of the ancients that he will rage at those irresponsible schoolmasters who infect the minds of the young with wrongheaded ideas and lead them away from the love of good literature. Dr Jodocus and the burgomaster Conrad, in turn, offer real obstacles to the advance of Batt's position with the result that the reader feels he is witnessing a genuine engagement of minds. Although we perceive that all the participants share the same fundamental attitude towards good literature, they do not wish for an easy, unquestioned victory for their side. Part of the dialogue's conflict arises out of this conviction, and part also from a clash in attitude not among the personae but rather between them and the 'barbari,' the enemies of humanist reform. This contention begins first as one of notions, and then evolves into one of opposing spirits.

When Erasmus, Hermans, and Batt first encounter Conrad and Dr Jodocus, reference is made to a drinking party held the night before at which all five men seem to have been present.[46] This does not prevent them from rising early to enjoy each other's company again. Hermans and Batt, who are both guests of Erasmus for a three-day sojourn at his place of retreat, had agreed from the start to spend the entire time 'in pure amusement, in the freest of murmured talk.'[47] Conrad, on the other hand, must steal what time he can from the busy affairs concerning the civic life of Bergen in order to join his companions. Erasmus is even taken by surprise when sees Conrad from the canal bridge. 'What has a burgomaster,' he asks, 'to do with the country, what have you to do with this leisured retreat, you, the busiest man alive?'[48] In return, Conrad envies Erasmus because he has chosen to follow a calling that leads to a happiness he is not at liberty to experience. 'I am envious,' he admits, 'of your delightful life, you happiest of all men alive! While we poor wretches are tossed hither and thither by the raging sea of public affairs, you are strolling about all the time with your Muses, entirely at leisure and unoccupied.'[49] No wonder, then, that Erasmus has declined every invitation of Conrad luring him into the city away from his beloved woods. Erasmus replies by teasingly accusing the burgomaster of succumbing to the temptations of money-making and ambition, thereby permitting himself to get caught up in a life leading away from true happiness.[50]

In the above passages, we find an opposition between business and leisure suggestive of the rest-work antagonism in the *De contemptu mundi*, where the monastery's work is reduced to a form of rest or play while secular existence is characterized by its fleeting joy and constant anxiety amounting to a kind of work.[51] The new variation in the *Antibarbari* exchanges the monastic peace for the rural leisure of the scholar. This now becomes in Conrad's words the 'delightful life,' and, because Erasmus enjoys it, he is 'the happiest of all men.' By way of contrast, Conrad's involvement with political matters places him in a situation similar to the worldling in the *De contemptu mundi*. A 'raging sea' encircles both the politician and the worldling.[52] Curiously, Erasmus implies that the scholar's life of rural leisure is taken up with a good deal of playing as opposed to the serious business of city dwellers. When burgomaster Conrad is tempted away from his job, he is pursuing the desire 'to escape for a while from civil lawsuits with their clamour, whenever he had a mind to relax a little more freely and play, as Horace says, in carefree fashion.'[53] Furthermore, the students of letters want nothing to do with the self-importance of certain pretentious scholars or the narrow-mindedness of uneducated people. 'What have we to do with the rod of office,' asks Batt, 'or with the arrogance of philosophers?'[54] And when Conrad joins the group, he tells them: 'We will all amuse ourselves together. For Jodocus has left the stricter bit of his philosophy at home with his wife (he has a rather peevish one) and I have left the burgomaster at home.'[55] Such, then, is the opposition introduced at the beginning of the dialogue: on the one side, we have the study of literature graced with a leisure and merriment that is enjoyed by open and congenial minds; on the other side, the worry and pressure of business set next to the inflated importance associated with a false wisdom that begets a rigid and unsettled spirit. But, in almost typical fashion, while Erasmus separates work from play with his right hand, he begins to join them with his left. He first hints at this when mentioning how inseparable his own little group of three was from the presence of Conrad during their entire stay at Halsteren. This was so, confesses the author, 'because of the pleasure I took in his company and learning, or because I had business matters to go over with him.'[56] In this sentence, play and work are accommodated to each other and reconciled in the charm of a single person; later they will be found integrated in the scholar's pursuit of learning. To see how Erasmus brings this about will tell us a good deal about the philosophical grounds supporting the seriocomic art in his writings.

The antipathy between the life of leisure and that of work, so evident in the opening pages of the *Antibarbari*, is all but forgotten when the discussion opens in earnest, at which point a more crucial antagonism, the very conflict of the dialogue, arises: the contention between the cultured humanists and the 'barbari.' James Batt, the most articulate champion of Greek and Roman literature in this gathering, does not see his enemies merely as ignorant men. They are certainly that, but their small minds lean almost by instinct towards an arrogant self-satisfaction over the little they do know. Because they mistake themselves for models of learning, they will not admit the study of subjects they do not comprehend to be introduced into the schools. Only Christian authors, and, for the most part, those of the Middle Ages, win their approval. Batt, in addition to linking arrogance to the stupidity of his enemies, repeatedly charges them with licentious conduct. Failing to find pleasure in higher endeavours, they must need seek it in lower places like pigs at the trough. They are disgusted when girls are even mentioned in the tales of the poets, but they do not object in the least to 'forcing other men's wives, even Vestal virgins.'[57] But perhaps the vice that best characterizes them is their laziness. Sunk in their hopeless sloth, they remain insensate to the finer appeals which literature makes to the human spirit. "I wish I were allowed to choose a fine specimen out of those sties where so many fat healthy porkers idle away and are stuffed with the food of the people,' explaims Batt. 'I would rather sacrifice a biped than any four-footed pig.'[58]

Erasmus uses a number of Latin words to describe the indolence of the pseudo-learned clerics standing in the way of humanist reform. They are 'ignavi' (slothful), 'segnes' (sluggish), and given to what he calls an 'iners ocium' (a simple or unfruitful kind of idleness).[59] His usage of this last substantive elicits some interest, because, unlike the adjective 'ignavus,' which is always pejorative, 'ocium' can have two diametrically opposite meanings. It can mean a state of inactivity leading nowhere, or it can mean a state of leisure providing the necessary atmosphere for the earnest search for wisdom. Erasmus applies the word both to the humanists he defends and to the 'barbari' he assaults.[60] Furthermore, a strikingly similar profile is given by either side of this conflict when each is trying to sketch the other. For the humanists, the preoccupation of the 'barbari' is summed up by Batt in his story about the libertine whose whole time was given to whoring and to drinking contests: 'These were the fellow's studies – on these he lavished his toil, his care; in these he placed his pleasure, his leisure, his business, his happiness.'[61] When, however, Batt imagines the charges of the 'barbari' against the humanists, he makes use of the same kind of language: 'They ask if a person can really be considered Christian when he takes so much trouble and finds so much delight in irreligious exercises invented by wicked men to satisfy their pride, when he finds all his repose in these things and makes them into his leisure occupation, his business, his one solace?'[62] In the case of the licentious representative of the 'barbari,' Erasmus identifies his leisure with his work ('ocium'-'negocium'), because the man's entire happiness ('felicitatem') is confined to the one area of fleshly satisfaction. Whether feverish or torpid, all his activities are directed to this end. In the case of the student of humanist learning, Erasmus again identifies leisure with work, using the very same words ('ocium'-'negocium') and for the same reason: he finds in his studies his 'one solace' ('solatium omne'). We discover in this parallel assessment a recurrence of the thinking already noticed in the De contemptu mundi where two ways of life are distinguished by the pursuit of two kinds of pleasure, one spiritual, the other corporeal.[63] As work and rest were brought together in that other work, so are leisure and employment joined here, but, because the 'barbari,' in fact, do no real work at all, the work-rest paradox, when applied to them, is merely verbal. With the humanists, on the other hand, the integration of 'ocium' and 'negocium' reaches beyond words into things, in so far as it reflects a fundamental attitude espoused by all the personae of the Antibarbari, an attitude which in turn is caught up with the highest ideals projected in the book.

Just before the debate over the causes of the neglect of fine literature commences, mention is made of the political turmoil which at the moment besets Holland. This regional disaster, with its sacked towns and ruined villages, serves as the lead into the consideration of a similar catastrophe in the world of learning: the 'tragic and terrible deluge' whereby the 'joyful fruits of the finest culture' had been shamefully overwhelmed.[64] The sorrows afflicting the state are similar to those damaging the realm of the spirit. Later the two worlds are again brought together when Batt begins speaking about the Republic of Letters as if this were a city, a political entity, ready to wage war against the barbarian enemy besieging it.[65] Batt has prepared his listeners for this imaginative link between society and literature when he announces that the real perpetrator of the destruction of learning is the city itself, and, in particular, burgomaster William Conrad, for appointing and supporting the benighted tyrants who now rule over the pupils in the classrooms of Bergen.[66] The dialogue consistently affirms that the welfare of the nation depends on the quality of its education. As with Plato in the Republic, the body politic relates directly to the state of soul of its citizens, and souls do not, except where God's grace provides otherwise, attain to maturity in virtue without the assistance of a good education, which Erasmus equates with the reading of literature, especially those great pagan authors whom the *Antibarbari* presents as so many paths all leading to Christ.[67] Good letters mould character. Batt associates ignorance with pride and modesty with learning, and proves his point by contrasting the outspoken scholastic dogmatists to the more appealing humility of Socrates, Quintilian, and St Jerome.[68] While the 'barbari,' as we have seen, burn with carnal desire, the humanists, by means of their studies, are drawn away from preoccupation with such passions. Batt himself 'had in early youth been given to surreptitious affairs with girls, from which however he had soon been recalled by the study of letters.'[69] The connection between virtue and good literature is clearly implied in the conduct of the characters in this dialogue. To a man, they possess a spirit illustrating the fruit of their studies. The debate maintains a mellow, gentle tone, although Batt, on more than one occasion, is forced to bridle his flaring temper and to check an incipient abrasiveness. Despite his failing, the whole group shares the same ideal about conduct in the discussion of important questions. This ideal attains its happiest expression in that detached and genuinely courteous sense of wit which Erasmus takes care to sustain throughout the work.

The three main personages of the dialogue are presented to us as congenial, urbane men readily given to laughter. Our first look at Conrad shows us his 'usual cheerful smile.'[70] Jodocus 'is one of the merriest of men.'[71] The normal expression on Batt's face is called 'comic' or 'vultu faceto,' as the Latin has it.[72] These men seem to epitomize the Renaissance ideal of the 'vir facetus,' the man of wit. This concept gave birth to both a rhetoric and an ethos of its own, especially in the writings of Giovanni Pontano, the quattrocentro Italian humanist.[73] Because there is an art to telling a funny story, such a narrative, according to Pontano, can be subjected to rhetorical analysis. The art also depends on the genius of the teller, who has the gift of transforming even risqué or obscene material into a hilariously acceptable joke;[74] hence, it relates to the world of morality. The urbane pleasantry of the 'vir facetus' originates in the desire to please and to share with others rather than to offend them. The comedy proper to him does not call for a laugh at any price. Such a person, for instance, would not try to direct his humour aggressively at any individual, present or absent. The 'vir facetus,' as he loves the truth, will avoid flattery, and, as he wants to be friendly, will avoid boorishness. So he cultivates a kind of conversation that 'has a soothing, refreshing quality that ... is restful and relaxing in the best sense of the word.'[75] By reason of this attribute, he is also the 'vir festivus,' the man of cheer, whose wit partakes of the holiday spirit belonging to the origins of this last term.

As Pontano joins rhetoric and morality in his conception of the 'vir facetus,' so Erasmus couples the study of literature to the life of virtue in the *Antibarbari*. For more than half of the dialogue, Batt strives to prove that ignorance begets pride and arrogance while true learning inevitably leads to modesty. The enemy of the humanist carries within him a swinish appetite which is naturally aroused by his closed, uncultivated mind. The humanist does seek after pleasure, but only of the higher sort. Because this search makes its demands on the seeker and requires a discipline, it fosters virtuous habit. On the ideal plane, the person given to the higher enjoyment of literary art should become the pleasant man who incorporates in himself both the virtue so earnestly pursued and the balanced temper that frees him to exercise and enjoy the play of wit. All the characters of the dialogue indicate in their manner of arguing this inner poise and broadness of spirit allowing them to sport with one another and with a subject closest to their hearts.

In this study of the *Antibarbari*, we have seen an initial state of tension between the playful and the serious when Batt claims that, in leaving the city for the country, he and his friends have exchanged business for amusement. Their pastime debate, however, immediately rejoins the two ideas when Batt calls the subject of their entertainment the Republic of Letters and stresses the importance of good literature to society in general. In other words, the welfare of the body politic in which Conrad and Batt find their employment depends on a flourishing system of education where good authors, the subject of their recreation, are held in esteem. Again Batt couples the originally antagonistic notions in his view that the humanist finds through his readings both his leisure and his business. The frequently playful ways the interlocutors investigate a subject that is all-important to them reinforce this same bifocal outlook. Erasmus' willingness to treat didactic subjects comically even when he felt deeply about them stems from a conviction about the importance of play at all levels of learning. But perhaps even more important than this pedagogical outlook is the moral regard he shared with so many humanists for the 'vir facetus,' the man of wit and balance who resisted being so totally immersed in a subject that he failed to appreciate its lighter side. The author's very seriousness demanded the detachment of a light spirit just as his critique of the world of affairs called for a vital appreciation of those studies pursued in an ambience of leisure.

In the *Antibarbari*, Erasmus shows his concern for school curriculum and pedagogy; in the colloquy 'Puerpera,' he focuses upon an even more basic aspect of education: the part the mother is to play in this process from the moment of the child's birth. The woman's responsibility here is great but apparently unrecognized, or so the colloquy seems to say in its opening lines. When Eutrapelus congratulates Fabulla for learning 'so early the very difficult art of bearing children,' the young woman cannot take him seriously. 'How you always live up to your name,' she retorts.[76] 'Eutrapelus' means, literally, 'happy turn' and, more precisely, 'to be witty.' Fabulla evidently thinks her friend is joking because she does not believe that childbearing requires a special training. The task of Eutrapelus is indicated by the literal sense of his name: he has to turn the mind of Fabulla around so that she may appreciate to the fullest what her role in childbearing entails.

Early in the dialogue, Eutrapelus is seemingly distracted from the central topic of the discussion by the violent trend in the political events of the day. The king of Denmark has been exiled; the king of France has fallen into the hands of the Spaniards; King Charles 'is preparing to extend the boundaries of his realm.'[77] Eutrapelus then proceeds to recount in detail the rebellion, the anarchy, and the bloodshed going on around him. Everywhere he sees 'the seamless coat of Jesus is torn to shreds.'[78] Church authority and doctrine are both questioned while the Great Turk stands ready to pounce upon these divided and divisive Christians. One might wonder how this commentary on the struggles of the contemporary world comes into a colloquy whose main concern centres on the homely matter of bringing up babies. The description of a Christendom at strife, however, is not here by chance.

From the extensive references to a Europe at war with itself, the conversation moves to a battle of the sexes between the two personae. Basing his argument on the strength of the male and his courage in warfare, Eutrapelus pleads for the sexual superiority of man. Fabulla rejoins tellingly:

> You're worse than gladiators: you voluntarily surrender your bodies into the slavish necessity of killing or being killed. Now ... there's not a single one of you who, if he once experienced childbirth, would not prefer standing in battle line ten times over to going through what we must endure so often.[79]

Woman's courage is involved in the bearing of life, man's with the stifling of it. It is as if Erasmus were applying his remedy for the problem of human violence with its carnage and slaughter by returning to the origins of life with the intent of forming a new man less given to a violent temper. This formation is to begin immediately after birth. The *Antibarbari,* as we have seen, juxtaposes the wars in Holland and the desolate state of liberal education. A dialogue treating the early rearing of a child gives an extensive description of war-torn Christendom. This coupling is not mere coincidence. Erasmian education is intended to lead to freedom and upright moral action, not to what Fabulla calls 'the slavish necessity of killing.' But, while the lady shows only contempt for the soldier's life, she does not on that account disdain all forms of embroilment. She proves herself more than a match for Eutrapelus in the 'single combat' of this debate. The man is forced to yield in the battle of the sexes in order to return to the more important topic of raising children; and, in this matter, he wants not to beat her but to win her.

Fabulla needs no instruction concerning the true end of childbearing. She speaks no doubt for Erasmus when, after being congratulated by Eutrapelus for the happy delivery of her son, she replies, 'Congratulate me on a safe delivery if you like, Eutrapelus; on a happy one when you see my offspring prove himself an honest man.'[80] A happy delivery, or childbearing in the fullest sense, aims at sound moral conduct. This Fabulla understands. She fails, though, in some fundamental aspects, to see the importance of her part in this process, and Eutrapelus is quick to point out this lack of awareness to her. When he discovers that her child is in the next room being nursed, he straightway begins to argue against what he considers to be Fabulla's negligence as a mother. The remainder of the dialogue is, for the most part, taken up with Eutrapelus' plea for the wisdom of maternal breast-feeding, but it would be a mistake to read what is said here as a narrow preoccupation with a single domestic arrangement. Child nursing is presented within a much broader vision of Erasmus' philosophic comprehension of the union of soul and body.

The natural movement of Erasmus' mind appears to run more frequently in the direction of synthesis than analysis. His commentaries on the psalms unite the Old Testament to the New under the Messiah whom the earlier literature prefigures; his theological polemic against Luther strives to couple human nature with the deity, human will with divine grace, without doing violence to the freedom of either; and his pedagogical treatises defend the pagan classics as prolegomena to a mature life in Christ. So, in the 'Puerpera,' Erasmus concentrates on the intimate and fast union of body to soul. Eutrapelus says that, although others have called the body a tomb or a prison of the soul, Christ refers to his own body as a temple, and Peter calls his a tabernacle.[81] According to Aristotle, the soul is defined by its act upon the body: 'the soul does nothing except through the organs, that is, the instruments of the body.'[82] But, just as 'every natural movement of a body originates in mind,' so bodily activity affects the condition of the mind. Eutrapelus compares the distance of the stomach from the brain to that of a fireplace from a chimney top, 'but if you sit on it [the top],' he claims, 'you'll feel the heat.'[83] So it makes a difference 'which spirits and vapors fly up from the stomach to the brain and the organs of the mind.'[84] Fabulla likens this description of human digestion to the function of 'a still by which we draw off the juice evaporating from flowers and herbs.'[85] This image suggests a more extensive distillation whereby the sensate objects of sight, hearing, and the other organs of perception rise to a state of spiritual presence in the soul. What enters the body, then, what man eats and drinks, is of real importance, and this conclusion applies especially in the case of a newborn child. But, granting this intimate relationship of body to mind and soul, why must the infant nurse at his mother's breast? Eutrapelus' answer, while not abandoning the physical plane, does explore a fundamental area of Erasmian educational psychology.

Early in the colloquy, Eutrapelus recounts to Fabulla a bawdy anecdote in which a woman is described as being cut in two in the act of sex.[86] When the discussion later turns serious, the figure of self-division is applied again to Fabulla. Eutrapelus calls her only half a mother for shunning her obligation of nursing her little boy, and the divisive image is extended to the baby as well. The woman denies that she has divided her son by entrusting him to a nurse. The repetition of images evoking the bisection of woman and child indicates a break both in a nature and in the self. Nature, by making the mother's breasts 'two little swollen fountains ... flowing with milk' at the time of childbirth, reminds the woman of her duty.[87] Fabulla, out of custom, has, in a sense, divorced herself from that nature and denied her child at a most tender age the initial and intimate expression of her love for him. Instead of receiving his first nourishment in an act of communion and love, the child is given the breast of a stranger who is merely fulfilling her duty as an employee. This early frustration will later affect the docility of the child towards the authority of his master. All human growth, on every level, is fostered by love. Eutrapelus applies this notion to a later period in the child's formation: 'Now one of the main steps in the learning process is mutual affection between teacher and pupil.'[88] The love to be made manifest in the later rearing of the child must not be denied him at the most elementary and physical stage of his growth. If the woman refuses to do what her body and her child call for her to do, she will be alienating herself from her nature and her son.

To this reasoning of Eutrapelus, Fabulla answers, 'So far as I can see, childbearing is not so simple an affair as people commonly suppose.'[89] Her friend has convinced her that the earliest period of a child's formation has a great influence on all that follows and that her part in it is both serious and important. If the child is to grow in love, he must first experience it on this most elemental level. To refuse him this is to divide him and to alienate him unconsciously. The references to self-division in mother and child may well have something to do with the description, early in the colloquy, of a Christendom that has turned against itself. If the maternal obligation to nurse is forgotten and the child is left to another, the frustration which Erasmus associates with such neglect will encourage an early manifestation and growth of that irascible appetite descried in the introductory section of the dialogue. The body and soul of the future citizen of the peaceable kingdom is to be nurtured in love and meekness from the first hour of his life.

The *Declamatio de pueris statim ac liberaliter instituendis* takes up just about where the 'Puerpera' leaves off. The child has been weaned and has begun to talk. His formal education is to begin, as the title indicates, immediately ('statim'). The reader may question why this work is being treated as seriocomedy when its argument is obviously meant to be taken with great earnestness and its tone has nothing of the playful ambivalence so noticeable in Erasmus' most famous declamation, the *Moria*, nor the *joie de vivre* of his most outspoken declamation, the *Encomium matrimonii*. Still one cannot read the *De pueris*, for all of its seriousness, without laughing at the human absurdities satirized by Erasmus in his frequent comparisons between man and beast; furthermore, the work says a good deal about the civilizing role of play and its special importance to the early years of a child's education. It sets this refined form of pedagogy in opposition to the brutalizing method of child-beating which seems to have been the practice in many of the schools known to Erasmus.

No one reading the *De pueris* can help noticing the parade of animals through its pages. It begins with an adage about the futility of trying to teach the old parrot to speak: he must be taught when young, and so must the child.[90] Animals are endowed by nature with horns and beaks and claws to protect themselves, while man's only defence lies in his wit, which calls for much training and sharpening.[91] This imagery becomes amusing when we are asked to consider the folly of the affluent who labour at training dogs for the hunt and horses for the track but give not the slightest thought to the education of their sons.[92] Once he has established the absurdity in man's disregard of studies, Erasmus can send the ridiculous human creature to his 'schola animalium' to learn from the beasts. Animals, we are told, have taught mankind any number of arts. The hippopotamus has instructed men in the practice of blood-letting; the ibis has given men the enema; the hart has led men to the herb dictamum, which is extremely efficacious in the doctoring of wounds.[93] If the beasts can teach man in such useful skills, what prevents him from learning to instruct his children by following the example of his fellow creatures? Cats are at great pains to show their kittens how to hunt and to lay hold of mice and small birds. Deer teach their little fawns how to flee danger and to take to the high, rocky ground in times of peril. Among the nightingales we notice a veritable teacher-pupil relationship with the elder bird giving the pitch to the younger one and correcting the mistakes committed during the music lesson.[94] What more by way of motivation do humans need than this? Man's confidence over his own teachability surely must grow when he sees an elephant walking the tightrope, or a bear dancing, or an ass playing the fool.[95]

The playful quality in Erasmus' treatment of animals in the *De pueris* cannot escape us. As we might expect, he also uses the same imagery to voice his outrage and indignation over the neglect of parents in seeing to the proper education of their children. Erasmus tells us that the law is severe on fathers who abandon their infant babes in the woods and leave them to the mercy of the prowling night creatures. But there is a crime worse than this, against which the law remains silent. Far worse is it to neglect the child's education, for in so doing the father abandons the son to the child's own appetite.[96] In the mind of Erasmus, the newborn child is a kind of shapeless mass capable of being formed into a godlike creature or of being misshapen into a beast or worse.[97] A similar notion is found in the seventh book of Aristotle's *Ethics*, where the philosopher refers to the bestiality to which a man can sink and the godlike quality with which the continent man is adorned.[98] Failure to educate the child in the right manner results in changing him into a beast just as Odysseus' companions were turned into swine by Circe. In fact, this metamorphosis makes man something lower than any animal. Erasmus regards the human passions, allowed to go unchecked, as so many raging beasts which grow to lord it over the child until that which might have been divine becomes the lowest of animals.[99] The witchcraft that turns men into wolves serves to illustrate what parents do to their offspring by neglecting their education.

Perhaps the worst form of parental remissness occurs when the father and mother pay no attention to the kind of master to whom they entrust the early education of their children. The incompetent teacher, like the culpably ignorant antagonist of the *Antibarbari*, figures in the *De pueris* as the enemy of everything for which the work stands. On page after page, this bane of education is pummelled not so much for the teacher's ignorance as for the brutal approach he takes towards the tender young people entrusted to his charge. Erasmus recounts some harrowing tales of child-beatings where the victims are thrashed and tortured to a point of collapse or even of death. These ignorant wretches are blamed for quelling in the child at an early age all respect for literature and learning. It would appear that this deranged master with his fearsome inclination towards violence is held responsible for the deformation of child into beast. He is guilty because he sees in his pupil not a person to be educated in freedom but an object upon whom he can vent his anger. Incapable of controlling his own passionate feelings, he unloads the tempest within him upon his students and arouses within them the same irascible appetite. According to Erasmus, such fellows as these teachers are fit only to be butchers or hangmen.[100]

The remedy for this appalling abuse lies in the hands of those responsible for hiring schoolmasters and tutors and in a change of method and approach to pedagogy at the primary level. Erasmus sets up in opposition to the cane-wielding master his ideal of the teacher endowed with Christian meekness. He seems to believe that the aggressive temper which has infected European society and nourished its wars is to be checked and forestalled at the elementary stage of the child's education. Erasmian reform does not take place in the pulpit, in that it does not call for a basic revision of doctrine, but in the classroom, in that it requires the instilling of knowledge and discipline proper to a student at a moment when the person is most malleable. In the *De pueris*, Erasmus, to all intents and purposes, defines his idea of education as one that is diametrically opposed to the tyranny of a pedagogy relying on fear and physical beatings. The principle of accommodation, which Erasmus borrows from his theology, wherein God adapts himself to human understanding and need in the redemption, becomes the guiding norm for the adult's approach to the young. In planning his lessons, the teacher is to think first of the child's temperament and capabilities. Gentleness and love must characterize his method of teaching. In this spirit of charity, the instructor is to recall that children naturally incline to anything that suggests play or fun:

The young take to whatever is joyous and delightful ... Either I am mistaken or the ancients wanted to impress us with the same idea by attributing to the virgin Muses a striking beauty together with the harp and the songs and the dancing choruses and the games played in the surroundings of pleasant fields. As their companions, they added the Graces, for they thought that success in studies depends essentially upon the good feeling shared by master and pupil and from this disposition the ancients gave the name of 'humanitas' to the reading of literature.[101]

Erasmus appears to understand the term 'humanitas' in a double sense: it is something we are born with as well as something that is added to us.[102] What is added comes by way of education as an extension and growth of the creature made by God. This growth, of course, must respect the freedom of the nature. Erasmus remarks how absurd it is for a teacher to make slaves of those whom nature has made free.[103] This insight lies at the heart of his onslaught against a pedagogy that resorts to violence and tyrannical measures in the teaching of the young. Force, we are told, is used on slaves or on brutes, not on the free. 'It is no great charge,' writes Erasmus, 'to drive teams of asses and cattle but to endow the free with a liberating education – "liberos liberaliter instituere," howsoever difficult it be, is a thing of great beauty indeed.'[104] Now if applied force distinguishes a kind of training fit only for beasts, it would appear that the presence of play is one of the chief characteristics that defines an education worthy of free men. To be sure, Erasmus lays it down that not just any play will do but only those kinds which become those who are called to be free: 'Verum eorum qui liberales profitentur disciplinas, oportet et jocos esse liberales.'[105] Here he writes of word-play and pleasantries, but the same mentality obtains in the discussion of all games that accompany the learning process.

According to Huizinga, play is 'First and foremost ... a voluntary activity.' He goes on to stress this point. 'Here, then, we have the first main characteristic of play: that it is free, is in fact freedom.'[106] This insight at once parallels and underscores the relationship between play and the education of the free man in the thought of Erasmus. The notion applies especially to the child who first begins to read. Erasmus knows that the young are not blessed with a great deal of strength, but, at the same time, he is keenly aware of their remarkable resources of energy, particularly when they imagine themselves to be playing.[107] This appears to be the task which the good teacher must set for himself: he must lead the child to think of his study as a kind of game meant to be enjoyed, for the child's youth predisposes him to play.[108] Because the youngster has not the strength to endure laborious undertakings, the mentor must create the ambience within which the pupil can conceive of himself as playing.[109] Now the very subject matter of this study helps the master to create such an atmosphere. The chief source of the child's enjoyment is found in the literature itself. Of this Erasmus is convinced.

> To what does a child more gladly give his attention than to the fables of Aesop which, through laughter and jesting, manage to transmit the serious reflections of philosophy; the same profit is had in the tales told by the poets of antiquity. The child hears that the companions of Ulysses were turned into pigs and into the shapes of other animals by the cunning of Circe. The story draws his laughter, and, at the same time, he learns an axiom of moral philosophy: those who are not directed by sound reasoning but are swept away by the whim of their feelings are not men but beasts. What stoic speaks more seriously? And nevertheless the same teaching is taught by a ridiculous story. The lesson is so evident that I will not delay you with further examples. What is more pleasant than a pastoral poem? What more delightful than a comedy? As it focuses on manners it affects both the ignorant and the young; but what a great deal of wisdom is learned from this playing.[110]

The very literature the child reads partakes of a ludic nature by reason of the playful manner in which it teaches: 'per risum jocumque.'

'Because like rejoices in like,' observes Erasmus, '... the master in a certain manner must become a child again ['repuerescat'] in order to win the youngster's love.'[111] This amounts to one specific application of a more general principle announced in the *Concio de Jesu puero*: 'In the last analysis, Christianity is nothing other than a rebirth ['renascentia'] or becoming a child again ['repuerascentia']'[112] – a genuine and thorough rejuvenation. Christ himself established the child as his model disciple in chapter eighteen of Matthew (1–4), and Erasmus, in commenting on the passage, invokes once more the notion of like attracting like. He says that princes tend to draw to themselves people of a selfishness like their own, whereas Christ takes delight in those who resemble him in his humility and simplicity.[113] The reform that Erasmus envisages is to be wrought in the heart of a child by means of the reform of education. The child is conceived as free and, therefore, worthy of a liberating form of instruction. The role of play is stressed here. Erasmian pedagogy arises out of a theological conviction. We will see in the next chapter that his images representative of the life of grace correspond with his thought concerning education. He holds for the soul's freedom in complying with the attraction of grace; he reverts to the example of the infant child in describing man's active engagement in the divine life; and he shows a fondness for ludic metaphors when trying to join the deity's power with human participation and sharing in that power.

THE GOOD MAN AND THE GOOD LIFE: 'CONVIVIUM RELIGIOSUM'

The 'Convivium religiosum' takes up where the *Antibarbari* leaves off. At the close of the latter work, the personae stroll into dinner; at the opening of the former, the guests are invited to a repast, and most of the conversation takes place during an enjoyable midday meal. In some ways, the 'Convivium religiosum' reads like a continuation of the *Antibarbari*. We encounter in the colloquy the same rural setting and a similar gathering of companionable people, only now the cast of characters is made up entirely of laymen. The monks of the *Antibarbari*, William Hermans and Erasmus, have disappeared. Having cast off his own cowl, Erasmus now locates the paradise of delights, once restricted to the cloister, in the peaceful, rural villa of Eusebius, the pious, moderately wealthy layman. His gardens are reputed to be 'Epicurean'; his estate has a self-sufficiency likened to that of the Fortunate Isles; and his house displays enough religious and moral art to convince a guest that the 'place is hallowed.'[114]

Eusebius' villa has been called 'an earthly fiction of paradise' and the conversation that takes place there an illustration 'of Erasmus' vision of an ideal Christian society.'[115] In this second transmigration of the 'locus beatitudinis' from the monastery to the world at large, Erasmus' imagination and mind have leaned on the arrangements of the religious house for support. As in the *De contemptu mundi*, the quiet fields of the country are preferred to the smoke and the busyness of the city. Eusebius has constructed a wall to enclose his gardens in a manner suggesting the cloister itself. The art works which adorn the house's interior are of either a religious or a moral nature. Although married to a good woman, Eusebius chooses to invite guests to dinner who would lead us to think him a celibate: only men gather around his table. Once seated, the host says grace, a passage from scripture is read, and the entire conversation is dictated by this and other verses from the Bible. It is as if Erasmus in this colloquy were answering the rhetorical questions he once posed in a letter to Paul Volz: 'Why do we so closely confine the professed service of Christ, which he wished to be as wide open as possible? If we are moved by splendid names, what else, I ask you, is a city than a great monastery?'[116] In the 'Convivium religiosum' we behold not a great monastery, but a little one made up only of laymen.

As is to be expected, the passage of the Erasmian utopia from the cloister to the world is partially explained by the colloquy illustrating it. During the long discussion of scriptural passages, Sophronius, one of the guests, glosses a text from Proverbs (21:2): 'Every way of a man is right in his own eyes; but the Lord pondereth the hearts.' The first half of the verse, according to Sophronius, refers to the various callings open for a man to choose in life:

> Some find the priesthood to their liking, some celibacy, some marriage, some retirement, some public affairs, according to their different constitutions and temperaments ... Paul wants everyone to enjoy his own preferences ... No man should judge in questions of this sort but leave judgment to God, who pondereth the hearts.[117]

In his more youthful *De contemptu mundi*, Erasmus identified the happiness available to the Christian on earth with the monastery; here his spirit breaks from the cloistered setting and decrees the good life open to all. To limit this joy to one kind of place is to falsify the teachings of the gospel and to confuse an essentially spiritual message with notions not necessarily adhering to it.

Closely associated with Erasmus' thinking about the freedom man enjoys in electing a way of life is his understanding of the body and of all material things. In this colloquy the body is accepted as subordinated to the soul. Because of this hierarchy, material reality cannot be allowed to dictate to the spirit. The monastic precinct and ceremony can claim no hold on man; on the other hand, the body's subjection is not conceived of in terms of a base thraldom. Eusebius prefers to call his body a partner that is joined to him rather than a tomb which somehow impedes and suffocates his soul.[118] But this physical dignity is maintained only as long as matter remains servant to the spirit. So the corporal rites of the church are fulfilled when they reach out to their spiritual destination. The ceremony perceivable to the senses is joined to the hidden realm that transcends sacramental phenomena. The physical thing perishes; the grace lives on. Uranius calls his body an inn, not a house.[119] Nephalius thinks of his as a tent and is reminded of this by a passage in the Second Letter of Peter: 'I think it meet ... as long as I am in this tabernacle, to stir you up by putting you in remembrance, knowing that shortly I must put off this my tabernacle' (1:13–14). The tent is folded but the spirit moves on. In the 'Convivium religiosum,' body and soul are integrally mated, but the latter must enjoy a primacy in order for man to attain the freedom and dignity to which he is called.

As soul is harmoniously joined to body, spirit to matter, and grace to sacrament, so a tranquil unanimity adheres to the discussion of the eight diners at the table of Eusebius. As a group, they seem to embody the Erasmian ideal of peaceful, amicable enquiry into the nature of the truth. The ease of their conversation stands in marked contrast to the strident polemics of the theologians of the day. None of the personae in this dialogue are doctors of theology, but their meekness of approach to the issues at hand shames those professing expertise in the study of scripture. Here are the people whom Erasmus has in mind when he draws the plans for an education that will produce a man who has learned to master his pride and his aggressive temperament. They listen carefully to the words of the speaker and interpret what he says generously, without any intention of picking a quarrel. The graciousness of their manners blends in nicely with the quietly festive surroundings of Eusebius' villa. Erasmus' dream of peace is reflected in the conversation and amusements of these genteel members of an intellectual aristocracy.

Although the characters of the colloquy, when taken together, realize Erasmus' ideal of intelligent, friendly discourse, as individuals they leave something to be desired; and, indeed, this defect damages the work as dialogue art. The deficiency may arise from the very placidity of their dispositions. Because none of them is given to contention, we encounter no conflict in the

'Convivium religiosum.' Unlike the *Antibarbari*, where all the personae, and Batt especially, have at the antagonist, the champion of ignorance, no enemy is to be ferreted out at this table of saints, nor has Erasmus succeeded in the arduous task of fashioning for us characters whose goodness is joyously alive and who are capable of convincing the reader of their genuineness. Eusebius bores us by reason of the didactic uses to which Erasmus chains him. He must ever be prating about the right way of living and doing things. 'True gaiety,' he sings, 'comes from a clean, sincere conscience,' and he banishes in the same breath all 'silly, bawdy stories.'[120] But if, in our search for mirth, we must choose between Chaucer's Miller and Eusebius, the latter, I fear, will be left without an audience. The fact is that, while Erasmus has painted a festive setting conducive to a gentle comedy of manners, the imperative of his virtuous ideal has flattened the truly joyous potential of the 'Convivium religiosum.' Almost inevitably, the righteousness espoused in the dialogue becomes self-righteousness; furthermore, Eusebius and his guests find a moral or religious significance in every plant or artefact on the property: 'A wonderful variety,' exclaims old Timothy, 'and nothing inactive, nothing that's not doing or saying something.'[121] The garrulous propensity of things on this estate tells us that Erasmus has forgotten one essential in making the world his cloister. We hear nothing of that mystery-filled silence which first strikes the visitor to the walks and the galleries of a monastery.

Erasmus' preoccupation with the insemination of ideas in the 'Convivium religiosum' seems to have caused him to neglect the characterization of the personae in the dialogue. Although such a focus led him to err as an artist, it did enable him to achieve clarity in the representation of his thought. Where the colloquy fails in the embodiment of the perfect man, it does succeed in the theoretical description of him. This ideal arises out of the discussion of a verse from Proverbs: 'The king's heart is in the hand of the Lord, as the rivers of water: he turneth it whithersoever he will' (21:1). Eusebius first explains the text according to both its literal and its moral significance. He examines the heart of the king and the awesome effects of what Proverbs implies as its torrents. The commentator prudently reflects on the need to limit the monarch's power so 'that he may not easily break out into tyranny.'[122] Old Timothy seconds this reading and then requests to be allowed to accommodate the verse 'to a deeper meaning.' In a spirit of acquiescence typical of all at table, Eusebius encourages his guest to proceed, and Timothy begins:

> 'King' can be understood as the perfect man who, with his bodily passions under control, is governed solely by the power of the Holy Spirit. Moreover, to compel such a man to conform to human laws is perhaps inappropriate ... What need is there to prescribe to him who voluntarily does more than human laws require? Or what foolhardiness would it be to bind by human regulations the man who (as is evident by certain signs) is governed by the inspiration of the Holy Spirit?[123]

Such a creature as this, it would appear, is the man Erasmus has in mind in his educational reform. The liberal training in literature aims at this loftiest of all freedoms, that which originates in the Spirit of God and in docility to him. This liberty demands control of the bodily passions and a generosity exceeding the requirements of human legislation. Probably because this same passage displays a reluctance to submit the liberated Christian to human law, the Sorbonne condemned Erasmian freedom as heretical.[124] But the colloquy does not assert in this section or in any other part an irresponsible libertinism. Eulalius later confirms the spirit of commitment that is involved in this liberty when he comments on Pauline freedom. The liberty in question must not be thought of as beyond all restraint but as always being at the service of love. Paul, Eulalius tells us, refrained from eating foods used in sacrifices for the sake of the brethren, even though, in his own mind, he considered himself free to do so.[125] For the most part, the middle section of the dialogue's table talk is taken up with the description of the freedom of the perfect man in an attempt to elucidate this point of culmination in Erasmus' vision of reform. The entire quest can be captured in a single verse out of John's gospel: 'The truth shall make you free' (8:32).

In the 'Convivium religiosum' the discussion of the liberty peculiar to the fully developed Christian is introduced by a very free interpretation of the word 'king' as it appears in a verse out of Proverbs. The liberal education conceived by Erasmus leads to a certain freedom with words just as it allows a certain freedom with things. In both cases, this licence must stem from the Spirit and must be subordinated to the service of love. When, in the colloquy, Timothy tells his friends that 'king' can be taken as the perfect man, he presupposes, as does his creator, that the Old Testament cannot be read in isolation from the New or from its perfect man, Jesus, who alone completes every biblical saying and event antecedent to him. Timothy understands 'king' as the perfect man in the light of this final consummation of all Old Testament truth in Christ. In this view, then, the literal meaning of the Old Testament contains only an impoverished significance that waits to be enriched by the coming of the Word. What is said of these ancient Jewish texts might also be applied to the Erasmian statutes of pedagogy: only the presence of Christ can bring them to fruition. As we read in the title to the *Concio de puero Jesu*, the image of the Christ child presides over the early years of education while the picture of the matured Christ commands the goal and object of this process. In the 'Convivium religiosum,' Eusebius sees Christ as the source of all men's happiness and the beginning and end of all that they do.[126] The fullness of life in him is the happy conclusion to this growth in knowledge and freedom.

PART FOUR

TOWARDS A LUDIC THEOLOGY

SEVEN

The Play of Grace

꿎

At the opening of this entire discussion of the seriocomic, I said that its central argument arose out of a conviction that Erasmus' humorous expression is often liable to contain his most profound thought. His literary genius is such that it needs the freedom of a sportive and open atmosphere to declare itself fully. When we turn to his forcefulness as a theologian, we happen upon a similar phenomenon. I do not refer to his scholarly achievement as the editor of the Greek New Testament, his acknowledged contribution to the theology of his day. Rather I have in mind the stimulating quality of his thought when writing about God and the things of God. Locked in a debate with a professional theologian, Erasmus is held to a traditional form of exposition with its own vocabulary and method of argumentation within which he does not feel completely at home. He admits to Luther at the beginning of his *De libero arbitrio* that he 'always preferred to sport in the wider plains of the Muses rather than to brandish a sword in a hand-to-hand fight.'[1] It is my intention in this and the three remaining chapters to take Erasmus at his word and to follow him into those meadows where he prefers to romp, to catch the theologian at play in the realms of the poetic. I will consider him, not as a speculator at the level of the abstract, but as a poet at the level of the concrete. 'Poetry' is not used here in a precise sense but in its larger meaning as understood by the writers of the Renaissance. Sidney calls poetry 'a representing, counterfeiting or figuring forth – to speak metaphorically, a speaking picture ... to teach and delight.'[2] In these chapters, I will concentrate on the poetic and imaginative aspects of Erasmus' attempts to capture in words the elements at work in man's striving for salvation. Because he conceives of life and redemption in dramatic terms, the image of the 'theatrum mundi' will be a controlling figure in this discussion. It will command our attention in the present chapter and help to shape the concluding chapters that deal with the conflict and the terminus of the drama of the human spirit in its approach to God. But before focusing upon this world-as-theatre metaphor, I would like to underscore a problem, the frequent recurrence of which indicates the importance of trying to formulate a theology of play in Erasmus. At this point, we take up a question that will lead directly into the heart of Erasmian seriocomedy.

At almost every stage of this study, we have encountered some form of the Erasmian dialectical play of thought upon the pleasurable and the afflictive. It is seen in the early works where Erasmus celebrates the restful labour of the monks and writes to Colet about the beatific joy that does not abandon Christ even in his passion.[3] We find it as well in the *Concio de puero Jesu* when the child preacher talks of the great inversion which Christ achieves by making the bitter sweet and the sweet bitter.[4] It arises again in the antagonism and reconciliation between leisure and business in the *Antibarbari*.[5] In the same spirit of mind, Erasmus composes the 'Epicureus' and boasts of the satisfaction of a life given to generosity and sacrifice.[6] The consistency of this outlook is borne out by other works not examined here. Erasmus' ideal prince is urged to find his happiness in the labours of his office just as the 'farmer, the truck gardener, the smith, all get pleasure from their work.'[7] It surfaces frequently in his scriptural commentaries. Meditating on Psalm 22, Erasmus writes of Christ, the Good Shepherd, who leads his flock to shady pastures and to cool waters that make unpleasant things pleasant.[8] This paradoxical turn of mind derives from the Pauline descriptions of Christian existence: 'We live as chastened but not killed, as sorrowful yet always rejoicing, as poor yet enriching many, as having nothing, yet possessing all things' (2 Cor 6:9–10). The coincidence of pleasure and pain has even in Paul assumed the form of a play of mind in which two opposing notions are brought together in almost nonsensical contention. Somehow each side of the paradox (as sorrowful yet always rejoicing) is to be preserved if the statement is to be accepted as intended. Yet not just any kind of interpretation of it will do. For instance, it would be perverse to say that the sorrow itself is enjoyed. It seems more likely that

Erasmus would grasp the Pauline juxtaposition of the painful and the pleasureful in terms of joyously surmounting the sorrow so that, though it remains, it does so in a relatively diminished state due to an expansion of the spirit. But, in the final analysis, the paradox must be accepted through belief because the human intelligence cannot lay hold of its full significance. Erasmus can only explain the phenomenon by recourse to the operation of grace. 'The law of faith,' he writes, 'commands more arduous things than the law of works, yet because grace is plentifully added to it, not only does it make things easy which of themselves are impossible, but it makes them agreeable also.'[9] To the law of works, Erasmus opposes the law of faith with the abundant grace that makes the difficult easy and pleasant. This passage from the *De libero arbitrio* opens the way for the Erasmian play of mind involving Christian paradox and for the more extensive understanding of the whole of life in terms of the ludic.

'THEATRUM MUNDI'

At the beginning of part 2 of the *Moria*, Folly tells us about the gods in heaven sousing themselves in nectar and taking their seats 'at the place where heaven juts out farthest' and how they 'lean forward to watch what mankind is about. Nor could any other spectacle give them more enjoyment. Good lord, what a theater, how manifold the feverish fretting of fools!'[10] There follows a panoramic account of the frenetic business going on below with the human creatures taking very seriously what the gods find as a source for their amusement. Then Folly invites us to enjoy a heavenly vantage point on the moon and to look down, as Menippus once did, and see the innumerable broils of mankind: 'you would think you were looking at a great cloud of flies or gnats quarreling among themselves, warring, plotting, plundering, playing, frisking, being born, declining, dying. It is downright incredible what tumults, what tragedies can be stirred up by such a tiny creature, so frail and short-lived.'[11] The theatre seat in heaven reduces the importance of worldly activity to that of trafficking on an anthill. The seriousness with which the fools take these transactions only adds to the gods' enjoyment. Within this celestial perspective, human enterprise provides the plot for a kind of miniature drama played out in a toy theatre. And as importance vanishes, enjoyment sets in.

We might try to schematize the way in which Erasmus uses cosmic space in depicting his 'theatrum mundi' for us. Let us imagine a playhouse on earth to be a circle contained within a larger one that represents the world. The smaller circle designates the illusion of the stage in contrast to the world circumscribing it as reality. But imagine still a third circle that now holds within it the other two and stands for the heavens occupied by the gods. This added area causes a shift in our perception of reality. Earth now becomes the place of illusion, the stage, and heaven becomes the vantage point from which the play is beheld. The gods enjoy true consciousness, while the players below are lost in something like a dream because they have not the perspective by which they would be able to judge the importance of what they are doing. Purely secular concerns such as banking and trading undergo a deflation in value and take on an amusing aspect especially when engaged in with zealous preoccupation. This heavenly vision imagines mankind's work to be play. It introduces a perspective that opens the possibility for the transforming of labour into amusement by reducing its intensity.

It could be argued that in my reading of the celestial balcony scene too much is being made of a crowd of juvenile, drunken gods and their way of seeing things. The comedy of the passage, however, is most pertinent to its insight. The gods are entertained by the goings-on below because they are distanced from these generally frantic happenings. This is a spatial rendering of a state of soul that can be achieved even while one is on the stage itself. Thomas More, to whom Erasmus dedicated the *Moria*, is described in the prefatory letter as habitually playing 'the role of Democritus by making fun of the ordinary lives of mortals.'[12] In his letter to Ulrich von Hutten, Erasmus defines More's 'festivitas' in terms of his disengaged assessment of the play going on around him.[13] Again he is likened to Democritus. When More himself enters into the drama's action, it is as a player who adapts himself to the characters within the scene. More encourages the play of life when he presses Erasmus to write the *Moria*. The capacity for acting and for enjoyment, two major aspects of the ludic, meet in Erasmus' idealized portrait of his English friend. In fact, More seems to exemplify for Erasmus his own conviction, stated in the *Adagia*, that for the true Christian 'every day is a feast-day.'[14]

Folly's other major passage on the world-as-theatre topos

stresses the fictitious nature of human affairs. The viewing point in this scene is not heaven but earth. We are, as it were, on stage, and Folly asks us to consider the disguises that the players – especially the rich and the powerful – have assumed. She invokes the Silenus of Alcibiades as a working principle for understanding the nature of this illusory world:

> Hence, what appears 'at first blush' (as they say) to be death, will, if you examine it more closely, turn out to be life; conversely, life will turn out to be death; beauty will become ugliness; riches will turn to poverty; notoriety will become fame; learning will be ignorance; strength, weakness; noble birth will be ignoble; joy will become sadness; success, failure; friendship, enmity; what is helpful will seem harmful; in brief, you will find everything suddenly reversed if you open the Silenus.[15]

Folly gives the example of a king whom everyone admits to be rich and powerful. 'But suppose,' she says, 'he possesses none of the goods of the mind; suppose nothing is ever enough for him: then clearly he is the poorest of the poor.'[16] For all that, Folly thinks there is no point in disturbing the play by stripping off the royal disguise and revealing the king's true nature. That would be acting like a foolish man who drops down from heaven onto the stage of life and shouts 'that this figure whom everyone reverences as if he were the lord god is not even a man because he is controlled by his passions like an animal, that he is a servant of the lowest rank because he willingly serves so many filthy masters.'[17] Such misbegotten zeal manifests in Folly's mind a bad sense of time and place. Worst of all, this fool from heaven spoils the show.

In this passage, Folly speaks with her usual lack of care and consistency, but her creator has ironically introduced ideas that he takes seriously and repeats frequently in other of his writings. For the moment, let us fix our attention on the man from heaven. Folly calls his wisdom 'misplaced.' The Latin reads 'praepostera sapientia.'[18] Literally, this is a wisdom that places last things – death and eternity – first. The man from heaven has the far-sighted vision characteristic of the carousing gods and Menippus on the moon, a vision which reduces the importance of worldly affairs under the perspective of the heavenly and the eternal. In contrast to this vision, Folly's scurrying humanoids are the victims of their own myopia. They fail to see beyond the task at hand. This is a characteristic shortcoming of one sort of ever-appearing fool in the *Moria*. He is the king who never reaches to the spiritual meaning beyond his regalia;[19] he is the theologian whose eyes are riveted to his 'formalities, quiddities, ecceities' and a host of other supersubtleties;[20] he is priest and he is layman who both 'keep a sharp lookout to harvest their profits.'[21] This short-sightedness encloses the beholder within a world of illusion by a kind of hypnosis that centres the concentration on what is most immediate. As Erasmus writes in the 'Sileni Alcibiadis,' the mask is preferred to the truth, the shadow to the reality, the counterfeit to the genuine, the fleeting to the substantial, the momentary to the eternal.'[22]

Both passages treating the 'theatrum mundi' theme in the *Moria* tend to deflate the truth and importance of physical reality. The gods laugh at the frenzy aroused over material concerns in the one scene, and matter becomes, by reason of the Silenus imagery, a form of disguise which constitutes the fictive nature of the second. In this last passage, it is the heavenly perspective of the man who drops down from the sky that confirms the false and unreal texture of a world where riches and power motivate the characters playing on its stage. Matter has become the means by which the truth is hidden because it is divorced from and is an impediment to the realm of the spirit. Somehow the two must be reunited, and, even in the comedy of the *Moria*, a hint is given us about the means of restoration. The man who descends from heaven bears an obvious resemblance to Christ. In his commentary on Psalm 22, Erasmus sees the saviour as one who confronts the mighty of this world with the truth about themselves just as the anonymous intruder does in the *Moria*.[23] As Erasmus continues to reflect in his later life upon the theatrical nature of human existence, Christ becomes more and more important to this concept. He is the one who can turn the tragedies of history towards a comic resolution; he is the one who can make matter cohere with the spirit within the context of the 'fabula Christi,' the entire history of mankind conceived as a drama in which God enters the action and becomes, in a disguise that hides his divinity, the central figure of the play.[24] Furthermore, the triviality to which human existence is reduced in the Platonic vision is balanced by the deity's involvement in the stage of history. Somehow this play has a profoundly serious aspect involving the heart's blood of the creator.

As Chantraine has indicated, the 'fabula Christi' is an important image in Erasmian theology.[25] On the one hand, it depends on an allegorical interpretation of scripture by which the personages and events of the Old Testament foreshadow the person of Christ and the birth of his church in the New. It is he who sums up not only the two dispensations but also the entire history of mankind. The 'fabula' must not be taken as a mere figure or literary device; Erasmus uses the term, as the Greeks used their word 'drama,' to signify a unified action, something done, an ongoing movement that makes of this play the very substratum of reality.[26] Erasmus sees the whole of history as a drama with the protasis consisting of Adam's blessed state before the fall, an epitasis centring on the crucifixion, and a catastrophe reached with the resurrection of the just.[27] The act that commands the direction of the plot development concerns the entrance of God into history: the birth, life, death, and resurrection of Christ. Through the incarnation, divinity assumes the disguise of mortality ('Filius assumta carnis infirmitate divinam naturam dissimulans'), and, because of this, matter becomes sacramental and indicative of the life of the spirit. Christ's mortal body both dissembles his divine origin and reveals his divine love in his death on the cross. His humanity functions within the drama like the allegories of scripture: it both hides and makes known his godhead. Lifted up on the cross as a worm and no man, he draws all men to himself.

In the *Moria*, Erasmus bases his comparison between the theatre and human existence upon the deceit and deceptiveness which inevitably intrude into all facets of life on earth. The world is understood as a great court masque in which the players take upon themselves roles that are clearly separate from their real selves. Another but more magnificent kind of deceptiveness occurs on the stage where Christ holds the focal position. The Son of God takes on a real human nature which serves to disguise his divine origins. Man's body now becomes the mask of the god, the persona, the face-piece through which the deity speaks to reveal itself and behind which it conceals its unfathomable substance. Human flesh becomes accommodated to the designs of the Spirit, and the possibility of integration is now restored. So, for those who are called to be united with Christ, their very flesh becomes, as in the case of the master, a disguise of their participation in the divine life. The immortal fire lies hidden behind the all too evident fact of their mortality, but, in contrast to the deceitfulness of the player's role in the *Moria*, this mask is a real one, an essential part of the present human condition. Only faith can teach man that his mortality hides his destiny to live forever.

Just as God becomes man to accommodate himself to human understanding and needs, so man is to become like God who is Christ by accommodating himself to God's word and his grace. Paul describes this change of man into Christlikeness by means of theatrical terms which Erasmus paraphrases: 'Now, since you have been grafted onto Christ through baptism, put on the man himself. Let him whom you have professed shine forth in every life. Portray him whom you have taken into your hearts. He is sobriety, he is chastity, he is peace, he is love. Dress of this kind becomes the light of the gospel.'[28] This verse (Rom 13:14), which Erasmus expands, concludes Paul's development of man's coming to Christ in baptism as a passage from darkness to light. John Colet writes in a similar vein when reflecting upon the ancient rite of baptism in his own adaptation of Dionysius' *Ecclesiastical Hierarchy*:

> If you would be in his wedding garment, you must take order to come to him naked, that you may put it on; and to lay aside your former manner of living, that you may enter on that which is Christ's. This is the meaning and significance of the divesting himself of all garments by him who betakes himself to Christ ... The meaning of his turning to the east, when now quite stripped, and exposing himself to the rays of the risen 'Sun of Righteousness,' is that he, being now purified and single, should receive the single and pure ray, and put on the robe of light and righteousness, which the grace of the Holy Spirit in Christ has woven.[29]

In this explanation of certain ceremonies within an early baptismal liturgy, the person about to be christened plays at something which the rite means to effect. The catechumen is stripped, then immersed in the saving waters of baptism, then clothed 'in the white robe of righteousness' that identifies him with Christ. He is now called to play the role of his saviour, and he is literally dressed for the part.

It should be noted that, in the above passage from Colet, it is 'the grace of the Holy Spirit in Christ' which weaves this new dress; that is, grace, not human power, makes operative the change in life. In other words, the force that makes possible the virtuous activity entailed in the following of Christ originates in God and not in man. This truth tends to confirm another ludic aspect involved with Christian life and belief. In the epilogue to his *De libero arbitrio*, Erasmus offers a parable meant to illustrate how man cooperates with the movement of divine grace. He gives the example of a toddler who falls in the attempt to obtain a hanging apple. So the father must lift the child, maintain his balance, guide his step, and pick the fruit which hangs beyond his tiny reach.[30] Human participation with grace is conceived as a kind of child's play in which man's part by comparison with God's is minimal. Recall what Erasmus says in the *Concio de puero Jesu*, in which a boy delivers a sermon on the child as the new model for Christian living.[31] In the gospel of Matthew (11:16–17), Christ compares his own kerygma to the play of children: 'But to what shall I liken this generation? It is like children sitting in the market place, who call to their companions and say, "We have piped to you and you have not danced; we have sung dirges and you have not mourned."' The verses represent John the Baptist as the chanter of lamentations and Christ as the piper of a more joyous music. The ludic image is particularly apt here. The children are seated in the market-place and are set off from the serious world around them by their play. As the saviour's preaching points towards a kingdom not of this world, it too has to be distinguished from the secular interests surrounding it. Commenting on this passage, Erasmus attributes the audience's failure to respond to Christ's message to their lack of faith and their peevishness.[32] As the Latin puts it, they are 'morosos': captious, fretful, narrow-eyed, a kind we have seen and will see again on the stage of the *Moria*. People of such a constitution, as well as being resistent to the challenge of belief, are unfit for the world of play.

The image which Christ presents in Matthew's gospel of his own preaching manifests itself as a kind of music calling for a reaction; in this case, a playful response of dancing to the tune being piped. But the listeners, because they are 'morosi,' refuse to respond. To put it another way, Christ calls to them, and they refuse to enter into dialogue. They will not perform the roles they

are being asked to play. Their very refusal implies a freedom: they
are not forced to react. Therefore, the assent to dance means that
the listeners freely enter into the play of the music. The context of
this metaphor blissfully ignores the strongly deterministic cosmos that Luther urged against Erasmus. 'Yet the will of God,'
Luther argues, 'is immutable and infallible, and it governs our
mutable will, as Boethius sings: "Remaining fixed, Thou makest
all things move."'[33] Thus Luther banishes the interplay between
the divine and human wills which is a necessary ingredient, if we
are to talk seriously about the possibility of a genuine love
existing between God and man, a free appeal and a free reaction
to that appeal. Grace under this image would be the very music
that enables the listener to dance to its rhythms. At this point, we
reach the inner junction between play and belief. Huizinga
maintains that play 'only becomes possible, thinkable and
understandable when an influx of *mind* breaks down the absolute
determinism of the cosmos. The very existence of play continual-
ly confirms the supra-logical nature of the human situation.'[34]
Huizinga's insight into what he calls the 'supra-logical' nature of
play underscores its affinity with belief in what transcends
human intellection. In both the realm of the ludic and that of
faith, we encounter elements that simply resist submission to
cool reason. Erasmus' willingness to give playful expression to
his own faith springs, I believe, from an unconscious awareness
of this affinity. His metaphor of the world as theatre calls for an
interplay between Christ and the Christian. The saviour who
pipes to his audience is also the God who babbles in a kind of
baby talk so that his infant listeners will understand him.[35] These
images illustrate Erasmus' view of God as one who accommo-
dates himself to human needs. The role of man on this stage is to
adapt himself to his divine calling by putting on Christ.

Any development of the 'theatrum mundi' theme within a
Christian context can scarcely remain uninfluenced by the
church's liturgy. In the writings of Erasmus and Colet, we have
already seen the liturgical connection between assuming the role
of Christ and the rite of baptism. The very notion of human
history presented as a stage centring on Christ derives from the
celebration of the eucharistic liturgy that makes present ritually
the passion, death, and resurrection of Christ as the singularly
saving event of mankind. Two theologians of the twentieth
century have pointed out the ludic nature of the liturgy. Hugo

Rahner recalls to us the Venerable Bede's sensitivity to the playful aspect of the baptismal rite, which, seen from the outside, is merely colourful play-acting.[36] 'Only mother church,' Bede says, 'who is bringing forth new life understands these rites. To the eyes of those looking in without faith, one leaves the font the same as one enters it; everything that happens seems to be no more than a game.'[37] For Romano Guardini, the liturgy partakes of the ludic in so far as it escapes any observable purpose as the church joyfully squanders its time in the worship of a God who cannot be seen.[38] Erasmus is also very much aware of the resemblance between liturgy and theatre, but he urges his contemporaries not to allow the distinction between the two to break down. The music heard in theatres is by no means to win admission into the temple of God. The marches played in a military parade have no place in a church that claims to have present within it the peace-loving Christ.[39]

In formulating his definition of play, Johan Huizinga says that ludic activity must be distinguished from what we normally call 'ordinary' or 'real' life. He then shows that religious ritual contains all of the essential features of his definition. He does not conclude, however, that nothing happens within the rite because it is not 'real': 'The sacred performance is more than an actualization in appearance only, a sham reality; it is also more than a symbolical actualization – it is a mystical one.'[40] By this last term Huizinga seems to mean that the ' "representation" is really *identification*, the mystic repetition or *re-presentation* of the event. The rite produces the effect which is then not so much *shown figuratively* as *actually reproduced* in the action.'[41] Furthermore, the ritual act would appear to be mystical in the sense that it 'transports the participants to another world.'[42] In the same fashion, the modern theologian Alexander Schmemann writes of the faithful who have gathered together for the celebration of the eucharist: 'we have entered the Eschaton, and are now standing beyond time and space; it is because all this has first happened to us that something will happen to the bread and wine.'[43]

In chapter 1, a notion from the *Querela pacis* was mentioned in which the eucharistic cup was used as the foundation for Erasmus' hard, logical argument against bellicose Christians. Here I would like to take a closer look at the entire passage not so much with Erasmian pacifism in mind but rather with an eye on his settled conviction about the value of ceremony and the part it should play in his readers' lives. In this section of the declamation, Erasmus turns to the sacrifice of the Mass and stresses the point that its ritual amounts to something far more than idle spectacle:

> Shall not that heavenly bread and mystical cup join Christian men in friendship which Christ himself made sacred and which they renew daily and make present again in their offerings? If Christ accomplished nothing there, then why all of these ceremonies? If he delivered to us something of importance, why is it neglected by you as if he played out something ludicrous and theatrical? Does anyone dare approach this sacred table, the symbol of friendship, the banquet of peace, who is determined to wage war against Christians and prepares to destroy those men for whom Christ died to save and to draw their blood for whom Christ shed his?[44]

In the above passage, Erasmus, while aware of the ludic element in the liturgy, exhorts his readers not to reduce the sacred rites of the Mass to mere theatre. As in Huizinga's understanding of ritual, Erasmus insists that the eucharist is 'more than a symbolical actualization.' Something really happens within the rite because Christ is made present on the altar, and that presence is conceived as an active one in which Jesus stirs the soul through his grace. Because something happens within the rite, Erasmus expects something to happen within the participants. The action whereby the person of Christ is rendered present within the mystery aims, in turn, at affecting the world beyond the place of sacrifice in the sense that the change of bread and wine into the body and blood of Christ looks to another change in those receiving the sacrament. In the mystery of the eucharist, the food taken is for the nourishment of the spirit, and, according to the traditional teaching, spiritual nutriment does not act as normal food. In the consumption of ordinary diet, that which is eaten is changed into the substance of the consumer. In the case of spiritual food, the one who eats is changed into the image of what he takes. 'Whereas corporeal food and drink,' Erasmus writes, 'is turned into the substance of the eater and drinker, in this case [that of the eucharist] those who eat and drink are transformed into that which they have taken.'[45] Beyond the liturgy, then, the transforming action, begun with the change of the sacramental species, continues within the souls of the faithful in their gradual assumption of a likeness unto Christ. This metamorphosis, this putting on of Christ, is essential to the internal action of the 'fabula Christi,' and this likeness to the saviour leads inevitably to a confrontation, the external agon of the Erasmian drama which will be examined in the next chapter.

It is clear from the passages cited above that Erasmus lays great stress upon the inner operation of the eucharist, yet one notices in the quotation from the *Querela pacis* a tone of frustration bordering on despair that the sacrament seems to have so little effect, that man can partake of the body and blood of Christ and then fall to slaughtering his fellow Christians. For this reason, Erasmus assails that torpor of soul which holds the worshipper's attention at the sensory level when surrounded by ritual and prevents the mind from rising to the spiritual realm to which the symbolism of the liturgy invites its participants. In the *Enchiridion*, Erasmus urges his reader to the proper use of the visible elements in Catholic worship by understanding them as a means of ascending to a higher level. His general rule applies especially to sacramental devotion: 'we should always keep at hand, never to come to a standstill anywhere in temporary gratifications, but by the process of analogies ascend from that stage step by step ... to the love of the spiritual.'[46] This law of ascent constitutes the fifth rule of the *Enchiridion* and exhorts the reader 'to mount – as if by certain steps of Jacob's ladder – from body to spirit, from the visible world to the invisible, from the letter to the essence, from the sensible to the intelligible, from multiplicity to oneness.'[47] This is the movement beyond space and time of which Schmemann writes above, the entering into the Eschaton which Huizinga recognizes as a confirmation of the ludic nature of ritual. Again John Colet reflects the spirit and mind of Erasmus in his description of the rite of the eucharist. For Colet, the minister who presides over the liturgy plays the role of Christ, and the incense which he describes as moving down from the altar through the congregation and back to the sanctuary is seen as the flow of God's grace from heaven to earth and back again.[48] Grace descends in the incarnation and rises with the risen Christ and in the rising of all good souls. Erasmus will give this movement his most lyrical and play-filled expression when he writes of Christ who leaps beyond the hills towards heaven to the music of love. It is to a study of this heavenly music that we must now turn.

For more than two years, Erasmus dwelt as a young scholar at s'Hertogenbosch, the home of another eminent Dutchman, Hieronymus Bosch. The similarity of their religious conceptions of the world about them becomes more striking than any temporal or spatial coincidence in their lives when we reflect upon the artist's triptych known as the *Haywain*. Because the painting embodies the 'theatrum mundi' theme, it will serve as a conclusion to the treatment of this subject. The triptych, furthermore, is concerned with heavenly music, the topic which will occupy us for the remainder of this chapter. As such, the painting will also provide a junction between the theatre of the world and the music played upon this stage.

The left panel of Bosch's painting represents the Garden of Eden and the banishment of Adam and Eve; the right panel shows us a scene of apocalyptic retribution enacted in Hell. The borders of the masterwork suggest the entire stretch of human history, or, as David L. Jeffrey states in his illuminating essay on the triptych, it 'provides a sweeping insight into all three time zones of our *historia salvationis*.'[49] While the extreme panels depict time past and time future, the larger central piece focuses on the present in the form of what Jeffrey sees as a Corpus Christi procession that is led by a wagon or pageant on which is played out a drama conceived as an agon between heavenly and earthly music. A couple, in plain sight, give their attention to a page of music, a song meant to symbolize an inner harmony by which the soul is loved more than the body. A relaxed and peaceful attitude can be discerned on the faces of these two. Another couple appears to be engaged in a different kind of music. Like their counterparts, these two have a tutor, but he does not expose himself to the light – he hides in a bush. Jeffrey reads the scene as a 'conflict between ... two loves ['caritas' and 'cupiditas'] which rages on the little "stage" atop the hay.' This leads him to conclude that the *Haywain* depicts the 'greatest drama of all, all the world is indeed the stage, all its people players.'[50] In both Bosch and Erasmus we see the tendency to look at human existence from a dramatic viewpoint and an inclination to describe that drama's conflict as taking place within man; furthermore, both of these Dutch geniuses resort to musical imagery in their description of man's interior life. This latter characteristic resurfaces in the writing of a modern theologian who, in the conclusion to his essay on grace, makes use of a ludic metaphor when he cites lines from Wallace Stevens' 'The Man with the Blue Guitar':

> ... But play you must
> A tune beyond us yet ourselves ...

'The blue guitar,' writes Cornelius Ernst, 'becomes here the instrument of poetic transfiguration' rousing us 'from our dream of reality' and waking us 'to the reality in the dream.'[51]

CELESTIAL MUSIC: THE BACKGROUND

When Erasmus turned to writing his commentary on Psalm 38, the poem's title caught his attention and inspired him to write a treatise on mystical music that extends over fourteen columns in the Leiden edition of his *Opera omnia*. The title reads in the Latin: 'In finem pro Idythun ipsi David.' 'Finem' he understands not as a conclusion but rather as a consummation which indicates fulfilment.[52] And so Erasmus interprets the David here to be not just the original composer of these verses but, more important, the Christ who is the full realization of the Old Law. Following Jerome or Augustine, he takes Idythun to mean 'transiliens' (springing over or leaping across).[53] We have, then, in the title to Psalm 38, the elements that will serve as the basis for a discourse on heavenly music: the Christ of whom the harp-playing David sings and whose own song is accompanied by a rising movement indicated in the word 'transiliens.' In other words, the music coincides with a leap to its rhythms, a sublime ascent towards the things of heaven. In our discussion of Erasmus' commentary on Psalm 83, a passing reference was made to the music of the spirit in the Song of Degrees which also implies a rising motion.[54] It would appear that Erasmus' more extensive development of the idea of ascent in Psalm 38 was suggested by Augustine's sermon on the same song. The theme of a sublime form of inner rhythm and melody is shared by a number of fathers and theologians, and the subject was traced in the first chapter. We return to the tradition here and will focus upon those authors to whom Erasmus either directly or indirectly refers in his exposition of Psalm 38.

In his description of the power of instrumental music to calm the agitated mind, Erasmus recalls the passage from 1 Samuel (16:14–23) where David eases the tormented spirit of Saul by his skilful playing on the harp.[55] Erasmus imagines Christ's own resurrection to take place as an awakening to a song sung by the Father:

> That harp went silent for a short time with the body of Christ hidden in the tomb. But the Father did not endure a prolonged silence for so delightful a harp. He arouses the sleeping one, crying out in mystical song: 'Rise up, my glorious one; awaken harp and lyre.' To whom the harp quickly replies: 'I will arise at daybreak.'[56]

This musical setting for the resurrection finds scriptural support in 1 Corinthians (15:52), where the dead arise on the last day to the sound of a trumpet. In Joel (2:15), the trumpet is used to summon the community, but, in Matthew (24:31), it calls forth the elect of God from death. It is scripture too which associates the playing of music with prophecy. In 1 Chronicles (25:3), a musician named Idythun (Jeduthun) is said to prophesy 'with a harp to give thanks and to praise the Lord.' The Bible also commends an inner, spiritual song in Colossians (3:16). Commenting on this verse, Erasmus claims that it is this internal music of love echoing in the heart, and this alone, in which God takes special delight.[57]

As well as being aware of the scriptural sources for the affirmation of music's place in both religious worship and the spiritual combat, Erasmus knew of the high regard which song enjoyed in the philosophy of the Greeks. In the commentary on Psalm 38, he calls attention to the Platonic teaching that the World Soul was created according to musical measures. Because of this melodic pattern, the individual soul takes pleasure in the harmony of well-modulated song, and, for the same reason, it is offended by discordant sound.[58] Pythagoras is believed to have been taken by the notion that a wonderful kind of musical harmony exists among the stars seen in the night sky. He and his followers revolted at the notion that such huge bodies are moved at so great a speed in silence, so they postulated a heavenly music that sets the planets in motion and keeps time with the harmonious will of him who created and governs the great spheres of the heavens.[59] When treating the power of music,

Erasmus moves from Greek philosophy to the Greek myth of Orpheus. The Orphic legend reflects an almost holy regard for music and the changes which it can effect.[60]

Another avowed source of Erasmus' discourse on heavenly music is Boethius, whose classifications are mentioned when the harmony existing both inside and outside of man is brought up. Erasmus refers to what Boethius had called 'musica humana,' 'that blending of elements and properties in the human body, the joining together of body and soul, as well as the rhythmical measure of the soul's powers as related to one another.'[61] Because music, in the mind of Boethius, is 'the unifying of many things and the concord of separated things,' the unity within man constitutes a musical harmony.[62] Erasmus is also aware of two other kinds of music as Boethius distinguishes them. 'Musica instrumentalis' is that which is normally played on string or wind instruments, and we have already seen the 'musica mundana' or the music of the spheres, of the happily blended elements, and the course of the earth's seasons.[63] None of the above types, however, satisfies Erasmus in defining the kind of music he writes about in the introduction to his commentary on Psalm 38. 'Musica humana,' although it mirrors the harmony of its source, God himself, is, at its best, conformed to human reason. Man's mind will frequently be out of time with the rhythms of grace associated with the promptings of the Holy Spirit.[64] Erasmus, therefore, out of deference to that Spirit, calls this music spiritual: 'Sed nostra musica spiritualis est.'[65] Furthermore, it is spiritual because it is sung to God, who is a spirit, and through it the whole of man achieves a harmonious conformity to the divine will.

So Erasmus writes about the music of the spirit, a melody of divine origin which escapes the categories laid down by Boethius. Because the music is so deeply involved with man's inner life of grace, it would appear that Augustine, rather than Boethius, will provide the context for understanding Erasmus' treatment of heavenly song. It should be reiterated that Augustine wrote a sermon on Psalm 38, and we know that Erasmus was familiar with it. At one point in his own commentary on the same psalm, he quotes rather freely from that sermon.[66] A crucial difference in the readings of Erasmus and Augustine lies in the former's extensive development of Christ as the new David, the divine minstrel who transcends earthly realities in an ascent to the things that exist beyond this world, but, on one important point,

Augustine provides the insight that leads Erasmus into his own peculiar development of the theme of divine music. Augustine, in explaining the term 'Idythun,' yokes the notion of leaping beyond to the motif of spiritual music.[67] It will prove helpful to probe Augustine's conception of this song of ascent because we find in him an earlier theology of music similar to what we read in Erasmus.

Because Augustine's treatment of heavenly music focuses upon the transformation which this divine rhythm brings about, something must be said about his imaginative representation of this change. Augustine thinks of grace as the moving presence of the Holy Spirit. This motion can be understood as resulting in man's conversion to God, but it is more strikingly represented under the metaphor of heavenly ascent. To describe this rising action, Augustine, in his *Confessions*, calls forth a moral cosmos and invents for it a kind of spiritual law resembling some of the observations of modern physics, only here we find greater attention paid to levity than to gravity. Imaginatively, Augustine presents God's redemptive influence upon the soul under the figures of place and motion. More literally, he is speaking about the spirit's finality and inner rest: 'In Thy Gift we find our repose; there do we enjoy Thee. Our repose – that is our "place."'[68] Location is conceived as the terminus of the will's desire. Augustine introduces the notion of weight into this passage, but by it he does not mean necessarily 'an inclination toward the lowest level' but rather the impetus directed towards one's proper place.[69] This law of the spiritual cosmos includes a benign form of levity in opposition to the tug of gravity or the weight of concupiscence which pulls down into the steep abyss. It is the love ignited by the Holy Spirit that 'inclines upward,' a sublime levity that overcomes the drag of fleshly desire and allows the soul to be set on fire, a fire that moves upward 'to the "peace of Jerusalem."'[70]

Now the soul's ascent to Jerusalem is powered by grace or the attraction by which the beloved finds her delight in her divine lover. Figuratively, grace induces love's impetus, a goad freighted for ascent: 'pondus meum amor meus.'[71] Like Erasmus, Augustine understands the ascent to consist of a spiritualizing process that answers to Christ's love in the incarnation: 'He descended ... that we might ascend.'[72] This ascent dictates an exchange of natures whereby man assumes the life of the Spirit out of love for him who assumed man's flesh. Such a transformation results in the subjection of concupiscence to a divinely instilled charity.[73] As in Erasmus, this transformation means that the pleasures of the flesh are exchanged for the joys flowing from the presence of God in the soul: 'For this joy is within, where the voice of praise sings, and is heard; with this voice He is praised who is to be freely loved "with the whole heart, the whole soul, the whole mind," and who kindles His lover with love for Himself by the grace of the Holy Spirit. What else is the new canticle but the love of God?'[74] Of a sinner, grace creates a lover, and that weight which is identified with love may also be understood as the soul's joy: 'For delight is a kind of weight in the soul. Therefore, delight orders the soul.'[75]

In the preceding paragraph, we touched upon one passage from Augustine where the soul's fulfilment is described as a joyous song of praise. In addition, an important element of his doctrine of spiritual ascent is summed up in a quotation from the *De musica*. It would not be inappropriate here to ask ourselves what such an insight is doing in a treatise on rhythm. Augustine in book 6 of the *De musica* discusses the reform or reordering of the soul in rhythmical terms because this is how he conceives the action of the Spirit within man. To begin with, he believes that God, in creating the world, did so on numerical principles, and, in proof of this, he cites the Book of Wisdom (11:20): 'Thou hast ordered all things in number and measure and weight.'[76] For one student of Augustine this number is described as 'the symmetrical arrangement of architectural elements, the rhythmic movements of the dance, the measures and harmonies of musical sounds.'[77] For another scholar, 'numerus' or rhythm is essential to the structure of both the individual and the cosmos. It is, as it were, the very music of being without which no created thing would be beautiful.[78] Emmanuel Chapman traces this quality of 'numerus' in creation back to the harmony of the divine and eternal number existing in the deity. For Chapman, measure and number result from successive repetitions of unity, the striving of things to obtain oneness.[79] Repetition implies likeness, and this similarity in things can exist because of a self-subsistent likeness in the godhead: 'The super-eminent immutable and eternal likeness is the Second Person of the Blessed Trinity.'[80] Ultimately, the rhythms of the universe derive from an origin within the harmonious being of God.

In a rhapsodic passage from his *De libero arbitrio*, Augustine sings his paean to number:

Seek, then, what moves the members of the artisan himself; it will be number ... And if you withdraw work from the hands, and from the soul the intention of making, and that movement of the member be referred to pleasure, it will be called dancing. Seek, therefore, what gives pleasure in dancing: number will make answer to you: behold it is I.[81]

Augustine urges the reader to transcend the lure of merely sensuous number in order to seek out the source of this beauty. This search calls for nothing less than the transformation of the soul, its re-creation in Christ; and, just as God lies at the initiation of the first creation, so he must set in motion this second one: 'Qui fecit, ipsi reficiat; et qui creauit, ipse recreet.'[82] The God, then, who creates the world according to musical measure will restore order to the soul in the same fashion; hence, in the *De musica*, Augustine treats this return of order to the human spirit as the inducement of a delight in higher things. From the enjoyment of ephemeral beauty, the soul is led by God to a love of eternal number which, in turn, makes possible this new order to be established within man.[83] By a creative act of the Holy Spirit, traditionally understood as uncreated grace, the soul is fired with a love of eternal beauty and attuned to a heavenly music, the attraction of God himself.

When we turn from God's agency in this change of soul to the type of activity it inspires man to perform, we find again a theology that lends itself to ludic expression. In fact, one of Augustine's sermons brings together the two central images which have provided the bases for the discussion of this chapter: 'theatrum mundi' and the music of transformation. In 'Sermo 9' (*Sermones de vetere testamento*), Augustine discourses on the ten-stringed lyre, which, in a sense, has replaced the ten commandments of the Old Law because the New Law originates in the music of love. To illustrate this point, Augustine refers to the games of Roman society in which the gladiator excelled with his sword and the minstrel with his harp. But, in the games ordained by God in his world theatre, the gladiator and the minstrel are one and the same.[84] The striking of one note on love's harp slays a herd of vicious beasts.[85] The image captures the very essence of Christian seriocomedy as the struggle for virtue is conceived in musical terms. In the Old Testament, this ten-stringed instrument was carried as a law and a burden. In the New Testament, the harp is played in so far as the weight of the old commandment has been made light by love.[86] Augustine combines the ideas of play and work here. At times the law becomes a burden even for the Christian, and then the instrument can only be carried; but God's law is fully comprehended when it is loved, and then this inner affection is discussed as the music of the heart.

Carl Johann Perl has written of Augustine's fascination with the Alleluia or the Jubilation, a musical sequence in the liturgy of the Mass. Augustine frequently refers to it in his commentaries on the Psalms. Perl cites a passage from the exposition of Psalm 32 which highlights an interesting facet in the musical theory of a man who laboured so mightily to be clear and enlightening in his teaching. The power of the writing calls for extensive quotation.

'Rejoice in the Lord, O ye righteous, for praise is comely to the upright. Praise the Lord with kithara, sing unto Him with the psaltery of ten strings. Sing unto Him a new song.' Put off oldness: ye know the new song. A new man, a New Testament, a new song. A new song belongeth not to men that are old: none learn that but new men, renewed through Grace from oldness, and belonging now to the New Testament, which is the kingdom of Heaven. For that sigheth all our love, and singeth a new song. A new song let us sing, not with the tongue, but with the life. 'Sing unto Him a New song: sing skilfully unto Him.' Every man asketh how he should sing unto God. Sing unto Him, but sing not unskilfully. He would not that His Ears be offended ... Sing 'with jubilation' ... What is it to sing with jubilation? To be unable to understand, to express in words, what is sung in the heart ... And whom beseemeth that jubilation, but the Ineffable God? For He is Ineffable, Whom thou canst not speak; and if thou canst not speak Him, and oughtest not to keep Him silent, what remaineth to thee but jubilation; that the heart may rejoice without words, and the boundless extent of joy may have no limits of syllables? 'Sing skilfully unto Him with jubilation.'[87]

In this passage, the dogmatic Augustine owns to a belief in an ineffable God whose infinitude we cannot express. Here again we encounter the supra-logical area mentioned earlier in this chapter, that sublime darkness or cloud in which man can only rejoice, that profound reality the mystery of which we cannot sound but only sing.

THE DIVINE MINSTREL

Erasmus takes as his opening for a discussion of music the original singer of psalms, the prophet David, who prefigures the object of all prophecy and the singer of the perfect song, Jesus Christ. Just as the literal history of Israel takes on a spiritual meaning in the light of Christ's life and death, so the audible song of the prophet finds its fullest realization in the spiritual music that is Christ's. Erasmus recounts the life of the saviour within a musical allegory. He is the minstrel who plays a song of love using his own body as his harp, a body fashioned most delicately by the Holy Spirit within the womb of the chaste virgin.[88] Christ's entire life on earth is conceived as a song of praise played to his Father on the harp that is his body.[89] This body, because it is an instrument of power to cure the sick, to clean lepers, to liberate the possessed from their demons, reflects the presence of the deity in his divine song.[90] And all this serves as but a prelude to one moment of arresting lyrical beauty.

> Never did this harp play so melodiously as when the supreme artist, in his extremity, with limbs stretched out on the cross, struck those final notes so gracious to his Father's ears and so salutary for us ... What more admirable than that voice beseeching the Father for those who were the authors of his execution and who attacked him with more weighty charges as he hung in the throes of death? 'Father,' he said, 'forgive them, for they know not what they do.' Surely, this was the voice of perfect charity; nor was it ineffective. The minstrel was heard for the reverence due him. Hardly can the cord of love be further extended; most powerfully the taut string of courage brought forth that parting sound when the excellent harpist with a mighty cry entrusted his spirit into his Father's hands and soon after died – willingly he laid down his life. The sound of this

instrument so prevailed that at his cry the veil of the Temple was rent from top to bottom, the earth quaked, rocks split, monuments blew open, many were shaken from death, bystanders were terrified, the centurion was converted, and the sun was covered in darkness. What like unto this has human music ever produced?[91]

As music enjoys a sway over human passions so strong that it can allay man's anger, so this dying note of the Son affected the love of the Father when his wrath towards mankind was transformed into mercy, and from this change flows the grace that inaugurates the conversion of man from his sins.

The music that fades with Christ's last breath awakens again with his resurrection and lives on now by means of the faithful ministers who come after him and through the words of scripture whose verses prolong the melody of love. The song is heard from the lips of preachers who proclaim Christ's heavenly message out of love for God and not for their own comfort and profit.[92] The good harpist must rise above his own desires and passions lest inner unruliness bring dissonance to the song he would play.[93] The music of Christ's love in the scripture is capable of transforming the reader into the very image of the Lord. The word of God, like the sacrament of the eucharist, contains within itself the power to change man into the likeness of Christ, provided it be read in the light of the Spirit who has inspired it. The music of Christ's word raises the feeble spirit of man, frees him from his servitude to vice, awakens him to the love of his saviour.[94] The object of the study of scripture, Erasmus tells the aspiring theologian, is to be 'converted, seized, inspired and transformed into those things you are learning.'[95]

Because music requires harmony, this spiritual music whose organ is the heart of man calls for an interior concord that leads outward towards a peaceful union of all in Christ. This inner song relates also to the audible music played and sung in the churches. Erasmus took sharp issue with the practice of playing military music during ecclesiastical services because he believed such works aroused the aggressive instinct in the house of prayer and love.[96] The audible music must accord with the inner music of the heart and must quiet and not stir up violent emotion. The melody sung in the church should reflect the melody of grace that causes love to rise in the hearts thereby joining the faithful together in unity.[97] In this divine motion by which the heart of man is rendered peaceable, we touch the cornerstone, the *sine qua non*, of all the thought and activity directed towards the Erasmian utopia of a Christendom united by its faith. The heart is the instrument on which the Spirit of God plays and turns this organ of flesh into a thing of spiritual refinement. The strings of this harp are the human affections of hope, fear, joy, and sorrow. If these are tuned to conform to worldly ends, then the song will be off pitch, out of tune. If, on the other hand, they are strung out of a compassionate regard for God, out of a fear of offending him and a joy in pleasing him, then the music of the heart will be harmonious.[98] This inner condition in which the passions are subjected to the divine will contributes to the concert of praise sung by all members of the church together.

Because Erasmus conceives of the metamorphosis of the carnal man into the spiritual man as a result of the music played in the heart by the Spirit of God, the mystical song can be understood as an attempt to explain the action of grace. Music, by reason of its power to change man, functions within Erasmus' commentary on Psalm 38 much as rhythm operates in Augustine's *De musica*. In both works, we read of an internal flow or movement originating not in man, the recipient, but in God. Erasmus, although he does not outright identify this spiritual music as grace, indicates, even in a formal treatise on the subject, an inclination to grasp this mysterious reality under the figurative veil of an inward rhythmical current. In the introduction to the commentary on Psalm 38, I have counted five places where Erasmus uses the word 'pulsare' (to beat) and its cognates within a musical context: 'pulsantes citharam,' 'fides pulsare,' 'per organa flatu ... et pulsu constat,' 'musicam ... pulsatilem,' 'pulsantes ... chordam.'[99] Now, when we turn to the *Hyperaspistes*, a theological tract written in answer to Luther's *De servo arbitrio*, Erasmus frequently uses the same word to describe the action of grace: 'gratia pulsans,' 'pulsanti gratiae,' 'auxiliante gratia pulsante.'[100] 'Pulsare' can mean an ongoing rhythmical beat or a single act of striking; but, in the light of the author's image of Christ as the divine minstrel and his depiction of the Holy Spirit reviving the heart of man through a heavenly music, it would appear that the preferred reading of 'pulsare,' when coupled with 'gratia,' in most cases favours a rhythmical image. Furthermore, in the commentary on Psalm 38, Erasmus draws a finer distinction with regard to the music played by the Spirit within the heart. When the motion influences the heart's petition in prayer to conform to God's commands, it is called a woodwind music, 'flatilem musicam,' referring to the breath lifting the prayer to heaven.[101] When the motion directs the soul's action to conform to God's will, it is called a string, or strumming, music, 'pulsatilem [musicam].'[102] Erasmus succinctly capsulizes the thought of this passage: 'verbum resonat, opus pulsat,' 'the word resonates, the deed throbs, pulses.'[103] The inner music of grace moves and coincides with the inclination of the will to pray and to act in a kind of spiritual dance. The Spirit sounds and the heart re-sounds in harmony. The divine rhythm informs and shapes the work to be accomplished. 'Opus pulsat.' The deed is transformed as a dance between partners; the work thus undergoes a metamorphosis and assumes a playful aspect. This divinely inspired rhythm is that 'musica spiritualis' which makes it possible for the whole man to conform himself to the will of God.[104] So grace, as mentioned at the start of this chapter, changes the arduous into what is pleasant. It gives rise to a great hope that so refreshes in the act of re-creating that 'those things which seem bitter to the lovers of the world become sweet.'[105]

Portrayed under a musical allegory, Christ's redemptive action answers to Erasmus' belief in a primacy of grace that does not cancel human engagement in the process of conversion. The soul is, as it were, lifeless, an alien to the realm of the supernatural before the minstrel's music sounds. With the striking of the harp, the soul moves, or rather leaps, in ballet fashion. Because he is the player of mystical, soul-transforming music, Christ is also the great leaper in a dance that transcends the tyranny of matter and selfish desire. His spouse, the church, beholds him dancing across the highlands and addresses him in the words of the Beloved: 'The voice of my dear one! Behold he comes, leaping upon the mountains, bounding over the hills' (Cant 2:8).[106] Christ pitches his tent in the region of the sun and, then, enticed by a love for mankind, descends into the womb of the Virgin.[107] Having lived and died and risen from death, he leads mankind in a return to the Father he has never left.[108] The stages in the story of redemption that recount Christ's descent to earth and to hell and his ascent back to heaven are described in the Bible, according to Erasmus, as a race or a leap. We have already mentioned that Plato recognizes the earliest manifestation of the play impulse in the infant's urge to jump: 'They leap and bound, they dance and frolic.'[109] The psychiatrist Erik H. Erikson finds in this instinct to leap the briefest and best formulation of play that he knows.[110] This, too, is the play of grace: the music that so absorbs the spirit and fills it with song that it becomes a new creature transcending secular interest in a great leap of love. This, too, is the cosmic dance of Christ with his spouse. Because the music affects the change from the carnal to the spiritual and the leap to this music represents a rising from what is earthly to what is heavenly, the two images stand for one and the same reality. Both aim at a ludic expression of the act of total conversion; both the primacy of grace and the soul's active engagement are preserved in these images. Without the music, there is no leap, no dance. But the soul's involvement, however genuine, is not just work. In acceptance of God's gracious gift freely bestowed, man freely acquiesces and turns to the rhythms of the divine impulse, entering as he does into love's responsive motion, the play of Wisdom when the mountains came to be (Prov 8:30).

EIGHT

The *Moria* and Its Agon

⚜

Because the *Moria* is written as a declamatory speech, it has attracted many of its readers to attend to its rhetorical patterns and devices. The work of Walter Kaiser and Jacques Chomarat has proven especially instructive because of the importance they have made of Erasmus' rhetorical structure.[1] The text of the *Moria*, however, represents not just an isolated speech but one that is delivered before a live audience whom Folly considers to be her fellows in the celebration of the ridiculous and the absurd. We are to imagine a scene in which Folly steps to the rostrum or the pulpit so quickly and unexpectedly that her audience breaks out laughing. Some argue that she wears, in addition to her fool's motley, an academic gown. For their evidence, these critics point to Folly's avowal that she is wearing an 'unusual' costume.[2] Be that as it may, we find at the start of the *Moria* a *mise en scène* complete with stage, audience, and a persona who is dressed for her role. There are, in a sense, two stages: Folly's rostrum separating her from her listeners and the hall including the entire festive assembly upon which the reading audience silently eavesdrops.

The *Moria*'s setting and theatrical opening do not in themselves justify a dramatically oriented reading of the work, but they do invite further investigation into the possibilities of such an approach. Folly's speech, when divided into its three topological parts, reveals a plot movement, a gradual ascent to the higher reaches of foolishness.[3] At the start, Folly seems to mingle indiscriminately with her followers. At the beginning of the second part, she invites her audience to be seated on the moon and to look down on the stage of fools from above. By the end of her talk, she has led us to behold transcendent folly in the ecstasy of the sanctified and blissful souls in heaven. In addition to this plot line, there is in the speech a more dramatic element: an agon or conflict which is first announced humorously and diffusively in the opposition of words and ideas but which gradually polarizes and develops into a tension involving a serious vein in the work that lies just beneath its surface.

The conflict in the *Moria* is first noticed in its line of thought. The text abounds with contradictory statements, non sequiturs, and paradoxes. These aberrations and conundrums all issue from the head of the bemused lady entertaining her listeners. She is not unlike the person whom Roland Barthes asks us to conjure up at the beginning of *Le plaisir du texte*. He wants us to imagine a droll individual who no longer fears the charges directed at his or her self-contradiction and bad logic.[4] Folly herself fits this description and, perhaps, betters it because of the zestful pleasure she takes in her nonsense. This is particularly true in the opening pages of the work, for, as Folly advances deeper into her talk, we notice occasional fits of bad temper that flash out against her enemies, especially the Stoics and the furiously insane. By the middle sections, Folly begins – most nonsensically – to manifest her most heated rage against her own fools. The ideational conflict here becomes dramatic in the sense that it is now being absorbed by a character who is designed to mirror in a whimsical, haphazard manner the main issue of the stage of the world which her speech describes. In the latter part of the previous chapter, the internal action of the Erasmian 'fabula Christi,' the transformation of the soul through grace, occupied the centre of interest; now, the concern will be to find what the *Moria* says about the external confrontation that exists on this stage. We anticipated some part of this discussion in the last chapter's comments upon the friction between the imprudent man of heaven and the other players in this 'theatrum mundi.' This encounter, occurring slightly more than halfway through the opening part of the speech, adumbrates later passages of contention that work to clarify the major issue of the *Moria*.

It may appear too sanguine to hope to make clear the main contention of a work so addmittedly equivocal as the *Moria*. Rosalie L. Colie, in her study of Renaissance paradox, finds in the constantly shifting ground of the text reason for concluding that 'Erasmus, or Folly, has left his (or her) discourse open-ended, stretching into infinity.' She believes that Folly has abandoned the reader 'to make his own decisions about value.'[5] I think it is true enough to say that Folly abandons us, but could we say the same about Erasmus? Doubtless, the work is open-ended, but does Erasmus walk away indifferently, or has he taken pains to offer us a choice? In the prefatory letter to Thomas More, Erasmus addresses his friend as the one who qualifies best as a reader of the *Moria*. More is quick to appreciate a joke and slow to take offence at a playful approach to literary exercise. He would seem to understand precisely what Erasmus means when he says that 'just as nothing is more trivial than to treat serious matters in a trivial way, so too nothing is more delightful than to treat trifles in such a way that you do not seem to be trifling at all.'[6] Erasmus hints at making his *Moria* something more than an idle *jeu d'esprit* or an inane bit of fun. Later, when driven to defend the book against its critics, he tells Martin Dorp that the *Moria* 'is concerned in a playful spirit with the same subject as the *Enchiridion*.'[7] Earlier in the same paragraph, Erasmus writes that, in the *Enchiridion*, he 'laid down quite simply the pattern of a Christian life.'[8] We have cause to expect, then, that within this trifle, this playful romp that is the *Moria*, we should come upon some evidence of a Christian form of existence, and, if this is true, we will most likely find there as well the makings for the conflict mentioned above.

In my own understanding of the movement of the work, I see it opening in a happy, carnival spirit, at least on the surface, and passing to a middle section characterized by an aggressive satire the tone of which clearly distinguishes it from the preceding part. At the end, the initially festive mood returns and reaches new heights in the uncontrolled and boundless joy experienced by the saints. In his letter to Dorp, Erasmus mentions that the purpose of the *Moria* is 'to embrace the whole world of things under the name of foolishness and to show that the whole sum of human felicity depends on Folly.'[9] This is a large order that constrains the author to include foolishness as it ranges from ordinary absurdity to the sublime self-forgetfulness of the holy ones. The difficulty here lies in the transition from the lower stages to the higher, and it is precisely to these junctions that modern criticism points when finding fault with Erasmus' control of his subject.

Perhaps the most severe criticism of the *Folly* fastens on the moment when the lady fool loses her congenial tone of voice and turns with unmistakable ire on the theologians and the religious orders. One critic thinks the change severe enough to demand a new persona, a new mask, as it were.[10] Another thinks that the mask is abandoned altogether and that, in this part, 'Erasmus (not Folly) is clearly the speaker.'[11] Further dissatisfaction is caused when Folly abandons her caustic satire and begins talking about scripture and the things of heaven. The introduction of the sublime at this juncture constitutes, according to one interpretation, 'an awkward transition from the life of reason to that of faith.' Erasmus seems to run away from 'the problems that beset the stage of life' by retreating to heaven.[12] No one denies that Erasmus moves from the trivial to the serious in the *Moria*, but his modern critics question the success of his passage from one to the other. In the present chapter, I will confine myself to the elucidation of the contending elements in the *Moria* and, in the next one, turn to the movement of its plot line from the ridiculous to the sublime. In so doing, we will examine a most difficult and demanding kind of literary sleight of hand that substitutes a speechless ecstasy for an irresponsible vacuity. There, perhaps, is the severest test for the Erasmian seriocomic temper.

IDEATIONAL CONTENTION

In the first part of her discourse, Folly sets out to celebrate her sway over the lives of both gods and men. Being true to her character, she follows nonsensical lines of argument which she manages to camouflage partially from the reader by means of a constantly varied pace and tactic. No care whatsoever is given to consistency. Folly will make the wise man the object of her attack and then turn around and say that it is she who leads to the heights of wisdom.[13] She will refer to the stupidity of Socrates and in the next breath say his wisdom got him into trouble.[14] She will flout the rules of logic by means of her equivocation and false assumptions. She informs us that fools are to be preferred to the wise because the former are driven by their passions and the latter are guided by reason, and she proves her case for folly's excellence by appealing to the common run of humanity who are driven by appetite.[15] Folly claims that 'no branch of learning was ever discovered except at [Folly's] inspiration,' only to refute this statement later by avowing that after the golden age 'evil spirits ... began to invent the learned disciplines.'[16] She first says that all

the players on the stage of life, as if by instinct, take to a costume
and a mask that hide the inner self, and then she goes on to argue
that nature abhors disguises.[17] The most obvious conflict in the
opening section of the *Moria* issues from the carefree self-
contradiction of Folly herself. What first appears as a rollicking
sense of good humour in the character will grow taut in the
middle part of her speech when the contradiction of the thought
begins to manifest a division and opposition within the notion of
folly itself.

Folly pays so little attention to the significance of what she is
saying that meaning becomes unmoored in a sea of countless
possible interpretations. The paradox of part 1 involves the witty
exercise of Erasmus' mind by which he tricks the reader into
following a line of thought that appears, upon close analysis, to
be mindless and incoherent. But the spirit of play, championed
by the speaker, is infectious, and the sympathetic reader, who
readily gives himself to the joke, is taken into its vacuity so that he
experiences the power of the folly that rules all things. Amidst
this jocular reign of disorder, Folly will on occasion facetiously
play at the attempt to put things right by drawing distinctions
which would seem to deliver her from self-contradiction and to
clarify her thought. This is most apparent when she divides the
notion of foolishness itself into two opposing factions. Pierre
Mesnard has called this 'la distinction capitale' of the book, the
radical division that will make sense out of some of Folly's most
glaring instances of absurdity.[18] Such a view is defensible only if
we see this first separation of the notion of folly as premature yet
anticipatory of the crucial distinction that is made in part 3. In the
first section of her speech, Folly is simply too fun-loving and
irresponsible to be bothered about being clear; furthermore, the
basis for her initial distinction between the two follies really fails
to make a genuine separation between them.

A little over two-thirds of the way through part 1 of her speech,
Folly puts forth an argument against her own position which she
imagines to come from the school of the sour, disgruntled Stoics:
'"Nothing," they say, "is more miserable than madness."'[19] To
extricate herself from this charge, Folly claims that there are two
kinds of mental disorders:

one which is sent up from the underworld by the avenging
Furies whenever they dart forth their serpents and inspire

in the breasts of mortals a burning desire for war, or un-
quenchable thirst for gold, or disgraceful and wicked lust,
or parricide, incest, sacrilege, or some other such plague, or
when they afflict the guilty thoughts of some criminal with
the maddening firebrands of terror. There is another kind
far different from the first, namely the kind which takes its
origin from me and is most desirable. It occurs whenever a
certain pleasant mental distraction relieves the heart from
its anxieties and cares and at the same time soothes it with
the balm of manifold pleasures.[20]

Folly's madness consists of a pleasing kind of distraction that
brings relief from care and comforts the mind with a feeling of
ease and satisfaction. Such a madness, we are told, is far removed
from the other sort, the furious insanity originating in Hades and
defined as an affliction.

Within two paragraphs of separating the notion of folly into
two compartments, Folly, in one more act of inconsistency,
begins to confuse and to bring together what she has just divided
in two. She includes within the category of fools belonging to her
those aficionados whose happiness is confined to the exercise
and challenge of the hunt. These madmen of hers experience
'exquisite pleasure ... when the quarry is to be butchered!' The
passage mocks the ritual in which the slain animals are cut up as if
the spectacle were some new religious ceremony. Folly says that
these fools are lowering themselves 'almost to the level of the
animals they hunt.'[21] Such fellows belong to Folly because their
madness brings them pleasure, but they take that pleasure in
violent acts more proper to the insanity originating in the hell of
the Furies.

Further evidence of Folly's inability to restrain the abrasively
insane from joining her ranks occurs in part 2 of her speech. She
refers to the classrooms given over to the charge of her grammari-
ans as torture chambers. There the insane mentors oversee flocks
of boys and 'grow old in their labors, grow deaf from the noise,
waste away in the stink and stench, and yet through my [Folly's]
favor they imagine they are the luckiest of mortals – so powerful
is their flattering delusion while they terrify the timid band of
pupils with threatening words and scowls and beat the poor
wretches bloody with rods, switches, and straps, raging wildly
with every imaginable sort of arbitrary cruelty.'[22] In their mad-

ness, these schoolmasters think that this 'most wretched slavery of theirs seems a life fit for a king, so much so that they wouldn't trade their tyrannical rule for the empire of Phalaris or Dionysius.'[23] These demented teachers belong to Folly's band because they believe their life to be comforting, but, alas, this comfort amounts to a sadistic joy in violence and squalor. Something similar can be said of the theologians whose arrogant interpretations of the gospel of peace so vitiate the sacred text that it is thought to advocate conversion by the sword and the bloody execution of delinquent Christians.[24] The most scandalous instance of the perversion of Christ's message into a code of terror and aggression is found in the lives of the violent popes whose pleasure it is to interdict, suspend, excommunicate the erring members of the faithful and to start wars in which the follower of the crucified is urged 'to unsheathe cold steel and thrust it into his brother's guts without any offense against the highest duty of charity.'[25] A thinly veiled form of horror has been introduced into Folly's plea on behalf of the satisfactions that attend her.

The juxtaposition of pleasure and pain, commented on so frequently in this study, takes on a garish and perverse quality in the above passages. For these violent fools, the infliction of pain appears to be a source of satisfaction. Folly's argument on behalf of herself and her devotees, which begins so happily and congenially, takes on a grimly self-defeating aspect when the line of reasoning ventures into the world of the learned and the powerful. Something of the method in the speech's madness is revealed when we trace the change even in part 1 from a convivial, mindless starting point towards the gradual introduction of arresting ironies suggestive of the sorrow in human existence. Early in the book, Folly celebrates the foolishness of the sexual act as proof of her universal hold upon gods and men. In these chapters, all is revelry and mirth. But, as the speech continues, Folly's plea on behalf of the happiness that she brings mankind becomes involved with arguments that indirectly recall the perilous and chilling aspects of the human condition. Folly alone relieves us from the tedium of living; she alone eases the grief of growing old; she alone brings the numbness and empty-headedness that makes dying endurable.[26] Without her illusions, men and women would not be able to put up with the great void that confronts them. Here Folly's boon comes to mankind in the dubiously beneficial form of darkness and ignorance. The only antidote she can offer for the gloom of mortality is another kind of gloom discernible in the eyes of pale, withered faces.

In the final analysis, many of Folly's self-contradictions can be resolved after the distinction fundamental to the work has been established. The initial function of this disorder is to introduce a carnival spirit of riot. But the slow, almost imperceptible, degeneration of the argument that claims that Folly alone brings pleasure to all the ages of man opens a more solemn and thought-provoking phase of the speech. Folly would have us believe that she is the arch-enemy of pain and mortality, but, before the end of part 1, she has thoughtlessly insinuated her collusion with death. She reasons ironically that the older her dear fools grow 'the nearer they come to childhood, until like children, without being bored by life or afraid of death, they depart from this life.'[27] The look of madness in the eyes of the aged is exchanged for the hollow, skeletal grin of death. Michel Foucault claims that at the dawn of the Northern Renaissance 'the mockery of madness replaces death and its solemnity. From the discovery of that necessity which inevitably reduces man to nothing, we have shifted to the scornful contemplation of that nothing which is existence itself.'[28] The 'contemptus mundi' has evolved into a 'contemptus vitae.' Although there is no need to attribute such a pessimism to Erasmus, his goddess Folly, in pleading her own case, will inadvertently touch upon the anguish and frustration that accompanies man's life on earth. When Erasmus travelled through the Alps into Italy in the late summer of 1506, he composed a long poem, the 'Carmen Alpestre,' on the advent of old age and its inevitable encounter with death. Three summers later, when leaving Italy through those same mountain passes, the germinal inspiration for the *Moria* seized him, and, in the light of the work's full development, it is not difficult to see a relationship between the prose declamation and the poetic lamentation. In the first part of the *Moria*, death and folly are joined when the latter is described as a kind of sedative for the absolute and frightening demands of the former. As such, Folly is the joyous companion of man's nothingness.

Folly's attempt, therefore, to distinguish clearly what she claims to be her own satisfying and comfortable foolishness from a furious and abrasive sort does not succeed. As Wayne A. Rebhorn observes, 'in this world the life-giving, beneficent form of folly cannot be separated from the destructive kind.'[29] The lady fool's boast that she is the source of all pleasure admits of an insane delight in violence, in suffering, in death. Obviously, another distinction must be found with regard to foolishness in general if we are to arrive at the contention which is the source of so much of Folly's self-contradiction. This distinction is not made until part 3 of the work, but it is anticipated in part 1 when Folly sets out to prove that she can lay claim to what appears to be her opposite: the virtue of prudence. She first boasts that prudence, because it has to do with experience, belongs to the fool who is ready for any undertaking rather than to the wise man who is restrained from bold action by his modesty and his timidity. Then Folly examines prudence from another point of view, from a definition that sees it 'as consisting in good judgment.'[30] She then goes into her famous description of life as theatre and reflects on the incident of the intruder from heaven who bungles onto the stage, spoiling the illusion created by the players when he starts to unmask them and to tell them what they really are. This, in Folly's eyes, is the height of imprudence and bad judgment because true prudence 'recognizes human limitations and does not strive to leap beyond them; it is willing to run with the herd, to overlook faults tolerantly or to share them in a friendly spirit. But, they say, that is exactly what we mean by folly.'[31] Ergo, folly is the equivalent of prudence. As usual, Folly confuses the issue when she calls the celestial unmasker 'a raving lunatic' and then proceeds to explain herself: 'Just as nothing is more foolish than misplaced wisdom, so too, nothing is more imprudent than perverse prudence.'[32] So Folly, in order to prove that prudence belongs to her, uses the example of a fool capable only of imprudence. By implication, we have in this passage two kinds of foolishness and two kinds of prudence, and, in each case, the one is at loggerheads with the other.

I have already adverted to Erasmus' Latin for what his translator calls a 'misplaced wisdom.' I return to it now because it provides a clue to what amounts to the decisive distinction in the entire work. 'Sapientia praepostera' can mean literally a wisdom that places last things first or first things last. 'Praepostera' in the present context is inextricably connected with scales of values and the radical reversal of such scales. The man whose vision is described by these words descends onto the stage of life from heaven. What the players seem to value most he values least; his own scale is the reverse of theirs. Conformed to the law of the Silenus, the focus of his sight pierces the façade and reaches to the truth within. What appears to be life turns out to be death for him; beauty becomes ugliness; wealth turns to penury. The contrary is true for most of the players about him. The heavenly is set in contention with the earthly, and this struggle, announced indirectly in part 1 of the *Moria*, is developed in the later sections as the major conflict of the work.

THE NOTIONAL CONFLICT DRAMATIZED

At the start of the second part of her speech, Folly tells her listeners that she will enumerate for them the forms of foolishness assumed by 'those who have the appearance of wisdom in the eyes of mortals.'[33] She is only a few sentences into her catalogue when we notice that her delivery begins to take on a satirical bite. We have already seen how she concentrates on the demented schoolmaster who wallows in filth and violence to his heart's content. She then goes on to ridicule the mad grammarian who 'would consider himself perfectly happy if he could live long enough to determine once and for all how the eight parts of speech can be distinguished from each other.'[34] This life commitment to the perfecting of the imperfectible, while derided by Folly, is not completely rejected by her. In her concluding remarks to this kind of delusion, she lays claim to the fool whom she has mocked. 'Would you,' she asks, 'rather call this madness or folly? It makes little difference to me, as long as you grant that through my favor a creature who would otherwise be the most miserable wretch imaginable is elevated to such heights of happiness that he would refuse to change places with the kings of Persia.'[35] A similar contention between negative and positive attitudes is present in Folly's references to the lawyers and the dialecticians. She finds them ludicrous for being so loud-mouthed and quarrelsome in their fights 'to the bitter end over some hair-splitting quibble.'[36] But these too enjoy the happiness that only Folly can bring by reason of their self-love and the pleasure they take in verbal duels over nothing. In part 2, Folly engages in a scathing attack on the chairs of learning and the thrones of power, while, at the same time, owning to and taking credit for the evils that infect these places. The self-contradiction, so characteristic of part 1, now assumes a more emotive and personal quality as Folly both contends against and embraces the aberrations of her learned followers.

The further we read into part 2 of the *Moria* the less likely we are to remain sensitive to Folly's close connection with these particular fools of hers and the more we will become aware of the grudge she nurtures against them. Her caustic irony is impossible to miss when she tells us that the theologians of the schools are especially beholden to her 'for benefits of no little importance. They are so blessed by their Selflove as to be fully persuaded that they themselves dwell in the third heaven, looking down from high above on all other mortals as if they were earth-creeping vermin almost worthy of their pity.'[37] The theologians resemble the drunken gods looking down from heaven, only now the affable spirit has vanished and the vision of the beholders has become mistaken and deluded. Not only has the mankind for whom Christ died been demeaned to vermin, but the august science of theology has been reduced to an obsession with 'most subtle subtleties.'[38] The complaint against the theologians on page after page of this most prolonged attack on any single profession focuses on their propensity to fix their attention on trivia. They are preoccupied with 'petty quibbles,' 'supersubtleties,' and 'most delightful trifles.'[39] They exemplify better than any class of scholar what Erasmus means when he mentions in the prefatory letter to the *Moria* that 'nothing is more trivial than to treat serious matter in a trivial way.'[40] The inconsistency of Folly, then, that is peculiar to her in part 2, takes the shape of a cantankerous indisposition towards the learned and authoritative occupations because they are so cluttered with her own devotees.

As indicated earlier, the change in Folly's tone from congeniality to a livid disdain of certain kinds of foolishness has disturbed some modern critics. It provides further evidence in proof of A.E. Douglas' conclusion that the *Moria* is bereft of coherence.[41] Why should this champion of the ridiculous suddenly turn on her own in a volte-face for which we are not prepared? Furthermore, how can we justify the change in the texture of the speech away from the equivocation so characteristic of part 1 to the unmistakable clarity and univocal assertions of part 2? Although Folly's utterances are open to a multiplicity of readings in the earlier sections of the speech, it would be erroneous to expect a similar storehouse of possible interpretations in part 2. The treatment of war and violence in the first part, for example, has an ambivalence which cannot be found in the second part's tirade against the warring popes. Whatever can be said about this passage, the point of its grievance lies beyond dispute. From what literary perspective, then, are we to understand Folly's change of attitude from one of good-natured camaraderie to open hostility and her change of delivery from ambiguity to openness?

At the beginning of part 2, Folly tells us of the drunken gods who, from their heavenly theatre seats, look down on the human comedy. Earlier in the speech, Folly mentions a similar vantage point, a watchtower, for beholding the tragedies of humankind, and, again, this same kind of outlook is associated with the gods, in this earlier case, with Jupiter.[42] Such a comprehension of the whole belongs to heavenly beings, and it is to such a place of vantage that Folly invites her audience at the opening of part 2. 'If you could look down from the moon,' she says, 'as Menippus once did, and see the innumerable broils of mortals, you would think you were looking at a great cloud of flies or gnats quarreling among themselves, warring, plotting, plundering, playing, frisking, being born, declining, dying.'[43] As I pointed out in the previous chapter, the vision situated in heaven contrasts decisively with the way of seeing characteristic of the humanoids flitting across their insect mound. The recurrent aberration indigenous to the learned professions in part 2 originates in their myopia: they are all guilty of reducing truth to some kind of quibble. Heavenly sight, on the other hand, never loses touch with the great sweep and reach of its transcendent goals. To a worldling this is madness, a 'praepostera sapientia.' It is this form of madness that Folly introduces in part 2, and this introduction results in a personality split of the character.

In part 2 of the *Moria*, Folly dramatizes in her own person the essential cleavage or division in the notion of foolishness itself that permeates the entire work and becomes explicit only at the end. When she turns irately on her own devotees, she exposes the ugly side of their lives after having assured them earlier that only Folly could make them oblivious of their painful existence. In part 1, she pleaded for the keeping up of appearances, and costumes were understood as disguises. Now she would have the monarchs in her entourage remember the religious and moral significance of the regalia. The cardinals of the church likewise are urged to realize the meaning of the clothes by which they are invested into their high office and to reflect within themselves:

'What does the whiteness of this garment mean? Isn't it the most eminent and flawless innocence of life? What does the scarlet underneath mean? Isn't it the most burning love of God? And then what is meant by the scarlet outside, flowing down in such wide undulations and completely covering the Most Reverend Father's mule? – though, for that matter, it would be enough by itself to cover a camel. Isn't it charity reaching out far and wide to help everyone, that is, to teach, exhort, console, reproach, advise, settle wars, resist wicked princes, and freely give not merely riches but even life-blood for Christ's flock – though why should any riches at all belong to those who act in the place of the poor apostles?' – if they considered these things, I say, they would not strive to get that office and would gladly relinquish it, or at least they would lead very laborious and anxious lives, such as those ancient apostles lived.[44]

Dress no longer serves as disguise but as a symbol of service, as a kind of extension of the dedicated inner self. Folly has assumed a moral consciousness that now wants to unmask the ridiculous charade perpetrated by those who are supposed to be wise and holy. She functions in part 2 precisely as the man from heaven did in part 1 when he landed on the stage of life and began exposing the vice hidden behind the imposing façade of the rich and powerful lord. She now is possessed of the same heavenly folly, or the 'praepostera sapientia,' which drove the celestial creature to ruffle the decorum of the stage by making a great scene. There can be no doubt that Folly in these passages is seized by a Christian view of things; she even takes on the voice of Jesus himself when she berates the monks for becoming preoccupied with ceremony:

But Christ, interrupting their boasts (which would other-wise never come to an end), will say, 'Where did this new race of Jews come from? The only law I recognize as truly mine is the only one I hear nothing about. Long ago, not speaking obliquely in parables but quite openly, I promised my Father's inheritance not to hoods, or trifling prayers, or fasts, but rather deeds of faith and charity. Nor do I acknowledge those who too readily acknowledge their own deeds: those who want to appear even holier than I am can go dwell in the heavens of Abraxasians if they like, or they can order that a new heaven be built for them by the men whose petty traditions they have placed before my precepts.'[45]

On the one hand, I must admit that the tone of the passages just cited is coloured by a moral righteousness that seriously threatens the decorum of a comical personage. In normal circumstances, such rectitude undoes the ambience of disorder within which the clown thrives. On the other hand, Erasmus' fool is called upon to speak on behalf of every kind of foolishness under the sun, and, in the author's mind, the folly of Christ constitutes one of the two major areas in the division of this topic. This division only becomes explicit at the end. What is openly declared in the final paragraphs remains implicit in the middle section, although the words of Folly clearly suggest a dialectic of opposites within the concept of foolishness throughout part 2. The tone of righteousness, if it does not sit well with our understanding and expectations of the foolish character, at least remains true to a kind of ridiculousness, a folly, that is, which will not adapt to 'prevailing circumstances' and which insists on disturbing the play in which it finds itself.[46] Folly, by demanding that the actors be what they seem to be, causes a great scene. In dramatic terms, part 2 of the *Moria* is what Aristotle would call an act of anagnorisis or discovery in which the fundamental conflict between Christ and the world is emotionally laid bare by the caustic manner which the speaker adopts towards a great number of her own devotees. And this enmity is nothing other than the very agon of what we called in the previous chapter the 'fabula Christi,' the Erasmian version of the theatre of life.

THE TWO FOLLIES

Erasmus seems to have been aware of the danger of allowing his fool to preach seriously for too long; therefore, he decided to reduce the intensity of her zeal upon arriving at the last and most religious stage of her speech. In part 3, Folly abandons her voice of indignation and accusation as she jocularly prepares to marshal a host of scriptural verses in her defence. Regardless of the change in her tone, the enmity between two kinds of folly is present here, even if in a less strident form than in the second part. Two opposed ways of exegesis clash when Folly's apparently careless and whimsical reading is set next to the interpretations executed in the pretentious manner of Nicolas de Lyra. We witness a contest between heavenly foolishness, represented by Folly, and a base, secular wisdom portrayed by the pompous theologians. De Lyra and his tribe stand the gospel on its head 'just as if Christ had reversed his position and ... had recanted his former teaching.'[47] They do to scripture what the lax bishops do to Christian life when they turn law and religion upside down. They gloss a passage in Luke (22:35–6) to mean that Christ, the champion of meekness, embraced the cause of violence. The sword is invoked to the point where the 'interpreter of the divine mind musters the apostles fully equipped with spears, slings, siege-machines, cannons, to preach Christ crucified.'[48] One old man arrogantly pronounces as the scriptural truth that Christians must execute heretics and justifies his doctrine of force by misinterpreting verses in Paul and Exodus.[49] In this manner, the foolish theologians, with their worldly wisdom, profane the sacred instruction of the Bible and reduce the thought of Christ to mere secular pragmatism.

By way of contrast, Folly does not seem to take her own exegesis seriously. She first tells us that she would like to don the garb of a theologian, as if to mimic that learned gentleman as she earlier did the Sophist;[50] later she begs the reader to show her the same indulgence as that given to the great teachers of theology if her quotations are not accurate.[51] She appears to do humorously what the theologue does gravely: to distort the meaning of scripture to suit her own purpose. For instance, she recalls a verse from Ecclesiastes (1:17) in which the sacred writer says that he gave his heart 'to understand wisdom and knowledge, delusions and folly.'[52] From this one dictum, she argues that the author shows his great deference to foolishness by saving for it the last and most excellent place in the sentence out of a regard for the ecclesiastical order of precedence which dictates that in a procession the highest dignitary should come last. However pleasant we may find the argument, it can hardly be defended. A custom of the present forces an interpretation on the sacred text. On the surface, Folly, the exegete, seems just as incompetent as her bungling opponent. Yet, even if she does give the impression of playing, she has long ago abandoned the role of the Sophist. A serious meaning can now more readily be extracted from her light and frothy discourse if we focus not so much on her statements taken in isolation as on the direction in which these statements lead.

Folly's first quotations in defence of foolishness are all drawn from the Old Testament, and almost every text implies an opposition between wisdom and folly with the two terms approximating the contrast between good and evil. Folly, of course, ignores the drift of this meaning and constantly gives a benign interpretation to foolishness. In the immediate context of the individual verse, this cannot be justified, but, if we relate her reading to something she later says, then a new light is thrown upon her line of thinking. From the Old Testament she moves into the New, to Pauline folly, and finally to the folly of the incarnation: 'Do not all witnesses cry out with one voice that all mortals are fools, even the pious? And that even Christ, though he was the wisdom of the Father, became somehow foolish in order to relieve the folly of mortals when he took on human nature and appeared in the form of a man? Just as he became sin in order to heal sins.' The 'Verbum caro factum est' of John's gospel (1:14) here becomes 'Christum ... stultum esse factum.'[53] For the Word to become flesh is for Wisdom to become foolish. Because of the incarnation, the scriptural antagonism between the fool and the wise man is resolved, and foolishness is redeemed, justified, exalted. Through the force of this paradox alone, Folly's ridiculous readings of the Old Testament passages take on new meaning. Erasmus held that all scripture finds its fulfilment in Christ, and Folly's defence of biblical foolishness is justified only in the light of this fulfilment. Furthermore, by contending against and putting down the worldly wisdom of the interpreter who turns upside down all Christian standards, Folly reinverts the scale and sets matters straight again.

The folly of the Word become flesh is intensified by Christ's passage from this world through the sacrificial agony of the cross. This passage becomes the norm whereby men are made Christian. They are baptized in Christ's death and resurrection. The ritual of baptism in which the neophyte is submerged in water to rise a new man in the Lord symbolizes the life that is to be led thenceforth. In a paraphrase of 1 Corinthians (1:21 and 27), Folly proclaims 'that God was pleased to save the world through folly because it could not be redeemed by wisdom.'[54] This foolishness becomes the one and only path to salvation: 'Nor did he [Christ] choose any other way to heal them [mankind] but through the folly of the cross.' These words, crucial to Folly's argument, again echo 1 Corinthians (1:21) and deserve careful notice. In the Latin the sentence reads: 'Neque alia ratione mederi voluit [Deus], quam per stulticiam crucis.'[55] 'Ratio' here has the force of 'mode' or 'fashion': a way of grasping that gives the intellect a distinctive form. The 'ratio crucis' designates an outlook, a manner of thinking, incomprehensible to a mind shaped by the appetite for that which is embedded in and restricted to the temporal. We may call this latter kind of comprehension a 'ratio carnis' or 'ratio mundi' – a mind that is sculpted by the will to have all now, and it is diametrically opposed to the fool in Christ.

Folly uses Plato's myth of the cave to introduce her most explicit account of the antagonism between the two kinds of foolishness. The prisoner who escapes the cave, beholds the light, and returns to tell his fellows of things as they are resembles the man from heaven in part 1. Both are possessed of truth and, in revealing it, are considered mad. The prisoners in the darkness wonder at the shadows and laugh when they are told that they have been mesmerized by illusions. There can be no meeting of minds here. Christian foolishness leads the soul away from purely earthly interests, and the world's madness remains enamoured of the ephemeral. Folly concludes that because 'these two groups are in such utter disagreement on all matters, the result is that each thinks the other is insane – though that word applies more properly to the pious than to ordinary men, if you want my opinion.'[56] In these final paragraphs of her speech, Folly shows a special favouritism towards Christian foolishness. The highest realms of human happiness are described in terms of a madness inspired by the love of Christ and of his Father. God grants the victory in this contention of follies to his own fools; he singles out the weak to overcome the strong and chooses the fool to confound them who think themselves wise. As Erasmus states when commenting on 1 Corinthians (1:25), God's 'secret force overcomes his opposition by means of its opposites.'[57]

The antagonism between two follies, which has been traced through the *Moria*, constitutes, as has been said before, the agon of Erasmus' stage of life. The conflict, although portrayed in metaphorical language, is a very real one, an intrinsic part of history itself. 'In this world,' Erasmus writes, 'there are two worlds, at variance with each other in every way: the one gross and material, the other celestial, having its thoughts centred even now, as far as may be, on that which is to come hereafter.'[58] To pass from one world to the other, from the earthly to the heavenly, from the self to Christ, necessitates an inversion of ideas, values, words. We are told in the *Enchiridion* 'that in Christ all things are changed and their names are reversed.'[59] 'Sileni Alcibiadis' repeats this teaching: 'The reversing of values brings about a reversed use of words. What is sublime they [the followers of the world] call humble; what is bitter they call sweet; the precious is called vile, and life, death.'[60] In this radical opposition between Christ and the world and the two follies which each represents, we discover the resolution of many of Folly's contradictions. What appears to carnal sight as death is to the eyes of faith a passage to life. When Folly tells us she is the source of wisdom, the truth in this paradox can only be grasped within the context of the latter stages of her talk when divine foolishness is revealed as the height of human bliss. The same may be said of Folly's claim to prudence and to unending youth. In part 1, Folly unconvincingly appropriated to herself the benign form of madness as distinguished from its malevolent strain. We saw that she failed to maintain successfully such a distinction. In part 3, however, the benign foolishness reaches its true fulfilment in the folly of Christ and his followers.

But it would be erroneous, I believe, to conclude, as some do, that Folly herself has been transformed by the close of her speech. She is spokeswoman for all foolishness, both worldly and divine, and to claim that she has been converted by her own peroration would be to wrest from Folly the essentially Protean cast of her character. Moreover, the contest between two kinds of madness goes on after Folly's voice has died and she steps down from the rostrum. Her parting words exhorting us to drink up may be understood sacramentally as a behest to partake of the drink that leads to the fullness of life or as an invitation to lift the cup of good red wine. The struggle between believing and temporizing, invisible and visible, heaven and earth, developed within the book, is not settled at the end. The mind, in a sense, is undone by this speech and is indirectly prodded to reach out for faith to achieve wholeness. Reason alone will not do. The human predicament is not unlike that of the man in the theatre of whom Folly tells us. He took great pleasure from sitting alone in the empty show house caught up in the mad belief that a play was being acted before him on the deserted stage; and he resented it when his friends cured him of his delusion.[61] This passage suggests the choice we are left with after Folly has fled the scene. Which do we prefer? The 'fabula Christi,' the stage with Christ at its centre, or the empty one? The mind, left to its own resources, cannot reach a satisfactory answer to this question, but one folly or other has to be chosen. And therein lie the danger and the risk.

NINE

In Defence of the *Moria*:
Cohesion of the Ridiculous with
the Sublime

❦

In the introduction to the previous chapter, mention was made
of the modern critics who find fault with the *Moria* because of
its lack of coherence. One aspect of this problem, the change of
tone in part 2, has already been discussed in the treatment
of the work's agon. Folly's abrasive speech in the middle section of her address manifests emotionally and dramatically the
contention between two forms of madness that is intrinsic to the
work as a whole. There remains the question of Folly's ascent
from the trivial to the sublime and the success or failure of
Erasmus to achieve such an admittedly difficult transition. Does
he effect a true cohesion of the light with the serious, of laughter
with the sacred, of the worldly with the heavenly? The stress of
chapter 8 of this study lay upon the antagonism between heaven
and earth as norms for living but not as entities in themselves.
Now, in the present chapter, we will seek a basis for relating the
carnival joy characteristic of part 1 to the heavenly ecstasy of part 3.
So the *Moria* will be studied here against a theological and cultural
background relevant to understanding the work's movement
from a Saturnalian hilarity to an all-transcending enthralment. In
order to do this, I would like first to look briefly at the initial
complaints about the *Moria* published in Erasmus' lifetime and
then to study more carefully selected passages from the author's
own defence of his book. The early voices of disapproval, although
they betray more distress and alarm, do resemble the modern
uneasiness about the work's unifying web. Just as some modern
critics find fault with Erasmus' passage from reason to faith, so
his contemporaries balk at what they consider to be the profanation of the divine when Folly juxtaposes the human experience of

madness to man's communion with his God. Both then and now, the *Moria* excites a resistance to its bold joining of an earthly phenomenon to a heavenly mystery.

THE EARLY CHARGES AGAINST THE *MORIA*

Erasmus completed his first draft of the *Moria* in the summer of 1509. In the following year he composed the prefatory letter to More, and, not long after that, Richard Croke's unauthorized edition appeared. Erasmus then sent his own corrected version through the press for publication at Paris in July of 1512.[1] Barely two years had passed when Martin Dorp, an ambitious theological student, wrote a letter to Erasmus informing him that the theologians of Louvain had been appalled by the *Moria*. The little work 'has upset everything' by undoing all that Erasmus had previously accomplished.[2] This instance of the book's rejection by academe anticipates the ensuing attacks on it by theologians all over Europe from Edward Lee, the Englishman, to Petrus Sutor, the Frenchman, Jacobus Stunica, the Spaniard, and Alberto Pio, the Italian.[3] Not long after Erasmus' death, the Sorbonne got around to condemning the book officially, and, as Clarence Miller points out, the *Moria* met a good deal of opposition in Italy. The book 'appeared on the indices of Milan and Venice (1554), of Paul IV (1559), of Trent (1564), of Sixtus V (1590), and Clement VIII (1596).'[4] These condemnations indicate a kind of gravity that Erasmus in his lifetime wanted the *Moria* to be spared.

The book does more than just touch on matters related to the learned teachers of divinity. It attacks the decadent scholastic method of exegesis and, by inference, the theologians who practise it. It also calls for the revision of theological studies by satirizing the prevalent obsession with trivial questions. Finally, Folly herself assumes the guise of triviality in the role of a Sophist only to lead the reader to a revelation of genuine Christian foolishness at the close of her speech. The book thus reverses the current trend of taking matters of weight and placing them under a glass that focuses only on minutiae. All of this provides matter enough to stir the conservative and backward theologians of the day.

In the letter written late in the summer of 1514, Martin Dorp complains to Erasmus especially about the way the *Moria* treats the faculty of theology 'for which it is so important to retain the respect of common folk.'[5] Along with his professors, Dorp seems to have taken Folly's assault on the theologians as a personal affront; furthermore, he indicates his disappointment in Erasmus, whom he addresses as 'Doctor of Divinity,' for having betrayed the profession to which they both belong by indulging himself irresponsibly in the ridiculous. 'What has *Moria*,' he seems to ask, 'to do with theology?' The only way for Erasmus to make amends would be by exchanging his motley for a dress of greater dignity and 'by writing and publishing a *Praise of Wisdom*.' This 'prolific subject' would be worthy of Erasmus' genius and beneficial to his favourite study.[6]

We can detect in Dorp's critique of the *Moria* an affectation of professional gravity concerning his office of theologian that borders on the precious. This can be attributed to the inexperience of a man in his late twenties aspiring to the doctoral degree in theology. His zeal on behalf of Louvain's divinity faculty doubtless was influenced by his situation as a doctoral candidate there. In fact, Thomas More suggests that Dorp was really representing not his own mind but the wounded feelings of his teachers when he wrote against the *Moria*.[7] Later events tend to confirm this opinion because Dorp lived to regret this controversy with Erasmus.[8] In his reply to Dorp's charge of disrespect, Erasmus felt no need to belabour his defence. He mentions that only a few theologians have complained about the book and ascribes their dissatisfaction to an ignorant reading of the text. He implies that these pompous critics have no literary finesse and perception.[9] Erasmus was perhaps exaggerating the ease with which one familiar with the study of letters can arrive at the meaning of the *Moria*. In his own day, not a few were to take the book in a sense which its author claimed he never meant.

Treatment of the theologians is one thing; treatment of Christ and his saints and the heavenly realm is quite another. The charges of the adversaries here range from those of impropriety in Dorp to those of blasphemy in Stunica, Sutor, and Pio.[10] This last-named critic accused Erasmus of making fun and sport of things divine to the extreme of strangling the Christian faith by basing it entirely on foolishness.[11] Erasmus' answer to this indictment, whenever it was urged against the *Moria*, always

includes an appeal to the scriptural precedent of Pauline foolishness.[12] Indeed, the idea of Christian folly that Paul develops in
the early chapters of 1 Corinthians serves as indispensable
background for arriving at the inspirational matrix of the *Moria*;
and the last section of 2 Corinthians, where Paul defends his
ministry against the intrusion of false teachers, bears a striking
resemblance to the fool's sermon. In the eleventh and twelfth
chapters of this letter, Paul delivers an apologia for his mission
to the Corinthians and stresses the notion of his own foolishness
for doing what Dame Folly does in her sermon. Paul's apologia,
like Folly's, abounds in ironic double-meanings and includes a
heated polemic against his enemy impostors who can only give a
surface imitation of him, the real apostle. Finally, Paul's foolishness points the way for Folly to take when it drives him to
describe his ascent to the third heaven.

Erasmus had turned to Paul in justification of his idea of
foolishness as early as 1515 when he replied to the objections of
Martin Dorp; but the Pauline model failed to satisfy the theologians disturbed by the *Moria*. Numerous other attacks were
launched against it after Erasmus' letter to Dorp, attacks that
were to occupy the author's attention time and again during the
last twenty years of his life. Dorp's initial grievance was to be
repeated and intensified: 'And then Christ, and the life in Heaven
– can the ears of a good Christian endure to hear foolishness
ascribed to him, while life in Heaven, it says, is likely to be
nothing but a form of lunacy?'[13] Something in the metaphor and
the sound of the word jarred the ears of the learned. Aquinas had
defined folly as a sin, the daughter of lust, and as something
characterized by engrossment in the things of sense.[14] In her
frequent references to inebriating drink, to the blissful delusions
of lovers, and the simple, happy fools who are led by their natural
instincts, Folly's suggestions of Saturnalian excess evoke the
same meaning of foolishness given it by Aquinas. This involvement in a kind of carnivalesque celebration lends a colouring to
Erasmian folly that does not show up so readily in Paul's use of
the term. In this sinful connotation of the word, we isolate a
major cause of the trouble between the *Moria* and the irate
theologians. How, then, would Erasmus justify this tainted
image in his application of it to Christ and the heavenly life, and
what is the religious insight so commanding that it subjects moral
consideration to its arresting truth?

METAPHOR AND DEITY IN THE PATRISTIC
TRADITION

Erasmus understood his adversaries' charges of disrespect and blasphemy as essentially a problem with words and their associations. So in his reply to Dorp he spells out the difficulty as plainly as he can. He imagines a case where someone calls Christ 'a robber, an adulterer, a drunkard, a heretic.'[15] Of course, the good Christian would be shocked. Here is a choice of metaphor in which sin is attributed to the holy one much more baldly than the *Moria* puts it. Yet Erasmus goes on to defend this strange kind of diction provided only that it be done with tact.

> But suppose one expressed this in appropriate language; suppose one worked up to it, as though one were leading the reader by the hand up to this point gradually, until he saw how in his triumph through the cross he robbed Hell of its plunder which he restored to the Father; how he took unto himself the synagogue, like the wife of Moses (the wife of Uriah over again), that a peace-loving people might be born from her; how he was intoxicated with the new wine of charity when he gave himself for us; how he brought in a new kind of teaching, very different from all the current convictions of wise and foolish alike.[16]

As Erasmus develops each of these metaphors, he attempts to salvage the opprobrious word by making a spiritual interpretation of it in which he elevates what is normally immoral activity from a human to a divine level and so redeems it. At the same time, a genuine resemblance is struck between Christ and the sinner. In each example, the saviour becomes involved with sin just as he does in the *Moria*, but Erasmus sees no harm in the comparison because of the way in which it is treated.

No matter how great the delicacy a writer exercises in carrying out this paradoxical approach, today's readers may have trouble trying to make sense out of seeing Christ first as a sinner only to arrive at understanding the apparent sin as the excess of love. For Erasmus, this outlook originates in the saviour's and the scripture's role as a Silenus – both despised yet filled with hidden treasures; and he makes use of the ancient doll image in this very context when defending the *Moria* against Dorp.[17] The allegorical interpretation which Erasmus proposes in his reply to Dorp has been termed 'unhelpful' recently, because Erasmus is reacting to complaints that 'now strike us as crass and irrelevant.'[18] It is even possible that Erasmus' answers will strike us the same way. At any rate, Douglas Duncan dissuades us from the adoption of that reading of the *Moria* which its author encourages in the Dorp letter:

> one does not arrive at its [the *Moria's*] beautiful seriousness by peeling off layers of jest. A metaphor appropriate to the allegorical 'opening up' of obscene stories in the Old Testament is less appropriate to the holding in balance of conflicting facets of truth which Erasmian irony usually requires.[19]

Yet the Erasmian interpretation of Christ, the adulterer, for instance, calls for the very balancing 'of conflicting facets of truth' which Duncan advocates in his own critique. Erasmus' allegorical understanding of scripture and literature in general is not irrelevant but rather most important to the understanding of a text like the *Moria* because it reflects not only the author's habit of reading but also his manner of composition.

I have cited Duncan's rejection of Erasmus' own general explication of the *Moria* to illustrate a problem which many of us may run into when asked to take this approach to the text. Duncan's study focuses brilliantly on the Lucianic aspects of Erasmian irony, but, in his own defence of the *Folly*, Erasmus leads us into areas which demand more than just a knowledge of Lucian in order to see what the author is getting at. We are not likely to be familiar with this proposed way of reading, especially when it favours the application of a rule of paradox to a point where the inversion or reversal of meaning may seem as contrived to us as it once seemed disrespectful to Erasmus' enemies in the schools of theology. Nevertheless, a very ancient tradition of literary theology exists that readily supports this view. Its peculiar strain of thought and expression deserves a closer examination if we are to appreciate fully the connection between the *Moria's* celebration of human enjoyment even to its zenith and the book's religious spirit. We will, therefore, return to the four epithets which Erasmus attributes to Christ with our attention fixed on the scriptural and hermeneutical background to them and the habit of mind supporting them. More space will be afforded to two of these images – Christ the adulterer, and Christ the drunkard – because they relate most directly to the Saturnalian abandon characteristic of the *Moria*.

In his explication of Christ the adulterer, Erasmus says that Jesus ravishes the Synagogue, which he personifies as the wife of Moses, or 'the wife of Uriah over again.' This interpretation of the adultery of David with Uriah's Bathsheba discloses Erasmus' familiarity with the patristic and medieval penchant for finding Christ prefigured not in the faithful Hittite soldier but in the scheming, lustful king. This way of looking at the episode goes back to Augustine, who in his *Contra Faustum* distinguishes between the historic and the prophetic content of this Old Testament narrative. Augustine condemns the David of history for dispatching Uriah and stealing his wife but commends the true David prefigured in the account, the Messiah who will come to subdue the devil (Uriah) and take from him his spouse (Bathsheba), whom he will purify as his church.[20] A similar understanding of this text is found in Gregory the Great, only now Bathsheba stands for the Law and Uriah for the Jewish people with Christ still prefigured by David. As long as the Law remains joined in wedlock to the Judaic religion, it is held prisoner to carnal sacrifices. The new David, in ravishing the Law and winning her away from her fleshly partner, transforms his spouse when he spiritualizes her and reveals to her the destiny she was intended to fulfil.[21] Following the lead of the two great Latin fathers, medieval exegetes read the marriage of David and Bathsheba as prophecy. The scheme of Augustine is found in Gerhoh of Reichersberg and Honorius and is briefly summed up by John of Salisbury:

> Finally who, on the face of it, was more just than Urias? Who more base and cruel than David, whom the charms of Bathsheba allured to betrayal, murder, and adultery? All of which changes its aspect when Urias is understood to represent the devil, David Christ, and Bathsheba the Church besmirched by the stain of sin.[22]

The dramatic change of which Salisbury writes depends on Christ's power to reverse the course of history and to deliver his people from sin. This same volte-face occurs in the *Moria* when Christ saves a world of fools by becoming their fellow.

208 Towards a Ludic Theology

The Christian allegorization of the Old Testament originates with the acceptance of Christ as the *raison d'être* and fulfilment of that narrative: every one of its chapters, in some way, suggests and leans towards him. The purely ethical consideration is subordinated to this all-embracing concept, or rather, the moral decorum is upended by the manifestation of the divine in human affairs. We begin, I think, to comprehend more clearly this radical habit of mind when we consider the scriptural bases of two of the epithets used by Erasmus – Christ the heretic, and Christ the thief. In the gospel of John, Jesus angers his religious opponents because he takes their sacred law into his own hands and like a heretic breaks it. Their rage against him is summed up in the charge that will lead to crucifixion: 'he does not keep the Sabbath' (9:16). Throughout the narrative, John sustains an antagonism between Christ, the divine 'logos' in whom all things are made, and the Jewish leaders, fighting to defend their narrow understanding of religious and moral life. They see Christ as one who brazenly invades their Temple, cries out in its sacred precincts, and, like a god, violates their law. Similarly, when Christ compares himself to a robber in the synoptic gospels and his Second Coming to a thief's nocturnal forcing of a house, he clearly suggests the intrusive power of divinity in its dealing with mankind in general and with individual souls in particular.[23] The figure declares that the immorality of the robber on the human level cannot apply to God in his dealings with man, the creature, who is but clay in the hands of his maker. The same applies for all of Erasmus' epithets concerning Christ. If we think of him only as human, they remain strained; but, when the reader accepts him as divine, they begin to make sense because, within this religious perspective, God can come like a thief to take man's life, inebriate him past satiety, and transport him lovingly out of his senses. Ethical unseemliness on a human level disappears when an act under the image of immorality indicates God's intervention. Augustine writes that what is usually considered sinful in ordinary people becomes in scripture a symbolic manifestation of some sublime truth when predicated to the person of God or a prophet.[24] So Christ, foreshadowed by David, the adulterer, answers to that aspect of the deity which Folly identifies as its power to draw the soul beyond itself in heavenly ravishment.

The problem we are treating has to do with language and its propriety when speaking about God and the things of God. What we have discovered so far is that the norm that holds when man discusses man does not necessarily apply when man wants to talk about the deity. Patristic and medieval exegesis, in the willingness it shows to involve God in apparent sin, can only be understood, as we have just seen, by distinguishing the human and divine levels of being. This distinction is fundamental to the present investigation and is found in a principal source to this idiosyncratic use of words – the writings of Dionysius the Areopagite. In his *Enchiridion*, Erasmus counsels the reader to become familiar with Dionysius, who is an able guide to the correct method of interpreting biblical allegory.[25] The same author can also prove helpful in leading us to an understanding of the diction of the *Moria*.

In chapter 1, mention was made of the dissimilar similitude, a term coined by Dionysius and explained by Richard of St Victor and others as vital to the correct understanding of what we mean when we speak about God. Now we must explore that paradoxical term to a greater depth. Dionysius establishes as the groundwork for his negative theology man's inability to know and speak about the divine super-essence as it exists in itself.[26] Nonetheless, man can perceive and discuss God in the likeness which things bear to him. This similarity runs from creatures to their creator and not vice versa. Man, for instance, resembles something in God, but God does not resemble man. As the earth reflects the sun and takes on some of its warmth without the fiery star being like the watery planet with regard to the diffusion of light and heat, so creatures inevitably mirror something that originates in their creator without his fullness resembling their limitations.[27] Aquinas expresses the likeness and the difference here succinctly: 'Two things enclosed within the same order may reflect one another's likeness, but the likeness between cause and effect is not thus mutual: we can say that a copy is like the original, but not conversely. We can speak of the creature resembling God in some way, but not of God resembling the creature.'[28] So, when man speaks about God, he must be aware of the feeble basis for his analogy. He must not think that the things to which his works refer can be equated with the deity. We saw in chapter 1 that the words which might appear to be the most decorous, like 'heaven' and 'light,' are beset with a handicap: they could mislead the uninitiated into thinking that God is the heaven or the light we see and know. For this reason, Dionysius formulates his theory of dissimilar similitudes or likenesses which 'verge towards the absurd, and pernicious and impassioned.'[29] The divine revelation, then, is twofold: 'one ... proceeding through likenesses that are similar, and of a sacred character, but the other, through dissimilar forms, fashioning them into entire unlikeness and incongruity.'[30] Although Dionysius considers the sacred diction – words like 'godhead' and 'mind' – to be more reverent, he thinks it inferior to the material, dissimilar representation – the divine Messiah, for example, revealed under the image of a worm (Ps 22:7).[31] Dionysius favours such an incongruous metaphor because it seems to possess a greater power to elevate the mind than do the similitudes. The latter, since they might be mistaken for divinity itself, are, in a sense, more dangerous, more capable of inducing a kind of idolatry. The writers of holy scripture appear to have foreseen this difficulty. In order that men be not deceived, they introduce their readers to this paradoxical usage of language through the formulation of a base imagery that is meant to prod the soul to reach beyond the humble, earthen reality towards the heavenly. The inspired author has no fear that the lowly simile will be confused with God. All the same, such a figure is not entirely deprived of religious decorum because it is taken from God's creation, and, in so far as it has being, it participates in the beautiful: 'all things,' Dionysius announces, 'are very beautiful.'[32]

Even the incongruous and the lowly images bear some resemblance to God and paradoxically exercise a stronger attraction towards the heavenly. The same way of thinking extends to the metaphor of the sinner or the sinful excess. No act, according to Dionysius, can be evil under every one of its aspects. Despite his waywardness, the man 'who desires the very worst life, as wholly desirous of life and that which seems best to him, by the very fact of desiring, and desiring life, and looking to a best life, participates in the Good.'[33] Because even anger participates in this good, the scripture speaks of God's wrath, and because the intoxicating drink of wine originates in a creation that is good, Dionysius writes of the scripturally based divine carousals and inebriation.[34] So we have, in both the Bible and in Dionysius' interpretation of it, the deity and things divine represented under the metaphor of sinful action. In the same spirit, the *Moria* celebrates a festive madness of intemperate and mindless enjoyment only to have this image serve as an analogue for and introduction to the final vision of celestial ecstasy.

The Dionysian explanation of metaphor as it applies to the deity is formulated in the light of scriptural revelation upon which the author develops his theory. The figure of divine intoxication just mentioned is not infrequent in the Bible and in biblical commentary. The wine cellar of the Song of Songs and the numerous medieval glosses thereon represent two manifestations of this particular image. Christ compares his teachings to new wine (Matt 9:17), changes water into wine in symbolic gesture (John 2), and promises to drink the fruit of the vine in his kingdom (Luke 22:18). In the celebration of the eucharist, the wine signifies the form which the grace of the sacrament takes. The wine in holy communion announces the joy that God brings to the soul cleaving to him. The church understands the eucharist and reads its meaning through its very symbols. St Cyprian of Carthage stood firm against an enclave of prohibitionists who wanted to replace the wine of communion with water. He argued that water is not capable of producing a state of inebriation and reminded his reader of the sublime forgetfulness which the sacramental drink induces.[35] St Gregory of Nyssa writes of a heavenly intoxication whereby the soul is drawn out of itself. He speaks of a sleep in which the senses are lulled to rest under the influence of a supernatural attraction.[36] Erasmus, commenting on a verse from Acts (2:13), follows the same tradition when he writes of a spiritual drunkenness that brings on a forgetfulness of the sinful ways of one's earlier life ('inducit oblivionem praeteritorum malorum').[37] Likewise, in defending his *Moria*, Erasmus writes of Christ as 'intoxicated with the new wine of charity when he gave himself for us.'[38] The image of drink as developed in the book perhaps best captures the relationship between its festive language, which threatens to violate all decorum, and the essence of its spiritual utterance.

The cup flows generously in the *Moria* as the principal manifestation of that uninhibited and relaxed quality which drew the fire of the theologians when into this ambience of carnival the things of heaven were introduced. The complainers would have had no trouble finding passages of intoxication that border on riot. Folly herself was nursed at the breasts of Methe (Drunkenness), the daughter of Bacchus, that god who 'spends all his time partying, singing and dancing, having a good time.'[39] The nectar of the gods causes the ridiculous behaviour of the immortals when they gather at supper.[40] It was after a drinking bout that Plutus, Folly's drunken father, begot her on the goddess Neotes

(Youthfulness).[41] The lady fool defines her own madness as a kind of perpetual intoxication[42] and reminds us that the beginnings of life depend upon the drunken and absurd amusements of sex.[43] She orders the drinking of healths and the passing of cups to get any party started;[44] she prescribes wine[45] and a concoction of ignorance, thoughtlessness, and often forgetfulness to alleviate the tedium of old age.[46]

At the close of her speech and just before she sends her followers back to their tankards, Folly tells us that she hates a fellow drinker with a memory. Wine and oblivion are joined in this valediction just as they were in the body of the talk when Folly likened her spirit to 'perpetual intoxication' and added to that description thoughtlessness and forgetfulness, both effects of drinking. Now this mindless aspect comes to mean something more than mere vacuity in the later stages of the book. Even more important, two kinds of oblivion make up the essential parts of Folly's account of the redemption. Her view implies a certain lack of attention on the part of both the saviour and the saved in a compounding of follies, each different, yet both associated with the forgetfulness of the drinker.

When Folly analyses the causes for salvation, she first centres her attention on man, the recipient of the redemptive act. What in him draws down the divine mercy? The lady fool believes that man can win it only by pleading folly and ignorance.[47] She reinforces her argument with the testimony of the dying Christ's prayer to his Father to forgive his tormentors because 'they know not what they do.'[48] Two kinds of foolishness meet here, the human and the divine, the latter characterized by a form of forgetting similar to what we noticed about ecstasy. Folly cites the words of Paul to Timothy where the Apostle admits that he was granted God's mercy because he had acted in ignorance without full awareness of himself or his deeds.[49] Christ, the outcast, in his desolation, submits to death as if he were unaware of his origins. On the cross, one folly cancels the other, and foolish man's sin is forgotten in the sleep of the Fool's death.

Earlier, mention was made of the Saturnalian quality of riotous excess in the *Moria* when its theme of drinking and insobriety was interpreted as a metaphor for the limitless love of Christ in the sacrifice of his life for his fellow men. In his letter to Dorp, Erasmus suggests that the foolishness we associate with Christ has 'an element of weakness, something attributable to our natural affections, which when compared with that pure and eternal wisdom might seem less than wise.'[50] On the one hand, Erasmus seems to see in Christ a foolish outpouring of affection and, on the other, a divine serenity that remains foreign to such excess. The same dialectic of opposing qualities in the godhead is expounded by Dionysius when he writes about 'the Divine Peace and Repose' which paradoxically 'proceeds to all, whilst remaining entire within,'[51] and of 'the unmoved' who 'goes forth to all, and is *moved.*'[52] Divine wisdom, within itself, is appreciated as totally independent and sufficient – all perfect, all placid; but, when Dionysius reflects on God's motion beyond himself, the language of serenity is exchanged for a wording that borders on the foolish:

> One might make bold to say even this, on behalf of truth, that the very Author of all things, by the beautiful and good love of everything, through an overflow of His loving goodness, becomes out of Himself, by His providences for all existing things, and is, as it were, cozened by goodness and affection and love, and is led down from the Eminence above all, and surpassing all, to being in all, as befits an extatic [sic] superessential power centred in Himself. Wherefore, those skilled in Divine things call Him even Jealous ... as though the objects of His providential care were objects of jealousy for Him.[53]

The idea of a God who is cozened and jealous runs counter to one who transcends all things and is, therefore, totally remote. Erasmus, in the *Moria*, plays on this same paradox by portraying Christ as 'the wisdom of the Father' who foolishly assumes human flesh and becomes obedient to the Father's 'ratio crucis.'

CARNIVAL AND THE CHRISTIAN EXPERIENCE

Our investigation has led us through the history of the usage of metaphor and diction peculiar to works in the Judaeo-Christian tradition where the apparently indecorous is used to indicate the presence of beauty beyond our powers to express. A knowledge of the tradition, as well as helping us to understand Erasmus' defence of the *Moria* in the letter to Dorp, also serves as background for seeing how the bemused and jocular passages of part 1 cohere with the climax of part 3 in the sublime. We have already seen that Erasmus, in the Dorp letter, claimed to be following the same intention in writing the *Moria* that he had followed in the *Enchiridion*, the only difference being that the former was composed 'in a playful spirit.'[54] The *Enchiridion* overtly enunciates what the *Moria* joyously celebrates. Likewise, we have seen in chapter 7 that the *Enchiridion* exhorts its reader to mount from earthly to celestial reality.[55] We saw in the last chapter that Folly's speech was plotted according to a rising motion that begins with worldly joys and ascends towards the heavenly. This is the scaling action 'by the process of analogies' of which the *Enchiridion* speaks.[56] But what is the resemblance or the basis of the analogy between carnival riot with its vicious connotations in part 1 and the experience of the blessed that dominates the close of the work?

In her explication of Christian foolishness, Folly paraphrases 2 Corinthians (5:21) and claims that Christ 'became sin in order to heal sins.'[57] We are confronted here with a paradoxical figure, an external equation which in the end proves to be the opposite of what it literally says; yet the metaphor manages, despite all of its contrariety and puzzlement, to cast light upon the subject it is used to modify: 'Christ is sin.' For Erasmus, this would be one of those absurd sayings of scripture the inner sense of which is meant to be probed in order to taste the meat. To be sure, Christ is the criminal on the cross, the condemned, the outcast, the despised. But there is more. The crucifixion is the manifestation of the divine largess, infinity's invasion of human existence in the form of immeasurable, ungauging love. The word 'virtue' will simply not suffice to explain adequately the immensity of this reality. In this sense, God's presence in history overturns even man's most respectable efforts at conceiving his own moral life. The generosity of Christ's offering of himself for mankind resists being put into the words in which the ancient philosophers had couched ethical activity. In fact, it runs counter to such a terminology. Aristotle devotes the entire seventh book of the *Nicomachean Ethics* to the refinement of the concept of 'enkrateia,' a notion signifying human self-possession. The idea is not foreign to the New Testament, but it is not a master concept. In fact, a dominant idea arising from the Pauline meditation on the cross runs head-on into the concept of self-possession. M.A. Screech, in showing Erasmus' dependence on Origen for his theology of

foolishness, indicates that the divine folly is made manifest in the
kenosis of Christ, the self-emptying process which Paul beholds
in the birth and the death of the saviour.[58] The notion of kenosis,
in so far as it rubs against the psychology of a Greek understanding of virtue, bears a resemblance to vice, without, of course,
being so. The concept does not so much change the content of the
moral order as revolutionize our whole way of viewing this order.

Virtue conceived as self-possession lends itself less readily to
the Christian grasp of moral accomplishment than does virtue
understood as self-emptying. When Erasmus paraphrases the
scriptural passage (Phil 2:5–11) upon which the latter concept is
based, he dwells on the twofold aspect of the process: while the
Second Person of the Trinity humbles himself by taking on the
finite nature of man and undergoes a most painful and ignomini-
ous death as a criminal, his Father inaugurates the glorification of
the Son which rises out of his debasement. The action of the
Father, however, does not lessen the pain of emptiness and
abandonment in the heart of Christ upon the cross. In his last
agony, Christ hangs upon the gibbet, naked without and within,
the accused without honour, forsaken, it would seem, even by
his Father, and his person becomes the inspiration and source of
Christian living. The time of his dying is the hour of darkness, of
ignorance, of meaninglessness. To the folly of this void, then,
Christ subjects himself. This is the 'nada' of the mystics, the
non-being, the 'nihil,' out of which God recreates mankind, just
as he did in the beginning when out of nothing – 'ex nihilo' – he
made all things.

The Christian experience of kenosis reveals its painful aspect in
the crucifixion. But there is another side to this spiritual dyna-
mism, a side which the *Moria* treats when Folly describes the
heavenly delights of her blessed fools. The insanity ascribed to
celestial happiness is characterized by an outgoing impetus
answering to the traditional Christian understanding of ecstasy.
Man in beatitude, Folly tells us, will 'be outside himself, and will
be happy for no other reason than that he is located outside
himself, and will receive unspeakable joy from that Highest Good
which gathers all things to Himself.'[59] This is the madness of the
lover who loves so intensely that he 'no longer lives in himself but
rather in that which he loves, and the farther he gets from himself
and the closer to it, the happier he is.'[60] The life of the pious on
earth anticipates this condition, especially in their inclination to

exist beyond themselves, 'as if their minds were living somewhere else, not in their bodies.'[61] Even Folly, in her portrayal of
the heavenly madness, becomes so involved in her depiction that
she forgets herself.[62] All of this self-emptying indicates a form of
mental absence. Elsewhere in his writings, Erasmus says that the
proper attitude for the contemplation of the things of God
requires a mind emptied of everything else – 'omissis omnibus,
vacuus.'[63] This void in the soul supports the likeness between
beatitude and a comical kind of folly, a likeness based not only on
the superficial resemblance between vacancy of spirit and the
vacuity of the nonsensical fool, but more positively on the shared
quality of the truly comical and the intensely contemplative
moments in that each arrives, as it were, from nowhere –
spontaneous, unprogrammed, divorced from hard logic and
carefully planned thinking.

We have just seen the self-emptying quality of both Christian
joy and suffering. It is, as it were, the common ground and
unifying link to the pleasure and the pain which Erasmus
habitually runs together. Folly says that the saints 'throw away
their possessions, ignore injuries, allow themselves to be deceived, make no distinction between friend and foe, shudder at
the thought of pleasure, find satisfaction in fasts, vigils, tears,
and labors, shrink from life, desire death above all else – in short,
they seem completely devoid of normal human responses.'[64]
Obviously, this is madness to man's practical sense of things,
and, indeed, we need not think that Erasmus agrees with the
exaggeration in these statements. The joy that his saint finds in the
arduous is not sadistic or perverse. Folly tells us that the holy one
is emptied of personal appetite and envy, because he is oriented
towards 'living somewhere else.'[65] This notion is derived from a
dictum of St Bonaventure: 'the soul ... more truly belongs where
it loves than where it simply animates.'[66] This outgoing state of
soul, so typical of Christian madness in the *Moria*, also provides
the basis for the likeness or analogy between parts 1 and 3.

In part 1 of her speech, Folly establishes a set of antagonistic
elements similar to the psychological opposition already noted
between the Christian kenosis and the classical 'enkrateia.'
Folly's consistent enemy in part 1 is the Stoic 'who is completely
deaf to all human sentiment, who is untouched by emotion, no
more moved by love or pity than "a chunk of flint or a mountain
crag." '[67] This Senecan wise man eliminates 'all emotional pertur-

bations, as if they were diseases' and sets up a new ideal of manhood: a marble statue, 'utterly unfeeling and quite impervious to all human emotion.'[68] Against this self-encrusted concept of human happiness, Folly sends her own benign followers: the lover, the tippler, the boon companion. Which of these two types the Christian saint in heaven resembles should not be difficult to discover. Folly's celestial madness is amatory, ecstatic, and self-forgetting. Her depiction of the Stoic represents the very antithesis of the heavenly experience because the barren philosopher is sealed within himself without feeling or love. It is evident that the images of the book's early parts which relate most closely to its climax are paradoxically found among the disciples of Folly, who in their lovemaking, their drunkenness, and their recklessness better anticipate the final leap beyond reason than do their more respectable and ethical counterparts: the self-contained, the sober, the cautious. A soul in bliss fixes her gaze on the delightful object of her love, not unlike the husband who sees nothing but goodness in his beloved. A soul in bliss loses all awareness of herself, not unlike the old reveller who forgets himself and his boredom in drink. A soul in bliss has gone beyond the limits of the reasonable, not unlike the fool 'who is never restrained from any undertaking whatsoever – either by modesty (because he has none), nor by danger (to which he pays no attention).'[69] The orientation outward, characteristic of the lover, serves as the basis of the analogy between human and divine madness.

This analogy between the excesses of carnival joy and the ecstasy of the heavenly experience, based as it is on the common element of a strongly felt extroversion, amounts, in a sense, to but a superficial likeness. All the same, it contains an arresting and vital idea. Erasmus' conception of human fulfilment within a Christian frame of things bears this outward likeness to festivities connected with uninhibited licence. But the word 'carnival' itself means a farewell to meat, and this, in a transferred sense, is what the *Moria* is saying. It leads away from the flesh, not in itself, but as the norm for human conduct. The body of man in the work is not suppressed in the end but rather absorbed by the spirit which itself is absorbed by God.[70] This union does not mean disappearance, because the absorption results in an even stronger affirmation of individual identity. The remarkable thing about this picture is the intense joy which illuminates it. Christian existence is grasped as carnival because Erasmus' faith teaches him that the life of grace ultimately provides in reality that expansive happiness, that freedom and release, which man looks for in the extravagance of Saturnalian riot. The resemblance between carnivalesque pleasure and the consummation of Christian existence is valid because the latter partakes of a mind-stunning rapture beyond the power of words to tell.

THE *MORIA* AS CARNIVAL

The present study of Erasmus' *Moria* began in the preceding chapter with a discussion of the conflict between Christian and worldly folly, only to find, it would appear, in this chapter, a resemblance between the two in their common propensity towards extraversion and excess. The earthly folly of which we treat is of a specific nature and not to be taken in a broad, general sense. The foolishness that best bears comparison with Christian folly is carnivalesque, a festive joy which, like the heavenly one, delights in opposing itself to the powers of this world. Mikhail Bakhtin tells us that the 'carnival celebrated temporary liberation from the prevailing truth and from the established order; it marked the suspension of all hierarchical rank, privileges, norms, and prohibitions.'[71] Folly, herself, disrupts the society of her own day by attacking its highest spheres of power and then by inveighing against the notion of power itself in deferring to the divine weakness. In its own way, the *Moria* answers to that description of absolute comedy which Stephen Greenblatt draws of Marlovian drama with its will to play that flouts 'society's cherished orthodoxies, embraces what the culture finds loathsome or frightening, transforms the serious into a joke and then unsettles the category of the joke by taking it seriously.'[72] To be sure, the presence of Saturnalia has been modified by Erasmus, but its essence remains all the same. The *Moria* has been insightfully studied as a 'sermon joyeux' typified by a zany, turnabout logic and placed in its natural setting – the world of carnival.[73] This festive spirit of the work requires further reflection.

The *Moria*'s comedy is consciously universal in its range. As was pointed out in the last chapter, Erasmus wanted the *Moria* to reach out to folly in all of its manifestations.[74] He specifically mentions as examples of his all-inclusive topic kings, pontiffs, apostles, and Christ. In the course of his declamation, Erasmus pokes fun at his own people, his own calling, and himself as well.

This is the festive laughter of carnival and not that significative comedy of Baudelaire which depends on a presumption of superiority in the laughter for its success.[75] Bakhtin describes the more festive laughter as 'directed at all and everyone, including the carnival's participants. The entire world is seen in its droll aspect, in its gay relativity.'[76] For this reason, the same author can claim that the *Moria* is 'one of the greatest creations of carnival laughter in world literature.'[77]

The presence of grotesque imagery in the *Moria* tends to confirm the carnivalesque nature of the work. Its droll depiction of old men and old women falling in love like youngsters, its comparisons of men wiggling their ears like asses and strutting about like apes, inspired the lively imagination of the young Hans Holbein to realize visually the Erasmian grotesquerie present in the *Moria*.[78] The game of sex, which even the grave and solemn are forced to play should they desire offspring, is set down as a madness universal. Hence, 'endless jokes are provided by Priapus, that worthless fig-wood puppet' with its obscene proportions.[79] Silenus, the god who hides a mystery of depth, nevertheless is represented as a 'white-haired wooer' who 'dances a *frisky jig*.'[80] Animal imagery abounds even in the final section of the speech where Folly expounds on Christian foolishness. Christ shows a special love for animals the farthest removed from the sly fox, and so he rides the ass in his hour of triumph and calls his followers sheep, than whom, Folly assures us, 'No other animal is more stupid.'[81] And, in almost her next breath, she goes on to say that Christ himself 'delighted in the title "lamb."'[82]

Bakhtin maintains, 'The essential principle of grotesque realism is degradation, that is, the lowering of all that is high, spiritual, ideal, abstract; it is a transfer to the material level, to the sphere of earth.'[83] This degradation is seen corporeally when the 'upward' in question is the face or the head, and the 'downward' is the belly, the buttocks, or the genital area. The degradation is considered cosmically when heaven is lowered to earth. Bakhtin, in reference to this cosmic degradation, holds that the carnival spirit supports even the profanation of the sacred. The Erasmian sense of carnival would appear to find in the incarnation – the 'Christum ... stultum esse factum' – the basis for the grotesque style of the *Moria* that tends to support rather than scandalize faith although the imagery is meant to shock the intelligence. At the core of Erasmus' belief stands the Christ, the God become man and lowered to the shame and hideous torment of the cross. It is he who, in the words of Isaiah, has no beauty but who, in the words of John, draws all things to himself. The Erasmian grotesque agrees with Bakhtin's delineation of this genre in that it consists in degradation. But Erasmus, following a Christian tradition, seems to take his grotesque even further when the ambivalence of his art joins together in one reality an ugliness with a strange beauty.

According to Bakhtin, the mocking language of carnival that parodies the world outside of it aims both at burial and revival.[84] In imitation of the seasonal cycle on which it is based, the carnival commemorates the dying of nature and its rebirth. Because of this transformation, life and death are intimately linked, and mortality itself is conceived as pregnant. So the descent and degradation of the grotesque in a Saturnalian environment calls for a corresponding revitalization. The collusion of Folly with death in the *Moria* reveals a similar mentality in that the supreme foolishness of the crucified Christ leads to life. The wisdom of the Father takes on foolishness that he might 'relieve the folly of mortals.'[85] So Folly's paradoxical assertion about death being life[86] is proven true in the logic *à l'envers* of carnival. He who is highest becomes the lowest that he might lift up the powerless. The movement of Christian belief based on the descent and elevation indicated by the incarnation and resurrection lends itself readily to the Saturnalian order of things, and Erasmian comedy indicates a spontaneous recognition of the resemblance. An awareness of this order is implied in Erasmus' translation of Lucian's *Saturnalia* and is shown to be assumed into his art of composition in pieces like the 'Scarabeus aquilam quaerit' and the *Concio de puero Jesu*. The *Moria*'s victory of Christian foolishness over the frigid, self-centred wisdom of the Stoic provides still another example of Erasmus' fondness for the overthrow that characterizes carnival.

The main concerns of the grotesque comedy under discussion have to do with overturning, bringing down, and lifting up. The festive laughter provoked in such action is associated with what Baudelaire calls 'le comique absolu.'[87] In commenting on this distinction, Morton Gurewitch says that the absolutely comic, 'embodying the spirit of the grotesque, defies utilitarian common sense and shuns the moralization of laughter.'[88] The *Moria*, in its higher ranges, deftly refutes the opinion of those many critics who wish to reduce Erasmus to a moralist pure and simple. The interest of the work is less to teach than to celebrate. It is adventurous and daring and, in the spirit of 'le comique absolu,' shows little concern for the golden mean and far more for the extreme. The work takes us to the regions of madness and peers into the void of human existence. When Erasmus shows us that man's folly and his mortality are one and the same, he entertains a kind of nihilism that threatens to silence all mirth. 'Yet,' according to Gurewitch, 'when comedy, on that very verge, can play with sepulchral laughter directed against itself as well as against the nature of things, virtually a blooming miracle occurs.'[89] Such a statement again suggests the descending and rising motion of grotesque humour. The laughter which Baudelaire claims has ensued from the fall can, he says, play a salutary role in man's redemption.[90]

In celebrating nonsense, the *Moria* would appear to be a champion of meaninglessness. This vacuity is first asserted by Folly's careless self-contradiction in the opening passages of her speech. In the middle sections, significance is again threatened when Folly turns on herself by attacking her own followers. The nonsense reaches its culmination at the close of the speech in Folly's paean to an ecstasy the meaning of which is unfathomable and where the Self loses its psychological awareness in the Other. At this moment of climax, sense vanishes within the infinite, the moral is lost in wonder, and righteousness is overwhelmed by the riotous.

TEN

'The Uproars of Comedies
Always End in Marriage'

The title for this chapter is taken from Erasmus' colloquy 'A Fish Diet,' where the interlocutors, a fishmonger and a butcher, are conversing about the affairs of princes.[1] As in a comedy, so in the serious affairs of the great, marriage tends to resolve the difficulties that confront the people concerned. Once again, Erasmus returns to a favourite image of life as theatre and, in this case, the joining of a happy outcome to a marital tie reflects the author's belief concerning the end towards which history moves. The destiny of the human race is a union between Christ, the saviour, and his spouse, the people mystically united in that mystery we call the church. The comic dénouement to this cosmic drama is held and supported by Erasmus' belief and not by any optimistic assessments based upon observing the conduct of his contemporaries. He brooded over the religious upheavals of his times and despaired of a settlement of the disputes without divine intervention. His understanding of the end of the life of the individual likewise is a realist's view of the human predicament and of man's susceptibility to fearful torment in his passage from the stage of life.[2] Only belief in the divine power to transform and to make new stimulated within Erasmus the hope that looked forward to the festive restoration of all things in Christ.

The restoration that is looked for is conceived as a coupling between the saviour and his spouse, the church. The matrimonial image of the end of history seems to have influenced Erasmus' thinking about the human institution of marriage. In fact, marriage on the human plane and marriage at the mystical level tend to complement one another: each casts a light on its counterpart. The nuptial union of man's soul with his God indelibly impressed upon Erasmus' mind the sacred character of the union between the sexes. Because he saw the creator's hand in the movement of one sex towards the other, he spontaneously made use of this natural image in exploring the mystery of the higher coming together of the soul and of the church with the deity. In this final chapter, then, we shall examine the comic pieces of Erasmus that treat of marriage with an eye to seeing how they accord with and anticipate the final consummation between Christ and the people of God. In a kind of résumé of the preceding chapters, we shall study the colloquies dealing with marriage and the declamation in praise of it in order to show how these frothy 'opuscula' portray in a comical manner an outlook and attitude that conform with Erasmus' belief about the ultimate end awaiting mankind.

The present chapter is not intended to be only a résumé of the comic materials found in the colloquies and the declamations now gathered under the single rubric of 'marriage.' It is this but also something more. Erasmus' spirited compositions on the subject of wedlock drew more fire from his enemies than any other topic on which he wrote. His *Encomium matrimonii*, when it was finally published in 1518, initiated a series of debates which was to last for years.[3] Erasmus' constant ruse was to defend the piece as trivial, a product of his 'schola declamationis,' not worth the time and consideration that the theologians were giving it. The author makes fun of those graybeards for taking a light, comical work so seriously; but, as we shall see, the content of the *Encomium matrimonii* elicits a response from the theologians because it focuses on matters that concern them. Erasmus' tactic in the controversy is to maintain, for the most part, a comic tone, not because the subject lacks seriousness, but because he wants to deliver the issue from the tribunal of the prejudiced and the intolerant. He wants the freedom to introduce fresh ideas on a subject that had been restricted for too long within a celibate caste system. The strategy of playing down the importance of the *Encomium matrimonii* is really an attempt to introduce a less ponderous, less authoritarian, and less violent tone into a debate over questions that deeply concerned the church. Erasmus seems to have sensed the dangerous consequences of the bad-tempered polemics of his day. By studying his marriage works and his defence of them, we can better understand how his playfulness contends against the violent anathemas hurled at the author by his opponents.

Furthermore, the investigation of Erasmus' thought about and literary treatment of marriage may serve to correct the impression that his Platonic ideas compromised his Christian belief. There is no doubt that, in his concern for the soul and its fulfilment, Erasmus is sometimes distracted from the incarnational element of his faith. From some of his statements, we might feel obliged to conclude that the body exists merely to be denied and subjected as a thrall to the interest of the spirit. Such a judgment fails to take into consideration the positive role, for instance, that corporeal activity plays in Erasmus' conception of the growth and budding sense of affection in the infant child. The 'Puerpera' insists upon the importance of maternal breast-feeding because Erasmus has a keen sense of the body's importance in the transmission of love. In the *Querela pacis*, he stresses the intimate knitting of soul to body.[4] Still, a tendency to discard the flesh rather than to incorporate it into the whole of the human being sometimes disturbs the consistency of his thought. In the *Moria*, for instance, Folly, on the one hand, will castigate the Stoic for stifling his emotions, the very 'guides to those who are hastening to the haven of wisdom'; on the other hand, she will tell us that the saints are known to be such because 'they pay no attention to the body'[5] and seem to be incapable of natural affection towards their own kind. Of course, Erasmus could deny his approbation of what Folly says, but the unsettling dichotomy between body and soul does find frequent expression in his serious works, as David Marsh's essay has made apparent.[6] All the same, this is not the whole story, and I hope that a look into the comic writings pertaining to love and the state of wedlock will redress the balance by showing us an Erasmus who conceives of corporeal functions in terms of the body's cooperation with and participation in the life of the spirit.

THE MARRIAGE COLLOQUIES

In Erasmus' 'Marriage Group' of colloquies are found two that heighten the opposition between the celibate calling of the cloister and the state of matrimony. These dialogues, the 'Virgo misogamos' and the 'Virgo poenitens' are really two scenes from a single little drama about the seventeen-year-old Catherine, who believes that she has been called to become a nun. She confesses this to Eubulus, a young man who is very much interested in her. From a literary point of view, the debate between Eubulus and Catherine over her entering a convent is marred by the author's didactic interests. Weighing down the 'Virgo misogamos' with his own complaints about monastic life, Erasmus has Eubulus deliver these opinions in a series of rather tedious sermonettes. As a character, Catherine suffers by comparison with Margaret, who livens chapter 11 of the *De contemptu mundi*. This latter young lady, in a similar situation, shows much more independence of mind in following her religious vocation and betrays none of Catherine's preoccupation with saving her precious virginity. In the 'Virgo poenitens,' Catherine does come to life as she recounts to Eubulus the merry events that led her into the convent and back home again. Along the way, we encounter boozing monks, reluctant parents, and a covey of nuns who appear to have staged a vision for the novice in the form of a 'horrible-looking specter.'[7] The second colloquy improves upon the first because Catherine's own account of what happened to her has replaced the sermonizing of Eubulus. In the end, we are not told just why Catherine has left the convent. This remains a secret for Eubulus to divine.

In the 'Virgo misogamos,' marriage is described by Eubulus as a kind of religious community without the rigidity and severe regulation that are found in the convent. In the *Colloquies*, Erasmus does not attempt to make a one-sided case for matrimony by confining himself to its joys and perfections. The 'Coniugium impar' rages over the guile of an old, pox-ridden troll who has foisted himself upon an unsuspecting girl, and, in 'Coniugium,' Xanthippe, a disillusioned young wife, complains about her husband's drinking, whoring, and gambling. Yet, one senses in the 'Marriage Group' as a whole an optimistic approach to the possibilities of the wedded life that encourages a comic spirit which achieves its fullest expression in 'Proci et puellae.'

It may well be that, as a character, Maria, the girl whose hand is sought by Pamphilus in 'Proci et puellae,' is the most memorable female persona in the *Colloquies*. Her lively sense of humour never abandons her even when she argues in defence of her virginity. With good reason has Craig R. Thompson said that she is 'a delightful creature, comparable in poise, intelligence, and wit to the women in Shakespeare's romantic comedies. It would be hard to point to another girl of her qualities in pre-Elizabethan literature.'[8] What adds to the delight of the dialogue is Pamphilus, the suitor whom Erasmus has coupled with Maria. He is her match in wit and he develops his arguments in a playful spirit for the most part. He thereby avoids the heavy-handed, moral tones of Eubulus in 'Virgo misogamos.'

The drama of the colloquy begins when Pamphilus assumes the part of a wooer who has been so stricken by love that he has despaired of life and died. Only Maria can revive him, and, unless she does, she will prove herself the most cruel of women. Maria gives no credit to these hyperboles. Dead men do not walk and eat as Pamphilus does.

MARIA. Poor you! Yet all the time you're putting on weight. And do dead men talk, too?
PAMPHILUS. Like me, in a very thin, squeaky voice.
MARIA. When I heard you wrangling with your rival not long ago, though, your voice wasn't so thin and squeaky. But I ask you, do ghosts even walk? Wear clothes? Sleep?
PAMPHILUS. They even sleep together – though after their own fashion.
MARIA. Well! Witty fellow, aren't you?[9]

Amid the give and take of this banter, the author himself seems to join the game he has created by means of his characters and begins to play with and to entertain ideas dear to him. Listen to Pamphilus insist on the death that Maria has caused him to die.

PAMPHILUS. Men seized by a divine inspiration neither hear nor see nor smell nor feel, even if you kill them.
MARIA. Yes, I've heard that.
PAMPHILUS. What do you suppose is the reason?
MARIA. You tell me, professor.
PAMPHILUS. Obviously because their spirit is in heaven, where it possesses what it ardently loves, and is absent from the body.
MARIA. What of it?
PAMPHILUS. What of it, you unfeeling girl? It follows both that I'm dead and that you're the murderer.
MARIA. Where's your soul, then?
PAMPHILUS. Where it loves.[10]

Erasmus introduces into this light conversation the notion of ecstasy that we saw in the *Moria*. The lover lives not in himself but in the other, the object of his love. The arguments of Pamphilus do not defeat Maria. She concedes playfully that her suitor is dead but not because of her.

When Pamphilus ceases to plead the case of his living death, he soon turns to a direct proposal of marriage. One senses throughout the latter part of the dialogue that Maria is more than ready to accept Pamphilus, but she, nonetheless, plays a waiting game and refuses to grant her lover's request until the marriage can be formally arranged with the approbation of their parents. As a delaying tactic, she broods over the loss of chastity consequential to marriage. In return, Pamphilus lays stress on married chastity, which he conceives as a way of advancing to a kind of virginity. Maria cannot fathom this. Is virginity to be lost in order to be won? Pamphilus sees no reason why not. We have here an example of Erasmian paradox certain to awaken the anger of his enemies, and, on the other hand, a comic insight into the destiny of married love as ordained by God. Carnal knowledge is not understood as a necessary impediment to chastity. Pamphilus, in fact, argues for sexual intercourse as downright virtuous.

PAMPHILUS. Which more truly deserves praise for chastity, the man who castrates himself or the one who, while sexually unimpaired, nevertheless abstains from sexual love?
MARIA. My vote would go to the latter. The first I'd regard as mad.
PAMPHILUS. But don't those who renounce marriage by a strict vow castrate themselves, in a sense?
MARIA. Apparently.
PAMPHILUS. Now to abstain from sexual intercourse isn't a virtue.
MARIA. Isn't it?
PAMPHILUS. Look at it this way. If it were a virtue per se not to have intercourse, intercourse would be a vice. Now it happens that it *is* a vice *not* to have intercourse, a virtue to have it.
MARIA. When does this 'happen'?
PAMPHILUS. Whenever the husband seeks his due from his wife.[11]

The paradoxical play on ideas with intercourse being virtuous and abstention vicious seems almost consciously designed to arouse the celibate clergy, and, of course, it succeeded. Erasmus, in answering the censures of the Sorbonne concerning 'Proci et puellae,' appealed to the dialogue's dramatic nature. Pamphilus is speaking as a young man in love; he is not the mouthpiece for his creator.[12] So, in one sense, Erasmus divorces himself from his character and considers it absurd to entertain a notion that carnal knowledge leads to virginity. He is rather of the mind of his other persona, Maria, who can only ridicule Pamphilus' suggestion. In spite of the joke and its absurdity, the young man's argument follows a line of Erasmus' own thought when he states the similarity between marriage and virginity and draws attention to the teaching that Christian marriage is meant to serve a form of chastity and not unbounded lust.

The comic spirit of 'Proci et puellae' arises out of Erasmus' deep conviction about the soundness of human emotion and affection. Faith in man as created by a benign God lies at the source of his optimism. Erasmus does not deny Adam's fall and the weakness that ensues from it. He is most ready to admit that man is capable of viciousness in the extreme, but he does not allow this awareness to undermine his faith in the latent goodness of human nature. He enjoys expressing this belief in paradox. Unlike many of his clerical contemporaries, Erasmus conceives of the act of love between man and woman in the most positive terms. It too partakes of the restoration of fallen man. In the 'Coniugium,' Eulalia emphasizes to the disillusioned Xantippe the vital part played by sexual intercourse in reviving a flagging marital love.

'Coniugium' opens with Xantippe complaining to Eulalia about her husband Nicholas and wishing that there were some way of being rid of him. Drunk and disgusting, the man comes home, rolls into bed and snores out the night. The plot of the dialogue follows Eulalia's argument to Xantippe on behalf of salvaging her friend's deteriorating marriage. Eulalia counsels Xantippe to cease her constant carping about the behaviour of her husband. As Xantippe admits, her verbal abuse has driven Nicholas to the threat of murderous blows in retaliation for her tongue-lashings. Although the colloquy advocates an attitude of submission in woman alien to the modern outlook, it also sees her role as the one who forms and reforms man. The metamorphosis is explained in comical and sexual terms.

Eulalia tells Xantippe how she trained her own husband once she had noticed that there would be problems if she did not. She would adapt herself to him in order to avoid any unpleasantness. She paid special attention to 'what soothed and irritated him, as do those who tame elephants and lions or suchlike creatures that can't be forced.'[13] Xantippe enjoys the comparison.

> XANTIPPE. That's the sort of creature I have at home!
> EULALIA. Those who approach elephants don't wear white, and those who approach bulls don't wear red, because these beasts are known to be enraged by such colors. Likewise tigers are driven so wild by the beating of drums that they tear their own flesh. And trainers of horses have calls, whistles, caresses, and other means of soothing mettlesome animals. How much more fitting for us to use those arts on our husbands, with whom, whether we like it or not, we share bed and board for our entire lives.[14]

The animal imagery of this passage reflects the comic spirit in which the theme of metamorphosis, wrought by adaptation and love, is developed within the 'Coniugium.' The training in character is not one-sided. Man mends woman too, and the transformation again is presented wittily. Eulalia tells the tale of a young wife's rebellious flouting of the desires of her spouse. The husband accompanies her home where he begs the assistance of his father-in-law. The girl's father draws her aside and turns on her irately. He berates his daughter in such scalding terms that she falls on her knees and begs his pardon for being such an unfeeling spouse. The father has played his part well, and the daughter mends her ways. This story unravels in the manner of a domestic comedy and concludes with the two people enjoying the happiness of loving union. Even the strategic turning point in the girl's conduct is achieved by a cunning father 'capable of playing any comedy without a mask.'[15] The game serves as remedy to a serious problem in life.

When Eulalia focuses on woman's power to change man, she emphasizes the charm of her sexual attraction. She refers again to classical mythology and recalls the powers of Circe to change men into beasts and then claims that Xantippe can turn Nicholas 'from drunk to sober, spendthrift to thrifty, idler to worker.'[16] In order to effect such a change, all carping must cease and anger must give way to love. The victory of love over wrath is confirmed in sexual intercourse.

> EULALIA. ... Above all, in my judgment, you must be careful not to start an argument in the bedroom or in bed, but try to see that everything there is pleasant and agreeable. If that place, which is dedicated to dispelling grudges and renewing love, is profaned by any contention or bitterness, every means of recovering good will is clean gone. Some women are so peevish that they even quarrel and complain during sexual intercourse and by their tactlessness render disagreeable that pleasure which ordinarily rids men's minds of whatever vexation may be therein – spoiling the very medicine that could have cured their ills.[17]

The act of sexual love dissolves the spirit of rancour so harmful to the marital union and makes firm the knot which God has tied.

The comic vision of marriage in both 'Proci et puellae' and 'Coniugium' understands sexual love as a transforming power. It is conceived as issuing from the hand of its creator and working towards the goal for which he designed such love. The man and the woman are to cleave together so that out of two people a oneness may be formed. The procreative act by implication is an extension of the creative act and is involved deeply with a scheme of being that is cosmic. The above colloquies presuppose this way of thinking without ever declaring such ideas openly. Erasmus becomes more explicit about his thought on marriage in the *Encomium matrimonii* and in his apologiae on behalf of this work.

THE *ENCOMIUM MATRIMONII*

The *Encomium matrimonii* partakes of a comic spirit even more expansive than that of the marriage colloquies. The exaggeration found in its introductory paragraphs tells us clearly that we are not encountering here a serious treatise. We are rather reading an informal letter from one friend to another. The addressee has just lost his mother, and the sadness following upon this loss has caused both him and his sister to flee the world and commit themselves to the barren rule of the celibate life. The writer of the letter makes it clear from the start that he intends to dissuade his friend from this desperate move. He mentions that he first heard of it while dining at the home of one Antonius Baldus and that, as the news broke, the dining table was turned from a place of convivial joy to one of sorrow with tears breaking out on all sides. This excessive reaction to a friend's retirement into religious solitude warns us that the author's approach to his work is something other than tense and high-strung.

After his introduction, our anonymous correspondent begins his unqualified panegyric to matrimony. As instituted by God, as honoured by Christ, as exalted by the church, marriage has been removed from the realm of the profane and made sacred. Even the laws of men – Hebrews, Greeks, Romans – have all sought to revere and protect the marital bond and to reward those couples who have contributed a large number of children towards the well-being and prosperity of the community. More fundamentally, the law of nature itself has instilled in all living things the desire to propagate. Plants and animals as well as men follow the instinct to reproduce their own kind; and propagation, especially in the case of man, has been surrounded with delight because of the charms of his spouse. The woman is the joy of man not only in the marriage act but in the entire course of his life. So writes our panegyrist:

> When you are at home, the lady will be there to dispel the tedium of loneliness. When going abroad, she it is who attends your departure with a kiss and who longs for you in your absence and who greets you joyfully when you return, she, the sweet companion of your youth and the charming comfort of your old age. Any companionship is naturally pleasant to man. Will not this be the most pleasant of all where everything will be shared together?[18]

The roseate picture extends even to in-laws. 'Nature,' he writes, 'can give us only one mother, one father. By marriage, another father, another mother are added who, because they have entrusted to you their own flesh, must needs become dear to you by reason of this singular tie.'[19]

Granting that we have in the *Encomium matrimonii* a tribute to the wedded state that moves beyond the limits of serious credibility, there is nothing in this sportive exaltation of the subject to arouse the indignation of the clergy, were this all there were in the piece. Present, however, as the weft to the warp of praise, is an equally exaggerated attack on the celibate life. From the outset it is described as sterile, and, from this inauspicious beginning, matters grow steadily worse. Sterility suggests an incompatibility with life and the life-bearing process. The incompatibility evolves into a positive hostility as celibacy is linked to disease, to the plague, and to death.[20] If the Mosaic Law cursed sterility because it yielded no offspring, what are we to think of a way of life which refuses the responsibility of producing and rearing children? As the enemy of life, the celibate is condemned for being in a violent rebellion against nature. Even the pagans know this and reflect this awareness in the tales they tell. The fable of those giants of old who laboured to build mountains into the sky that they might wage war against the gods is taken as a metaphor for those proud creatures who reject their own nature as men in following the angelic life of celibacy that they might win heaven. In so doing, they become enemies of God for attempting to advance beyond their own limitations. The ancient poets also tell the story of Orpheus, who, by the sound of his music, was able to move rocks. 'What does this signify?' asks Erasmus, or rather the character within his fiction. 'It means that a wise and eloquent man of spirit was able to restrain his fellows who were living like senseless stones and practising the customs of beasts – such men, I say, he restrained from their irresponsible habit of concubinage and drew them to accept the most holy laws of matrimony.'[21]

We need proceed no farther to discern what in the *Encomium matrimonii* might arouse the temper of the established priesthood. In the last example of men living according to a religiously sanctioned custom of animals – 'ritu ferrarum' in the Latin – we discover a thinly veiled reference to the immoral habits of many priests in sixteenth-century Europe. When the celibate character is described as self-centred, hardened to a crusted state of insensitivity, hostile to a natural, God-given instinct, and opposed to life itself, Erasmus could hardly expect that this portrait would go unnoticed or unanswered by his priestly confrères. In the light of the contents of the *Encomium matrimonii*, the attack of Jean Briard at Louvain, the Sorbonne condemnation, and Josse Clichtove's polemic all seem inevitable.

Erasmus' *Encomium matrimonii* caused its author no end of trouble and made enemies for him in the ranks of many formidable champions of Roman Catholicism. Under the pressure of their assaults, Erasmus never recanted, never formally disowned the work. He felt no need. In his mind the little book had been misinterpreted from the start. So he writes to Briard in the *Apologia de laude matrimonii* and fourteen years later to Clichtove in the *Dilutio*.[22] In this latter reply, he points to the dramatic nature of the *Encomium matrimonii*. It is, he claims, a declamation, and the voice of the one declaiming is that of a character created by Erasmus whose ideas are not necessarily to be identified with those of the author. Erasmus accuses Clichtove of mistaking him for the persona who exists only in a fiction. 'Do not imagine,' he tells his opponent, 'that Erasmus is speaking to someone else. No. A layman talks to a layman.'[23] In this way the author attempts to deflect the charge of heresy from himself and towards his character. Furthermore, Erasmus says that it is the intent of his declamation to discuss matters that are arguable, so his persona does not pronounce, as it were, *ex cathedra*, but speaks modestly as befits one who does not possess the truth.[24] Rather he seeks it. Finally, because the declamation is a rhetorical exercise by which the minds of students may be trained, it contains some false arguments in order that the pupils may keep a sharp lookout for them and learn to refute them.[25] If, then, Clichtove remains insensitive to the declamatory nature of the *Encomium matrimonii*, he will inevitably misinterpret it.

Another cause for misunderstanding arises from an incorrect reading of the terms 'celibate' and 'celibacy.' Erasmus informs Clichtove that celibacy means the single life but not necessarily a life of continence. 'Horace,' he says, 'calls himself celibate even though he was far from being continent.'[26] The best Latin usage indicates that the word signifies the bachelor state, a freedom from wedlock, and nothing more. Erasmus attacks Clichtove for confusing the issue and for making it seem that his book ridicules continence and not the single life. Whenever my 'declamation speaks against celibates,' he complains, 'it is thought I mean the continent.'[27] Nothing could be further from the truth. On the surface, Erasmus insists that 'to be celibate' does not mean 'to be continent.' Just beneath that surface, of course, we detect the suggestion that not only does 'to be celibate' not mean 'to be continent' but also that the real celibate is not. 'Monks and priests,' writes Erasmus, 'by their vows, do not reject incontinence – that is permitted to no one – but only marriage.'[28] In defending the innocence of his book, Erasmus manages to question the innocence of those vowed to a life of perpetual chastity.

Another ruse used by the humanist to free his book from the charge of heresy is to deny that it had any pretensions whatever to being theological. 'I write,' he says at the beginning of his *Dilutio*, 'a declamation, a rhetorical exercise, having nothing to do with the rule of faith or morals.'[29] Much as he would like to remove the *Encomium matrimonii* from the domain of theology, the subject matter of the work, although not developed weightily and seriously, teems with suggestions that invite further discussion and probing by theologians. For instance, when Erasmus' speaker says that living virtuously means 'to follow the lead of nature,' the theologian would question, as Clichtove did, the author's understanding of nature.[30] On arguing about this passage, the two men were forced to discuss nature graced and nature fallen, the good and evil aspects of the sex drive, and the moral nature of the shame associated with the organs of reproduction. All this is fair game for the theologian. Obviously, the *Encomium matrimonii* cannot be divorced from a theological interest. So it is by no means clear how we are to understand Erasmus when he writes: 'I declare, I do not theologize' and 'I argue as a rhetorician sometimes, sometimes as a statesman ... always as one thinking and discussing, otherwise I would be working out a theological proof.'[31] In this last citation, one who examines is contrasted to one who proves; the rhetorician engages in the former, the theologian in the latter. One meaning of Erasmus' denial of writing theology in the *Encomium matrimonii* issues from this distinction: where the theologizer solemnly pronounces, his little book wittily and light-heartedly converses. Listen to Erasmus' description of Clichtove's book attacking him: 'Now a theologian laboriously answers in a ponderous tome the first part of my little declamation and attaches to his work the magnificent title of *Propugnaculum ecclesiae*, as if this affair were of the utmost seriousness.'[32] At the very start of his refutation of Clichtove, Erasmus laughs at his opponent for suiting himself in armour to do battle with shadows. Because Erasmus' encomium of marriage was not written in total seriousness, the author considered that a serious defence of it would be incongruous. In both the original work and the ensuing defences of it, Erasmus repeats that, for the most part, he is playing and will not be drawn into the thick of an earnest and grave theological slugfest.

Of course, it may be objected, as it has been so often in the past, that Erasmus, in wanting to give this debate a ludic turn, loses all credibility as a theologian and perhaps even as a sincere Christian. Once again the presupposition seems to be that the man of truth asserts seriously, even majestically, and dismisses anyone wanting to engage him in a play of mind. Yet, how often, in the study of the theological debates of the sixteenth century, we encounter tracts inspired less by a truly religious conviction than by decidedly wounded feelings. All authors, even those dedicated to the cause of religion, can easily mistake their own wrath for that of heaven, especially during a violent controversy. Northrop Frye's observation about the devil with whom every writer must contend applies in particular to authors arguing over doctrinal issues:

> There is also in every poet, as in every man, an ego that wants to harangue and buttonhole, to sound off and impress, to impose opinions and project fantasies, to make enemies squirm and friends glorious by association. The only indecency known to literature is the exhibition of the author's naked ego.[33]

Often enough in the steamy atmosphere of the great Reformation polemic, we experience more heat than light, more anger than grace, more aggression than sound and generous persuasion. On this point, we may profit from the different stances assumed by the two contenders in the dispute we are reviewing.

Clichtove, the grave defender of Christian orthodoxy, assumes the traditional role of the learned professor dedicated to the faith and the pursuit of serious study. At first sight, this gives him a considerable advantage over the elflike Erasmus; however, like all serious people, especially when caught in an argument over religion or politics or whatever they hold dear, Clichtove tends to become too serious. He grows so outraged that he loses the perspective and clarity necessary to convince the less serious reader. By contrast, the playful Erasmus is moderate and even-tempered. Clichtove, in a myopic and prurient reading of Erasmus' text accuses it of being sexually titillating. Erasmus points to the circumspection and propriety of the work in this regard.[34] The severity of Clichtove's attack may be traced back to the severity of his belief. He associates the sex drive with sin, while Erasmus sees it as natural.[35] Clichtove is more ready to stress the shameful side of this appetite and the bodily parts pertaining to it. Erasmus also admits to the shame but adds that a good deal of this embarrassment 'arises from the words and instructions of grownups who shout at children to cover up and not shame themselves.'[36] Throughout the debate Erasmus is surprisingly self-contained. The wit and humour of the man indicates that he has preserved the distance necessary for beholding the subject he is treating. Clichtove, on the other hand, becomes so incensed that he sometimes loses his hold on his own position. For instance, in one place he maintains that the rule of sacerdotal celibacy is of divine origin and, therefore, absolute and unchangeable.[37] Erasmus reminds him that the Greek church does not know this law and that for many years the Latin church was ignorant of it too.[38] When we set the light spirit of Erasmus against the heavy one of Clichtove, we begin to see a kind of wisdom in the former's playfulness.

Furthermore, it should be noted that Erasmus engages in a parody of himself when he launches his exaggerated attack on celibacy. He too is one of the horrible company of bachelors. He is detached enough to make sport of himself. This freedom and play are meant to involve the reader and not merely to distract him. Recall that in the *Encomium matrimonii* he includes defective arguments to keep his reader's mind awake. Elsewhere he says, 'Things should be written not in such a manner that everyone understands everything but that they be forced to investigate and discover certain things on their own.'[39] Erasmus' style, with its play on words, its ironic, double-pronged statements, is aimed at engaging the reader's attention. Sometimes he will shock by using a paradox. In the *Encomium matrimonii* he maintains that a man 'does not castrate himself who lives the single life but rather the man who cherishes and lives the married life.'[40] He later explains to Clichtove his own understanding of the paradox. 'I mean,' he writes, 'that a great amount of chastity can be had in marriage if it does not serve lust.'[41] The thought here approaches the paradoxical argument of Pamphilus in 'Proci et puellae' when he tells Maria that virginity is won by losing it. Erasmus entertains the possibility of a form of purity in marriage to get his reader to entertain it too. Virginity as described by Augustine is an integrity of body.[42] What Erasmus hints at is an integrity of soul. The kind of integrity achieved by the marriage act itself is suggested by Thomas Aquinas when treating the nature of friendship: 'Friendship is more permanent when the give and take is equal and identical, for instance, pleasure for pleasure.'[43] What solidifies friendship for Aquinas is shared pleasure. In another passage he says that 'there seems to be the greatest friendship between husband and wife, for they are united ... in the act of fleshly union, which produces a certain gentle association.'[44] The marriage act itself, then, as long as it remains an act of love in which pleasure is shared and not exploited, fosters that same spiritual integrity that the virgin seeks by her 'integritas carnis.'

In defending his *Encomium matrimonii,* Erasmus often argues playfully about a position that he appears to take seriously. Yet he makes no claim that his stand is necessarily the correct one. He does not dogmatize. 'I declaim,' he tells us and immediately adds, 'I do not teach theology,' as if he wishes to divorce his rhetorical piece from the discipline of theology.[45] A few paragraphs later, however, he calls the *Encomium matrimonii* a 'theologica declamatio.'[46] It seems that Erasmus is being as careless about consistency as Folly was in her own declamation. But upon closer examination, we find that Erasmus has not contradicted himself here. If we return to the first of these two passages, we discover that he has not separated the work from theology but rather from authoritative pronouncement. 'Declamo,' reads the Latin, 'non doceo Theologiam.' 'Theology' is the object of both declaiming and teaching. In the first case, an idea is meant to be entertained and discussed openly; in the second, the idea is presented for our acceptance as a matter already settled. Clichtove is irritated because Erasmus writes on a topic like celibacy as if the issue had not already been divinely instituted and fixed for all time. Erasmus has no business writing a declamation that involves the practice of celibacy; that is, he should not have opened a case which has already been tried and judged.

In chapter 4, while considering the decorum of treating religious matters comically, I laid stress on the significance of the 'schola declamatoria,' Erasmus' classroom for debate where theological topics, already reduced to the frivolous, could be reclaimed in a joyous spirit that both exposed the folly of theologians and exulted in the limitless expanses of heavenly reality. Erasmus introduces theological issues into this lower school out of a desire to encourage a more open-minded and less intolerant ambience in a discipline that was already suffering from a tendentious will on the part of its practitioners to dominate and to libel. The 'schola' provides a playground adjacent to the more imposing halls of theology where the august subject, debased by contention, could be purged of the myopic absurdities to which it was being subjected and where the truly magnificent stretch of its vision could be hinted at. Clichtove's morose understanding of marriage illustrates the debasement to which theology could be reduced. Erasmus, by persisting in his spirit of play and by refusing to reply in kind to the outraged Clichtove, attempts to confine the debate to the 'schola declamationis' where it belongs. But as long as we remain within the limits of an argument directed against a theologian with a cramped understanding of human sexuality, we shall fail to see the symbolic richness towards which Erasmus' thought drives. To enjoy this higher perspective, we must relate what has been said in the 'schola declamatoria' to passages in the scriptural commentaries and other serious works.

BEGINNING AND END

Until now we have considered Erasmus' playfully optimistic views of the potential that lies within human sexuality. The marriage act functions as an agent in love's metamorphosis whereby the distant, erring, disgruntled spouse is made a benign partner. Virginity is lost in wedlock only to be retrieved. One form of integrity is given in love that the partners may win another through chastity. Still, it would be wrong to conclude that Erasmus' view of marriage was so uncritical as to make it naïvely optimistic. One whole section of the *Encomium matrimonii* dwells on the risks a man runs in marrying and, thereby, brings us much closer to the complex realities of the institution.[47] Although we have been tracing one positive and dominant line in his thought, we need not deny that on occasion a kind of puritanical uneasiness about the marriage act arises in Erasmus, as when he insists that its pleasures are licit only if the couple have a child in mind, a sort of stricture not unlike the English mother's advice to her daughter for the wedding night: 'Just close your eyes and think of England.'[48] Even here, though, there is a more positive way of understanding Erasmus' insistence on relating nuptial pleasure to its progeny, and we will see this presently. Suffice it to say that we are not attempting an exhaustive study of Erasmus' views of marriage but rather focusing on that aspect of his teaching which perceives the union of man and woman as integral with and symbolic of other unions of a creative nature. In an area where human failure dictated fear rather than hope, Erasmus based his optimism upon a divine order of things within which sex plays an important part. This holds on the supernatural as well as the natural level. Sex occupies a place at the beginning of God's redemptive plan, and, because it lies at the source of life, it symbolizes the terminus and fruition of that plan within Erasmus' providential view of history. In these senses, it is present to God's redeeming action both in its beginning and in its end.

Before looking at Erasmus' commentary on the beginnings of salvation history, an observation must be made about his tendency to see human sexuality not merely as the stimulus to mate in the isolated act of copulation. Rather, the instinct is understood as a process beginning with the marital act and terminating in the rearing of the offspring. In the *Encomium matrimonii*, when celebrating the tendency of all things to wed, Erasmus juxtaposes the gentleness of the lion in mating with the fierceness of the tiger in defending its cubs.[49] The act of begetting merges with the act of protecting as part of a single drive oriented towards life. This becomes even clearer in the case of man. He calls that coition holy which circumscribes and cradles the child only. The marriage embrace has, as it were, at its centre a third party, the child to be born. The learning of integrity in the act of sex, which Erasmus toys with in 'Proci et puellae,' is repeated solemnly in the commentary on Luke: 'Sanctus est coitus, qui nihil nisi prolem ambit.'[50] The love for the spouse is fused with the love for the child. The one should not be separated from the other. If we recall the sad history of Erasmus' own childhood, when the priest who begot him was not permitted to raise him, we will see one reason based on experience which fostered this conviction.

There is a trinitarian overtone to the passage in which the love of two people is said to involve a third. Erasmus even calls the sexual instinct numinous: 'Numen autem appello naturae instinctum, cuius conditor est deus,' he writes in his reply to Clichtove.[51] Pierre Mesnard, when translating the sentence, equates the 'numen' of the Latin with 'une force transcendante' of the French.[52] This seems to be going too far if we take the word in its context. 'Numen' here refers to the divine will as reflected in the order of nature. But when we turn to Erasmus' commentary on Luke's infancy narrative, Mesnard's use of 'transcendante' appears less of an exaggeration because there the heavenly power acts directly upon the sexual, first in the conception of John and then more miraculously in the conception of Jesus. Divine creativity is joined to human creativity.

Erasmus reflects on the birth of John the Baptist in his commentary on the first chapter of Luke's gospel. The divine initiative that fully obtains in the incarnation of the Second Person of the Trinity is foreshadowed in the conception of his precursor. The marriage of John's parents, Zachary and Elizabeth, is called sacred 'not so much by reason of the joining of their bodies' but because their souls are twinned in goodness.[53] The age of the man and the sterile condition of the woman call for a heavenly intervention if conception is to take place. This is no ordinary birth but one in which Erasmus finds God's special providence. The fecundity no longer hoped for by Elizabeth serves as the token of heaven's presence to the couple's physical union. 'Chaste are those embraces,' writes Erasmus, 'which a divine promise and not a violent appetite binds.'[54] Sexual pleasure ebbs from this description of the marital act and is replaced by a selfless joy that originates in God's creative love. The angel tells Zachary in the temple that Elizabeth will bring forth a child not for her husband alone but for the whole people and for the God whose care makes possible the unexpected event.[55] The happiness which the aging pair experience in the coming of life through their wrinkled bodies will diffuse itself in the person of the child who will grow to introduce the good news of salvation. In this way, private joy becomes public, and the fruit of human intimacy reaches out to a fulfilment far beyond the grasp of man and woman alone.

In Erasmus' account of the incarnation, the deity becomes the sole initiator of the human birth of the Second Person of the Trinity. As a first step in reviewing his ideas upon the coupling of the divine and human natures, we will consider Erasmus' understanding of the part played by the Virgin Mary in salvation history. We have already seen his negative attitude towards the excessive and misguided devotions to Mary in the *Colloquies*. This should not prevent us from appreciating the very important position which Erasmus attributes to the Mother of God. It is towards her that the entire biblical account leans, in the sense that from her will issue the Messiah. She joins the Old Testament to the New, for both sing of her; she is *the* woman, a new Judith, a new Esther, a new Eve.[56] She is at once the paradisal garden and the true Jerusalem, both its temple and holy of holies because she will bear within her Israel's redemption in the flesh.[57] In the *Paean virgini matri dicendus*, the recollection of Mary's role within the drama of salvation draws from Erasmus his most poetical prose. She is the promised land which bears the fruit of redemption and the noble house which the Son of God, the wisdom of the Father and the architect of wonders, has fashioned himself.[58] And she, in turn, will fashion him.

Erasmus sees the incarnation as a marriage between God and mankind that is realized through the duality of natures come together in the single person of Jesus Christ. This union is made possible when God himself intervenes and stirs up life in the womb of the Virgin Mary. Erasmus writes of the joining of the Holy Spirit with the Virgin in terms of a wedding:

> It is piously and reverently said by those of orthodox belief that God the Father begot for a second time his Son through Mary whom he loved as his spouse. Between God and the Virgin the angel Gabriel served as the marital go-between so that he might solicit the Virgin's consent without which there can be no legitimate union. Upon the reception of that consent, the power of the Most High, in an embrace full of mystery, settled upon the Virgin and through the Holy Spirit, whose creative presence takes the place of the semen, makes her pregnant with the heavenly child, who draws his double nature from both his parents: divine on his father's side and human on his mother's.[59]

Although human initiative has been suspended in the conception of Christ, Erasmus emphasizes the divine willingness to work through humanity represented by the most pure person of Mary and through the channels of the nature which he had created. He describes the joining of heaven and earth in the ardent language of love. The maiden languishes out of burning desire for her beloved, not unlike the young woman of the

Canticle of Canticles, and the deity finds her so beautiful that the brightness of her eyes causes the Word to leap from the Father's bosom into her womb.[60] In the *Obsecratio ad Mariam*, Erasmus addresses the Virgin Mother in the same language: 'The sheer fragrance of your goodness – your incomparable purity, lowliness, and kindness – enticed to earth the Only Begotten of the Father, like one drunk from love.'[61] The Spirit's overshadowing of Mary, this coming together of the divine and human natures, is expressed in the terms of the marital coitus, but in this case, the union does not violate but rather consecrates the woman's modesty: 'Sanctus hic divinae naturae cum humana coitus, non violabit pudicitiam tuam, sed consecrabit.'[62] Here is the ultimate resolution of that antipathy between chastity and fecundity, an antipathy which Erasmus continues to dissolve in both his comical and serious works.

Erasmus' use of the word 'coitus' within the context of the incarnation drew a thundering reply from Martin Luther. Erasmus, writes Luther, 'must be condemned as a dreadful blasphemer of God and the Virgin.'[63] Even if the word could yield a more acceptable meaning, he argues, people will inevitably think of its obscene reference. So it will not help the cause of Erasmus for him to try to make the statement agree with church teaching. The other foul sense will always be present. The Christian cannot help but be vehemently offended by so base a usage of words within so holy a setting. Luther then turns on Erasmus, the trafficker in ambiguities, the devil who sows tares in the wheatfields of faith by reducing the mystery of God's union with Mary to the level of myth, where Mars beds with Rhea and Jupiter with Semele. 'Through the use of such figures,' he warns, 'Christians would begin to doubt and, through doubting, give up believing altogether, and so religion itself would be driven out of the heart before anyone could notice.'[64] Luther's violent reaction here indicates an obstacle separating him and his adversary in their ways of thinking and speaking about God's communication with man.

Not only does Erasmus differ with Luther in his thought about the incarnation, but he differs also in his understanding of the usage of words. In answering his opponent's charges, Erasmus makes some important distinctions. An act which is foul in itself because of its evil nature is not to be confused with an act which, although good in itself, demands, by reason of modesty, care and delicacy in speaking about it.[65] It would seem that in Erasmus' mind the reality indicated by 'coitus' could be either good or bad depending on the parties engaged therein, but that the act as intended by God and nature is good. Whether or not the words describing this act are obscene depends directly, not on moral principle, but on usage. Usage determines the proper words for both good and bad acts. Church tradition, Erasmus claims, justifies his use of 'coitus.' He then cites Ambrose, Prudentius, John Damascene, the *Catena aurea*, and Aquinas, all of whom borrow from the vocabulary describing the human sexual process in their accounts of the incarnation.[66] Erasmus claims to have followed in the line of such writers when he paraphrased the angel's words to Mary concerning the birth of Jesus in the gospel of Luke.

> The heavenly Father decreed his Son to be born again in a new manner. There will be no need of mortal man's seed for this divine conception, but the Holy Spirit will descend into you from on high and in your womb, as in a heavenly workshop, will bring to completion the shaping of this holy foetus. Instead of a physical, marital embrace, the Most High will overshadow you and adapt his immense power to the working of human nature so that it will be able to sustain this intercourse. Where violent passion arises in coition, what is born there is born unclean and subject to sin. What will be born of you, however, because it will be conceived through the most holy embrace of the Almighty and through the intervention of the Holy Spirit who sanctifies all things and through a most pure virgin whom in this instance God chose to be clean from the least taint of sin – that child, then, will be holy, just as it will be conceived.[67]

Erasmus' persistence in holding to sexual imagery in the face of Luther's exasperating cry of scandal highlights a difference in their ways of understanding the incarnation. The proximity of the Spirit to Mary and the part which this Person of the Trinity plays within the human sexual process indicate how closely Erasmus situates the operations of nature and grace. In the above passage, the deity adapts itself to the ways of the humanity it has created. The heavenly does not do violence to the earthly but, in this case, restricts and conforms its power to the natural condition. In this way, the divine and the human coalesce and symbolize how the higher order perfects the lower one. On the other hand, Luther rebels at the thought of a proximity between nature and grace. He accuses Erasmus of degrading the incarnation to the level of the sexual intercourse which mythology tells us took place between Mars and Rhea, but Luther offers no proof to show us why the presence of sexuality should render the incarnation fictional. This constitutes an obvious weakness in his argument, because the absence of sexuality, not its presence, would cast doubt upon the reality of Christ's manhood. Luther does not seem to mind Erasmus' speaking of a union between Mary and the Spirit. But he is rattled and accuses his opponent of obscenity when Erasmus indicates that this is a marriage involving Mary's sex. Luther seems unwilling to allow Mary to react as a woman to this intervention of the Spirit: it seems as if he cannot abide the thought that sooner or later this union must draw on the sexual process of reproduction so that a child can be born. This glaring difference between the two authors in the way they consider the incarnation reiterates the impasse they met in their debate on grace. Both insist on the divine initiative in redemption; they fall out, however, over the question of how man is involved within the saving act.[68]

This, then, is the Erasmian doctrine of the incarnation: the Holy Spirit, in a most sacred but most real manner, penetrates the Virgin and stirs within her a life that is both human and divine. The Spirit takes hold of the flesh in a way that foreshadows the spiriting of human matter in the resurrection. To be sure, the body of Christ, born of the Virgin, differs from the risen body, but both thrive as a result of the Spirit's intervention, and both indicate the terminus intended within the redemptive plan. Salvation history moves towards the resurrection of a body absorbed by spirit, a body not known to mortal man. The overshadowing of Mary by the Holy Spirit anticipates this new fusing of the lower and higher realms in the full maturation of the new man. Erasmus' belief in such a union clears him from the charge of being a Platonist hiding behind the trappings of Christian orthodoxy. His notion of man's ascent to the spiritual plane of living does not discard the body but insists on its presence within the process. This faith in a new marriage of flesh to spirit is most evident in his paraphrase of the fifteenth chapter of Paul's first letter to the Corinthians.

Erasmus' interest in a doctrine is often betrayed by the way he expands the scriptural verses pertaining to it. For instance, he takes a single verse from 1 Corinthians, 'And when thou sowest, thou dost not sow the body that shall be, but a bare grain, perhaps of wheat or something else' (15:37), and develops the notion through twenty-two lines of the Leiden edition. In Paul, a simple parallel is drawn between the body lowered into a grave and the grain of wheat sown in a field. Erasmus' meditation on the verse stresses the vile and insignificant condition of the seed by comparison with its state as it rises a wheat stalk in full maturity. We behold not only a rebirth but a growth into something far different from what it was, a change manifesting a totally new appearance. In paraphrasing this verse and those following, Erasmus lays a heavy stress on the wondrous change from seed to full flower: 'longe alia specie renascitur semen ... in meliorem speciem ... non tamen eadem specie renascantur.'[69] But the growth to loveliness demands a death and burial. What descends into the grave a corpse that had been susceptible to animal passion and appetite arises out of the ground no longer a prisoner to the earth but a body now most sensitive to spiritual reality: 'quod hic paulatim a sensibus et affectibus corporeis defecatum, mox per resurrectionem renascens, quodammodo transfiguratum est in animum.'[70] This is the new marriage of flesh to spirit in which the body no longer weighs down the soul but partakes now fully in the satisfaction of man's highest longings.

The image of the grain of wheat is central to the preaching of the gospel message. In the fifteenth chapter of 1 Corinthians, it illustrates the Christian hope in the resurrection. In the twelfth chapter of John, the notion of fecundity is added to the paradox of life in death. Erasmus' paraphrase of John 12:24–5 emphasizes the amazing fertility of a single grain that dies and returns a hundredfold with an abundance of wheat stalks. The great rush of vegetal life enriches a whole countryside with waves of golden wheat.[71] Erasmus' commentary upon the natural phenomenon points towards a new and forceful coming to life within the spiritual realm. But this new vitality is of divine, not human origin. For Erasmus, the birth of John the Baptist from aged and sterile parents symbolizes a new principle of generation open to those who, for the sake of the kingdom of God, have castrated themselves. Like the seed in the parable, human sexuality itself must undergo a death before it can enter into the realm of beatitude. Then the eschatological marriage of Christ to his spouse, the church, can assert itself.

Before looking at Erasmus' view of the eschatological marriage at the level of the re-creative act of divine salvation, we must first sum up his idea of sex as a principle within the scheme of creation. The sex drive is both natural and God-given.[72] It is inscribed deep within man's psyche, but not within man alone.[73] All living things partake of the movement that leads to mating. The *Encomium matrimonii* celebrates the tendency of all life to beget and to multiply. The work urges us to look closely at the creatures surrounding us and to discover on all levels of being the sexual desire that brings these same creatures together.[74] Erasmus goes on to mention Pliny's account of how the male tree extends its branches towards the female, straining towards union. Without this leaning movement of the former, the latter would remain barren.[75] His enthusiasm leads him to attribute the impetus towards union to inanimate things, to precious stones, as if in anticipation of the discovery of valence within atoms.[76] Finally this tendency to wed becomes cosmic when Erasmus sees the whole of nature joined together in a great chain of being with heaven playing the role of the father to mother earth made fertile in the shower of his rains: 'by reason of this marital union, all things cohere and stand together, and, without this, creation itself would come apart, disintegrate, and collapse into nothingness.'[77]

Erasmus tends to see a marital principle deeply involved both with the divine creative process and with the divine sustaining action. Furthermore, he believes that the same God who creates man lies also at the source of man's rise to a life of grace after he has fallen: 'Man is just as powerless to re-create himself as he is unable to call himself into being.'[78] His need of a redeemer in the one case is as great as his need of a creator in the other. Because the same God is found at the source of both creation and salvation, Erasmus shows a willingness to discern a similarity in the divine *modus operandi* in the order of nature and in that of grace. Grace is not violently forced on man, but the human and the divine motions coalesce because the same deity inaugurates and supports both levels of operation and, indeed, orders them in parallel ways. Of course, the divine movement is more predominant in the salvific than in the natural act. So, for Erasmus, the marital principle, which acts as a norm in creation, appears again on the higher plane of man's redemption and transformation. Erasmus' way of conceiving salvation in terms of a marriage between Christ and the church is rooted in Pauline eschatology, but part of his description of the mystery of these espousals reveals some dependence upon John Colet, the acknowledged partner in his theological studies.[79] Colet's vision of the divine marriage will serve as an introduction to Erasmus' writings on the same subject by providing a kind of setting for the latter's thought.

Although Colet appears to be far less sanguine than Erasmus with regard to the bond of flesh between man and woman in marriage, he relies heavily upon its symbolic value when he writes his *De sacramentis ecclesiae*. In that treatise, the marital tie becomes the controlling image through most of the discussion. A kind of paradox is maintained throughout the work. On the one hand, Colet denies that marriage is a sacrament in its own right and sees the coming together of man with woman as debilitating and unworthy of the Christian male's virility; on the other hand, he identifies the spiritual marriage between Christ and his spouse with the sacrament of holy orders and as an ever-present aspect of the life fostered by sacramental grace.[80] To appreciate the pervasive force of Colet's notion of marriage we must first go to his reading of Genesis 1:27.

Colet sees an intrinsic link between the first and the second part of this verse: 'And God created man to his own image; to the image of God he created them. Male and female he created them.'[81] The image to which Genesis refers is understood by Colet in terms of the sexual differentiation mentioned in the second part of the verse: 'Male and female he created them.' The sexual distinction and union is literally comprehended as reflecting a mysterious reality within God himself. The Father's generation of the Son is grasped and described in sexual terms: 'God, the Father, has begotten for himself the co-eternal Son by means of an everlasting generative act so that he conceives within himself and from himself and, as it were, comes together ['coit'] within himself so that he might bring forth the Son likewise within himself and, in an ineffable manner, he can be said to be both Father and Mother.'[82] This internal activity of God suggests to Colet his way of proceeding when he turns to creating a world or to saving the fallen race of mankind. 'It was settled,' writes Colet, 'that he who created men should also re-create them.'[83] And a few lines later, he sharpens his meaning: 'God created and re-created for himself his human spouse.'[84] The divine husband in this marriage between heaven and earth is the Second Person of the Trinity, who within himself unites the Godhead to humanity and the male to the female when he joins the power of the deity to the weakness and mortality of the flesh.[85]

The marriage between man and woman, while it symbolizes the union of Christ with his spouse, only feebly indicates the richness of the higher mystery. Seen from the divine point of view, God instituted human marriage as a faint image of the intended marriage between Christ and the church. Christ, therefore, is called by Colet 'the first among husbands ['primus maritus'] after whom every marriage in heaven and on earth is named.'[86] His union reaches that perfection towards which all unions strive. The wonderful marital hyperboles in John Donne's love poems reach an actual fruition in the marriage of Christ and his spouse.

> She is all states, and all princes I,
> Nothing else is.
> Princes do but play us; compared to this,
> All honor's mimic; all wealth alchemy.
> 'The Sun-Rising' (lines 21–4)

Like the lovers at the close of 'The Canonization,' the pattern of this marriage between God and humankind is sought after by lesser lovers whose hearts have been distracted by trifles from the true object of all desire.

As in the case in human wedlock, the union between Christ and the church is ordered towards the begetting of offspring, only now a spiritual rather than a physical birth obtains. Colet draws his conclusion concerning this new kind of generation from the writings of Paul: 'Just as all die in Adam so all live in Christ ... The first Adam was made a living soul; the new Adam is a life-giving spirit ... The first man was of earth, earthy; the second man of heaven, heavenly' (1 Cor 15:22, 45, and 47). From these verses, Colet argues that 'there is no begetting in Christ which is not heavenly and spiritual.'[87] This bringing to life is understood in sexual terms. The embrace between Christ and his church leads to a birth in the spirit:

> From these holy espousals and the divine coition, man can
> be perfected to the highest degree by embracing his God,

and she who was sterile becomes wonderfully fertile by means of her compassionate lying together with the Son of God. Out of this seminal conception, she is able to bring forth the rich fruit of sanctity and justice which are the good works that Paul often calls offspring reaching unto life eternal. To the Galatians [5:22–3] he writes: 'But the fruits of the spirit are charity, joy, peace, patience, greatness of soul, goodness, kindness, gentleness, faith, modesty, continence, chastity.'[88]

Growth in virtue and in the life leading to salvation is here understood as resulting from the Son's embrace of a woman who, in receiving, begets. Nothing could be further from a Pelagian conception of grace and redemption.

As was said earlier, Erasmus' view of the tie between man and woman differs from Colet's. He sees the union as a sacred one from its inception and as a sacrament under the new dispensation.[89] But once Erasmus begins to discuss marriage as a sign, we sense a likeness of outlook between the Dutchman and his English friend. In his *Institutio christiani matrimonii*, Erasmus refers to marriage as a symbol of the hypostatic union of the divine and human natures in the one person of Christ. 'In either case,' he says, 'you are told of unity: in the first, of the unique joining of God to man; in the second, of an image of this unity: "And they will be two in one flesh" [Gen 2:24]. Here, two natures are joined but not confused; there, two sexes copulate without loss of identity.'[90] The similarity between Colet and Erasmus lies in the willingness of both authors to explore spiritual reality within a sexual framework. Erasmus speculates on the marital tie between the divine and human natures. Once made, it can never be broken. Through Christ, God is forever with us. The same, according to Erasmus, applies to the marriage between man and woman. He even hesitates over the power of death to dissolve the bond and speculates that, if the marriage tie can be undone, there is reason to believe that it never was a real union.[91] It would appear that Erasmus is consciously exaggerating in voicing such opinions, but beneath the overstatement lies the firm belief in the undying nature of the marriage between God and man. The permanency of this bond affects the way in which Erasmus thinks about unity within the church.

As in Colet, so in Erasmus, the marriage of man and woman,

with the subsequent begetting of children, symbolizes the heavenly Father's eternal generation of the Son.[92] Matrimony also points to the union of God and the Virgin Mary out of which the Son of God is born again for the sake of mankind.[93] This marital bond between God and man reaches its fulfilment in the coming together of Christ and his spouse, the church. Erasmus reflects on the nature of this union and the benefits ensuing from it:

> But where is the fruit of this coming together? In this guise, the heavenly spouse went forth from his bridal chamber, adorned in the robe of our flesh, first, to expel his rival, and then to claim as his own his spouse, the church whom he delivered by his own death and washed clean in his own blood and endowed with the mystical gifts of his Spirit. This same husband has caused his wife to bring forth a numerous and happy progeny, and now daily he begets children through his spouse by means of the dispersion of his heavenly semen of the divine word, as James the Apostle writes: 'Of his own will he has begotten us by the word of truth that we might be, as it were, the first-fruits of his creatures' [1:18]. For, if Paul speaks correctly: 'In Christ Jesus, did I beget you' [1 Cor 4:15] and, again, 'My dear children with whom I am in labour until Christ is formed in you' [Gal 4:19], how much more justly can this parental role be attributed to Christ, the father and author of the children of this new way of coming to life, that is, of those 'who are born not of blood, nor of the will of man, nor of the will of the flesh, but of God' [John 1:13]?'[94]

Christ, the begetter of the new creature who partakes of the divine life of grace, does so through the church by means of the sacrament of baptism. The matrimonial sign here gives way to that of the saving waters which become instrumental in awakening new life. 'Through marriage,' Erasmus writes, 'we are born into this world; through baptism, we are reborn unto Christ.'[95] Within the walls of the physical church, the new creature is nourished and refreshed at the sacramental table by the food and drink which is Christ's body and blood; and so the many are joined in one body as the two partners become one in marriage. Erasmus meditates on the words of John the Baptist in the gospel:

'He who has the bride is the bridegroom' [John 3:29]: by an indissoluble tie has he coupled himself to the church just as members of a body are joined to the head. When you hear 'head' and 'members' spoken, you listen to two distinct and separable words, but, in reality, these constitute a single thing by reason of their intimate union ['communione']. And so the spouse in the gospel prays for his bride from whom he cannot bear to be torn: 'Yet not for these only do I pray, but for those also who through their word are to believe in me, that all may be one, even as thou, Father, in me and I in thee; that they also may be one in us. Holy Father, keep in thy name those whom thou hast given me, that they may be one even as we are.' And later in the same passage: 'I in them and thou in me; that they may be perfected in unity' [John 17:20–1, 11, 23].[96]

Notice how easily Erasmus' thought moves from marital inter-penetration to the spiritual coupling of Christ and his bride and finally to the theological archetype. for all of this imagery: the mutual indwelling within the Trinity itself. Love, by its nature, follows a pattern traceable back to its absolute source.

In Erasmus' paraphrase of the fifth chapter of Ephesians, he once again shows the link in his own thought between the matrimonial symbolism he uses with regard to the redemption and the inner nature of the Trinity. The sexual union between man and woman not only indicates Christ's marriage with his spouse but also reaches into the wonder of the Godhead itself. This last element which introduces the union between Father and Son goes beyond what is explicitly stated by Paul. Erasmus reflects on the verses from Genesis (2:24) cited by the Apostle: 'For this cause a man shall leave his father and mother, and cleave to his wife; and the two shall become one flesh.' There is present here, according to the paraphrase, an ineffable and immense mystery. By cleaving together and becoming one flesh, Adam and Eve constitute a type or figure 'which is mystically fulfilled in Christ and the church. Whoever searches into this indivisible tie,' Erasmus continues, 'will come to grips with an awesome secret. For just as Christ was one with his Father, in the same manner, he desired to be one with all of his own.'[97] This is the basis for and the fullness of the marital imagery of Erasmus. The oneness between man and woman originates in the unity between the divine persons and thereby becomes the image for understanding the nature of that bond existing between Christ and his church.

Earlier in his paraphrase of the fifth chapter of Ephesians, Erasmus lays down man's love for his fellow creatures as the necessary condition for the continuance of God's good will towards his children: 'He will preserve an everlasting charity on your behalf provided that you maintain among yourselves a mutual love for each other.'[98] This is but Erasmus' way of attempting to show the intimate relationship between the love of Christ for his church and the oneness he believes should exist in the mystical body that grows and flourishes out of that love. Just as it is unthinkable that the Son should be separated from the Father or that Christ should be parted from his spouse, so the church would fail to understand her calling if she thought that the love of her children for each other were separable from the love which they claim for Christ. Erasmus knows that Christ identifies himself with his own:

> And in order to comprehend the total sharing of goods and troubles of all in this mystical marriage, he speaks thus in the gospel: 'What you have done to the least of my own, you have done to me'; and, in the Acts of the Apostles, he cries out to Paul who rages against the children of his spouse: 'Saul, Saul, why do you persecute me?' He would hardly say *Why do you persecute my own*, unless the bride were to be identified with the husband. This marriage knows no divorce.[99]

Because Christ identifies himself with the members of his mystical body, those members are to regard each other with a love that cannot be detached from the affection which they claim for Christ himself. This charity of brother for brother participates in that intense union between Father and Son and realizes the fullness of the marital embrace between Christ and his church. Out of this belief rose Erasmus' dedicated opposition to those kings who saw no contradiction between their profession as followers of Christ and their willingness to slaughter their own brethren on the field of battle. Out of this same conviction, Erasmus stood up against the beady-eyed dogmatist, the bellicose inquisitor, and the cantankerous heretic, all of whom preferred their own peculiar notions of doctrinal purity to the unity of Christ's church.

Much of what has been said on these last pages is found in its most concentrated form in a passage that occurs towards the end of the *Moria*. Folly, about to deliver her own account of the essence of celestial happiness, puts a question to her audience:

> What, then, is that future life in heaven for which pious minds long so eagerly? I'll tell you: the spirit, stronger at last and victorious, will absorb the body. And it will do so all the more easily, partly because it is in its own kingdom now, partly because even in its former life it had purged and refined the body in preparation for such a transformation. Then the spirit will be absorbed by that highest mind of all, whose power is infinitely greater, in such a way that the man will, [sic] be outside himself, and will be happy for no other reason than that he is located outside himself, and will receive unspeakable joy from that Highest Good which gathers all things to Himself.[100]

Essential to the understanding of this passage is a correct knowledge of the meaning of absorption as it is used here. M.A. Screech has shown that the concept does not mean disappearance or loss of identity.[101] The body does not dissolve when absorbed by the spirit nor does the individual vanish by reason of his union with God, although the state of being outside oneself certainly implies a psychological loss of self-awareness due to the preoccupation with the beloved. The absorption of which Folly speaks consists of a loving interpenetration suggestive of the coition and marital tie that Erasmus discovers between Mary and the Spirit in the conception of Christ. Such a coupling would appear to be one of the necessary elements of love in its fulfilment. This is that mutual indwelling, the 'mutua inhaesio,' which Aquinas sees as an effect of true love.[102] So in the Erasmian description of beatitude the whole of man enters into the beauty of God, and the Spirit in turn penetrates the heart of the human lover in a total realization of that union prefigured by the coupling of man and woman within the sacrament of matrimony.

NOTES

BIBLIOGRAPHY

INDEX

Notes

✣

ABBREVIATIONS

AD   Erasmus *The 'Adages' of Erasmus: A Study with Translations* trans Margaret Mann Phillips (Cambridge: Cambridge University Press 1964)

AS   Erasmus *Ausgewählte Schriften* 8 vols (Darmstadt: Wissenschaftliche Buchgesellschaft 1967–80)

ASD   Erasmus *Opera omnia* (Amsterdam: North Holland 1969–)

AW   Erasmus *Ausgewählte Werke* ed Annemarie Holborn and Hajo Holborn (Munich: C.H. Beck 1933)

COL   Erasmus *The Colloquies of Erasmus* trans Craig R. Thompson (Chicago: University of Chicago Press 1965)

CSEL   *Corpus scriptorum ecclesiasticorum latinorum* (Vienna: 1866– ; New York: Johnson 1960–6)

CCSL   *Corpus christianorum series latina* 53 vols to date (Turnholt: Brepols 1953–)

CWE   Erasmus *The Collected Works of Erasmus* 17 vols to date (University of Toronto Press 1974–)

EE   Erasmus *Opus epistolarum Des. Erasmi Roterodami* ed P.S. Allen, H.M. Allen, and H.M. Garrod, 12 vols (Oxford: Clarendon 1906–58)

L&E   Erasmus and Martin Luther *Luther and Erasmus: Free Will and Salvation* trans and ed E. Gordon Rupp, A.N. Marlow, Philip S. Watson, and B. Drewery (Philadelphia: Westminster 1969)

LB   Erasmus *Desiderii Erasmi opera omnia* ed J. Clericus, 10 vols in 11 tomes (Leiden 1703–6)

PF   Erasmus *The Praise of Folly* trans Clarence H. Miller (New Haven: Yale University Press 1979)

PG   *Patrologiae, cursus completus, series graeca* ed J.-P. Migne, 164 vols (Paris 1857–1912)

PL   *Patrologiae, cursus completus, series latina* ed J.-P. Migne, 221 vols (Paris 1879–90)

WA   Martin Luther *D. Martin Luthers Werke: Kritische Gesamtausgabe*
      62 vols to date (Weimar: H. Böhlaus Nachfolger 1883–)
WA Br Martin Luther *D. Martin Luthers Werke: Kritische Gesamtausgabe,*
      Briefwechsel 16 vols (Weimar: H. Böhlaus Nachfolger 1930–80)
WA Tr Martin Luther *D. Martin Luthers Werke: Tischreden* 6 vols (Wei-
      mar: H. Böhlaus Nachfolger 1912–21)

CHAPTER ONE

1 Huizinga *Erasmus and the Age of the Reformation* 78
2 von Balthasar *Seeing the Form* 494
3 Moltmann *Theology of Play* 10–11
4 Huizinga *Erasmus and the Age of Reformation* 190
5 Walter J. Ong, preface to *Man at Play* by Hugo Rahner, xiv. For a
  study which resolves the opposition between the sacred and the
  more sublime manifestations of play, see Gerardus van der
  Leeuw's *Sacred and Profane Beauty.* Far from being alien or
  disruptive to man's religious aspiration, play for van der Leeuw 'is
  the prerequisite for those forms of existence which strive toward
  a communion with the other, and finally for a meeting with God'
  (112). A helpful survey of the history of the relationship
  between play and divinity in Western thought is found in David L.
  Miller's *Gods and Games: Toward a Theology of Play.* This work also
  contains an extensive bibliography. Three collections of studies on
  the ludic are worth noting here. *Yale French Studies* devotes
  number 41 (September 1968) to 'Game, Play, Literature' and
  contains illuminating articles by Jacques Ehrmann, Eugen Fink,
  Michael Holquist, Mikhail Bakhtin, and Roger Caillois. Volume 18,
  number 2 (Summer 1974) of *Philosophy Today* focuses upon play
  in the thought of such authors as Jean-Paul Sartre, Eugen Fink, and
  Friedrich Nietzsche. The *Canadian Review of Comparative Litera-*
  ture devotes its June issue of 1985 (vol 2, no 2) to 'Game and the
  Theories of Game' and contains a most informative annotated
  bibliography of play and literature (310–53).
6 Rahner *Man at Play* 23
7 Guardini *The Spirit of the Liturgy* 97
8 *Ratio seu compendium verae theologiae per Des. Erasmum Roterdamum*
  in *AW* 274 line 26
9 See Erasmus' colloquy entitled 'Convivium religiosum': 'Etenim si
  ethnicis quoque religiosa erat mensa, quanto magis oportet esse
  sacram Christianis, quibus habet imaginem quandam illius sacro-
  sancti conuiuii, quod Dominus Iesus postremum egit cum suis
  discipulis' (*Colloquia* ed L.-E. Halkin, F. Bierlaire, and R. Hoven
  ASD I-3: 240 lines 276–9).
10 Charles Baudelaire 'De l'essence du rire' *Oeuvres complètes* 375. See

also Morton Gurewitch's comment on Baudelaire's distinction
between the 'significantly comic' and the 'absolutely comic' in
Comedy 190.

11 *Antibarbari* trans Margaret Mann Phillips CWE 23: 21 lines 20–5
(ed Kazimierz Kumaniecki ASD I-1: 42 lines 16–20)

12 *CWE* 23: 21 line 7 (*ASD* I-1: 41 lines 20–1)

13 Batt couples the rhetorician with the theologian (*CWE* 105 lines
17–18) and with the man of divinity (*CWE* 74 lines 12–16). See
also *ASD* I-1: 124 lines 17–18 and 96 lines 15–17.

14 *CWE* 23: 72 lines 23–4 (*ASD* I-1: 94 lines 31–2)

15 'Nec tamen in aliud faui litteris humanioribus nisi vt famularentur
grauioribus disciplinis, et in his praecipue theologiae' (Ep 1805
EE 7: 15 lines 20–1). When, as in this note, no translator is
mentioned, the translation is my own.

16 Ep 337 *EE* 2: 101 lines 398–414

17 Chomarat *Grammaire et rhetorique chez Erasme*. He succinctly states
his view of a theologian's *métier*: 'bâtir un édifice intellectuel à
partir de l'Ecriture' (1:18). Chomarat is disinclined to set Erasmus
among the theologians because he appears to lack a systematic
approach: 'Erasme ne s'intéresse guère a des questions comme
celles dont s'occupe la théologie systématique' (18). He grants
that Erasmus furnished the theologians with 'les instruments de
travail' (20), and by this I suppose he means his edition of the
New Testament in Greek. Expertise in scriptural studies, however,
and concern for piety do not make a theologian: 'Fondamentale-
ment, Erasme n'est pas un théologien' (20). Chomarat then
proceeds to make his case for Erasmus the rhetorician, and then
concludes: 'Etudier en Erasme le grammairien et le rhéteur n'est
donc pas le considérer sous un aspect mineur, mais au contraire
aller au centre' (24). Chomarat, out of a preoccupation with
Erasmus the rhetorician, dismisses him as a theologian. A
similar line of reasoning is found in Enno van Gelder, who,
according to Georges Chantraine ('Erasme theologien?' *Revue
d'histoire écclésiastique* 64: 811–20), argues that Erasmus is not a
theologian 'parce qu'il est humaniste' (813). Chantraine himself,
along with E.W. Kohls (*Die Theologie des Erasmus*), finds in the
corpus of Erasmus' writings a structured theology. See his
'Mystère' et 'Philosophie du Christ' selon Erasme. André Godin (*Erasme
lecture d'Origène* 508–9) strongly disagrees with his systematiz-
ing of Erasmian thought. Perhaps some of this disagreement could
be forestalled by clearly stating the kind of theology in which
Erasmus engages. Henri de Lubac in his *Exégèse médiéval* says of
Erasmus: 'sa vocation à lui, son génie propre, n'est pas d'un
théologien d'école, ni d'un philosophe: il s'en rend parfaitement
compte' (2-2: 432). If the words 'scholastic' and 'dogmatic' do

not precisely qualify the theology of Erasmus, surely terms such as 'biblical' and 'rhetorical' do.

18 #3619 *Table Talk, Luther's Works* 54: 245 (*WA Tr* 3: 460 lines 39–40)

19 *De servo arbitrio, L&E* 103 (*WA* 18: 601 lines 19–20)

20 *De servo arbitrio, L&E* 102 (*WA* 18: 601 lines 13–14)

21 In one passage, Luther addresses Diatribe as Mistress Reason: 'O domina Ratio' (*WA* 18: 674 line 13). The lady is given to dreaming: 'Diatribe somniat hominem esse integrum et sanum' (674 lines 6–7); she prates her foolish and absurd ideas: 'ut qui sciamus, eam non nisi stulta et absurda garrire' (673 lines 10–11). Prone to thoughtlessness and error, she confuses issues and contradicts herself: 'Nimis nimia est incogitantia Diatribae nostrae' (676 lines 14–15). 'Perpetuo obliviscitur Diatribe statum caussae' (686 lines 17–18). 'Hoc modo perpetuo disputat Diatribe contra suum ipsius institutum' (679 lines 8–9). She pretends and pretends again: 'Fingat, refingat ... Diatribe quantum uolet' (715 lines 17–18).

22 Lanham *The Motives of Eloquence* 5

23 *AW* 260 lines 5–6

24 Boyle *Erasmus on Language and Method in Theology* 121

25 'De vtilitate colloquiorum' *ASD* I-3: 742 lines 26–7

26 Schiller *On the Aesthetic Education of Man* 60

27 *Aesthetic Education* 96

28 Erasmus writes of the song of Christ living on in his church with the same powers which the saviour manifested during his life on earth: 'Quamquam idem citharoedus et hodie canit nobis in litteris sacris, canit per pios Doctores, si modo nos aures purgatas adhibeamus. Et hodie, sanat aegrotos, pellit Daemones, excitat mortuos, dum excutit languorem animis, dum insanis cupiditatibus liberat, dum ab impia vita revocat ad studium pietatis' (*Enarratio psalmi 38, LB* 5: 420C).

29 'Addamus et quintam regulam huic quasi subsidiariam, ut in hoc uno constituas perfectam pietatem, si coneris semper a rebus visibilibus, quae fere vel imperfectae vel mediae sunt, ad invisibilia proficere iuxta superiorem hominis divisionem' (*AW* 67 lines 22–5).

30 Chantraine *'Mystère' et 'Philosophie du Christ'* 355

31 The habit of mind fostered in the Christmas preface derives from the teaching of Paul in Romans: 'Ever since the creation of the world his invisible nature, namely his eternal power and deity, has been clearly perceived in the things that have been made' (1: 20).

32 Sartre *Being and Nothingness* 580. This passage in *Being and Nothingness*, completed in 1943, derives from an entry in *The War Diaries of Jean-Paul Sartre*. Some sentences from this earlier composition are incorporated verbatim into *Being and Nothing-*

ness. In the diary entry for Monday, 11 March 1940, Sartre sets in
contention the notions of seriousness and play. For him the
'serious man himself is merely a consequence,' an object which is
determined 'like the atom or like the star' (*War Diaries* 326).
From an inner desire to escape the world and to look down on it
from an ivory tower, Sartre originally thought of life as game or
masquerade. There was something in him of the contemplative. In
the same entry, he mentions his mother's fondness for repeat-
ing to him 'that a few centuries earlier I [Sartre] should have
become a monk' (325). By 1940 he had abandoned this escapist
mentality for the conviction of the importance of freedom, and this
conviction in Sartre's mind involves the ludic: 'as soon as man
grasps himself as free, and wishes to use his freedom, all his
activity is a game' (326). Still, the religious background to this
way of thinking is revealed when he writes of refusing to escape
and continuing to play: 'And, after all, being-in-the-world isn't
being of the world' (327). Sartre renounces the ivory tower but
does not want his 'life to stop being a game.' The entry
concludes with a quotation from Schiller: 'Man is fully a man only
when he plays' (327).

33 Sartre *Being and Nothingness* 580
34 Plato *Laws* 2.653d–e
35 'Laetantur oculi quaerentium aliquid uidere luminosum; laetantur
aures quaerentium cantum ... *Laetetur cor quaerentium dominum*'
Augustine (*Sermones de vetere testamento* 28.1 *CCSL* 41: 368 lines
10–13.
36 'Cordi autem nostro dominus et lux est et uox est et odor est et
cibus est' (*Ser* 28.2 *CCSL* 41: 368 lines 16–17).
37 'Cibus est qui reficit nec deficit; cibus est qui cum sumitur non
consumitur; cibus est qui esurientes satiat et integer manet' (*Ser*
28.2 *CCSL* 41: 369 lines 31–3).
38 In the *Confessions*, Augustine relates the words of the inner voice of
the deity addressing him: 'Cibus sum grandium: cresce et
manducabis me. Nec tu me in te mutabis sicut cibum carnis tuae,
sed tu mutaberis in me' (7.10.16 *CCSL* 27: 103–4 lines 18–20).
39 'Ista lux uidetur ab omnibus, pascit omnium oculos. Et aspectus
uidentis reficitur, et lux integra perseuerat. Si duo uideant, tanta
permanet; si plures uideant, eadem permanet' (*Ser* 28.3 *CCSL* 41:
369 lines 49–52).
40 'Intellectus ergo manens in corde meo migrat ad tuum, nec deserit
meum' (*Ser* 28.5 *CCSL* 41: 371 lines 98–9).
41 'Ecce enim uerbum dei ... manens incommutabiliter apud patrem,
ut procederet ad nos, carnem quasi sonum quaesiuit, ei se
inseruit et ad nos processit et a patre non recessit' (*Ser* 28.5 *CCSL* 41:
371 lines 103–8).

42 *LB* 5: 420F–421A. The Erasmian theme of cosmic music and dance is treated in chapter 7 of the present study.

43 In paraphrasing Christ's words in Matthew (lines 17–19), Erasmus lumps together the faithless and the morose spirits: 'Tibiis cecinimus vobis laeta, nec saltastis, lugubria cecinimus vobis, nec planxistis. Diversis viis idem tentatum est a nobis [Jesu et Johanne]. Neutra profectum est apud quosdam incredulos ac morosus' (*Paraphrasis in evangelium Matthaei*, *LB* 7: 67F). For more about this passage, see chapter 7.

44 Marie-Dominique Chenu *Nature, Man, and Society in the Twelfth Century*. The essays in this collection have been selected from Chenu's *La théologie au douzième siècle*. I have relied most heavily upon chapter 3 of the English version, entitled 'The Symbolist Mentality,' and upon Chenu's seminal article 'Théologie symbolique et exégèse scolastique aux xii⁰–xiii⁰ siècles' in *Mélanges Joseph de Ghellinck, S.J.* 2: 509–26. Henri de Lubac draws a similar contrast between symbolic and dialectical theology in chapter 10 of his *Corpus mysterium: L'eucharistie et l'église au moyen âge* (Paris: Aubier 1949) 240–77.

45 Henri de Lubac *Exégèse médiévale* 2: 432 and 427–8

46 Thomas Aquinas *In liber primum sententiarum* Prologue 1.5

47 Chenu 'Théologie symbolique' 525–6

48 Thomas Aquinas *In lib prim sent* Prologue 1.5 trans Thomas Gilby *Theological Texts* 21–2

49 Thomas Aquinas *Questiones quodlibetales* 7.6.15

50 Thomas Aquinas *Summa theologiae* 1a.84.7 ad 3

51 Chenu *Nature, Man, and Society* 138

52 Hugh of St Victor *In hierarchiam coelestem S. Dionysii Areopogitae* 2; trans in Chenu *Nature, Man, and Society* 103 (*PL* 175: 941B–C)

53 *Nature, Man, and Society* 131

54 *Nature, Man, and Society* 131

55 *Nature, Man, and Society* 83 and 101

56 Eliade *Symbolism, the Sacred, and the Arts* 3

57 Richard of St Victor *In apocalypsim Joannis libri septim* 1.1 trans in Chenu *Nature, Man, and Society* 140 n 77 (*PL* 196: 689A–B)

58 Thomas Aquinas *Summa theologiae* 1.1.9 ad 3 trans Thomas Gilby *Summa* (Blackfriars) 1: 35

59 Hugh of St Victor *Didascalicon* 6.3 trans Jerome Taylor *The Didascalicon of Hugh of St Victor* 138 (*PL* 176: 801C). In this passage Hugh quotes from Gregory the Great's *Moralium libri* (*PL* 75: 513C)

60 Chenu 'Théologie symbolique' 516 and 524

61 'Théologie symbolique' 520

62 Hugh of St Victor *In hierarchiam coelestem* 1.1, *PL* 175: 924B–925A

63 *Piers Plowman* c-Text, passus 20, lines 459–60

64 Ong 'Wit and Mystery: A Revaluation in Medieval Latin Hymno-dy' *Speculum* 22: 310–41
65 Cited by Ong in 'Wit and Mystery' 312
66 Hugh of St Victor *Explanatio in canticum beatae Mariae*, PL 175: 415C
67 Cited by Ong in 'Wit and Mystery' 313
68 Thomas Aquinas *In librum Boetii de Trinitate expositio* 2.1 ad 5. In the *Poetics* (1459a), Aristotle claims that mastery of metaphor indicates an ability which cannot be taught and is a characteristic of genius by reason of the intuitive power to see the similarity in things which are different.
69 Thomas Aquinas *Summa theologiae* 1.1.8 ad 1 trans Thomas Gilby *Summa* (Blackfriars) 1: 31
70 ASD IV-2: 76 lines 375–80
71 ASD I-1: 53 lines 16–20
72 See Chomarat 'La vérité et la violence' in *Grammaire et rhetorique* 2: 1118–53. For other studies of Erasmus' pacifism, see James D. Tracy *The Politics of Erasmus* and Pierre Brachin 'Vox clamantis in deserto: Réflexions sur le pacifisme d'Erasme' *Colloquia Erasmiana Turonensia* 1: 247–75
73 McConica 'Erasmus and the Grammar of Consent' *Scrinium Erasmianum* 2: 77–99. In his 'Erasme et la "Respublica christiana"' (*Colloquia Erasmiana Turonensia* 2: 667–90), Otto Schotten-loher likewise stresses the importance of consent within the church as a sign of the truth (683).
74 Boyle *Rhetoric and Reform*
75 *Querela pacis* ed O. Herding ASD iv-2: 72 lines 274–5
76 ASD IV-2: 77 lines 387–8
77 ASD IV-2: 77 line 389
78 ASD IV-2: 66–7 lines 162–8
79 ASD IV-2: 74 lines 294–6
80 ASD IV-2: 96 lines 833–6
81 ASD IV-2: 84 lines 526–8
82 ASD IV-2: 82 lines 497–8
83 ASD IV-2: 82 lines 481–2
84 ASD IV-2: 90 lines 673–6
85 ASD IV-2: 61 lines 11–14
86 ASD IV-2: 96 lines 847–8
87 *Paraph in Matt*, LB 7: 78B
88 Prefatory letter to the *Moria*, PF 3 (ASD IV-3: 67–70)
89 *De libero arbitrio*, AS 4: 140
90 *De libero arbitrio*, L&E 80 (AS 4: 140)
91 *De libero arbitrio*, L&E 96 (AS 4: 190)
92 *De libero arbitrio*, L&E 80 (AS 4: 140)
93 Thomas Aquinas *Summa theologiae* 1a.2ae.68.8 trans Thomas Gilby *Theological Texts* 254

94 *In Joannem* 6.5 (*Opera* 10: 414)
95 *De libero arbitrio, L&E* 55–6 (*AS* 4: 64)
96 *In Joannem* 6.5 (*Opera* 10: 414)
97 von Balthasar *Seeing the Form* 251
98 *Seeing the Form* 76
99 *Seeing the Form* 77
100 *Seeing the Form* 77
101 Plato *Laws* 2.653d
102 Plato *Timaeus* 40b
103 Eliot 'Burnt Norton' lines 52–4 *Four Quartets* 15
104 Philo *Who Is the Heir of Divine Things?* in *Philo of Alexandria* 4: 393
105 Philo *On the Account of the World's Creation Given by Moses* 42.126, in *Philo of Alexandria* 1: 98–9
106 Miller *Measures of Wisdom* 71. The reader will find in this work an exhaustive exposition of the themes of sacred music and dance in ancient times. The sources and development of the theme of cosmic music are traced by Kathi Meyer-Baer in her *Music of the Spheres and the Dance of Death.* See also Eleanor Irwin's 'The Songs of Orpheus and the New Song of Christ' and Patricia Vicari's '*Sparagmos*: Orpheus among the Christians.' Both of these articles are found in *Orpheus: The Metamorphoses of a Myth* ed Warden, 51–62 and 63–83.
107 Ignatius of Antioch *Epistola ad Ephesios* trans James A. Kleist *The Epistles of St Clement of Rome and St Ignatius of Antioch* 67 (*PG* 5: 660A–B)
108 *Ep ad Eph, Epistles* 61 (*PG* 5: 648A–B)
109 *Ep ad Eph, Epistles* 61–2 (*PG* 5: 648B)
110 Clement of Alexandria *The Exhortation to the Greeks* in *Clement of Alexandria* 11
111 *Exhortation* 13
112 *Exhortation* 15
113 Basil *De spiritu sancto* 9.23.20c trans James Miller in *Measures of Wisdom* 383 (*PG* 32: 109B–C)
114 Gregory of Nazianzus *Orationes* 44.10 *PG* 36: 617C–620A
115 Dionysius the Areopagite *De ecclesiastica hierarchia* 3.3.5 *PG* 3: 432A–B
116 *De eccles hierarchia* 3.3.3 and 3.3.12 (*PG* 3: 482D–429B and 441C–444B)
117 *De eccles hierarchia* 3.3.1 trans John Parker *The Works of Dionysius the Areopagite* 2: 91 (*PG* 3: 428B)
118 Clement of Alexandria *Exhortation* 7
119 Dionysius the Areopagite *De coelesti hierarchia* 2.2 trans John Parker *Works of Dionysius* 2: 5 (*PG* 3: 137A–B)
120 Colet *Ioannes Coletus super opera Dionysii* trans J.H. Lupton 7
121 *Super opera Dionysii* 9
122 *En ps 33, LB* 5: 380E–F
123 *Paraphrasis in epistolam Pauli ad Corinthios priorem, LB* 7: 863B–C)

124 *Paraph in epist ad Cor 1*, LB 7: 863D–E. For a modern interpretation of divine impotence, see the study of Dermot Cox, *The Triumph of Impotence*.
125 Medard Kehl 'Hans Urs von Balthasar: A Portrait,' introduction, *The von Balthasar Reader* 48
126 von Balthasar *Theodramatik* 1: 15
127 *Theodramatik* 1: 19
128 *Theodramatik* 1: 20
129 *Theodramatik* 1: 19

CHAPTER TWO

1 *Carmen* 3, lines 35–8, *The Poems of Desiderius Erasmus* 141–2
2 *Carmen* 23, lines 37–40 and 87–8, *Poems* 207–10
3 Ep 39 trans R.A.B. Mynors and D.F.S. Thomson CWE 1: 78 line 108 (EE 1: 141 lines 97–8)
4 Ep 30 EE 1: 120–2
5 CWE 1: 56 lines 44–5 (EE 1: 122 lines 42–3)
6 Ep 6 CWE 1: 8 lines 5–10 (EE 1: 79 lines 5–9)
7 According to the conjecture of S. Dresden, the composition of the *De contemptu mundi* was begun at Steyn (*De contemptu mundi* ed S. Dresden ASD V-1: 35)
8 ASD V-1: 44. The rather simplistic view of equating life in the monastery with virtue and life in the world with vice is corrected in chapter 12 of the *De contemptu mundi* (ASD V-1: 82–6). There Erasmus admits that the spirit of the world can infiltrate the cloister and that the true monastery exists wherever virtue flourishes: 'et in monasterio te esse puta vbicunque versaberis inter eos qui veritatem, qui pudicitiam, qui sobrietatem, qui modestiam amant (ASD V-1: 85 lines 229–31).
9 ASD V-1: 39 lines 12–14
10 ASD V-1: 30
11 ASD V-1: 58
12 ASD V-1: 45–6 lines 154–61
13 ASD V-1: 48 lines 228–36
14 ASD V-1: 64 lines 685–92
15 ASD V-1: 64 lines 692–8
16 ASD V-1: 44 lines 109–10
17 Telle *Erasme de Rotterdam et le septième sacrement* 18
18 ASD V-1: 44 lines 131–7; cf Vergil 'Eclogue 9' lines 39–43
19 ASD V-1: 73–8
20 ASD V-1: 73–4
21 ASD V-1: 49 lines 254–63
22 ASD V-1: 60 lines 562–3
23 'Pauperie nostra nihil locupletius, seruitute nihil liberius, labore

nihil quietius; inedia satura, angustiae spaciosissimae, maeror
iucundissimus, amaritudo perquam suauis, vigiliae somno quouis
gratiores' (*ASD* V-1: 62 lines 634–7).

24 'Et forte in contemplatione quidam labor est, sed melior requie, sed
otio suauior, sed somno dulcior, sed cunctis voluptatibus
delectabilor' (Peter of Celle *Liber de panibus* 7 PL 202: 962A).

25 Aelred of Rievaulx *De speculo caritatis* 1.19 in *Opera omnia* 1: 35

26 Peter of Celle *Liber de panibus* 7 PL 202: 962B

27 *ASD* V-1: 76 line 1

28 'Le résultat de la contemplation est en effet une seconde création,
une régénération totale, et l'on peut donc penser à une véritable
re-création. Mais en même temps il est sans doute question de
récréation, de joie céleste' (*ASD* V-1: 77 n 1).

29 *ASD* V-1: 77 n 4

30 *ASD* V-1: 62 line 636

31 *ASD* V-1: 78 lines 36–66

32 *ASD* V-1: 78 lines 64–6

33 *ASD* V-1: 79 lines 74. Bernard's exact words read: 'crucem quidem
videntes, sed non etiam vnctionem' (*PL* 183: 520D). In the
sentence following, Bernard pursues the kind of paradoxical
reflection which will become dear to Erasmus: 'vere crux nostra
inuncta est, et per gratiam Spiritus adiuuantis, suavis et delectab-
ilis est poenitentia nostra, et, vt ita dicam, amaritudo nostra
dulcissima.'

34 ASD V-1: 60, lines 575–6. Bernard, in 'Sermo 55' on the Canticle of
Canticles, refers to himself as both a monk and a citizen of
Jerusalem – 'monachus et Ierosolymita' (*PL* 183: 1045C). The monastery is conceived as Jerusalem by reason of the affiliation of its
inhabitants with the heavenly Jerusalem: 'But our citizenship is in
heaven' (Philip 3:20).

35 Erasmus' memorization of the complete works of Horace and
Terence is reported by Beatus Rhenanus in his introduction to the
Froben edition of Erasmus' *Opera* published shortly after his death
(1538–40).

36 Ep 447 *EE* 2: 301 lines 346–7

37 Schäfer 'Erasmus und Horaz' *Antike und Abendland* 16: 54–67.
Schäfer's article makes a thorough analysis of the Roman poet's
influence on Erasmus but also recognizes where the two part
company by reason of the latter's Christian conviction.

38 Ep 337 *EE* 2: 93 lines 99–100

39 *Ad censuras colloquiorum, LB* 9: 937A

40 Horace 'Satire 1' *Satires* 6 lines 24–5

41 *Satires* 478 line 343

42 Ep 337 trans R.A.B. Mynors and D.F.S. Thomson *CWE* 3: 115 lines
113–15 (*EE* 2: 94 lines 106–9)

43 Horace *Satires* 486 line 451
44 *ASD* IV-3: 68 line 37; Ep 222 *EE* 1: 461 lines 43–4
45 'Ad Gulielmum Copum medicorum eruditissimum de senectute carmen' *Carmen* 83 *Poems* 283–9. For a clear explication and appreciation of the 'Carmen Alpestre,' see D.F.S. Thomson's article 'Erasmus as a Poet in the Context of Northern Humanism' *De Gulden Passer* 47: 187–210.
46 *Carmen* 7 *Poems* 147–8
47 *Carmen* 24 *Poems* 211
48 *Carmen* 24 *Poems* 210–17
49 *Carmen* 83 *Poems* 290 lines 229–30
50 Ep 138 *CWE* 1: 296 lines 52–3 (*EE* 1: 321 lines 46–7)
51 Ep 61 *CWE* 1: 127 lines 96–102 (*EE* 1: 183 lines 90–5)
52 *ASD* I-1: 1–138
53 Epp 106–11 *EE* 1: 242–60
54 Ep 109 *CWE* 1: 207 lines 19–20, 24–5, and 38–9 (*EE* 1: 250 lines 15–16, 21–2, and 33–4)
55 The *Disputatiuncula de tedio, pavore, tristicia Iesu* published in the *Lucubratiuncula* (Antwerp: Th Martens, 15 February 1503) consists of a conflation and amplification of two letters (nos 109 and 111 of the *EE*) to Colet that carry Erasmus' main argument in the debate with his friend.
56 Of course, Erasmus, in the several vehement debates that arose between him and people like Luther and Alberto Pio, did not always maintain his composure; nevertheless, a friendly and unheated manner of contention always remained for him an ideal to be sought after. For a review of Erasmus' part in polemical argument, see the articles of Myron P. Gilmore, 'De modis disputandi: The Apologetic Works of Erasmus' *Florilegium Historiale* 62–88, '*Apologiae*: Erasmus's Defenses of Folly' *Essays on the Works of Erasmus* 111–23, and 'Erasmus and Alberto Pio, Prince of Carpi' *Action and Conviction in Early Modern Europe* 299–318.
57 Ep 110 *CWE* 1: 211 lines 6–8 (*EE* 1: 254 lines 6–7)
58 Ep 108 *CWE* 1: 203 line 33 (*EE* 1: 247 line 30)
59 Ep 111 *CWE* 1: 212 line 10 (*EE* 1: 254 lines 9–10)
60 *EE* 1: 255 lines 11–40
61 Ep 109 *EE* 1: 253 lines 151–4
62 *CWE* 1: 210 lines 131–6 (*EE* 1: 252 lines 119–25)
63 *CWE* 1: 209 lines 104–8 (*EE* 1: 252 lines 94–7)
64 *CWE* 1: 208 lines 78–85 (*EE* 1: 251 lines 70–6)
65 *CWE* 1: 209 lines 95–6 (*EE* 1: 251 lines 84–6)
66 Hans Urs von Balthasar echoes certain aspects of what Erasmus is trying to say here about Christ's joy and sorrow in his passion. Balthasar does not understand the essence of Christian sacrifice as destruction but rather as transfiguration. See *Seeing the Form*

115. Balthasar believes that faith teaches man to see that 'bliss and sacrificial self-abandonment are identical' (236). Because Christ 'dies out of love, his death is not a limitation, but a mighty expression of his love' (237–8).

67 *Paraph in Matt* LB 7: 24E
68 Ep 116 CWE 1: 229 lines 4–8 (EE 1: 268 lines 2–6)
69 CWE 1: 230 lines 14–15 (EE 1: 268 lines 12–13)
70 CWE 1: 230 line 33 (EE 1: 268 line 28)
71 CWE 1: 230 line 38 (EE 1: 269 lines 32–3)
72 CWE 1: 230 lines 38–40 (EE 1: 269 lines 33–5)
73 CWE 1: 232 lines 109–10 (EE 1: 270 lines 93–6)

CHAPTER THREE

1 Robinson's study *Lucian and His Influence in Europe* begins with an analysis for Lucian's art as a writer and then goes on to assess his influence. He devotes a large section (165–97) to the hand of Lucian in the composition of Erasmus' own seriocomic works. Duncan's main interest in his *Ben Jonson and the Lucianic Tradition* involves Lucian's part in the formulation of Jonson's comic style, but, in arriving there, he includes an interesting chapter on the link between Lucian and Erasmus (26–51). J.A.K. Thomson's 'Erasmus in England,' *Vorträge der Bibliothek Warburg* 9, which appeared in 1931, anticipates the work of both Robinson and Duncan when it shows the affinity between Erasmian and Lucianic irony.
2 Once he began to read Greek, Erasmus devoted a considerable part of his attention to the writings of Lucian. Together with his friend Thomas More, he translated into Latin several of Lucian's dialogues. His absorption of the Lucianic manner in dramatic colloquy doubtless stems from this exercise. For a complete account of Erasmus' part (the lion's share) in this enterprise, see C.R. Thompson *The Translations of Lucian by Erasmus and St. Thomas More*.
3 Lucian *Menippus* trans A.M. Harmon *Lucian* 4: 109
4 Lucian *The Dance* trans A.M. Harmon *Lucian* 5: 285
5 Douglas Duncan understands this Lucianic equanimity in terms of an open-eyed practical understanding: 'all creeds are equally prone to absurdity, especially when valued by the common sense norms of the market-place' (*Ben Jonson* 17).
6 *Lucian* 5: 283
7 Robinson *Lucian and His Influence* 189
8 Duncan *Ben Jonson* 15
9 Ep 187 trans R.A.B. Mynors and D.F.S. Thomson CWE 2: 103 lines 22–3 (EE 1: 417 lines 21–2)

10 Lucian *Toxaris* trans A.M. Harmon *Lucian* 5: 203

11 Ep 187 *EE* 1: 417 lines 19–28

12 Ep 193 *CWE* 2: 116 line 32 (*EE* 1: 425 lines 28–9)

13 Cedric H. Whitman *Aristophanes and the Comic Hero* 234

14 Whitman *Aristophanes* 258

15 *Adagia* 3.7.1 *LB* 2: 869A–883F

16 The tale of the eagle and the beetle can be found in Aesop, but it seems that Erasmus had Aristophanes in mind in developing his own version (*LB* 2: 883D–E). When, for instance, his heroic beetle reaches the pinnacle of success by triumphing over eagle and Jupiter, Erasmus quotes lines from *Peace*, the Aristophanic play that celebrates a similar victorious beetle:

> It is the only living thing with wings,
> So Aesop says, that ever reached the Gods.
> O father, father, that's too good a story
> That such a stinking brute should enter heaven!
> It went to take revenge upon the eagle,
> And break her eggs, a many years ago.

(*AD* 262; for the English version of these lines, Margaret Phillips follows the translation of B.B. Rogers).

17 *AD* 234 (*LB* 2: 870F)

18 *AD* 248 (*LB* 2: 877A)

19 *AD* 252 (*LB* 2: 879A)

20 *AD* 251 (*LB* 2: 878B)

21 Whitman *Aristophanes* 107

22 *AD* 259 (*LB* 2: 882B)

23 *Adagia* 2.10.5 *LB* 2: 686D–E

24 Plato *Symposium* 193a trans Michael Joyce in *The Collected Dialogues of Plato Including the Letters* 545

25 *Symposium* 193c *Dialogues of Plato* 546

26 Colet *De corpore Christi mystico* in *Ioannis Coleti opuscula quaedam theologica* 188

27 Ed Clarence H. Miller *ASD* IV-3: 88 line 304

28 Cooper *An Aristotelian Theory of Comedy* 125

29 *Adagia* 3.3.1 *AD* 269 (*LB* 2: 770D)

30 *AD* 270 (*LB* 2: 771A)

31 *AD* 271 (*LB* 2: 771D)

32 *AD* 272 (*LB* 2: 771E)

33 Richard of St Victor *In cantica canticorum explicatio* 27 *PL* 196: 485A

34 *AD* 272 (*LB* 2: 771E–F)

35 *PF* 43 (*ASD* IV-3: 104 lines 579–81)

36 Aristotle *Poetics* 4.1449a trans Ingram Bywater *On the Art of Poetry* 15

37 *PF* 43 (*ASD* IV-3: 104 lines 581–4)

38 Plato 'Letter VI' 323d

39 Plato *Republic* 7.514ff
40 *AD* 279 (*LB* 2: 775A)
41 Trans Raymond Himelick *The Enchiridion of Erasmus* 140 (*AW* 96 line 5)
42 The *Phaedo* tells us that the earth occupies the middle of the heavens (108e and 109a), and the *Phaedrus* looks 'aloft to the region where the gods dwell' (246e) and continues: 'Now within the heavens are many spectacles of bliss upon the highways where the blessed gods pass to and fro' (247a); trans R. Hackforth in *Collected Dialogues* 494.
43 Plato *Laws* 7.803c
44 *Enchiridion* 130 (*AW* 88 lines 23–8)
45 Plato *Phaedo* 109b trans Hugh Tredennick in *Collected Dialogues* 90
46 Plato *Laws* 10.899c
47 *Laws* 12.967b trans A.E. Taylor in *Collected Dialogues* 1512
48 Plato *Republic* 7.536b–c
49 *Laws* 1.644d–645c

CHAPTER FOUR

1 Ep 2093 *WA* Br 7: 30 lines 50–5. Luther in his *De servo arbitrio* also gets after Erasmus for mixing the sacred with the profane: 'Sed tu imprudenter et temere facis, qui puritatem sacrarum rerum misces, confundis, et assimilas cum prophanis et stultis questionibus impiorum' (*Luthers Werke in Auswahl* 3: 112 lines 10–12). In the following paragraph the charge is repeated: 'Et hic iterum confundis et misces omnia, more tuo, ut prophanis aeques sacra, nullo prorsus discrimine' (3: 112 lines 30–2).
2 In September of 1514, Martin Dorp wrote his well-known letter to Erasmus declaring the strong reaction of Louvain's theologians against the *Moria* especially for ascribing foolishness to Christ himself (Ep 304 *EE* 2: 10–16). The same complaint is lodged against the *Moria* by the Spanish theologian Jacobus Stunica. See Gilmore's '*Apologiae*' 113 and 122 n 22. In 1522 Erasmus replied to Stunica's accusation that the *Moria* blasphemes against God (*LB* 9: 359–60). Accounts of Erasmus' debates with Alberto Pio, the Prince of Carpi, over the *Moria* and other matters for the most part theological are found in Gilmore's '*Apologiae*' and in his 'Erasmus and Alberto Pio.'
3 In his *De officiis ministrorum* 1.23 (*PL* 16: 54B), Ambrose dismisses laughter from the study of theology. In the *Summa* (2a.2ae.168.2 ad 1), Thomas cites this passage from Ambrose in support of his own argument against blending laughter with the study of theology.
4 Bacon 'An Advertisement Touching the Controversies of the Church of England' *The Works of Francis Bacon* 2: 413

5 Robinson *Lucian and His Influence in Europe* 54
6 Knowles *The Tudor Age* 147
7 Pascal *Les provinciales* 218
8 Milton 'An Apologie against a Pamphlet' *Complete Prose Works of John Milton* 1: 882 and 903
9 Barber *Shakespeare's Festive Comedy*
10 Lucian *Saturnalia* trans A.M. Harmon *Lucian* 6: 99
11 *Lucian* 6: 107
12 *Lucian* 6: 97
13 Girard *Violence and the Sacred* 1–38
14 Elliott *Power of Satire* 7
15 *Erasmus and the Seamless Coat of Jesus* 34 (*LB* 5: 472E). This is a translation of Erasmus' *De sarcienda [amabili] ecclesiae concordia*, his commentary on Psalm 83. For the reference of a lid worthy of a pot, see *Adagia* 1.10.72 'Dignum patella operculum' *LB* 2: 387C–D.
16 'Les phénomènes engendrés par la chute deviendront les moyens du rachat' (Baudelaire 'De l'essence du rire' 372).
17 Tertullian *De spectaculis* 25–9. Tertullian inveighs against the contests of the circus in chapter 16 and against those of the theatre, the stadium, and the amphitheatre in the three ensuing chapters.
18 *De spectaculis* 24 lines 11–16
19 *De spectaculis* 10 lines 8–13. Tertullian then goes on to show in the next chapter that the general name for the games, 'liberalia,' indicates their origins in a festival dedicated to the god Liber. As they develop, different games honour different gods.
20 *De spectaculis* 16 lines 1–4
21 With reference to the games in general, Tertullian admits the following: 'Sint dulcia licebit et grata et simplicia, etiam honesta quaedam' (*De spectaculis* 37–8 lines 14–15).
22 *De spectaculis* 40 lines 17–20. This entire chapter (21) treats Tertullian's transformation of the festival. For the most part, however, it amounts only to an internal conversion. The pugilistic contest, for instance, becomes the spiritual combat.
23 As cited in Hugo Rahner *Man at Play* 77 (*Orationes* 5.35 *PG* 35: 709C–712A)
24 *Seamless Coat* 33–4 (*LB* 5: 472D–E)
25 *Seamless Coat* 35 (*LB* 5: 473B)
26 *Seamless Coat* 74 (*LB* 5: 493E–494A)
27 *Seamless Coat* 51 (*LB* 5: 481E)
28 *Seamless Coat* 67 (*LB* 5: 490A)
29 *Seamless Coat* 63 (*LB* 5: 488A–B)
30 *Seamless Coat* 66 (*LB* 5: 490A)
31 *Seamless Coat* 96 (*LB* 5: 491C)

32 At the opening of his discussion of the Saturnalian feast, Girard states: 'The fundamental purpose of the festival is to set the stage for a sacrificial act' (*Violence and the Sacred* 119). Earlier the author had said, 'If the sacrificial catharsis actually succeeds in preventing the unlimited propagation of violence, a sort of *infection* is in fact being checked' (30). This cure of the sick community would appear to be the reason for the coincidence of violent sacrifice and celebration.

33 Dresden 'Erasmé, Rabelais et la "Festivitas" humaniste' *Colloquia Erasmiana Turonensia* 1: 464–5

34 Dresden 'Erasmé' 467–71

35 COL 546 (ASD I-3: 728–9 lines 305–9)

36 Dresden 'Erasmé' 472–6

37 Kern *The Absolute Comic* 3

38 Ep 337 CWE 3: 115 line 100 (EE 2: 93 lines 93–4)

39 LB 9: 937A; 943A, C, and D

40 AW 280 lines 1–3; *In psalmum xxii enarratio triplex*: 'Allegorias in divinis literis ridere impietas est' (ed Ch Bene ASD V-2: 331 lines 69–70)

41 For Folly's initially superficial and humorous reading of scripture, see ASD IV-3: 178–82 lines 904–83. The *Sileni Alcibiadis* owns that the scriptures may at times appear absurd after a casual perusal of a specific passage. Examples are given from both the Old and the New Testaments. This ridiculous appearance of the shell indicates that it must be cracked open in order to reach the meat within (LB 2: 773C–E).

42 *Adagia* 3.3.1 AD 276 (LB 2: 773 D–E)

43 AW 179 lines 27–9

44 AW 280 lines 1–5. The interpretation which says that Peter denies Christ the man only because he knows him as God is found in the *Ratio* (AW 279 line 28).

45 Ep 1183 EE 4: 439 lines 35–40; Ep 1581 EE 6: 90 lines 113–19

46 COL 625 (ASD I-3: 741 lines 11–12)

47 COL 625 (ASD I-3: 741 lines 12–13)

48 COL 625 (ASD I-3: 742 lines 26–7)

49 Freud 'Der Dichter und das Phantasieren' *Gesammelte Werke* 7: 214

50 Richard L. DeMolen 'Pueri Christi imitatio: The Festival of the Boy-Bishop in Tudor England' *Moreana* 45: 17–28

51 DeMolen '*Peuri*' 18

52 J.H. Lupton *A Life of John Colet* 175

53 DeMolen '*Pueri*' 21

54 James D. Tracy in his article 'On the Composition Dates of Seven of Erasmus' Writings' (*Bibliothèque d'humanisme et Renaissance* 31: 362) suggests that Erasmus wrote the *Concio de puero Jesu* in 1503 rather than in 1511, the date usually assigned it, after he had

'sweated for weeks over the *Panygericus*' in honour of Phillip of Burgundy.

55 *LB* 5: 605D
56 *LB* 5: 599D
57 *LB* 5: 602C
58 *LB* 5: 602C
59 *LB* 5: 606B
60 *LB* 5: 608A–B
61 *LB* 5: 605D
62 *LB* 5: 602C
63 *LB* 5: 602F–603A
64 *LB* 5: 606A–B
65 *LB* 5: 601C
66 *LB* 5: 610A
67 As cited in V.A. Kolve's *The Play Called Corpus Christi* 133
68 *AW* 280 lines 1–2 and 274 lines 24–6

CHAPTER FIVE

1 Luther *WA Tr* 1: 185 lines 20–2
2 Ep 337 *CWE* 3: 115 lines 101–5 (*EE* 2: 93 lines 94–6)
3 Gurewitch *Comedy* 48
4 Pope 'Epilogue to Satires, Dialogue II' *Imitations of Horace* vol 4 of *The Poems of Alexander Pope* 324 line 198
5 In the introduction to Paul Pascal's English translation of the *Julius exclusus* 7–14, J. Kelly Sowards discusses the question of the dialogue's authorship and decides that it is a work of Erasmus' creation. Sister Geraldine Thompson in a long footnote (*Under Pretext of Praise* 88 n 1) presents an impressive list of Erasmian scholars who claim Erasmus as the author: P.S. Allen, W.K. Ferguson, A. Renaudet, Preserved Smith, J.J. Mangan, J.A. Froude, Roland Bainton, J.K. Sowards, and Sister Geraldine Thompson herself. Johan Huizinga, Margaret Mann Phillips, and Marcel Bataillon all abstain from the issue, while James D. Tracy, citing the work of the German Carl Strange, dissents from the majority opinion.
6 Sister Geraldine Thompson 'As Bones to the Body: The Scope of *Inventio* in the *Colloquies* of Erasmus' *Essays on the Works of Erasmus* 167
7 Kernan *The Plot of Satire* 26–31
8 *COL* 287 (*ASD* I-3: 470 lines 11–13)
9 *COL* 304 (*ASD* I-3: 486–7 lines 599–604)
10 *COL* 304 (*ASD* I-3: 487 line 615)
11 *COL* 310 (*ASD* I-3: 492 lines 816–18)
12 *COL* 293 (*ASD* I-3: 476 lines 201–4)

13 *ASD* I-3: 484 lines 503–7
14 *COL* 308 (*ASD* I-3: 490 lines 750–1)
15 *Adagia* 3.3.1 *LB* 2: 773E–774B
16 *Adagia* 4.1.1 *AD* 327 (*LB* 2: 959D)
17 *ASD* IV-2: 76 lines 373–6
18 *COL* 14 (*ASD* I-3: 156 lines 1007–9)
19 *COL* 391 (*ASD* I-3: 578 lines 53–4)
20 *COL* 421 (*ASD* I-3: 608 lines 165–6)
21 The story of Bockelson at Münster is told by Norman Cohn in *The Pursuit of the Millennium* 267–80.
22 Kernan *Plot of Satire* 30–1
23 *COL* 141 (*ASD* I-3: 327 line 73)
24 *COL* 141 (*ASD* I-3: 327 lines 76–7)
25 *COL* 142 (*ASD* I-3: 328 lines 96–8)
26 *COL* 142 and 144 (*ASD* I-3: 328 lines 111–13 and 330 lines 187–9)
27 *COL* 143 (*ASD* I-3: 329 lines 146–7)
28 *COL* 145 (*ASD* I-3: 331 lines 210–11)
29 *COL* 247 (*ASD* I-3: 431 lines 52–3)
30 *ASD* I-3: 654 lines 45–6
31 *ASD* I-3: 378 lines 110–11; 615 line 101; 686 line 7
32 *ASD* I-3: 424–9
33 *COL* 251 (*ASD* I-3: 434 lines 40–1)
34 *COL* 504 (*ASD* I-3: 687 lines 40–2)
35 *Adagia* 4.1.1 *LB* 2: 951F–954D
36 *COL* 360 (*ASD* I-3: 539 lines 62–3)
37 *Julius exclusus* 87–9
38 Richard S. Sylvester, the editor of *The History of King Richard the Third*, vol 2 of *The Complete Works of St. Thomas More* xciv, finds in Tacitus's character portrayal of Tiberius the model for More's own description of the dissimulation of Richard.
39 Frye *Anatomy of Criticism* 167
40 Baudelaire 'De l'essence du rire' 375 and 377
41 *COL* 344 (*ASD* I-3: 524 lines 1063–8)
42 *COL* 231 (*ASD* I-3: 417 line 16)
43 *ASD* I-3: 421 line 154
44 *COL* 232 (*ASD* I-3: 418 lines 40–50)
45 *COL* 232 (*ASD* I-3: 418 lines 57–8)
46 *COL* 234 (*ASD* I-3: 420 lines 112–13)
47 *COL* 237 (*ASD* I-3: 423 lines 232–3)
48 *COL* 237 (*ASD* I-3: 423 line 235)
49 *COL* 630 (*ASD* I-3: 746 lines 193–4)
50 *COL* 231 (*ASD* I-3: 417 lines 7–8)
51 *COL* 234 (*ASD* I-3: 421 lines 134–5)
52 L'Estrange, To the Reader *Twenty Select Colloquies of Erasmus* 3
53 Thomas Aquinas, Prologue *In librum Boetii de hebdomadibus expositio, Opera* 17: 339

CHAPTER SIX

1 Luther Ep 626 *WA Br* 3: 96 lines 18–25
2 *ASD* IV-2: 77 lines 387–9. See chapter 1
3 *Adagia* 4.1.1. *AD* 329 (*LB* 2: 960C)
4 *ASD* IV-2: 96 lines 847–8. See the discussion of the *Querela pacis* in chapter 1.
5 *COL* 539 (*ASD* I-3: 721 lines 44–7)
6 *COL* 538 (*ASD* I-3: 720 lines 3–4). See Thompson's introduction to the colloquy for a discussion of the characters' names (536).
7 *Adagia* 4.8.39 *LB* 2: 1132C–D. Erasmus cites the passage from the tenth book of the *Nicomachean Ethics* where Aristotle, in his discussion of happiness, quotes the saying of Anacharsis: '*Paizein d'opos spoudaze.*'
8 *COL* 549 (*ASD* I-3: 732 lines 439–40)
9 *COL* 539 (*ASD* I-3: 722 lines 60–1)
10 Cicero *De finibus bonorum et malorum* 2.26 trans H. Rackam 177
11 Epicurus cited by A.J. Festugière in his *Epicurus and His Gods* 21–2
12 *COL* 538 (*ASD* I-3: 721 lines 26–7)
13 *COL* 539 (*ASD* I-3: 722 line 50)
14 Festugière *Epicurus* 32–3
15 Cicero *De finibus bonorum et malorum* 1.14–16 trans Rackam, 51–5
16 See S. Dresden's introduction to the *De contemptu mundi* where he mentions Pineau as one of those commentators who deny that the Erasmian tranquillity has anything Christian about it. Dresden cites Telle's opinion that the monastic pleasure projected in the *De contemptu mundi* is thoroughly pagan (*ASD* V-1: 27–9). Dresden does not support this negative view because he thinks much better of the work: 'Peut-être sera-t-on surpris de voir comment le traité d'Erasme a été rapproché de la mystique' (*ASD* V-1: 30). Dresden then mentions the *De contemptu mundi*'s dependence upon St Bernard as a source. R. Bultot, in his 'Erasme, Epicure et le "De Contemptu Mundi"' (*Scrinium Erasmianum* 2: 205–38), likewise writes in favour of the Christian substance of Erasmus' treatise. He points out the failure of those who attack the work to comprehend the monastic meaning of '*otium*' as used by Erasmus (2: 218–19).
17 *LB* 5: 606A–B
18 *LB* 5: 1297E
19 *Seamless Coat* 98 (*LB* 5: 506D)
20 *ASD* V-1: 62 line 635
21 *COL* 541 (*ASD* I-3: 723 lines 111–12)
22 *COL* 545 (*ASD* I-3: 728 lines 290–3)
23 *ASD* I-3: 723 lines 110–12
24 *LB* 5: 313 C–D
25 *COL* 549 (*ASD* I-3: 732 lines 426–9)

26 *COL* 546 (*ASD* I-3: 729 line 310)

27 *COL* 547 (*ASD* I-3: 730 lines 365–6)

28 The following texts are among those listed by Festugière to demonstrate the value Epicurus placed on friendship: 'Of all the things which wisdom provides to make life eventually happy, much the greatest is the profession of friendship' (*Principal Doctrines* xxvii); 'Friendship must always be sought for itself though it has its origins in the need for help' (*Gnomologium vaticanum* xxiii). See Festugière *Epicurus* 37.

29 In the *De finibus* 2.24, Cicero argues against an Epicurean friendship that is based on utility: 'Manebit ergo amicitia tam diu quam diu sequetur utilitas, et, si utilitas constituet amicitiam, tollet eadem' (168).

30 *COL* 539 (*ASD* I-3: 722 line 50)

31 *ASD* V-1: 80 lines 85–90

32 *ASD* V-1: 80 lines 91–2

33 *LB* 7: 622B

34 *LB* 7: 616A–B

35 *LB* 7: 683C–E. Erasmus is here commenting on verse 32 of the fourth chapter of Acts.

36 Colet *De corpore* 194

37 In the 'Amicorum communia omnia,' the very first adage of the *Liber adagiorum*, Erasmus, relying on the authority of Cicero and Diogenes Laertius, attributes the saying to Pythagoras (*LB* 2: 14E).

38 Gilby's translation of the Commentary of book 8 of the *Nicomachean Ethics* lecture 4. See Thomas Aquinas *Philosophical Texts* 323.

39 Cunningham 'The Aged Lover Discourses in the Flat Style' *Collected Poems and Epigrams* 79

40 Ep 999 *EE* 4: 16 lines 103–6

41 Erasmus' love of friendly competition manifests itself in his debate with John Colet over the suffering of Christ in the garden before his death (Epp 108–11 *EE* 1: 245–60) and in the declamation contest he entered with Thomas More (Ep 191 *EE* 1: 422 lines 14–17). His gloss on Matthew 10:34 informs us of the personal and introspective direction which Christian violence should take (*LB* 7: 63E–F).

42 The most thorough discussion of the composition of the *Antibarbari* is found in Kazimierz Kumaniecki's introduction to his edition of the text (*ASD* I-1: 7–27). See also Margaret Mann Phillips' account in *CWE* 23: 2–15.

43 *CWE* 23: 19 lines 5–7 (*ASD* I-1: 38 lines 12–14)

44 *CWE* 23: 19 lines 11–12 (*ASD* I-1: 38 lines 18–19)

45 *CWE* 23: 39 line 17 (*ASD* I-1: 64 line 22)

46 *ASD* I-1: 42 lines 31–3

47 *CWE* 23: 23 lines 12–13 (*ASD* I-1: 44 lines 23–4)

48 *CWE* 23: 21 lines 16–17 (*ASD* I-1: 41 lines 27–9)

49 *CWE* 23: 21 lines 18–21 (*ASD* I-1: 42 lines 14–17)

50 *ASD* I-1: 42 lines 21–5

51 *ASD* V-1: 46 lines 185–7 and 62 line 635

52 *CWE* 23: 21 line 20 (*ASD* I-1: 42 lines 15–16)

53 *CWE* 23: 21 lines 5–7 (*ASD* I-1: 41 lines 19–21)

54 *CWE* 23: 23 lines 13–14 (*ASD* I-1: 44 lines 24–5)

55 *CWE* 23: 23 lines 16–18 (*ASD* I-1: 44 lines 25–7)

56 *CWE* 23: 21 lines 9–11 (*ASD* I-1: 41 lines 23–4)

57 *CWE* 23: 54 lines 6–7 *ASD* I-1: 77 lines 13–14)

58 *CWE* 23: 46 lines 14–17 (*ASD* I-1: 72 lines 2–5)

59 'Et fortassis erant qui simpliciter errantes negligerent studia
literarum; erant et qui laborem fugientes inertiam suam honesto
religionis nomine praetexerent, quando sub nulla vmbra melius
tegitur iners ocium et segnis ignauia' (*ASD* I-1: 46 lines 36–9).
'*Ignavia*, a cognate of '*ignavus*,' is a substantive meaning 'idleness.'
The adjectival form is found on page 77, lines 25–6 ('homines
ignauissimi'), page 78, line 24 ('ignaui simulque maligni hominis'),
and elsewhere.

60 For the pejorative use of 'ocium' as applied to the 'antibarbari,' see
note 59. Erasmus himself, however, is described as 'ociosus
interim ac vacuus' in his pursuit of the good life (*ASD* I-1: 42 line
16).

61 *CWE* 23: 87 lines 11–13. 'Haec erant hominis studia in his operam,
curam, voluptatem, *ocium et negocium*, in his felicitatem repone-
bat' (*ASD* I-1: 107 lines 27–8, emphasis mine).

62 *CWE* 23: 55–6 lines 36–3. 'An vero, inquiunt, is Christianus
censendus, qui disciplinis prophanis et ab impiis hominibus ad
superbiam excogitatis, tantum operae impertit, tantopere se oblec-
tat? *In his totus conquiescit, in his ocium, in his negocium, in his
solatium omne reponit?'* (*ASD* I-1: 79 lines 2–8, emphasis mine).

63 In the fourth chapter of the *De contemptu mundi*, Erasmus condemns the pleasures of the flesh (*ASD* V-1: 48–50). In the
eleventh chapter, he extols heavenly, spiritual joys over earthly
ones (*ASD* V-1: 74–6).

64 *CWE* 23: 23 lines 28–9 (*ASD* I-1: 45 lines 19–21)

65 Batt compares the master of the schoolroom to the king of a
country: 'Nihil est similius regno quam ludi literarii moderator'
(*ASD* I-1: 53 lines 16–17). He later refers frequently to the Republic
of Letters: 'Alii enim literariam Rem p. tanquam funditus
deletam cupiunt' (68 line 10). 'Postremi ita Rem p. saluam esse
volunt, vt afflictissimam velint, quippe in qua ipsi tyrannidem
occupent' (lines 12–13). 'Ex iis hostibus literaria Res p. grauissimos
perniciossissimosque patiatur' (lines 22–3), etc.

66 *ASD* I-1: 50–1 lines 27–31

67 For Erasmus, the ages immediately preceding the advent of Christ

were particularly blessed and are understood as leading to him by means of their letters and their wisdom. See *ASD* I-1: 84 lines 3–8. Good literature refines and makes virtuous the dull and boorish man: 'Quis igitur saxeos illos et agrestes homines ad humaniorem vitam, ad mansuetius ingenium, ad mores modestiores adduxit? nonne literae?' (*ASD* I-1: 87 lines 6–8).

68 *ASD* I-1: 87 line 13–88 line 27
69 *CWE* 23: 22 lines 16–18 (*ASD* I-1: 43 lines 22–3)
70 *CWE* 23: 21 line 12 (*ASD* I-1: 41 lines 24–5)
71 *CWE* 23: 74 line 2 (*ASD* I-1: 96 line 6)
72 'Tum ille vulto quo solet faceto' (*ASD* I-1: 49 line 24)
73 See the article by Georg Luck, 'Vir Facetus: A Renaissance Ideal' *Studies in Philology* 55: 107–21, upon which my own account of this humanist ethos depends.
74 According to Pontano, the wit of the 'vir facetus' is capable of transforming obscene material into a thing of delight: 'sic faceti homines, arte adhibita ac translationibus usi, rem naturaliter turpem dictis honestant et quod ipsum per se oscenum est in lepidum vertunt ac facetum' (Giovanni Gioviano Pontano *Iovannis Iovani Pontani de sermone libri sex* 125 lines 7–10).
75 Luck 'Vir Facetus' 120
76 *COL* 268 (*ASD* I-3: 453 lines 11–14)
77 *COL* 269 (*ASD* I-3: 454 lines 44–7)
78 *COL* 270 (*ASD* I-3: 454 lines 50–1)
79 *COL* 271 (*ASD* I-3: 456 lines 107–10)
80 *COL* 269 (*ASD* I-3: 454 lines 26–7)
81 *ASD* I-3: 462 lines 329–30
82 *COL* 279 (*ASD* I-3: 464 lines 398–9)
83 *COL* 275 (*ASD* I-3: 460 lines 267–8)
84 *COL* 276 (*ASD* I-3: 460 line 271)
85 *COL* 276 (*ASD* I-3: 460 lines 273–4)
86 *ASD* I-3: 453 lines 19–23
87 *COL* 282 (*ASD* I-3: 467 lines 517–19)
88 *COL* 283 (*ASD* I-3: 468 lines 546–7)
89 *COL* 283 (*ASD* I-3: 468 line 551)
90 *Declamatio de pueris statim ac liberaliter instituendis* 383
91 *De pueris* 385
92 *De pueris* 385
93 *De pueris* 399. All three of these examples – the hippopatamus, the ibis, and the deer – are found in Pliny's *Natural History* 8.40–1, 3: 69–73.
94 *De pueris* 399–401
95 *De pueris* 411–13
96 *De pueris* 395. Abandoning the child to its own appetite results in a condition diametrically opposed to the end which Erasmus has

in mind when he writes of the purpose of training the young. For him, a liberal education means the free submission of the passions to a will liberated from compulsion. For a full discussion of the part played by both nature and grace in human development, see Jean-Claude Margolin's 'L'idée de nature dans la pensée d'Erasme' in *Recherches erasmiennes* 9–44.

97 *De pueris* 391. In his 'Erasme et la notion de *humanitas*' (*Scrinium Erasmianum* 2: 527–45), S. Dresden suggests that Erasmus looked upon education as an extension of God's creative act. Erasmus' own words support the suggestion: 'homines ... non nascuntur sed finguntur' (*De pueris* 389). Dresden believes that Erasmus chose the verb 'fingere' here to denote a creative act but also to distinguish it from the divine action: '*creare* supposerait un dieu qui est à l'oeuvre et à qui tout est dû, *fingere* exprimerait, par ailleurs, une création humaine' (2: 530).

98 Aristotle *The Ethics of Aristotle* 7.1, 289

99 *De pueris* 391

100 *De pueris* 429

101 *De pueris* 447–9

102 See S. Dresden 'Erasme' 528–9.

103 *De pueris* 431

104 *De pueris* 427

105 *De pueris* 437

106 Huizinga *Homo Ludens* 7–8

107 *De pueris* 453

108 *De pueris* 447

109 *De pueris* 449

110 *De pueris* 445

111 'Quoniam ... *Simile gaudet simili*, praeceptor quodammodo repuerescat oportet, ut ametur a puero' (*De pueris* 443).

112 'Omnino Christianismus nihil aliud est quam renascentia, quam repuerascentia quaedam' (*LB* 5: 604A).

113 *Paraph in Matt LB* 7: 98C–D; *De puero Jesu, LB* 5: 604A–B

114 *COL* 77 (*ASD* I-3: 264 line 1029)

115 Boyle *Erasmus on Language* 131

116 Ep 858 trans R.A.B. Mynors and D.F.S. Thomson *CWE* 6: 89 lines 591–4 (*EE* 3: 376 lines 559–61)

117 *COL* 59 (*ASD* I-3: 244–5 lines 416–21)

118 *ASD* I-3: 247 lines 510–11

119 *ASD* I-3: 253 lines 674–5)

120 *COL* 56 (*ASD* I-3: 241 lines 320–1)

121 *COL* 53 (*ASD* I-3: 237 lines 183–4)

122 *COL* 58 (*ASD* I-3: 243 line 379)

123 *COL* 58–9 (*ASD* I-3: 244 lines 392–400 [alternate text MS E–O])

124 The Sorbonne censured Erasmus for opposing church precepts to Christian liberty (*LB* 9: 933B–935B).

125 *ASD* I-3: 248–9 lines 538–61

126 *ASD* I-3: 240 lines 291–4 and 234 line 90

CHAPTER SEVEN

1 *L&E* 36 (*AS* 4:6)

2 Sidney *A Defence of Poetry* 79–80

3 *De contemptu mundi, ASD* V-1: 62 line 635

4 'Itaque quod paulo ante dulce videbatur, nunc amarescit: quod amarum, dulcescit (*LB* 5: 608A–B).

5 See my discussion of the conflict in the *Antibarbari* between business and leisure in the second part of chapter 6 of the present study.

6 *ASD* I-3: 720–33

7 *The Education of a Christian Prince* trans Lester K. Born, 185 (*Institutio principis Christiani* ed O. Herding, *ASD* IV-1: 170 lines 103–4)

8 *LB* 5: 319F. In commenting on the 'aquas refectionis' of verse 2, Erasmus writes: 'sic recreat reficitque, ut ea quoque dulcia sint, quae videntur amara nil nisi mundum sapientibus' (*LB* 5: 320B).

9 *L&E* 50 (*AS* 4: 44)

10 *PF* 76 (*ASD* IV-3: 136 lines 196–200)

11 *PF* 78 (*ASD* IV-3: 138 lines 232–6)

12 *PF* 2 (*ASD* IV-3: 67 lines 15–16)

13 Ep 999 *EE* 4: 16 lines 121–30

14 *Adagia* 2.6.12 *AD* 268 (*LB* 2: 587B)

15 *PF* 43 (*ASD* IV-3: 104 lines 580–5)

16 *PF* 43 (*ASD* IV-3: 14 lines 587–8)

17 *PF* 44 (*ASD* IV-3: 104 lines 604–7)

18 *ASD* IV-3: 104 line 612

19 *ASD* IV-3: 169 lines 705–16

20 *PF* 89 (*ASD* IV-3: 148 line 409)

21 *PF* 115 (*ASD* IV-3: 176 lines 841–2)

22 *Adagia* 3.3.1 *AD* 279 (*LB* 2: 775A)

23 'De Regibus itaque qui sibi gerunt imperium, non Reipublicae commodis, nullus hominum auderet dicere, fures sunt et latrones, sed hoc ausus est dicere Dominus, qui nec mentiri novit, nec metuit quemquam' (*LB* 5: 317D).

24 'Filius assumta carnis infirmitate divinam naturam dissimulans' (*Adversus calumniosissimam epistolam Martini Lutheri, LB* 10: 1542D).

25 Chantraine *'Mystère' et 'Philosophie du Christ'* 274–95

26 'Fabula Graecis *drama* dicitur argumentum constans ex variis

personis, quarum unaquaeque suis fungitur partibus, tota actione sic ordine digesta, ut a satis tranquillo exordio incrudescat, ac tandem in laetum finem exeat' (*LB* 10: 1542D).

27 'Homo bene conditus, veluti protasis est, crux epitasis, resurrectio catastrophe' (*LB* 10: 1542E). In his 'L'idée de nature,' Jean-Claude Margolin mentions, as it were in passing, some underlying reasons for Erasmus' approach to existence as a kind of drama. When Margolin describes the Erasmian vision of cosmic harmony, he readily turns to a theatrical metaphor: 'Mais nous avons vu que la finalité ou l'harmonie du Monde n'impliquait pas une identité de structure ou de fonction des diverses natures spécifiques: c'est au contraire dans le jeu et dans la lutte des finalités différentielles entrecroisées, c'est dans la 'variété des choses' et dans la dialectique vivante des attirances et des répulsions que la dramaturgie du cosmos s'organise. Mais tout n'est pas joué d'avance' (41).

28 *LB* 7: 822C–D

29 Colet *Super opera Dionysii* 72

30 *AS* 4: 174

31 *LB* 5: 604A

32 *LB* 7: 67F–68B

33 Luther *De servo arbitrio*, *L&E* 120 (*WA* 18: 616 n 1)

34 Huizinga *Homo Ludens* 3–4

35 See *Ratio*, *AW* 274 line 26.

36 Rahner *Man at Play* 53

37 Bede *Homiliae* 2.12 *PL* 94: 198D

38 Guardini *Spirit of the Liturgy* 102 and 106

39 See Erasmus' letter to Nicolas Varius on the bellicose trumpets that were used in church (Ep 1756 *EE* 6: 420 lines 93–112). Jean-Claude Margolin cites this passage in his *Erasme et la musique* 62–3.

40 Huizinga *Homo Ludens* 14

41 *Homo Ludens* 15

42 *Homo Ludens* 18

43 Schmemann *Sacraments and Orthodoxy* 44

44 *LB* 4: 632D–E

45 *En in ps 22*, *LB* 5: 329C. The notion of this transforming power of spiritual food is found in Augustine's *Confessions* 7.10 (*CCSL* 27: 103–4), although the passage does not refer to the eucharist. We find this forceful characteristic applied to the sacramental meal in both Durandus Troarnensis (*Liber de corpore et sanguine Christi* 4.9 *PL* 149: 1389B–C) and Aquinas (*Summa theologiae* 3a. 73.3).

46 *Enchiridion* 104 (*AW* 69 lines 25–7)

47 *Enchiridion* 130 (*AW* 88 lines 25–8)

48 Colet *Super opera Dionysii* 86–7

49 Jeffrey 'Bosch's "Haywain": Communion, Community, and the Theater of the World' *Viator* 4: 330
50 Jeffrey 'Bosch's "Haywain"' 315 and 331
51 Ernst *The Theology of Grace* 93–4
52 'Quum audis *in finem,* quae vox frequenter in sacris litteris declarat non terminum, sed consummationem' (*LB* 5: 417A–B).
53 In his *Liber de nominibus hebraicis* 71, Jerome translates 'Idithum' as 'transiliens eos, sive saliens eos' (*PL* 23: 827). In the introduction to his homily on Psalm 38 (1), Augustine writes: 'Idithun interpretatur: Transiliens eos' (*Enarrationes in psalmos* ed Eligius Dekkers and Iohannes Fraipont *CCSL* 38: 401 lines 11–12).
54 *LB* 5: 490B–C
55 *LB* 5: 420B
56 *LB* 5: 420B–C
57 *LB* 7: 1013E–F
58 *LB* 5: 419F–420A. Plato's discussion of the role music plays in uniting the soul with the universe and in dispelling discord within itself can be found in the *Timaeus* 37d, 47b–e.
59 *LB* 5: 425D–E
60 *LB* 5: 420A–B
61 *LB* 5: 425D
62 'Est enim armonia plurimorum adunatio et dissidentium consensio' (*De arithmetica* 2.32 ed Godofredus Friedlein, 126 lines 16–17). This quotation is cited by David S. Chamberlain 'Philosophy of Music in the *Consolatio* of Boethius' *Speculum* 45: 81.
63 *LB* 5: 425D–E. To the music of the spheres, Boethius adds the harmony of the elements and the seasons as parts of 'musica mundana.' See Chamberlain 'Philosophy of Music.'
64 'At humana ratio frequenter discrepat a Spiritu Dei, ad cujus voluntatem nisi tendantur omnes animi nostri chordae, non potest reddi bene modulata cantio' (*LB* 5: 425D).
65 *LB* 5: 425E
66 '*Haec pietatis vox est, sed fucus iniquitatis,* ut eleganter dicit Augustinus' (*LB* 5: 453E). The Brepols text (*En in ps* 38.11) of this sentence substitutes 'excusatio' for 'fucus' (*CCSL* 38: 413 lines 45–6).
67 Augustine *En in ps* 38.1 *CCSL* 38: 402 lines 14–20
68 Augustine *Conf* 13.9.10 *CCSL* 27: 246 lines 7–8 trans Vernon J. Bourke *Confessions* vol 5 of *The Writings of Saint Augustine* 415–16
69 *Confessions* 416; 'Pondus non ad ima tantum est, sed ad locum suum' (*Conf* 13.9.10 *CCSL* 27: 246 lines 11–12)
70 *Confessions* 416 (*Conf* 13.9.10 *CCSL* 27: 247 lines 17–21)
71 *Conf* 13.9.10 *CCSL* 27: 246 line 16
72 'Descendit ergo ille ut nos ascenderemus,' *Epistolae* 140.4.10 *PL* 33: 542. Epistle 140 is sometimes called *On the Grace of the New Testament.*

73 'Reddite vicem; efficimini spiritus, et habitate in illo qui caro factus est, et habitavit in vobis' Augustine (*Ep* 140.4.11 *PL* 33: 542).

74 *Ep* 140.17.44 *PL* 33: 557 trans Sister Wilfrid Parsons, vol 11 of *The Writings of Saint Augustine* 95

75 Augustine *De musica* 6.11.29 *PL* 32: 1179 trans Robert Catesby Taliaferro *On Music* in vol 2 of *The Writings of Saint Augustine* 355

76 Augustine *De civitate Dei* 12.19 ed Bernardus Dombart and Alphonsus Kalb *CCSL* 48: 375 lines 19–20

77 Robert J. O'Connell *Art and the Christian Intelligence in St. Augustine* 15

78 Emmanuel Chapman *Saint Augustine's Philosophy of Beauty* 14

79 Chapman *Saint Augustine's Philosophy* 24–6. Chapman here gives his English rendition of Augustine's *De libero arbitrio* 2.16.41–3 *PL* 32: 1263–4.

80 Chapman *Saint Augustine's Philosophy* 34

81 2.16.42 *PL* 32: 1263–4. I have used Chapman's translation of this passage (25).

82 Augustine *En in ps* 38. 17 *CCSL* 38: 418 lines 8–9. In his own commentary on Psalm 38, Erasmus echoes the thought of Augustine: 'Tam nemo se potest refingere, quam nemo se potuit fingere' (*LB* 5: 449D).

83 Augustine *De musica* 6.11.33 *PL* 32: 1181

84 'In illis spectaculis non id est uenator quod cytharista; aliud agit uenator, aliud cytharista. In spectaculo dei unum est' Augustine (*Sermones* 9.13 *CCSL* 41: 132 lines 470–2).

85 'Et chordas tangis et bestias occidis. Id est, et cytharista et uenator' (*Sermones* 9.8 *CCSL* 41: 133 lines 483–4).

86 *Sermones* 9.8 *CCSL* 41: 122–3 lines 294–314

87 This passage from Augustine's *Expositions on the Book of Psalms* (1: 316f) is quoted by Perl in 'Augustine and Music' trans Alan Kriegsman *The Music Quarterly* 41: 498–9. Perl substitutes the word 'kithara' for 'harp' in the translation.

88 Augustine *En in ps 38 LB* 5: 419A

89 *LB* 5: 419A–B

90 *LB* 5: 419A–B

91 *LB* 5: 419C–E

92 *LB* 5: 421E–F

93 *LB* 5: 422B

94 *LB* 5: 420C

95 'Hic primus et unicus tibi sit scopus, hoc votum, hoc unum age, ut muteris, ut rapiaris, ut affleris, ut transformeris in ea, quae discis' (*AW* 180 lines 22–4).

96 Ep 1756 *EE* 6: 420 lines 93–112

97 Erasmus' letter to Adrian VI, which served as the preface to his edition of Arnobius' commentary on the Psalms, contains a splendid assessment of the power of sacred song to stir

the heart to virtue and love (Ep 1304, *EE* 5: 99–111, especially lines 376–444).

98 *LB* 5: 425B

99 *LB* 5: 'pulsantes citharam' (418E), 'fides pulsare' (422E), 'per organa flatu ... et pulsu constat' (425E), 'musicam ... pulsatilem' (426B–C) 'pulsantes ... chordam' (427B)

100 *LB* 9: 'Gratia pulsans' (1400B), 'pulsanti gratiae' (1467B), 'auxiliante gratia pulsante' (1468A). See also 'ex gratia pulsante ... pulsantem gratiam' (1339B); 'Quia pulsanti gratiae subducebant sese' (1385C); 'Imo pulsatus est gratia praeparante Pharao,' and 'flecti coeperat, et fortasse resipiscere poterat, si pulsantem gratiam fuisset amplexus' (1408B); and 'quod se gratiae pulsanti praebet si velit' (1413B).

101 'Nec absurdum fuerit flatilem musicam accipere, quae facit ut omnis oratio nostra congruat praeceptis Dei' (*LB* 5: 426B–C).

102 'pulsatilem, ut omnes actiones nostrae consonent illius voluntati' (*LB* 5: 426C).

103 *LB* 5: 426C

104 *LB* 5: 425E

105 See note 9 of this chapter.

106 *LB* 5: 420C–E

107 *LB* 5: 420F

108 *LB* 5: 421A

109 'No young creature whatsoever, as we may fairly assert, can keep its body or its voice still; all are perpetually trying to make movements and noises. They leap and bound, they dance and frolic, as it were with glee, and again, they utter cries of all sorts' Plato (*Laws* 2.653d–e; trans Taylor 1251).

110 Erikson *Toys and Reasons* 17

CHAPTER EIGHT

1 In his *Praisers of Folly* 46–50, Walter Kaiser call attention to the rhetorical nature of the *Moria*. Jacques Chomarat's *Grammaire et rhetorique* (2: 982–99) confines its attention to the strictly rhetorical aspects of the *Moria*. For all this stress of the rhetorical structure of the *Moria*, both of these writers readily admit the dramatic aspect of the work. Kaiser introduces the argument of his entire study by adverting to the motto of the Globe Theatre, '*Totus mundus agit histrionem*' (1), and later refers to 'the essentially dramatic character of Erasmus' mind' (99). Chomarat, in following Folly's argument, underscores her view of life as 'une comédie jouée sur un théâtre' (995).

2 In his edition of the *Moria* (*ASD* IV-3: 72), Clarence H. Miller discusses Folly's meaning when she refers to her unusual

attire – 'hoc insolito cultu' (line 20). Miller mentions the suggestion of Pierre Mesnard ('Erasme et la conception dialectique de la folie' *L'Umanesimo e 'la follia'* 53) that Folly is wearing an academic gown, which, of course, would be unusual for her. Miller leans in another direction: 'Her clothing is "insolito" not for her but for the setting of a formal and official eulogy in which she appears' (73). He opts for the motley worn by fools that is out of place in an academic context.

3 As Wayne A. Rebhorn observes in 'The Metamorphoses of Moria: Structure and Meaning in *The Praise of Folly*' *PMLA* 89: 463, most readers of the *Moria* divide it into 'three quite distinct sections: a long opening section comprising almost half of the work where the most outrageous of women holds forth with the most complex irony; a shorter middle section characterized by severe, straight-forward invective; and a few concluding pages devoted to Christian folly.' My own tripartite division of the *Moria* begins part 3 earlier than the section on the folly of the saints. I prefer to begin at the point where Folly turns theologian. There she abandons the invective that characterizes part 2.

Richard Sylvester, at the close of 'The Problem of Unity in *The Praise of Folly*' *English Literary Renaissance* 6: 125–39, stresses the tripartite structure of the *Moria* (136–9) and, like Rebhorn, speaks of Folly's metamorphosis in her progress through the three sections.

H.A. Mason divides the *Moria* into two parts: one concerned with play and the other given to seriousness. See *Humanism and Poetry in the Early Tudor Period* 76.

4 Barthes *Le plasir du texte* 9–10

5 Colie *Paradoxia epidemica* 20–1

6 *PF* 4 (*ASD* IV-3: 68 lines 42–4)

7 Ep 337 *CWE* 3: 115 lines 98–9 (*EE* 2: 93 lines 91–2)

8 *CWE* 3: 114 lines 94–5 (*EE* 2: 93 lines 87–8)

9 *CWE* 3: 126 lines 496–9 (*EE* 2: 103 lines 471–3)

10 After distinguishing the three basic parts of the *Moria*, Rebhorn notes the radical changes that take place in the persona at each change of section. He argues for the metamorphosis of Folly from a worldly to a heavenly fool in imitation of that change wrought within a Christian by what Erasmus calls 'gratiosam stulticiam' (*ASD* IV-3: 188 lines 122–3). I find this article filled with rich suggestions, but I cannot follow Rebhorn when he tells us that Folly undergoes a radical change. From beginning to end, she is the spokes-woman for all folly, both the worldly and the heavenly alike.

11 A.E. Douglas 'Erasmus as a Satirist' *Erasmus* 46. Although he does not single out the central section of the *Moria* in this remark, it obviously applies most aptly to it.

12 Thompson *Under Pretext of Praise* 84
13 Folly identifies the wise man as one led by reason and the fool as one given to emotion (*ASD* IV-3: 88–90 lines 316–21). So folly and wisdom would appear to be at loggerheads. Later, however, Folly claims that she had inspired the discovery of all branches of learning (*ASD* IV-3: 96 lines 463–4). Later still, we are told that evil spirits invented learning (*ASD* IV-3: 111 line 738).
14 *ASD* IV-3: 96–7 lines 477–86
15 *ASD* IV-3: 88–90 lines 316–28
16 *PF* 35 and 51 (*ASD* IV-3: 96 lines 463–4 and 111 line 738)
17 *ASD* IV-3: 104 lines 599–601 and 112 line 758
18 Mesnard 'Erasme et la conception dialectique' 58
19 *PF* 57 (*ASD* IV-3: 116 lines 863–4)
20 *PF* 58 (*ASD* IV-3: 116–18 lines 873–80)
21 *PF* 60–1 (*ASD* IV-3: 118–20 lines 918–19 and lines 924–35)
22 *PF* 79 (*ASD* IV-3: 138 lines 247–52)
23 *PF* 79 (*ASD* IV-3: 138 lines 253–5)
24 *ASD* IV-3: 182–4 lines 997–45
25 *PF* 114 (*ASD* IV-3: 174 lines 823–4)
26 *PF* 48 (*ASD* IV-3: 108 lines 671–7)
27 *PF* 22 (*ASD* IV-3: 84 lines 229–31)
28 Foucault *Madness and Civilization* 15–16
29 Rebhorn 'Metamorphoses' 471
30 *PF* 42 (*ASD* IV-3: 104 line 577)
31 *PF* 44 (*ASD* IV-3: 106 lines 615–18)
32 *PF* 44 (*ASD* IV-3: 104–6 lines 612–13)
33 *PF* 78 (*ASD* IV-3: 138 line 240)
34 *PF* 80–1 (*ASD* IV-3: 140 lines 273–6)
35 *PF* 81 (*ASD* IV-3: 140 lines 284–7)
36 *PF* 85 (*ASD* IV-3: 142–4 lines 354–8)
37 *PF* 87 (*ASD* IV-3: 146 lines 387–90)
38 *PF* 90 (*ASD* IV-3: 148 line 416)
39 *PF* 89, 93, and 95 (*ASD* IV-3: 148 line 408, 154 line 456, and 154 lines 485–6)
40 *PF* 4 (*ASD* IV-3: 68 lines 42–3)
41 'It has often been pointed out that for all its brilliant passages and incidental flashes of wit, the *Praise of Folly* suffers from a fundamental incoherence, and this incoherence results precisely from the combination in it of everything that can paradoxically (i.e. untruthfully) be said on behalf of Folly, with everything that Folly can say by way of satirizing the real follies of mankind' ('Erasmus as a Satirist' 46).
42 *ASD* IV-3: 106–8 lines 655–63
43 *PF* 78 (*ASD* IV-3: 138 lines 231–4)
44 *PF* 111 (*ASD* IV-3: 172 lines 757–67)

45 *PF* 100–1 (*ASD* IV-3: 162 lines 569–76)
46 *ASD* IV-3: 106 lines 613–15
47 *PF* 125 (*ASD* IV-3: 184 lines 30–2)
48 *PF* 126 (*ASD* IV-3: 184 lines 39–40)
49 *ASD* IV-3: 185–7 lines 49–55
50 *ASD* IV-3: 180 line 912
51 *ASD* IV-3: 186 lines 64–6
52 *PF* 120–1 (*ASD* IV-3: 180 lines 944–5)
53 *PF* 130 (*ASD* IV-3: 188 lines 106–10)
54 *PF* 128–9 (*ASD* IV-3: 186 lines 86–7)
55 *PF* 130 (*ASD* IV-3: 188 line 110)
56 *PF* 136 (*ASD* IV-3: 192 lines 228–30)
57 *LB* 7: 863C–D
58 *Adagia* 3.3.1 *AD* 288 (*LB* 2: 778F)
59 *Enchiridion* 140 (*AW* 96 lines 4–5)
60 *Adagia* 3.3.1 *AD* 279 (*LB* 2: 775A)
61 *ASD* IV-3: 118 lines 877–92

CHAPTER NINE

1 I follow Clarence Miller's account of the publication of the *Moria* (*Praise of Folly* ix–x). See also Miller's introduction to the *Moria* in *ASD* IV-3: 13–16, and M.A. Screech's review of various versions and editions of the work in his *Ecstasy and the Praise of Folly* xix–xx and 2–7.
2 Ep 304 *CWE* 3: 19 line 60 (*EE* 2: 13 line 54)
3 Myron P. Gilmore in his '*Apologiae*' (111–23) covers the debates that Erasmus had over the *Moria* with Dorp, Stunica, and Pio. He devotes most of his article to the heated controversy with Pio. See Clarence Miller's account of the attacks on the *Moria* in *ASD* IV-3: 24–9.
4 *ASD* IV-3: 28
5 *CWE* 3: 18 lines 28–9 (*EE* 2: 12 lines 25–6)
6 *CWE* 3: 20 line 83 (*EE* 2: 13 lines 74–6)
7 At the close of his letter to Dorp, More tells the young theologian that the reproaches he makes against Erasmus do not reflect Dorp's own irritation but that of others (Ep 15 *The correspondence of Sir Thomas More* 73 lines 1573–81).
8 For an account of Dorp's public recantation of his opposition to Erasmus, see Henry de Vocht *Monumenta Humanistica Louvaniensia* 159–65.
9 Ep 337 *EE* 2: 97–100 lines 258–347
10 For Erasmus' reply to these charges of blasphemy, see *Apologia adversus libellum Jacobi Stunicae, cui titulum fecit, blasphemiae et impietates Erasmi, LB* 9: 359C–360C, *Appendix respondens ad quaedam*

Antapologiae Petri Sutoris, LB 9: 805D–E, and *Responsio ad Albertum Pium,* LB 9: 1109E–1111F.

11 In the *Responsio* to Pio's charges, Erasmus cites what is probably the Italian's most sweeping attack on the *Moria*: '*Quid,* inquis, *ad jugulandam prorsus Religionem Christianam dici potuit atrocius, quam ipsam esse universam in stultitia fundatam?*' (LB 9: 1111A–B).

12 For instance, against Pio he cites the example of Pauline folly (LB 9: 1111B).

13 Ep 304 CWE 3: 18 lines 32–4 (EE 2: 12 lines 28–30)

14 Thomas Aquinas *Summa* 2a.2ae 46, 1–3

15 Ep 337 CWE 3: 127 line 534 (EE 2: 104 lines 507–9)

16 CWE 3: 127 lines 535–44 (EE 2: 104 lines 510–17)

17 EE 2: 104 lines 517–21

18 Duncan *Ben Jonson* 33

19 *Ben Jonson* 38

20 Augustine *Contra Faustum* 22.87 ed Josephus Zycha CSEL 25: 691–3

21 Gregory the Great *Moralium libri* 3.28.55 PL 75: 625C–627A

22 Gerhoh of Reichersberg *Commentarius aureus in psalmos,* PL 193: 1602D–1603B; Honorius *Selectorum psalmorum expositio,* PL 172: 283B–D; John of Salisbury *Policraticus sive De nugis curialium et vestigiis philosophorum* 1: 95–6 lines 30–4; trans Joseph B. Pike *Frivolities of Courtiers and Footprints of Philosophers* 82–3

23 See Matt 24:43, Luke 12:39, and Rev 3.3.

24 Augustine *De doctrina christiana* 3.12.18 ed Josephus Martin CCSL 32: 89 lines 16–18

25 AW 71 lines 21–4

26 In a very basic sense, Dionysius holds that God is 'namelessness – being after the manner of no existing being, and Cause of being to all, but Itself not being, as beyond every essence, and as It may manifest Itself properly and scientifically concerning Itself' (*De divinis nominibus* 1.1 *The Works of Dionysius the Areopagite* trans John Parker, 1: 2 [PG 3: 588B]). A dialectic runs through the core of Dionysian theology, as Hans Urs von Balthasar has observed: 'for Denys what is Incomprehensible is to be found in what is really comprehensible, for it is in every case the incomprehensible God in his totality who makes himself comprehensible in his communications' (*Studies in Theological Style: Clerical Styles* 185). In another place, Balthasar describes Dionysius' teaching in the same paradoxical fashion: 'God is and must be both all in all and nothing in anything' (179).

27 'The Good … is not entirely uncommunicated to any single created being, but benignly sheds forth its superessential ray, persistently fixed in Itself, by illuminations analogous to each several being' (Dionysius *De divinis nominibus* 1.2 *Works* 1: 3 [PG 3: 588C–589A]).

28 Thomas Aquinas *In librum Beati Dionysii de divinis nominibus commentaria* prologue trans Thomas Gilby *Theological Texts* 8
29 Dionysius *De coelesti hierarchia* 2.2 *Works* 2: 6 (*PG* 3: 137C–D)
30 *De coelesti hierarchia* 2.3 *Works* 2: 7 (*PG* 3: 140B–C)
31 *De coelesti hierarchia* 2.5 *PG* 3: 145A
32 *De coelesti hierarchia* 2.3 *Works* 2: 9 (*PG* 3: 141C)
33 Dionysius *De divinis nominibus* 4.20 *Works* 1: 57 (*PG* 3: 720C)
34 Dionysius *De mystica theologia* 3.1 *PG* 3: 1033B
35 Cyprian 'Ad Caecilium de sacramento Dominici calicis' *Epistola* 63 *Epistolae*, *PL* 4: 371–89. See particularly section 11 (382A–383A).
36 Gregory of Nyssa '*Homilia* 10' in *Commentarius in canticum canticorum*, *PG* 44: 992C–D
37 *LB* 7: 668D
38 Ep 337 *CWE* 3: 127 lies 541–2 (*EE* 2: 104 lines 514–15)
39 *PF* 17 and 24 (*ASD* IV-3: 78 lines 122–4 and 86 lines 270–2)
40 *ASD* IV-3: 88 lines 306–9
41 *ASD* IV-3: 78 lines 108–11
42 *ASD* IV-3: 132 lines 143–4
43 *ASD* IV-3: 80 lines 169–70
44 *ASD* IV-3: 92 lines 369–72
45 *ASD* IV-3: 82 lines 215–17
46 *ASD* IV-3: 108 lines 671–7
47 *ASD* IV-3: 188 lines 122–4
48 *ASD* IV-3: 188 lines 130–3
49 *ASD* IV-3: 188 lines 133–4
50 Ep 337 *CWE* 3: 126 lines 503–5 (*EE* 2: 103 lines 477–80)
51 Dionysius *De divinis nominibus* 11.1 *Works* 1: 113 (*PG* 3: 949A–B)
52 *De divinis nominibus* 9.9 *Works* 1: 108 (*PG* 3: 916C)
53 *De divinis nominibus* 4.13 *Works* 1: 48–9 (*PG* 3: 712A–B)
54 Ep 337 *CWE* 3: 115 lines 98–9 (*EE* 2: 93 lines 91–2)
55 *AW* 88 lines 25–8
56 *Enchiridion* 104 (*AW* 69 lines 25–7)
57 *PF* 130 (*ASD* IV-3: 188 lines 109–10)
58 According to Screech, Erasmus suggests 'that Christ in his manhood, emptied of his divine wisdom, was a kind of fool' (15). He also thinks that the self-emptying God of Erasmus is based on Origen's notion of divine folly (*Ecstasy and the 'Praise of Folly'* 22). Screech points out the heavy stress that Erasmus, in a long footnote to Hebrews 2:6 (*LB* 6: 985C–991D), lays on Christ's kenosis (25). The theme of kenosis runs through this most illuminating study of Erasmian folly and ecstasy. See also Screech 36, 38, 47, 232, and 241.
59 *PF* 137 (*ASD* IV-3: 192 lines 245–7)
60 *PF* 136 (*ASD* IV-3: 192 lines 234–6)
61 *PF* 132 (*ASD* IV-3: 190 lines 152–3)

62 'Verum ego iamdudum oblita mei' (*ASD* IV-3: 194 line 268)

63 *Enaratio in primum psalmum* ed A. Godin *ASD* V-2: 52 line 581

64 *PF* 132 (*ASD* IV-3: 189–90 lines 147–52)

65 *PF* 132 (*ASD* IV-3: 190 lines 152–3)

66 'Verius est anima ubi amat quam ubi animat' (Bonaventure
Soliloquium 2.2.12 in *Opera* 8 Quarrachi 1898, 49, col 1). Cited by
Screech *Ecstasy* 152

67 *PF* 46 (*ASD* IV-3: 106 lines 638–40)

68 *PF* 45 (*ASD* IV-3: 106 lines 627–35)

69 *PF* 42 (*ASD* IV-3: 102 lines 568–9)

70 *ASD* IV-3: 192 lines 241–5

71 Bakhtin *Rabelais and His World* 10

72 Greenblatt *Renaissance Self-Fashioning from More to Shakespeare* 220

73 Donald Gwynn Watson 'Erasmus' *Praise of Folly* and the Spirit of
Carnival' *Renaissance Quarterly* 32: 333–53

74 Ep 337 *EE* 2: 103 lines 471–3

75 Baudelaire 'De l'essence du rire' 373

76 Bakhtin *Rabelais* 11

77 *Rabelais* 14

78 Holbein drew his now famous illustrations in the margins of a copy
of Froben's 1515 edition of the *Moria*. See Betty Radice
'Holbein's Marginal Illustrations of the *Praise of Folly' Erasmus in
English* 7: 8–17. These drawings were copied by William
Stettler of Bern for Charles Patin's Basel edition of the *Moria* of 1676
(Miller *PF* 62–3). It would seem that the Stettler copies of
Holbein were used in the Leiden *Opera omnia* (*LB* 4: 401–504).

79 *PF* 27 (*ASD* IV-3: 88 lines 300–1)

80 *PF* 27 (*ASD* IV-3: 88 line 304)

81 *PF* 129 (*ASD* IV-3: 188 line 100)

82 *PF* 130 (*ASD* IV-3: 188 lines 103–4)

83 Bakhtin *Rabelais* 19

84 *Rabelais* 16–17

85 *PF* 130 (*ASD* IV-3: 188 line 107)

86 *ASD* IV-3: 104 lines 580–1

87 Baudelaire 'De l'essence du rire' 375

88 In Baudelaire 'le comique absolu' is distinguished from 'le comique
significatif.' Gurewitch has some illuminating things to say
about the opposition between the two, and the passage deserves
more mention than I have been able to squeeze into the text.
Here is the citation in greater fullness: 'The basic distinction
between the significantly comic and the absolutely comic is that
the former caters to common sense, morality, and social utility,
while the latter, embodying the spirit of the grotesque, defies
utilitarian common sense and shuns the moralization of laughter.
Also, the significantly comic generates a fairly moderate or

delayed laughter, while the absolutely comic produces an immediate hilarity "that has in it something profound, axiomatic and primitive, which more closely relates it to innocence and absolute joy than does the laughter occasioned by the comedy of manners"' Comedy (190).

89 Gurewitch Comedy 181
90 'Les phénomènes engendrés par la chute deviendront les moyens du rachat' (Baudelaire 'De l'essence du rire' 372).

CHAPTER TEN

1 ASD I-3: 506 lines 387–8
2 De praeparatione ad mortem LB 5: 1305C–F
3 The Encomium matrimonii was published at Louvain in 1518 by Thierry Martens d'Alost along with three other declamations by Erasmus (ASD I-5: 335). J.C. Margolin describes the controversies that followed from this publication in the preface to his edition of this text (ASD I-5: 370–81). In my reading of the Encomium matrimonii, I follow Margolin's edition in the ASD, based upon the editio princeps of Thierry Martens of August 1518. The Encomium matrimonii also appeared in the Froben edition (August 1522) of Erasmus' De conscribendis epistolis as an example of a letter of persuasion. The whole of this treatise on epistolary style has been translated in the Collected Works of Erasmus, vol 25, but I have decided against using its English version of the Encomium matrimonii because it translates from a text different from that of Margolin in the ASD I-5. In order to avoid confusion, I make my own translation whenever my argument calls for an Englishing of the text.
4 ASD IV-2: 62 lines 42–5
5 PF 45 and 134 (ASD IV-3: 106 lines 628–9 and 190 line 188)
6 Marsh 'Erasmus and the Antithesis of Body and Soul' Journal of the History of Ideas 37: 673–88
7 COL 113 (ASD I-3: 399 line 40)
8 COL 87
9 COL 88–9 (ASD I-3: 278 lines 34–9)
10 COL 89 (ASD I-3: 279 lines 62–73)
11 COL 96 (ASD I-3: 285–6 lines 297–309)
12 Declarationes ad censuras facultatis theologiae parisiensis, LB 9: 937D–F
13 COL 118–19 (ASD I-3: 304 lines 117–20)
14 COL 119 (ASD I-3: 304–5 lines 121–7)
15 COL 120–2 (ASD I-3: 306–7 lines 183–227)
16 COL 124 (ASD I-3: 310 lines 307–28)
17 COL 123–4 (ASD I-3: 309 lines 294–301)
18 ASD I-5: 406–8 lines 277–82

19 *ASD* I-5: 408 lines 301–3
20 Erasmus observes that all civilized societies detest infanticide: 'Nulla natio tam immanis est, quin exsecretur infanticidium' (*LB* 1: 420B). After mentioning laws punishing abortion and the Bible's opposition to onanism, he concludes that celibacy differs very little from this interference with the life-giving process: 'At quantulum ab hoc differunt, qui sibi perpetuam sterilitatem indicunt?' (*LB* 1: 420C). This passage does not appear in Margolin's North Holland edition. Both of the above editions, however, include the passage portraying celibacy as worse than pestilence, flood, and other human disasters because, like those tragedies, it proves itself hostile to human life. See *ASD* 1–5; 412–14 lines 365–75 and *LB* 1: 422F–423A.
21 *ASD* I-5: 394–6 lines 142–4
22 In both of these works, Erasmus argues that his adversaries have mistaken the *Encomium matrimonii* for a dogmatic pronouncement instead of a rhetorical exercise. In his answer to Briard, Erasmus chides Louvain's vice-chancellor for failing to understand the nature of a declamation: 'Quis enim nescit, Declamationes exercitandi ingenii gratia in fictis thematis versari?' (*Apologia de laude matrimonii, LB* 9: 108A).
23 *Dilutio eorum Iodocus Clithoveus scripsit adversus declamationem Des. Erasmi Roterodami suasoriam matrimonii* 82
24 *Dilutio* 86
25 *Dilutio* 95
26 *Dilutio* 77
27 *Dilutio* 80
28 *Dilutio* 77–8
29 Erasmus refers to the declamation as a practice in eloquence ('ad exercitationem dictionis') not focusing upon the rule of faith or morals ('non ad morum fideiue regulam pertinere') (*Dilutio* 70).
30 *Encomium, ASD* I-5: 392 lines 116–18
31 'Declamo enim, non doceo Theologiam' (*Dilutio* 93). 'Has partes tracto in argumentatione, interdum loquens ut politicus, interdum ut rhetor, interdum ut physicus, semper ut disputans, aliter locuturus in argumento Theologico' (*Dilutio* 86).
32 *Dilutio* 80–1
33 Frye *Natural Perspective: The Development of Shakespearean Comedy and Romance* 43
34 *Dilutio* 94
35 For Clichtove's negative approach to the sex drive, see the thirty-second chapter of book 2 in his *Propugnaculum ecclesie* 384–9. The position is summed up in the heading to this chapter: 'Celibatum in sacris literis multifariam commendavi: et stimulos libidinum non a natura condita sed a peccato primorum parentum

processisse contra Erasmi placitum' (384). Erasmus sees the
drive as natural and its rebellion as a sign of fallen nature: 'ego
pono stimulos gignendi esse naturae simpliciter acceptae, sicut
sitis et fames natura stimulant ad naturae conseruationem licet
rebellio ueniat e corruptione naturae' (*Dilutio* 87). For Erasmus,
the natural instinct is God-given: 'Numen autem appello naturae
instinctum, cuius conditor est deus" (*Dilutio* 87).

36 *Dilutio* 93
37 Clichtove's thought on the permanence of the law of celibacy is
involved with an idea concerning the nature of the sacerdotal
calling which makes it intrinsically incompatible with marriage.
Following a passage in Augustine, Clichtove maintains that,
while the marital state, when lived properly, may be said to be
clean in the eyes of men, if compared to the ministry of God, it
has to be called dirty: 'ea vite conditio rite obseruata secundum
matrimonii leges, etsi nobis hominibus munda sit: dei tamen
ministerio comparata, non est munda' (*Propugnaculum* 376). So
Clichtove, the theologian, has placed two sacraments of the
church at loggerheads with each other. For a discussion of
Clichtove that decidedly favours his stand against Erasmus, see
Emile Telle's *Erasme de Rotterdam et le septième sacrement* (336–9) and
the same author's introduction to his edition of the *Dilutio*.
38 *Dilutio* 97
39 *De copia* 1.18 *LB* 1: 19A
40 *ASD* I-5: 402 lines 218–19
41 *Dilutio* 91
42 Augustine *De sancta virginitate* 8 *PL* 40: 400
43 Thomas Aquinas, Commentary on the *Ethics* of Aristotle, bk 8,
lect 4, in Gilbey *Philosophical Texts* 323
44 Thomas Aquinas *Summa contra Gentiles, Book Three: Providence* 2: 123
trans Vernon J. Bourke 148
45 'Declamo enim, non doceo Theologiam' (*Dilutio* 93)
46 *Dilutio* 95
47 *ASD* I-5: 410–12 lines 320–57
48 This line is borrowed from Robin Farn's translation of Pierre Danino's
Les Carnets du Major Thompson. The English title reads: *Major
Thompson Lives in France and Discovers the French* (London: Jonathan
Cape 1955) 102. In his paraphrase of Luke (*LB* 7: 288c), Erasmus
subordinates the desire for sexual pleasure to the desire for offspring which alone seems to legitimize the physical enjoyment.
49 *ASD* I-5: 396 lines 159–63
50 *Paraphrasis in evangelium Lucae*, *LB* 7: 288c
51 *Dilutio* 87
52 Mesnard *La philosophie chrétienne* 389
53 *LB* 7: 284D–E

54 *LB* 7: 288B–C
55 *LB* 7: 286B
56 *Paean virgini matri dicendus, LB* 5: 1230A and 1231 A–B
57 *LB* 5: 1230D–E and 1231C–D
58 *LB* 5: 1230C and 1231D–E
59 *Adversus calumniosissimam epistolam Martini Lutheri, LB* 10: 1549C–D
60 'Tam fervida ut amore dilecti langueres, tam formosa ut Dei verbum e sinu Patris, in tuum ipsius uterum, nitor oculorum tuorum fecerit avolare' (*Paean, LB* 5: 1232B–C). The language of this passage resembles that of love poetry. Erasmus addresses the Virgin as one who has experienced the most intense love possible for a human being: 'Tu Sponsa, tu concubina, tu amica, tu columba unica. Tu amor es, tu ignis, tu propriae delitiae speciosi prae filiis hominum' (*LB* 5: 1232B). For Erasmus it would seem that the purer the love, the more intense it becomes.
61 *Obsecratio ad virginem matrem Mariam, LB* 5: 1236C
62 *Paraph in Luc, LB* 7: 290B
63 Luther Ep 2093 *WA Br* 7: 35 lines 276–7
64 *WA Br* 7: 37 lines 352–4
65 *Adversus Luth, LB* 10: 1548C–D
66 *LB* 10: 1549D–F
67 *LB* 10: 1550B–C. The passage is a copy of what is found in Erasmus' paraphrase of Luke 1:35 (*LB* 7: 290B–C).
68 Erasmus sums up his quarrel with Luther in one sentence: 'Neque quicquam interest inter te et me, nisi quod ego facio nostram voluntatem cooperantem gratiae Dei, tu facis nihil aliud quam patientem' (*Hyperaspistae diatribes* 1 *LB* 10: 1286B–C). According to this account, Erasmus sees man as more involved in the life of grace by his cooperating with the divine attraction. For Luther, man would appear to be completely passive, at least as far as Erasmus understands his position.
69 *Paraphrasis in epistolam Pauli ad Corinthios priorem, LB* 7: 909D–F
70 *LB* 7: 910D
71 *Paraphrasis in evangelium Joannis, LB* 7: 597D–E
72 See note 35 in the present chapter.
73 'Sed quid de scriptis legibus agimus? Naturae haec lex [i.e., the law to marry] est, non in tabulis aereis exarata, sed animis nostris penitus insita' (*ASD* I-5: 392 lines 114–15).
74 *ASD* I-5: 394 lines 123–5
75 *ASD* I-5: 394 lines 125–8
76 *ASD* I-5: 394 lines 128–9
77 *ASD* I-5: 394 lines 129–34. The Leiden edition (*LB* 1: 417F–418A) introduces God instead of nature as the subject of the first sentence in the passage: 'Nonne Deus ita res cunctas vinculis quibusdam connexuit, ut aliae aliis egere videantur?'

78 *En in ps 38*, *LB* 5: 449C–D
79 In a letter to Jacob Voogd, Erasmus refers to his fondness for studying theology with Colet: 'Sometimes I contemplate returning to England in order to spend a month or two studying divinity with my friend Colet, as I am well aware how profitable this might be for me' (Ep 159 *CWE* 2: 45 lines 59–62 [*EE* 1: 368 lines 53–6]).
80 Colet looks upon those in need of a union in the flesh as sick people (*Ioannes Colet opus de sacramentis ecclesiae* 76). In his eyes, only a spiritual marriage is good and is, in fact, to be identified with Orders: 'Idem est sacerdotium quod matrimonium' (*De sacramentis* 43).
81 Cited by Colet in *De sacramentis* 65
82 *De sacramentis* 61
83 *De sacramentis* 51
84 *De sacramentis* 51
85 As God, Christ is said to be masculine; as man, he is called feminine: 'fructificaverit Jesum, masculum et feminam, in quo erat masculus Deus et femineus homo' (*De sacramentis* 65).
86 *De sacramentis* 61
87 *De sacramentis* 55
88 *De sacramentis* 60
89 *Institutio Christiani matrimonii*, *LB* 5: 619F–620A
90 *LB* 5: 620D
91 'Ubi divortium incidit, ibi videtur numquam fuisse verum matrimonium' (*LB* 5: 620E); 'unius Matrimonii nodum sola mors dissolvit, ac vix haec quoque' (*LB* 5: 624B)
92 *LB* 5: 622D
93 *LB* 5: 622D
94 *LB* 5: 620F–621B
95 *LB* 5: 622B
96 *LB* 5: 621E–F
97 *Paraphrasis in epistolam Pauli apostoli ad Ephesios*, *LB* 7: 987E
98 *LB* 7: 984D–E
99 *Institutio christiani matrimonii*, *LB* 5: 621F–622A
100 *PF* 136–7 (*ASD* IV-3: 192 lines 240–7)
101 Screech (164) cites Erasmus' letter to Lypsius, where the author of the *Moria* explains what he means by the absorption which Folly celebrates: 'I said that the soul was swallowed by God because it is totally caught up into him by love; the soul is more where is loves (*amat*) than where it animates (*animat*). It is so caught up that it is made perfect (*perficitur*), not that it vanishes (*evanescat*) (*EE* 3, no. 848, 90, line 617f.).
102 Thomas Aquinas *Summa* 1a.2ae.28.2

Bibliography

✿

PRIMARY SOURCES: WORKS OF ERASMUS

Latin Works

Ausgewählte Schriften. 8 vols. Darmstadt: Wissenschaftliche Buchgesell-
schaft 1967–80
Ausgewählte Werke ed Annemarie Holborn and Hajo Holborn. Munich:
C.H. Beck 1933
Declamatio de pueris statim ac liberaliter instituendis ed and trans Jean-
Claude Margolin. Travaux d'humanisme et Renaissance 77. Gene-
va: Droz 1966
Desiderii Erasmi opera omnia ed J. Clericus. 10 vols in 11 tomes. Leiden
1703–6
*Dilutio eorum quae Iodocus Clithoveus scripsit adversus declamationem
Des. Erasmi Roterodami suasoriam matrimonii* ed Emile V. Telle. Paris:
Vrin 1968
*Opera omnia Desiderii Erasmi Roterodami recognita et adnotatione critica
instructa notisque illustrata.* 11 vols to date. Amsterdam: North Hol-
land 1969–
Opus epistolarum Des. Erasmi Roterodami ed P.S. Allen, H.M. Allen, and
H.M. Garrod. 12 vols. Oxford: Clarendon 1906–58
The Poems of Desiderius Erasmus ed C. Reedijk. Leiden: Brill 1956

Translations

The 'Adages' of Erasmus: A Study with Translations trans and ed Margaret
Mann Phillips. Cambridge: Cambridge University Press 1964
The Collected Works of Erasmus. 17 vols to date. University of Toronto
Press 1974–
The Colloquies of Erasmus trans Craig R. Thompson. Chicago: University
of Chicago Press 1965

Luther and Erasmus: Free Will and Salvation trans and ed E. Gordon Rupp
and A.N. Marlow. Library of Christian Classics 17. Philadelphia:
Westminster 1969. 33–97: trans of *De libero arbitrio*
The Education of a Christian Prince trans Lester K. Born. Records of Civili-
zation 27. New York: Octagon 1965
The Enchiridion of Erasmus trans and ed Raymond Himelick. Blooming-
ton: Indiana University Press 1963
*Erasmus and the Seamless Coat of Jesus: De sarcienda ecclesiae concordia
(On Restoring the Unity of the Church)* trans Raymond Himelick.
Lafayette: Purdue University Studies 1971
The Julius exclusus of Erasmus trans Paul Pascal, intro and notes by
J. Kelley Sowards. Bloomington: Indiana University Press, 1968
*La philosophie chrétienne: L'eloge de la folie, L'essai sur le libre arbitre, Le
cicéronien, La réfutation de Clichtove* trans and ed Pierre Mesnard. De
Pétrarque à Descartes 22. Paris: Vrin 1970
The Praise of Folly trans Clarence H. Miller. New Haven: Yale University
Press 1979

PRIMARY SOURCES: OTHER AUTHORS

Aelred of Rievaulx *De speculo caritatis*. In *Opera omnia* vol 1 of *Opera
ascetica* of *Corpus christianorum, continuatio mediavalia* ed A. Hoste
and C.H. Talbot. Turnholt: Brepols 1971. 3–162
Ambrose *De officiis ministrorum*. PL 16. 23–187
Aristotle *The Ethics of Aristotle* ed John Burnet. 1900. New York: Arno
1973
– *On the Art of Poetry* trans and ed Ingram Bywater. Oxford: Clarendon
1909
Augustine *Confessiones* ed Lucas Verkeijen. CCSL 27
– *Confessions* trans Vernon J. Bourke. Vol 5 of *The Writings of Saint
Augustine*. Fathers of the Church 21. New York: Fathers of the
Church 1953
– *Contra Faustum* ed Josephus Zycha. CSEL 25. 249–797
– *De civitate Dei* ed Bernardus Dombart and Alphonsus Kalb. CCSL
47–8
– *De doctrina christiana* ed Iosephus Martin. CCSL 32. 1–167
– *De libero arbitrio*. PL 32. 1222–1310
– *De musica*. PL 32. 1081–1194
– *De sancta virginitate*. PL 40. 395–428
– *De Trinitate* ed W.J. Mountain. CCSL 50–1
– *Enarrationes in psalmos* ed Eligius Dekkers and Iohannes Fraipont.
CCSL 38–40
– *Epistolae*. PL 33
– *Letters* trans Sister Wilfrid Parsons. Vol 11 of *The Writings of Saint Augus-
tine*. Fathers of the Church 20. New York: Fathers of the Church 1953

- *On Music* trans Robert Catesby Taliaferro. In vol 2 of *The Writings of Saint Augustine.* Fathers of the Church 4. New York: Fathers of the Church 1947. 151–379
- *Sermones de vetere testamento* ed Cyrillus Lambot. CCSL 41
- *Tractatus in Iohannis evangelium* ed Radbodus Willems. CCSL 36

Basil *De spiritu sancto.* PG 32. 67–218

Bede *Homiliae.* PL 94. 9–516

Boethius *De institutione arithmetica* ed Godofredus Friedlein. 1867. Frankfurt a. M.: Minerva 1966

Cicero *De finibus bonorum et malorum* trans H. Rackam. 2nd ed, rpt. Loeb Classical Library 40. Cambridge: Harvard University Press, 1967

Clement of Alexandria *The Exhortation to the Greeks* in *Clement of Alexandria* trans G.W. Butterworth. Loeb Classical Library. Cambridge: Harvard University Press, 1919. 1–263

Clichtove, Josse *Propugnaculum ecclesie: Adversus Lutheranos per Judocum Clichtove.* Cologne 1526

Colet, John *Ioannes Colet opus de sacramentis ecclesiae* ed J.H. Lupton. 1867. Ridgewood NJ: Gregg 1966
- *Ioannes Coletus super opera Dionysii* trans J.H. Lupton 1896. Ridgewood NJ: Gregg 1966
- *De corpore Christi mystico.* In *Ioannis Coleti opuscula quaedam theologica* intro J.H. Lupton. 1876. Ridgewood NJ: Gregg 1966. 183–95

Cyprian *Epistolae.* PL 4. 191–438

Dionysius the Areopagite *De coelesti hierarchia.* PG 3. 119–370
- *De divinis nominibus.* PG 3. 585–996
- *De ecclesiastica hierarchia.* PG 3. 369–584
- *De mystica theologia.* PG 3 997–1064
- *The Works of Dionysius the Areopagite* trans and ed John Parker. 2 parts. 1897–9. Merrick NY: Richwood 1976

Durandus Troarnensis *Liber de corpore et sanguine Christi.* PL 149. 1375–1423

Gerhoh of Reichersberg *Commentarius aureus in psalmos.* PL 193. 619–1814

Gregory the Great *Moralium libri.* PL 75. 509–1162

Gregory Nazianzus *Orationes.* PG 35. 395–1252; PG 36. 9–664

Gregory of Nyssa *Commentarius in canticum canticorum.* PG 44. 755–1120

Honorius *Selectorum psalmorum expositio.* PL 172. 269–312

Horace *Satires, Epistles and Ars poetica* trans H. Rushton Fairclough. Loeb Classical Library 194. Cambridge: Harvard University Press 1978

Hugh of St Victor *Didascalicon of Hugh of St. Victor* trans Jerome Taylor. Records of Civilization 64. New York: Columbia University Press, 1961
- *Expositio in hierarchiam coelestem S. Dionysii Areopagitae.* PL 175. 923–1154

- *Explanatio in canticum beatea Mariae.* PL 175. 413A–432B
Ignatius of Antioch *Epistola ad Ephesios.* PG 5. 643–62
- *The Epistles of St. Clement of Rome and St. Ignatius of Antioch* trans
James A. Kleist. Ancient Christian Writers 1. Westminster Maryland: Newman 1961
Jerome *Liber de nominibus hebraicis* PL 23. 771–858
John of Salisbury *Polycraticus sive De nugis curialium et vestigiis philosophorum* ed Clemens C.I. Webb. 2 vols. London 1909; Frankfurt a.
M.: Minerva 1965
- *Policraticus* trans Joseph B. Pike *Frivolities of Courtiers and Footprints of
Philosophers.* Minneapolis: University of Minnesota Press 1938
Langland, William *Piers Plowman: An Edition of the C-Text* ed Derek
Pearsall. Berkeley: University of California Press 1978
Lucian *Lucian* trans A.M. Harmon and K. Kilburn. Loeb Classical
Library. 8 vols. Cambridge: Harvard University Press, 1913–67
Luther, Martin *D. Martin Luthers Werke: Kritische Gesamtausgabe.* 62 vols
to date. Weimar: H. Böhlaus Nachfolger 1883–
- *D. Martin Luthers Werke: Kritische Gesamtausgabe, Briefwechsel.* 16 vols.
Weimar: H. Böhlaus Nachfolger 1930–80
- *D. Martin Luthers Werke: Kritische Gesamtausgabe, Tischreden.* 6 vols.
Weimar: H. Böhlaus Nachfolger 1912–21
- *Luther and Erasmus: Free Will and Salvation* trans and ed Philip S.
Watson and B. Drewery. Library of Christian Classics 17. Philadelphia: Westminster 1969. 99–334: trans of *De servo arbitrio*
- *Luthers Werke in Auswahl* ed Otto Clemen. 8 vols. Berlin: de Grunter
1959
- *Table Talk* trans and ed Theodore G. Tappert. Vol 54 of *Luther's
Works.* 55 vols. Philadelphia: Fortress 1967
More, Thomas *The Correspondence of Sir Thomas More* ed Elizabeth Frances Rogers. Princeton: Princeton University Press, 1947
- *The History of King Richard the Third* ed Richard S. Sylvester. New
Haven: Yale University Press 1963. Vol 2 of *The Complete Works of
St. Thomas More.* 14 vols to date. 1963–
Patrologiae, cursus completus, series graeca ed J.-P. Migne. 164 vols. Paris
1857–1912
Patrologiae, cursus completus, series latina ed J.-P. Migne. 221 vols. Paris
1879–90
Peter of Celle *Liber de panibus.* PL 202. 929–1046
Philo of Alexandria *On the Account of the World's Creation Given by Moses*
trans F.H. Colson and G.H. Whitaker. In vol 1 of *Philo of Alexandria.* 10 vols. Loeb Classical Library. Cambridge: Harvard University
Press 1949. 1–137
- *Who Is the Heir of Divine Things?* trans F.H. Colson and G.H. Whitaker. In vol 4 of *Philo of Alexandria.* 10 vols. Loeb Classical Library.
Cambridge: Harvard University Press, 1949. 269–447

Plato *The Collected Diaglogues of Plato Including the Letters* ed Edith
Hamilton and Huntington Cairns. Bollingen Series 71. Princeton:
Princeton University Press, 1961

Pliny *Natural History* trans H. Rackham. 10 vols. Loeb Classical
Library. Cambridge: Harvard University Press 1938–62

Pontano, Giovanni Gioviano *Ioannis Iovani Pontani de sermone libri sex* ed
S. Lupi and A. Risicato. Thesaurus mundi: Biblioteca scriptorum
latinorum mediae et recentioris aetatis. Lucani: Thesaurus Mundi
1954

Richard of St Victor *In apolcalypsim Joannis libri septem.* PL 196.
683A–888B

– *In cantica canticorum explicatio.* PL 196. 405–524

Tertullian *De spectaculis; De fuga in persecutione; De pallio* ed Joseph
Marra. Turin: Paravia 1954

Thomas Aquinas *Opera omnia.* 25 vols. Parma: Petrus Fiaccadorus
1852–73; New York: Musurgia 1948–50

– *Philosophical Texts* trans Thomas Gilby. London: Oxford University
Press 1951

– *Summa contra Gentiles, Book Three: Providence* trans Vernon J. Bourke.
1956. 2 vols. Notre Dame: University of Notre Dame Press 1975

– *Summa theologiae* ed Thomas Gilby et al. 60 vols. Cambridge: Blackfriars 1964–

– *Theological Texts* trans Thomas Gilby. London: Oxford University
Press, 1955

SELECTED SECONDARY SOURCES

Bacon, Francis 'An Advertisement Touching the Controversies of the
Church of England' *The Works of Francis Bacon* ed Basil Montague.
Vol 2. Philadelphia: Murphy 1887. 411–20. 3 vols 1887

Bakhtin, Mikhail *Rabelais and His World* trans Helene Iswolsky. Bloomington: Indiana University Press, 1984. Trans of *Tvorchestvo Fransua
Rable.* Moscow: Khudozhestvennia literatura 1965

Balthasar, Hans Urs von *Seeing the Form* trans Erasmo Leiva-Merikakis,
ed Joseph Fessio and John Riches. Vol 1 of *The Glory of the Lord: A
Theological Aesthetics.* 3 vols to date. San Francisco: Ignatius 1982–

– *Studies in Theological Style: Clerical Styles* trans Andrew Louth, Francis
McDonagh, and Brian McNeil, ed John Riches. Vol 2 of *The Glory
of the Lord: A Theological Aesthetics.* 3 vols to date. San Francisco:
Ignatius 1982–

– *Theodramatik.* 4 vols in 5 tomes to date. Einsiedeln: Johannes Verlag
1973–

Barber, C.L. *Shakespeare's Festive Comedy: A Study of Dramatic Form and
Its Relation to Social Custom.* 1959. Cleveland: World 1963

Barthes, Roland *Le plaisir du texte.* Paris: Editions du Seuil 1973

Baudelaire, Charles 'De l'essence du rire' *Oeuvres complètes* ed Marcel A. Ruff. Paris: Editions du Seuil 1968. 370–8

Boyle, Marjorie O'Rourke *Christening Pagan Mysteries: Erasmus in Pursuit of Wisdom*. Toronto: University of Toronto Press 1981

– *Erasmus on Language and Method in Theology*. Toronto: University of Toronto Press 1977

– *Rhetoric and Reform: Erasmus' Civil Dispute with Luther*. Harvard Historical Monographs 71. Cambridge: Harvard University Press, 1983

Branchin, Pierre 'Vox clamantis in deserto: Réflexions sur le pacifisme d'Erasme' *Colloquia Erasmiana Turonensia*. Vol 1. De Pétrarque à Descartes 24. Paris: Vrin 1972. 247–75. 2 vols 1972

Bultot, R. 'Erasme, Epicure et le "De Contemptu Mundi"' *Scrinium Erasmianum* ed J. Coppens. Vol 2. Leiden: Brill 1969. 205–38. 2 vols 1969

Chamberlain, David S. 'Philosophy of Music in the *Consolatio* of Boethius' *Speculum* 45 (1970) 80–97

Chantraine, Georges *Erasme et Luther: Libre et serf arbitre*. Paris: Lethielleux 1981

– 'Erasme theologien?' *Revue d'histoire écclésiastique* 64 (1969) 811–20

– 'Mystère' et 'Philosophie du Christ' selon Erasme: Etude de la lettre à P. Volz et de la 'Ratio verae theologiae.' Namur: Facultés universitaires 1971

Chapman, Emmanuel *Saint Augustine's Philosophy of Beauty*. Saint Michael's Mediaeval Studies – Monograph Series. New York: Sheed 1939

Chenu, Marie-Dominique *La théologie au douzième siècle*. Paris: Vrin 1957

– *Nature, Man, and Society in the Twelfth Century: Essays on New Theological Perspectives in the Latin West* ed and trans Jerome Taylor and Lester K. Little. Chicago: Chicago University Press 1968

– 'Théologie symbolique et exégèse scolastique aux xiie–xiiie siècles' *Mélanges Joseph de Ghellinck, S.J.* Vol 2. Gemblaux: Editions H. Duculot 1951

Chomarat, Jacques *Grammaire et rhetorique chez Erasme*. 2 vols. Les classiques de l'humanisme 10. Paris: Belles Lettres 1981

Cohn, Norman *The Pursuit of the Millennium: Revolutionary Millenarians and Mystical Anarchists of the Middle Ages* rev ed. New York: Oxford University Press, 1970

Colie, Rosalie L. *Paradoxia epidemica: The Renaissance Tradition of Paradox*. Princeton: Princeton University Press, 1966

Cooper, Lane *An Aristotelian Theory of Comedy with an Adaptation of the Poetics and a Translation of the 'Tractus Coislinianus.'* New York: Harcourt 1922

Cornford, Francis Macdonald *The Origin of Attic Comedy*. London: Arnold 1914

Cox, Dermot *The Triumph of Impotence*. Rome: Universita Gregoriana Editrice 1978

de Lubac, Henri *Corpus mysticum: L'eucharistie et l'église au moyen âge*. Paris: Aubier 1949

- *Exégèse médiéval: Les quatre sens de l'écriture*. 2 vols in 2 parts. Théologie 41, 42, and 59. Paris: Aubier 1959–64

DeMolen, Richard L. 'Pueri Christi imitatio: The Festival of the Boy-Bishop in Tudor England' *Moreana* 45 (Feb 1975) 17–28

Douglas, A.E. 'Erasmus as a Satirist' *Erasmus* ed T.A. Dorey. Albuquerque: University of New Mexico Press 1970. 31–54

Dresden, S[amuel] 'Erasme et la notion de *humanitas*' *Scrinium Erasmianum* ed J. Coppens. Vol 2. Leiden: Brill 1969. 527–45. 2 vols 1969

- 'Erasme, Rabelais et la "Festivitas" humaniste' *Colloquia Erasmiana Turonensia*. Vol 1. De Pétrarque à Descartes 24. Paris: Vrin 1972. 463–78. 2 vols 1972

Duncan, Douglas *Ben Jonson and the Lucianic Tradition*. Cambridge: Cambridge University Press 1979

Eliade, Mircea *Symbolism, the Sacred, and the Arts* ed Diane Apolstolos-Cappadona. New York: Crossroad 1988

Elliott, Robert C. *The Power of Satire: Magic, Ritual, Art*. Princeton: Princeton University Press 1960

Erickson, Erik H. *Toys and Reasons: Stages in the Ritualization of Experience*. New York: Norton 1977

Ernst, Cornelius *The Theology of Grace*. Theology Today 17. Notre Dame: Fides 1974

Festugière, A.J. *Epicurus and His Gods* trans C.W. Chilton. Cambridge: Harvard University Press 1956

Foucault, Michel *Madness and Civilization: A History of Insanity in the Age of Reason*. New York: Random House 1965

Freud, Sigmund 'Der Dichter und das Phantasieren' *Gesammelte Werke* ed Anna Freud, Edward Bibring, and Ernst Kris. Vol 7. London: Imago 1941. 213–23. 18 vols in 17 tomes 1952–68

Frye, Northrop *Anatomy of Criticism: Four Essays*. 1957. Princeton: Princeton University Press 1971

- *A Natural Perspective: The Development of Shakespearean Comedy and Romance*. New York: Harcourt 1965

Gilmore, Myron P. '*Apologiae*: Erasmus's Defenses of Folly' *Essays on the Works of Erasmus* ed Richard L. DeMolen. New Haven: Yale University Press 1978. 111–23

- 'De modis disputandi: The Apologetic Works of Erasmus' *Florilegium Historale: Essays Presented to Wallace K. Ferguson* ed J.G. Rowe and W.H. Stockdale. Toronto: University of Toronto Press 1971. 62–88

- 'Erasmus and Alberto Pio, Prince of Carpi' *Action and Conviction in Early Modern Europe: Essays in Memory of E.H. Harbison* ed Theodore K. Rabb and Jerrold E. Seigel. Princeton: Princeton University Press 1969. 299–318

Girard, René *Violence and the Sacred* trans Patrick Gregory. Baltimore: Johns Hopkins University Press 1977

Godin, André *Erasme lecture d'Origène*. Travaux d'humanisme et renaissance 190. Geneva: Droz 1982

Greenblatt, Stephen *Renaissance Self-Fashioning from More to Shakespeare*. Chicago: University of Chicago Press 1980

Guardini, Romano *The Spirit of the Liturgy* trans Ada Lane. London: Sheed 1937

Gurewitch, Morton *Comedy: The Irrational Vision*. Ithaca: Cornell University Press 1975

Huizinga, Johan *Erasmus and the Age of the Reformation with a Selection from the Letters of Erasmus* trans F. Hopman and Barbara Fowler. 1924. New York: Harper 1957

– *Homo Ludens: A Study of the Play-Element in Culture*. 1950. Boston: Beacon 1955

Irwin, Eleanor 'The Songs of Orpheus and the New Song of Christ' *Orpheus: The Metamorphoses of a Myth* ed John Warden. 1982. Toronto: University of Toronto Press 1985. 51–62

Jeffrey, David L. 'Bosch's "Haywain": Communion, Community, and the Theater of the World' *Viator* 4 (1973) 311–32

Kaiser, Walter *Praisers of Folly: Erasmus, Rabelais, Shakespeare*. Harvard Studies in Comparative Literature 25. Cambridge: Harvard University Press 1963

Kehl, Medard 'Hans Urs von Balthasar: A Portrait' introduction to *The von Blathasar Reader* by Hans Urs von Balthasar, ed Medard Kehl and Werner Löser, trans J. Daly and Fred Lawrence. New York: Crossroads 1982. 3–54

Kern, Edith *The Absolute Comic*. New York: Columbia University Press 1980

Kernan, Alvin B. *The Plot of Satire*. New Haven: Yale University Press 1965

Knowles, David *The Tudor Age*. Cambridge: Cambridge University Press 1959. Vol 3 of *The Religious Orders in England*. 3 vols 1948–59

Kohls, E.W. *Die Theologie des Erasmus*. 2 vols. Bale: Reinhardt 1966

Kolve, V.A. *The Play Called Corpus Christi*. Stanford: Stanford University Press 1966

Lanham, Richard A. *The Motives of Eloquence: Literary Rhetoric in the Renaissance*. New Haven: Yale University Press 1976

L'Estrange, Roger 'To the Reader.' *Twenty Select Colloquies of Erasmus*. Abbey Classics 17. Boston: Small, Maynard nd

Leeuw, Gerardus van der *Sacred and Profane Beauty: The Holy in Art* trans David E. Green. New York: Holt 1963

Luck, Georg 'Vir Facetus: A Renaissance Ideal' *Studies in Philology* 55 (1958) 107–21

Lupton, J.H. *A Life of John Colet, D.D., Dean of St. Paul's and Founder of St. Paul's School.* 1887. Hamden: Shoe String 1961

Margolin, Jean-Claude *Erasme et la musique*. De Pétrarque à Descartes 9. Paris: Vrin 1965

– *Douze années de bibliographie érasmienne (1950–1961)*. Paris: Vrin 1963

– 'L'idée de nature dans la pensée d'Erasme' *Recherches erasmiennes*. Travaux d'humanisme et renaissance 105. Geneva: Droz 1969. 9–44

– *Neuf années de bibliographie érasmienne (1962–1970)*. Paris: Vrin 1977

– *Quatorze années de bibliographie érasmienne (1936–1949)*. Paris: Vrin 1969

Marsh, David 'Erasmus and the Antithesis of Body and Soul' *Journal of the History of Ideas* 37 (1976) 673–88

Mason, H.A. *Humanism and Poetry in the Early Tudor Period*. London: Routledge 1959

McConica, James Kelsey 'Erasmus and the Grammar of Consent' *Scrinium Erasmianum* ed J. Coppens. Vol 2. Leiden: Brill 1967. 2 vols. 77–99

Mesnard, Pierre 'Erasme et la conception dialectique de la folie' *L'Umanesimo e 'la follia'* ed E. Castelli. Rome: Edizione Abete 1971. 44–61

Meyer-Baer, Kathi *Music of the Spheres and the Dance of Death: Studies in Musical Iconology*. Princeton: Princeton University Press 1970

Miller, David L. *Gods and Games: Toward a Theology of Play*. New York: World 1969

Miller, James *Measures of Wisdom: The Cosmic Dance in Classical and Christian Antiquity*. Visio: Studies in the Relations of Art and Literature 1. Toronto: University of Toronto Press 1986

Milton, John 'An Apologie against a Pamphlet' *Complete Prose Works of John Milton* ed Don M. Wolfe with preface and notes by Frederick L. Taft. Vol 1. New Haven: Yale University Press 1953. 862–953. 8 vols. 1953–82

Moltmann, Jürgen *Theology of Play* trans Reinhard Ulrich. New York: Harper 1971

O'Connell, Robert J. *Art and the Christian Intelligence in St. Augustine*. Cambridge: Harvard University Press 1978

Ong, Walter J. Preface to *Man at Play* by Hugo Rahner. New York: Herder 1967. ix–xiv

– 'Wit and Mystery: A Revaluation in Medieval Latin Hymnody' *Speculum* 22 (1947) 310–41

Parke, H.W. *Festivals of the Athenians*. Ithaca: Cornell University Press 1977

Pascal *Les provinciales* ed José Lupin. Paris: Gallimard 1966

Perl, Carl Johann 'Augustine and Music' trans Alan Kriegsman *Music Quarterly* 41 (1955) 496–510

Rahner, Hugo *Man at Play*. New York: Herder 1967

Rebhorn, Wayne A. 'The Metamorphoses of Moria: Structure and Meaning in *The Praise of Folly*' *PMLA* 89 (1974) 463–76

Robinson, Christopher *Lucian and His Influence in Europe*. Chapel Hill: University of North Carolina Press 1979

Sartre, Jean-Paul *Being and Nothingness: An Essay on Phenomenological Ontology* trans Hazel E. Barnes. New York: Philosophical Library [1956]

– *The War Diaries of Jean-Paul Sartre: November 1939–March 1940* trans Quintin Hoare. New York: Pantheon 1984

Schäfer, Eckart 'Erasmus und Horaz' *Antike und Abendland: Beiträge zum Verständnis der Griechen und Römer und ihres Nachlebens* 16 (1970) 54–67

Schiller, Friedrick *On the Aesthetic Education of Man in a Series of Letters* ed and trans Elizabeth M. Wilkinson and L.A. Willoughby. 1967. Oxford: Clarendon 1982

Schmemann, Alexander *Sacraments and Orthodoxy*. New York: Herder 1965

Schottenloher, Otto 'Erasme et la "Respublica christiana"' *Colloquia Erasmiana Turonensia*. Vol 2. De Pétrarque à Descartes 24. Paris: Vrin 1972. 667–90. 2 vols 1972

Screech, M.A. *Ecstasy and the 'Praise of Folly.'* London: Duckworth 1980

Sylvester, Richard 'The Problem of Unity in *The Praise of Folly*' *English Literary Renaissance* 6 (1976) 125–39

Telle, Emile V. *Erasme de Rotterdam et le septième sacrement*. Geneva: Droz 1954

Thompson, C[raig] R. *The Translations of Lucian by Erasmus and St. Thomas More*. Ithaca: Vail-Ballou 1940

Thompson, Sister M. Geraldine 'As Bones to the Body: The Scope of *Inventio* in the *Colloquies* of Erasmus' *Essays on the Works of Erasmus* ed Richard L. DeMolen. New Haven: Yale University Press 1978. 163–78

– *Under Pretext of Praise: Satiric Mode in Erasmus' Fiction*. Toronto: University of Toronto Press 1973

Thomson, D.F.S. 'Erasmus as a Poet in the Context of Northern Humanism' *De Gulden Passer* 47 (1969) 187–210

Thomson, J.A.K. 'Erasmus in England' *Vorträge der Bibliothek Warburg* 9 (1930–1). Rpt Neudeln, Liechtenstein: Kraus 1967. 64–82

Tracy, James D. 'On the Composition Dates of Seven of Erasmus' Writings' *Bibliothèque d'humanisme et Renaissance* 31 (1969) 355–64

– *The Politics of Erasmus: A Pacifist Intellectual and His Political Milieu*. Toronto: University of Toronto Press 1978

Vicari, Patricia '*Sparagmos*: Orpheus among the Christians' *Orpheus: The Metamorphoses of a Myth* ed John Warden. 1982. Toronto: University of Toronto Press 1985. 63–83 de Vocht, Henry *Monumenta Humanistica Louvaniensia: Texts and Studies about Louvain Humanists in the First Half of the XVIth Century.* Humanistica Lovaniensia 4. Louvain: Librarie Universitaire 1934

Watson, Donald Gwynn 'Erasmus' *Praise of Folly* and the Spirit of Carnival' *Renaissance Quarterly* 32 (1979) 333–53

Whitman, Cedric H. *Aristophanes and the Comic Hero.* Cambridge: Harvard University Press 1964

Index

�֍